BEST-EVER
VEGETARIAN

BEST-EVER
VEGETARIAN

THE DEFINITIVE COOK'S COLLECTION:
OVER 200 MOUTHWATERING
STEP-BY-STEP RECIPES

CONSULTANT EDITOR:
LINDA FRASER

PROSPERO
B·O·O·K·S
A DIVISION OF CHAPTERS INC.

This edition produced for Prospero Books,
a division of Chapters Inc.

© Anness Publishing Limited 1998

Produced by
Anness Publishing Limited
Hermes House
88–89 Blackfriars Road
London SE1 8HA

ISBN 1 89410 270 3

Publisher: Joanna Lorenz
Senior Cookery Editor: Linda Fraser
Project Editor: Sarah Duffin
Designer: Bill Mason
Illustrator: Anna Koska

Printed and bound in Italy

1 3 5 7 9 10 8 6 4 2

Contents

~

Introduction

WHETHER FOR HEALTH REASONS or due to ethical concerns, more and more people are rejecting animal products and turning instead to a vegetable-based diet and realizing that there is life after meat, after all. With the plentiful supply of fresh vegetables, fruit, herbs, nuts, grains, pulses (dried beans, peas and lentils) and pasta that is available to us, the possibilities of creating exciting and varied recipes have never been greater.

It is not only vegetarians who can enjoy vegetarian food. The fresh, light and innovative recipes that have come to the forefront of new-style vegetarian cuisine provide a tempting departure from many of the heavier, nonvegetarian dishes. This book gathers together some of the best recipes in the world, all of them packed with fabulous tastes and textures.

You are what you eat, and we are constantly being urged to choose a diet rich in complex carbohydrates found in cereals, grains, fruits and vegetables, which are abundant in vegetarian cooking. If you include dairy products in your diet, restrict your intake by choosing skim or low-fat milk and low-fat yogurts and cheeses. By limiting the use of oils to polyunsaturated types such as olive, sunflower, corn and peanut, you can reduce the level of fat in your diet considerably.

With options for everything from light snacks to special occasion dinners, every recipe here is delicious proof that eating the vegetarian way is not only nutritious, but entertaining and exciting too. Try them and enjoy them.

Fresh Vegetables

Thanks to the range of fresh produce now available, the choice for vegetarians has expanded enormously.

Asparagus
Asparagus spears have an intense, rich flavor—delicious served with melted butter.

Beans
Fava beans, green beans and runner beans can be steamed or lightly boiled in salted water until al dente.

Broccoli
Quick and easy to prepare, broccoli can be eaten raw with dips, or cooked.

Cabbage
There are many varieties of cabbage. Care should be taken not to overcook this vegetable.

Carrots
Carrots have a sweet and fragrant flavor. They are just as delicious eaten raw as they are cooked.

Cauliflower
Cauliflower has a pleasant, fresh flavor.

Celeriac
Celeriac has a hint of sweet celery.

Celery
With its distinctive flavor, celery is an ideal ingredient for soups.

Chiles
Members of the capsicum family, these can be very fiery.

Corn
Eaten on the cob with salt and butter, corn is absolutely delicious.

Cucumber
This has a crisp, refreshing taste.

Eggplant
Eggplant has a smoky flavor when cooked.

Fennel
Aniseed-flavored and delicious.

Garlic
These firm, round bulbs have a very distinctive flavor.

Leeks

A versatile vegetable with a subtle, oniony flavor.

Lettuce

There are many varieties of lettuce available. Most salads include this vegetable.

Mushrooms

Whether cultivated or wild, mushrooms are an essential ingredient for vegetarian cooking.

Onions

Onions come in many different varieties. They can be sautéed, roasted or eaten raw in salads.

Parsnips

A sweet root vegetable with a distinct earthy flavor.

Peas

Sweet tender peas are unbeatable. Make the most of them when they are in season.

Peppers

Green bell peppers have a fresh "raw" flavor, whereas red, yellow and orange peppers are sweeter.

Potatoes

Rich in carbohydrates, potatoes can be baked, boiled, fried, sautéed, mashed or roasted.

Pumpkins/Squashes

These have a fibrous flesh with a mild, slightly sweet flavor.

Rutabagas

These are ideal for adding to soups and casseroles.

Shallots

These small bulbs are ideal for using in sauces.

Spinach

Rich in iron, spinach can be eaten raw in salads or cooked.

Tomatoes

These come in a variety of sizes and form the basis of many vegetarian dishes.

Turnips

Sweet and with a nutty flavor, turnips range from very small to large, mature vegetables.

Zucchini

These are succulent and tender, with a delicate flavor.

Dairy Products

Both local and imported dairy products are now widely available. Most have low-fat versions.

Butter/Margarine

Butter is a natural dairy product made from cream. Margarine is a butter substitute made from vegetable fat.

Buttermilk

This is skim or low-fat milk with an added bacterial culture, to give it a natural tangy flavor.

Cheeses (hard and semi-hard)

Hard cheeses are often essential for cooking, and of course Parmesan is an important ingredient for many dishes.

Cheeses (soft)

Cottage cheese, curd cheese, mascarpone and ricotta are all soft, moist cheeses used in many dishes. Other soft cheeses of culinary note are mozzarella and tangy feta.

Cheeses (blue)

Blue cheeses such as Gorgonzola, Roquefort and Stilton are among some of the most popular cheeses used for sauces, soups and tarts.

Cream

This is available in many forms, including light, heavy, whipping, sour and crème fraîche.

Eggs

Rich in protein, eggs are used in both savory dishes and desserts.

Fromage frais

A creamy, fresh white cheese sold in pots.

Milk

This is available as skim, low-fat and full-fat, as well as condensed, powdered, and evaporated.

Quark

This soft white cheese is made from fermented skim milk.

Yogurt

Yogurt is available in various forms including active culture, low-fat, nonfat and strained plain ("Mediterranean-style").

Beans, Peas and Lentils

Dried beans, peas and lentils (pulses) are a good source of protein. They all need to be washed, and beans and peas should be soaked overnight before cooking. Beans should initially be boiled hard for ten minutes to destroy their toxins. Do not add salt until they are nearly cooked, as this toughens their skins.

DRIED BEANS AND SPLIT PEAS
Black-eyed peas

These are the only peas or beans that do not need soaking.

Lima beans

These are ideal for soups or pâtés, as they have a velvety texture.

Chickpeas

These round, beige-colored pulses have a strong, nutty flavor when cooked.

Navy beans

These are small, white and oval. They are ideal for slow cooking, as they absorb the flavor of herbs and spices easily.

Kidney beans

Kidney beans are dark red-brown beans with a strong flavor.

Green and yellow split peas

These tasty and nutritious peas are ideal for hearty soups and are frequently used in Indian cooking.

LENTILS
Brown and green lentils

These small lentils have a delicate flavor and retain their shape during cooking. Green lentils have a slightly stronger taste.

Red split lentils

Popular and easy to cook, these lentils are often used in vegetarian dishes.

TOFU

This is an unfermented soybean curd that is available in firm and silken varieties and can be used in all kinds of sweet and savory dishes as an alternative to dairy products.

Spices

The inclusion of spices in a recipe can literally transform a meal.

Cardamom
These pods are often used whole to add flavor to rice dishes.

Chili powder
The dried seeds of chiles are ground to make a very hot and spicy powder.

Cinnamon
Cinnamon is available whole or ground. The sticks are used for flavor and are not eaten.

Cloves
Cloves are used in spice mixtures for both sweet and savory dishes.

Coriander seeds
These are the roasted, dried seeds of the plant.

Cumin
Available as whole dark brown seeds and ground.

Fennel seeds
Small, light green seeds, similar in smell and taste to aniseed.

Fenugreek seeds
Fenugreek is used in many fish dishes and curries.

Ginger
Both fresh and ground ginger have a sharp, refreshing flavor. Fresh ginger root should be peeled before use.

Mustard seeds
Often used with vegetables and pulses, these have a nutty flavor.

Nutmeg
Whole or ground, nutmeg has a sweet, nutty flavor.

Peppercorns
Used in virtually all savory cooking, pepper has the capacity to enhance other flavors.

Saffron
This expensive spice is used for its aroma and color.

Turmeric
Turmeric is a bright yellow powder and is primarily used for its coloring properties.

Herbs

Beautiful fresh herbs from around the world are readily available. This herb checklist highlights both familiar and less well known items.

Basil
Well known for its affinity for tomatoes, basil has a spicy aroma that is a pungent mixture of cinnamon and anise.

Bay leaves
These are one of the oldest herbs used in cooking. When used fresh, they have a deliciously sweet flavor.

Chives
This herb has a very delicate, oniony flavor.

Cilantro (fresh coriander)
An intense, aromatic, sweet and spicy herb. The leaves can be used as a garnish.

Dill
A pungent, slightly sweet-tasting herb with anise overtones.

Marjoram
This is very similar to oregano, though more delicate in flavor.

Mint
A very versatile herb with a distinctive scent, mint is used in both sweet and savory dishes.

Oregano
An aromatic and highly flavored herb, oregano features strongly in Italian cooking.

Parsley
Both flat-leaf and curly varieties have a slightly bitter flavor.

Rosemary
Rosemary, with its dark, needle-like leaves, has an intense flavor and should be used sparingly.

Sage
The aromatic oils in sage impart a distinct and powerful flavor.

Savory
With its peppery flavor, savory makes a good seasoning.

Tarragon
This has a sweet, aniseed flavor.

Thyme
A robust aromatic herb with a warm, earthy flavor.

Dry Goods

Building up a pantry of everyday items such as flours, grains and pasta will ensure that you can produce a speedy meal at short notice.

Barley
With its distinctive flavor and slightly chewy texture, barley is used in soups or as an alternative to rice in risottos.

Buckwheat
Nutty in texture, this tasty alternative to rice is actually a grass.

Bulgur
This whole-wheat grain is steam-dried and cracked before sale, so it only needs a brief soaking before use. Keep it cool and dry in the pantry, and it will last for a few months.

Couscous
Also made from wheat, this grain is a staple in North Africa and is prepared in exactly the same way as bulgur.

Dried fruit
Rich in dietary fiber, vitamins and minerals, dried fruits are delicious in a wide selection of dishes, including muesli and pies. Because of their intense sweetness, they can be used as a healthy alternative to sugar in cooking.

Flours
As well as the usual white refined flour, try experimenting with other types including whole-wheat, buckwheat, soy, rice or rye for a more interesting, nutty flavor in your baking. Cornstarch is often used as a thickening agent for sauces.

Millet
High in protein, millet is used extensively in Southeast Asia and is cooked in the same way as rice.

Nuts and seeds
Nuts and seeds such as almond, cashew, brazil, sunflower, pumpkin and flax are a valuable source of protein, calcium and Omega 3 fatty acids. Bought in bulk for economy, they will keep in the freezer for several months.

Oats
Available as rolled, quick-cooking or steel-cut, this grain is an excellent source of complex carbohydrates, vitamins and minerals.

Pasta
While fresh pasta is generally preferred both for flavor and for speed of cooking, the dried product is a very valuable pantry ingredient. Italian pasta and Asian noodles are both useful.

Quinoa
Another good source of protein, quinoa is a soft grain from South America.

Rice
There are many different types of rice. Basmati is thought to have a superior flavor, fragrance and texture, and a mixture of basmati and wild rice (not a true rice, but the seeds of an aquatic grass) works well.

Sugars
Used sparingly, you can impart a distinctive flavor to your sweet dishes by adding dried sugars such as demerara, raw cane and confectioners' sugar, or liquid varieties including blackstrap molasses, honey and natural maple syrup.

Wheat, barley and rye flakes
These can be used in savory or sweet crumbles and biscuits to provide a variety of tastes and textures.

Bottled and Canned Goods

The pantry should be the backbone of your vegetarian kitchen. Stock it sensibly, and you'll always have the wherewithal to make a tasty, satisfying meal.

Canned beans, peas and lentils

Chickpeas, cannellini beans, green lentils, navy beans and red kidney beans survive the canning process well. Wash in cold running water and drain well before use.

Canned vegetables

Although fresh vegetables are best for most cooking, some canned products are very useful. Artichoke hearts have a mild, sweet flavor and are great for adding to stir-fries, salads, risottos or pizzas. Pimientos are canned sweet red peppers, seeded and peeled. Canned tomatoes are an essential ingredient to have in the pantry. Additional useful items to include are corn and water chestnuts.

Mustard

Whole-grain or Dijon mustards are widely used both in cooking and in salad dressings.

Oils

Peanut or sunflower oils are bland and will not mask or overpower delicate flavors. They are ideal for deep-frying. Fiery chili oil will liven up vegetable stir-fries, while tasty sesame oil will give them a rich, nutty flavor. A good olive oil will suit most purposes, except deep-frying; extra-virgin olive oil, being more expensive, is best kept for salads.

Olives

Green or black olives now come in a variety of marinades. Olive paste is useful for pasta sauces.

Passata

This thick sauce is made from sieved tomatoes. It is mainly used in Italian cooking.

Pesto

This classic Italian sauce combines fresh basil, pine nuts, Parmesan, garlic and olive oil and is useful for pasta or grilled or roasted vegetables.

Soy sauce/Shoyu

Soy sauce is a thin, salty black liquid made from fermented soybeans. Shoyu, or naturally brewed soy sauce, is fermented for far longer and so has fewer additives than soy sauce.

Stocks and flavorings

There are three kinds of vegetable stocks. Granules are ideal for light soups and risottos, bouillon cubes have a stronger flavor suited to hearty soups, while vegetable extracts have a robust taste that is delicious in casseroles.

Sun-dried tomatoes

These deliciously sweet tomatoes, baked in the sun and dried, are sold in bags or in jars, steeped in olive oil.

Tahini paste

Made from ground sesame seeds, this paste is used in Middle Eastern cooking.

Tomato paste

This is a concentrated tomato purée that is sold in cans, jars or tubes. A version made from sun-dried tomatoes is now available.

Vinegars

White or red wine and sherry vinegars are ideal for salad dressings. Balsamic has a very distinctive sweet/sour flavor that can be used in salad dressings or to liven up roasted vegetables and cooked grains.

SOUPS

Wild Mushroom Soup

Wild mushrooms are expensive, but dried porcini have an intense flavor, so only a small quantity is needed.

INGREDIENTS

Serves 4

1 ounce dried porcini mushrooms

2 tablespoons olive oil

1 tablespoon butter

2 leeks, thinly sliced

2 shallots, roughly chopped

1 garlic clove, roughly chopped

8 ounces fresh wild mushrooms

5 cups vegetable stock

½ teaspoon dried thyme

⅔ cup heavy cream

salt and freshly ground black pepper

sprigs of fresh thyme, to garnish

1 Put the dried porcini in a bowl, add 1 cup warm water and let soak for 20–30 minutes. Lift out of the liquid and squeeze over the bowl to remove as much of the soaking liquid as possible. Strain all the liquid and reserve to use later. Finely chop the porcini.

2 Heat the oil and butter in a large saucepan until foaming. Add the sliced leeks, chopped shallots and garlic and cook gently for about 5 minutes, stirring frequently, until softened but not colored.

3 Chop or slice the fresh mushrooms and add to the pan. Stir over medium heat for a few minutes, until they begin to soften. Pour in the stock and bring to a boil. Add the porcini, soaking liquid, dried thyme and salt and pepper. Lower the heat, half-cover the pan and simmer gently for 30 minutes, stirring occasionally.

4 Pour about three-quarters of the soup into a blender or food processor and process until smooth. Return the processed soup to the soup remaining in the pan, stir in the cream and heat through. Check the consistency and add more stock if necessary. Season with salt and pepper. Serve hot, garnished with thyme sprigs.

COOK'S TIP

Porcini are cépes, or boletus mushrooms. Italian cooks would make this soup with a combination of fresh and dried porcini, but if fresh ones are difficult to obtain, you can use other wild mushrooms, such as chanterelles.

Tomato and Fresh Basil Soup

*A pungent soup for late summer,
when fresh tomatoes are at their
most flavorful.*

INGREDIENTS

Serves 4–6

1 tablespoon olive oil

2 tablespoons butter

1 medium onion, finely chopped

2 pounds ripe Italian plum tomatoes,
   roughly chopped

1 garlic clove, roughly chopped

about 3 cups vegetable stock

½ cup dry white wine

2 tablespoons sun-dried tomato paste

2 tablespoons shredded fresh basil

⅔ cup heavy cream

salt and freshly ground black pepper

whole basil leaves, to garnish

1 Heat the oil and butter in a
large saucepan until foaming.
Add the onion and cook gently for
about 5 minutes, stirring, until the
onion is softened but not brown.

2 Stir in the chopped tomatoes
and garlic, then add the stock,
white wine and sun-dried tomato
paste, with salt and pepper to taste.
Bring to a boil, then lower the heat,
half-cover the pan and simmer
gently for 20 minutes, stirring
occasionally to keep the tomatoes
from sticking to the bottom of
the pan.

3 Process the soup with the
shredded basil in a blender or
food processor, then press through
a sieve into a clean pan.

4 Add the cream and heat
through, stirring. Do not allow
the soup to approach the boiling
point. Check the consistency and
add more stock if necessary, then
season with salt and pepper. Pour
into heated bowls and garnish with
basil. Serve at once.

Cream of Zucchini Soup

The beauty of this soup is its delicate color, rich and creamy texture and subtle taste. If you prefer a more pronounced cheese flavor, use Gorgonzola instead of dolcelatte.

INGREDIENTS

Serves 4–6

2 tablespoons olive oil

1 tablespoon butter

1 medium onion, roughly chopped

2 pounds zucchini, trimmed and sliced

1 teaspoon dried oregano

about 2½ cups vegetable stock

4 ounces dolcelatte cheese, rind
  removed, diced

1¼ cups light cream

salt and freshly ground black pepper

fresh oregano, extra dolcelatte and cream,
  to garnish

2 Add the zucchini and oregano with salt and pepper to taste. Cook over medium heat for 10 minutes, stirring frequently. Pour in the stock and bring to a boil, stirring.

3 Lower the heat, half-cover the pan and simmer gently, stirring occasionally, for about 30 minutes. Stir in the diced dolcelatte until melted.

4 Process the soup in a blender or food processor until smooth, then press through a sieve into a clean pan.

5 Add two-thirds of the cream and stir over low heat until hot but not boiling. Add more stock or water if the soup is too thick. Season with salt and pepper. Pour into heated bowls. Swirl in the remaining cream. Serve, garnished with oregano, extra cheese, cream and pepper.

1 Heat the oil and butter in a large saucepan until foaming. Add the onion and cook gently for about 5 minutes, stirring frequently, until softened but not brown.

COOK'S TIP

To save time, trim off and discard the ends of the zucchini, cut them into thirds, then chop in a food processor fitted with a metal blade.

Garlic, Chickpea and Spinach Soup

This delicious, thick and creamy soup is richly flavored and makes a great one-pot meal.

Serves 4

2 tablespoons olive oil

4 garlic cloves, crushed

1 onion, roughly chopped

2 teaspoons ground cumin

2 teaspoons ground coriander

5 cups vegetable stock

12 ounces potatoes, peeled and finely chopped

15-ounce can chickpeas, drained

1 tablespoon cornstarch

⅔ cup heavy cream

2 tablespoons light tahini (sesame seed paste)

7 ounces spinach, shredded

cayenne pepper

salt and freshly ground black pepper

1 Heat the oil in a large saucepan and cook the garlic and onion for 5 minutes, or until they are softened and golden brown.

2 Stir in the cumin and coriander and cook for another minute.

3 Pour in the stock and add the chopped potatoes to the pan. Bring to a boil and simmer for 10 minutes. Add the chickpeas and simmer for 5 minutes more, or until the potatoes and chickpeas are just tender.

4 Blend together the cornstarch, cream, tahini and plenty of seasoning. Stir into the soup with the spinach. Bring to a boil, stirring, and simmer for another 2 minutes. Season with cayenne pepper, salt and black pepper. Serve immediately, sprinkled with a little cayenne pepper.

Classic French Onion Soup

When French onion soup is made slowly and carefully, the onions caramelize to a deep mahogany color. The soup has a superb flavor and is a perfect winter supper dish.

INGREDIENTS

Serves 4

4 large onions

2 tablespoons sunflower or olive oil, or 1 tablespoon of each

2 tablespoons butter

3¾ cups vegetable stock

4 slices French bread

1½–2 ounces Gruyère or Cheddar cheese, grated

salt and freshly ground black pepper

1 Peel and quarter the onions and slice or chop them into ¼-inch pieces. Heat the oil and butter in a deep, medium-size saucepan, so that the onions form a thick layer.

2 Sauté the onions briskly for a few minutes, stirring constantly.

3 Reduce the heat and cook gently for 45–60 minutes. At first the onions need to be stirred only occasionally, but as they begin to color, stir frequently. The color of the onions gradually turns golden and then more rapidly to brown, so take care to stir constantly at this stage so that they do not burn on the bottom.

4 When the onions are a rich mahogany brown, add the vegetable stock and a little seasoning. Simmer, partially covered, for 30 minutes, then season with salt and pepper.

5 Preheat the broiler and toast the French bread. Spoon the soup into four ovenproof serving dishes and place a piece of bread in each. Sprinkle with the cheese and broil for a few minutes, until golden. Season with plenty of freshly ground black pepper.

White Bean Soup

A thick purée of cooked dried beans is at the heart of this substantial country soup from Tuscany. It makes a warming lunch or supper dish.

INGREDIENTS

Serves 6

1½ cups dried cannellini or other
   white beans
1 bay leaf
5 tablespoons olive oil
1 medium onion, finely chopped
1 carrot, finely chopped
1 celery rib, finely chopped
3 medium tomatoes, peeled and finely
   chopped
2 cloves garlic, finely chopped
1 teaspoon fresh thyme leaves or
   ½ teaspoon dried thyme
3 cups boiling water
salt and freshly ground black pepper
olive oil, to serve

1 Pick over the beans carefully, discarding any stones or other particles. Rinse thoroughly in cold water to ensure that they are clean. Soak in a large bowl of cold water overnight. Drain the beans and place them in a large saucepan of water, bring to a boil and cook for 20 minutes. Drain. Return the beans to the pan, cover with cold water and bring to a boil again. Add the bay leaf and cook for 1–2 hours, until the beans are tender. Drain again. Remove the bay leaf.

2 Purée about three-quarters of the beans in a food processor or pass through a food mill, adding a little water if necessary, to create a smooth paste.

3 Heat the oil in a large saucepan. Stir in the onion and cook until it softens. Add the carrot and celery, and cook for 5 minutes more.

4 Stir in the tomatoes, garlic and thyme. Cook for 6–8 minutes more, stirring often.

5 Pour in the boiling water. Stir in the beans and the bean purée. Season with salt and pepper. Simmer for 10–15 minutes. Serve in individual soup bowls, sprinkled with a little olive oil.

COOK'S TIP

Canned cooked beans, such as cannellini or borlotti, may be substituted in this recipe. Simply drain the beans and omit Step 1.

Asparagus Soup

Home-made asparagus soup has a delicate flavor, quite unlike that from a can. This soup is best made with young asparagus, which are tender and blend well. Serve it with wafer-thin slices of bread.

INGREDIENTS

Serves 4

1 pound young asparagus

3 tablespoons butter

6 shallots, sliced

1 tablespoon all-purpose flour

2½ cups vegetable stock or water

1 tablespoon lemon juice

1 cup milk

½ cup light cream

2 teaspoons chopped fresh chervil

salt and freshly ground black pepper

1 Cut 1½ inches off the tops of half the asparagus and set aside for a garnish. Slice the remaining asparagus.

2 Melt 2 tablespoons of the butter in a large saucepan and sauté the sliced shallots for 2–3 minutes, until soft.

3 Add the asparagus and sauté over low heat for 1 minute.

4 Stir in the flour and cook for 1 minute. Stir in the stock or water and lemon juice and season with salt and pepper. Bring to a boil, half-cover the pan, then simmer for 15–20 minutes, until the asparagus is very tender.

5 Cool slightly and then process the soup in a food processor or blender until smooth. Press the puréed asparagus through a sieve into a clean saucepan. Add the milk by pouring and stirring it through the sieve with the asparagus so as to extract the maximum amount of asparagus purée.

6 Melt the remaining butter and sauté the reserved asparagus tips gently for 3–4 minutes, to soften.

7 Heat the soup gently for 3–4 minutes. Stir in the cream and the asparagus tips. Continue to heat gently, then serve sprinkled with chopped fresh chervil.

Fresh Tomato, Lentil and Onion Soup

This delicious, wholesome soup is ideal served with thick slices of whole-wheat bread.

INGREDIENTS

Serves 4–6

2 teaspoons sunflower oil

1 large onion, chopped

2 celery ribs, chopped

¾ cup split red lentils

2 large tomatoes, peeled and roughly chopped

3¾ cups vegetable stock

2 teaspoons dried herbes de Provence

salt and freshly ground black pepper

chopped parsley, to garnish

1 Heat the oil in a large saucepan. Add the onion and celery and cook for 5 minutes, stirring occasionally. Add the lentils and cook for 1 minute.

2 Stir in the tomatoes, stock, dried herbs, salt and pepper. Cover, bring to a boil and simmer for about 20 minutes, stirring occasionally.

3 When the lentils are cooked and tender, set the soup aside to cool slightly.

4 Purée in a blender or food processor until smooth. Season with salt and pepper, return to the saucepan and reheat gently until piping hot. Ladle into soup bowls to serve and garnish each with chopped parsley.

Minestrone with Pesto

Minestrone is a thick, mixed vegetable soup using almost any combination of seasonal vegetables. Short cuts of pasta or rice may also be added. This version includes pesto sauce.

INGREDIENTS

Serves 6

3 tablespoons olive oil

1 large onion, finely chopped

1 leek, sliced

2 carrots, finely chopped

1 celery rib, finely chopped

2 cloves garlic, finely chopped

2 potatoes, peeled and cut into small dice

6¼ cups hot vegetable stock or water, or a combination of both

1 bay leaf

1 sprig of fresh thyme, or ¼ teaspoon dried thyme

¾ cup peas, fresh or frozen

2–3 zucchini, finely chopped

3 medium tomatoes, peeled and finely chopped

2 cups cooked or canned beans, such as cannellini

3 tablespoons pesto sauce

salt and freshly ground black pepper

freshly grated Parmesan cheese, to serve

1 Heat the oil in a saucepan. Stir in the onion and leek, and cook for 5–6 minutes. Add the carrots, celery and garlic, and cook over moderate heat for 5 minutes. Add the potatoes and cook for 2–3 minutes more.

2 Pour in the hot stock or water and stir well. Add the herbs and season with salt and pepper. Bring to a boil, reduce the heat and cook for 10–12 minutes.

3 Stir in the peas, if fresh, and the zucchini. Simmer for 5 minutes. Add the frozen peas, if using, and the tomatoes. Cover the pan and simmer for 5–8 minutes.

4 About 10 minutes before serving, uncover the pan and stir in the beans. Simmer for 10 minutes. Stir in the pesto sauce. Simmer for another 5 minutes. Remove from the heat and let stand for a few minutes. Serve with the grated Parmesan cheese.

Pumpkin Soup

This beautifully flavored, golden-colored soup would be perfect for an autumn dinner.

INGREDIENTS

Serves 4

1-lb piece of peeled pumpkin

4 tablespoons butter

1 medium onion, finely chopped

3 cups vegetable stock or water

2 cups milk

pinch of grated nutmeg

1½ ounces spaghetti broken into small pieces

6 tablespoons freshly grated Parmesan cheese

salt and freshly ground black pepper

1 Chop the piece of pumpkin into 1-inch cubes.

2 Heat the butter in a saucepan. Add the onion and cook over moderate heat until it softens, 6–8 minutes. Stir in the pumpkin pieces and cook for 2–3 minutes more.

3 Add the stock or water and cook until the pumpkin is soft, about 15 minutes. Remove from the heat.

4 Process the soup in a blender or food processor. Return it to the pan. Stir in the milk and nutmeg. Season with salt and pepper. Bring the soup back to a boil.

5 Stir the broken spaghetti into the soup. Cook until the pasta is done. Stir in the Parmesan, sprinkle with nutmeg and serve at once.

Split Pea and Zucchini Soup

Rich and satisfying, this tasty and nutritious soup will warm a chilly winter's day.

Serves 4

6 ounces (2 cups) yellow split peas
1 medium onion, finely chopped
1 teaspoon sunflower oil
2 medium zucchini, finely diced
3¾ cups vegetable stock
½ teaspoon ground turmeric
salt and freshly ground black pepper
crusty bread, to serve

3 Add the remaining zucchini to the pan. Cook for 2–3 minutes. Add the stock and turmeric and bring to a boil. Reduce the heat, cover and simmer for 30–40 minutes. Season.

4 When the soup is almost ready, bring a large saucepan of water to a boil, add the reserved diced zucchini and cook for 1 minute. Drain and add to the soup. Serve hot with warm crusty bread.

1 Place the split peas in a bowl, cover with cold water and let soak for several hours or overnight. Drain, rinse in cold water and drain again.

2 Cook the onion in the oil in a covered pan, shaking occasionally, until soft. Reserve a handful of diced zucchini to use later.

COOK'S TIP

For a quicker alternative, use red split lentils for this soup—they need no presoaking and cook very quickly. Adjust the amount of stock, if necessary.

Carrot and Cilantro Soup

Nearly all root vegetables make excellent soups, as they purée well and have an earthy flavor that complements the sharper flavors of herbs and spices. Carrots are particularly versatile. This simple soup is elegant in both flavor and appearance.

INGREDIENTS

Serves 4–6

1 pound carrots, preferably young
   and tender
1 tablespoon sunflower oil
3 tablespoons butter
1 onion, chopped
1 celery rib, plus 2–3 pale leafy
   celery tops
2 small potatoes, peeled
4 cups vegetable stock
2–3 teaspoons ground coriander
1 tablespoon chopped fresh
   cilantro
1 cup milk
salt and freshly ground black pepper

1 Trim and peel the carrots and cut into chunks. Heat the oil and 2 tablespoons butter in a large flameproof casserole or heavy saucepan and sauté the onion over gentle heat for 3–4 minutes, until slightly softened.

2 Slice the celery and chop the potatoes. Add them to the onion in the pan, cook for a few minutes and then add the carrots. Cook over gentle heat for 3–4 minutes, stirring, and then cover.

3 Reduce the heat even further and sweat for about 10 minutes. Shake the pan or stir occasionally so the vegetables do not stick to the bottom.

4 Add the stock and bring to a boil. Half-cover the pan and simmer for another 8–10 minutes, until the carrots and potatoes are tender.

5 Remove 6–8 tiny celery leaves for garnish and finely chop the remaining celery tops (about 1 tablespoon once chopped). Melt the remaining butter in a small saucepan and sauté the ground coriander for about 1 minute, stirring constantly.

6 Reduce the heat, add the chopped celery tops and cilantro and sauté for about 1 minute. Set aside.

7 Process the soup in a food processor or blender and pour into a clean saucepan. Stir in the milk and the cilantro mixture. Season, heat gently, taste and adjust seasoning. Serve garnished with the reserved celery leaves.

COOK'S TIP

For a more piquant flavor, add a little lemon juice just before serving.

Curried Celery Soup

An unusual combination of flavors, this soup is excellent served with warm whole-wheat rolls or whole-wheat pita bread.

Serves 4–6

2 teaspoons olive oil

1 onion, chopped

1 leek, washed and sliced

1½ pounds celery, chopped

1 tablespoon medium or hot curry
   powder

8 ounces potatoes, washed and diced

3¾ cups vegetable stock

1 bouquet garni

2 tablespoons chopped fresh mixed herbs

salt

celery seeds and leaves, to garnish

1 Heat the oil in a large saucepan. Add the onion, leek and celery, cover and cook gently for about 10 minutes, stirring occasionally.

2 Add the curry powder and cook for 2 minutes more, stirring occasionally.

3 Add the potatoes, stock and bouquet garni, cover and bring to a boil. Simmer for 20 minutes, until the vegetables are tender.

4 Remove and discard the bouquet garni and set the soup aside to cool slightly.

5 Purée in a blender or food processor until smooth.

6 Add the mixed herbs, season to taste and process briefly. Return to the saucepan and reheat gently until piping hot. Ladle into soup bowls and garnish each with a sprinkling of celery seeds and some celery leaves.

VARIATION

For a tasty change, use celeriac and sweet potatoes in place of the celery and standard potatoes.

Fresh Pea Soup

This soup is known in France as Potage Saint-Germain, a name that comes from a suburb of Paris where peas used to be cultivated in market gardens. If fresh peas are not available, use frozen peas, but thaw and rinse them before use.

INGREDIENTS

Serves 2–3

2 tablespoons butter

2 or 3 shallots, finely chopped

3 cups shelled fresh peas (from about 3 pounds garden peas) or thawed frozen peas

3–4 tablespoons whipping cream (optional)

salt and freshly ground black pepper

croutons, to garnish

1 Melt the butter in a heavy saucepan or flameproof casserole. Add the shallots and cook for about 3 minutes, stirring occasionally.

2 Add 2 cups water and the peas, and season with salt and pepper.

3 Cover and simmer for 12 minutes for young or frozen peas and up to 18 minutes for large or older peas, stirring occasionally.

4 When the peas are tender, ladle them into a food processor or blender with a little of the cooking liquid and process until smooth.

5 Strain the soup into the saucepan or casserole, stir in the cream, if using, and heat through without boiling. Season with salt and pepper and serve hot, garnished with croutons.

Pea, Leek and Broccoli Soup

*A delicious and nutritious soup,
ideal for warming those chilly
winter evenings.*

INGREDIENTS

Serves 4–6

1 onion, chopped

8 ounces leeks (trimmed weight),
    sliced (about 2 cups)

8 ounces unpeeled potatoes, diced

3¾ cups vegetable stock

1 bay leaf

8 ounces broccoli florets

1½ cups frozen peas

2–3 tablespoons chopped fresh
    parsley

salt and freshly ground black pepper

parsley leaves, to garnish

1 Put the onion, leeks, potatoes,
stock and bay leaf in a large
saucepan and mix together. Cover,
bring to a boil and simmer for 10
minutes, stirring.

2 Add the broccoli and peas,
cover, return to a boil and
simmer for another 10 minutes,
stirring occasionally.

3 Set aside to cool slightly and
remove and discard the bay
leaf. Purée in a blender or food
processor until smooth.

4 Add the parsley, season with
salt and pepper and process
briefly. Return to the saucepan and
reheat gently until piping hot.
Ladle into soup bowls and garnish
with parsley leaves.

Gazpacho

This cold soup is popular all over Spain, where there are hundreds of variations. It uses tomatoes, tomato juice, green pepper and garlic, and is served with a selection of garnishes.

INGREDIENTS

Serves 4

3–3½ pounds ripe tomatoes

1 green bell pepper, seeded and
    roughly chopped

2 garlic cloves, crushed

2 slices white bread, crusts removed

4 tablespoons olive oil

4 tablespoons tarragon wine vinegar

⅔ cup tomato juice

good pinch of sugar

salt and freshly ground black pepper

ice cubes, to serve

For the garnishes

2 tablespoons sunflower oil

2–3 slices white bread, diced

1 small cucumber, peeled and finely diced

1 small onion, finely chopped

1 red bell pepper, seeded and finely diced

1 green bell pepper, seeded and
    finely diced

2 hard-boiled eggs, chopped

1 Peel and quarter the tomatoes, then remove the cores.

2 Place the green pepper in a food processor and process for a few seconds. Add the tomatoes, garlic, bread, olive oil and vinegar and process again. Add the tomato juice, sugar, salt and pepper and process.

3 The mixture should be thick but not too heavy. Continue processing until it is the right consistency. Press the liquid through a sieve into a bowl and chill for at least 2 hours but no more than 12 hours, or the texture will deteriorate.

4 To prepare the bread cubes to use as a garnish, heat the oil in a frying pan and sauté them over moderate heat for 4–5 minutes, until golden brown. Drain well on paper towels.

5 Place each garnish in a separate small dish, or alternatively arrange them in rows on a large plate.

6 Just before serving, stir a few ice cubes into the soup and then spoon into serving bowls. Serve with the garnishes.

Cold Leek and Potato Soup

Serve this flavorful soup with a dollop of crème fraîche or sour cream to add richness to the broth. Sprinkle with a few snipped fresh chives.

INGREDIENTS

Serves 6–8

1 pound potatoes, peeled and cubed

6¼ cups vegetable stock

4 medium leeks, trimmed

⅔ cup crème fraîche or
sour cream

salt and freshly ground black pepper

3 tablespoons snipped fresh chives,
to garnish

1 Put the potatoes and stock in a saucepan or flameproof casserole and bring to a boil. Reduce the heat and simmer for 15–20 minutes.

2 Make a slit along the length of each leek and rinse well under cold running water. Slice thinly.

3 When the potatoes are barely tender, stir in the leeks. Season with salt and pepper and simmer for 10–15 minutes, until the vegetables are soft, stirring occasionally. If the soup appears too thick, thin it with a little more of the stock or water.

4 Purée the soup in a blender or food processor, in batches if necessary. If you would prefer a very smooth soup, pass it through a food mill or press through a coarse sieve. Stir in most of the cream, cool and then chill. To serve, ladle into chilled bowls and garnish with a swirl of cream and some snipped chives.

VARIATION

To make a low-fat soup, use low-fat fromage frais instead of crème fraîche or sour cream, or simply thin the soup with a little skim milk.

APPETIZERS

Guacamole

*This is quite a fiery version,
although nowhere near as hot as you
would be served in Mexico!*

INGREDIENTS

Serves 4

2 ripe avocados, peeled and pitted

2 tomatoes, peeled, seeded and finely
    chopped

6 scallions, finely chopped

1–2 fresh chiles, seeded and finely
    chopped

2 tablespoons fresh lime or lemon juice

1 tablespoon chopped cilantro

salt and freshly ground black pepper

cilantro sprigs, to garnish

1 Put the avocado halves in a
large bowl and mash them
roughly with a large fork.

2 Add the remaining ingredients.
Mix well and season with salt
and pepper. Serve garnished with
cilantro sprigs.

Lima Bean, Watercress and Herb Dip

This is a refreshing dip that is especially good served with fresh vegetable crudités and breadsticks.

INGREDIENTS

Serves 4–6

1 cup cottage cheese

14-ounce can lima beans, rinsed
  and drained

1 bunch scallions, chopped

2 ounces watercress, chopped

¼ cup mayonnaise

3 tablespoons chopped fresh mixed herbs

salt and freshly ground black pepper

watercress sprigs, to garnish

vegetable crudités and breadsticks,
  to serve

1 Put the cottage cheese, lima beans, scallions, watercress, mayonnaise and herbs in a blender or food processor and blend until fairly smooth.

3 Cover and chill for several hours before serving.

4 Transfer to a serving dish (or individual dishes) and garnish with watercress sprigs. Serve with vegetable crudités and breadsticks.

2 Season with salt and pepper and spoon the mixture into a dish.

COOK'S TIP

Try using other canned beans such as cannellini beans or chickpeas in place of the lima beans.

Saffron Dip

Serve this mild dip with fresh vegetable crudités—it is particularly good with florets of cauliflower.

INGREDIENTS

Serves 4

small pinch of saffron strands

7 ounces fromage frais

10 fresh chives

10 fresh basil leaves

salt and freshly ground black pepper

vegetable crudités, to serve

1 Pour 1 tablespoon boiling water into a small heatproof bowl and add the saffron strands. Let infuse for 3–4 minutes, stirring occasionally.

2 Beat the fromage frais until smooth, then stir in the infused saffron liquid.

3 Use a pair of scissors to snip the chives into the dip. Tear the basil leaves into small pieces and stir them in.

4 Season with salt and pepper. Serve immediately with vegetable crudités.

VARIATION

Leave out the saffron and add a squeeze of lemon or lime juice instead. Alternatively, replace the saffron strands with ground saffron powder.

Spiced Carrot Dip

This is a delicious dip with a sweet and spicy flavor. Serve wheat crackers or tortilla chips as accompaniments for dipping.

INGREDIENTS

Serves 4

1 onion

3 carrots, plus extra to garnish

grated zest and juice of 2 oranges

1 tablespoon hot curry paste

²⁄₃ cup plain yogurt

handful of fresh basil leaves

1–2 tablespoons fresh lemon juice, to taste

red Tabasco sauce, to taste

salt and freshly ground black pepper

3 Stir in the yogurt, then tear the basil leaves roughly into small pieces and stir them into the carrot mixture.

4 Add the lemon juice and Tabasco and season with salt and pepper. Serve within a few hours at room temperature. Garnish with grated carrot.

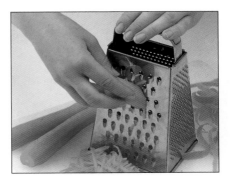

1 Finely chop the onion. Peel and grate the carrots. Place the onion, carrots, orange zest and juice and curry paste in a small saucepan. Bring to a boil, cover and simmer gently for 10 minutes, until tender.

2 Process the mixture in a blender or food processor until smooth. Let cool completely.

Eggplant Dip with Crisp Bread

This delectable Middle Eastern dish is flavored with tahini (sesame seed paste), which gives it a subtle flavor.

INGREDIENTS

Serves 6

2 small eggplants

1 garlic clove, crushed

4 tablespoons tahini

¼ cup ground almonds

juice of ½ lemon

½ teaspoon ground cumin

2 tablespoons fresh mint leaves

2 tablespoons olive oil

salt and freshly ground black pepper

Lebanese flatbread

4 pita breads

3 tablespoons toasted sesame seeds

3 tablespoons fresh thyme leaves, chopped

3 tablespoons poppy seeds

⅔ cup olive oil

3 Broil the eggplant, turning them frequently, until the skin is blackened and blistered. Remove the skin, chop the flesh roughly and let drain in a colander. Wait for 30 minutes, then squeeze out as much liquid from the eggplant as possible.

4 Place the eggplant flesh in a blender or food processor. Add the garlic, tahini, almonds, lemon juice and cumin. Season, then process to a smooth paste. Chop half the mint and stir in.

5 Spoon into a bowl, sprinkle the remaining mint leaves on top and drizzle with olive oil. Serve with the Lebanese flatbread.

1 Start by making the Lebanese flatbread. Split the pita breads through the middle and carefully open them out. Mix the sesame seeds, chopped thyme and poppy seeds in a mortar. Crush them lightly with a pestle to release the flavor.

2 Stir in the olive oil. Spread the mixture lightly over the cut sides of the pita bread. Broil until golden brown and crisp. When completely cool, break into pieces and set aside.

Chickpea Falafel with Cilantro Dip

Little balls of spicy chickpea purée, deep-fried until crisp, are served with a zesty cilantro-flavored mayonnaise.

INGREDIENTS

Serves 4

14-ounce can chickpeas, drained

6 scallions, finely chopped

1 egg

½ teaspoon ground turmeric

1 garlic clove, crushed

1 teaspoon ground cumin

4 tablespoons chopped cilantro

oil for deep-frying

1 small fresh red chile, seeded and
    finely chopped

3 tablespoons mayonnaise

salt and freshly ground black pepper

sprig of cilantro, to garnish

1 Put the chickpeas in a food processor or blender. Add the scallions and process to a smooth purée. Add the egg, ground turmeric, garlic, cumin and about 1 tablespoon of the chopped cilantro. Process briefly to mix, then season with salt and pepper.

2 Working with clean, wet hands, shape the chickpea mixture into about 16 small balls.

3 Heat the oil for deep-frying to 350°F, or until a cube of bread added to the oil browns in 30–45 seconds. Deep-fry the falafel in batches for 2–3 minutes, or until golden. Drain the falafel on paper towels. Place in a serving bowl and keep warm.

4 Stir the remaining chopped cilantro and the chile into the mayonnaise. Garnish with the cilantro sprig and serve alongside the falafel.

Hummus with Panfried Zucchini

Panfried zucchini are perfect for dipping into homemade hummus, served with pita bread and olives.

INGREDIENTS

Serves 4

8-ounce can chickpeas

2 garlic cloves, coarsely crushed

6 tablespoons lemon juice

4 tablespoons tahini (sesame seed paste)

5 tablespoons olive oil, plus extra to serve

1 teaspoon ground cumin

1 pound small zucchini

salt and freshly ground black pepper

paprika to garnish

pita bread and black olives, to serve

1 Drain the chickpeas, reserving the liquid from the can, and put them in a blender or food processor. Blend to a smooth paste, adding a small amount of the reserved liquid, if necessary.

2 Mix the garlic, lemon juice and tahini together and add to the blender or food processor. Process until smooth. With the machine running, gradually add 3 tablespoons of the olive oil through the feeder tube or lid.

3 Add the cumin. Season with salt and pepper. Process to mix. Scrape the hummus into a bowl. Cover and chill until required.

4 Remove the ends from the zucchini. Slice the zucchini lengthwise into even-size pieces.

5 Heat the remaining oil in a large frying pan. Season the zucchini with salt and pepper and cook them for 2–3 minutes on each side, until just tender.

6 Divide the zucchini among four individual plates. Spoon a portion of hummus onto each plate and sprinkle with paprika. Add two or three pieces of sliced pita bread and serve with olives.

VARIATION

For a stronger nutty flavor, substitute smooth peanut butter for the tahini paste. This is also delicious served with panfried or broiled eggplant or red pepper slices.

Marinated Vegetable Antipasto

This colorful selection of fresh vegetables and herbs makes a great appetizer when served with fresh crusty bread.

INGREDIENTS

Serves 4

For the peppers
3 red bell peppers
3 yellow bell peppers
4 garlic cloves, sliced
handful of fresh basil
½ cup olive oil
salt and freshly ground black pepper

For the mushrooms
1 pound portobello mushrooms,
   thickly sliced
¼ cup olive oil
1 large garlic clove, crushed
1 tablespoon chopped fresh rosemary
1 cup dry white wine
fresh rosemary sprigs, to garnish

For the olives
1 dried red chile, crushed
grated zest of 1 lemon
½ cup olive oil
8 ounces (1⅓ cups) Italian black olives
2 tablespoons chopped fresh flat-leaf
   parsley
basil leaves, to garnish
1 lemon wedge, to serve

1 Place the peppers under a hot broiler. Cook until they are black and blistered all over. Remove from the heat and place in a large plastic bag to cool.

2 When the peppers are cool, remove their skins, halve the flesh and remove the seeds. Cut into strips lengthwise and place them in a bowl with the sliced garlic and basil leaves. Season, then cover with oil and marinate for 3–4 hours, tossing occasionally. Garnish with basil leaves.

3 Place the mushrooms in a bowl. Heat the oil in a pan and add the garlic, rosemary and wine. Bring to a boil, then simmer for 3 minutes. Season. Pour over the mushrooms.

4 Mix well and let cool, stirring occasionally. Cover and marinate overnight. Serve at room temperature, garnished with rosemary sprigs.

5 Place the chile and lemon zest in a small pan with the oil. Heat gently for about 3 minutes. Add the olives and heat for 1 minute more. Pour the olive mixture into a bowl and let cool. Marinate overnight. Before serving, sprinkle with parsley and garnish with basil leaves. Serve with the lemon wedge.

Spicy Potato Wedges with Chili Dip

The spicy crust on these potato wedges makes them irresistible, especially when served with a zesty chili dip.

INGREDIENTS

Serves 2

2 baking potatoes, about 8 ounces each

2 tablespoons olive oil

2 garlic cloves, crushed

1 teaspoon ground allspice

1 teaspoon ground coriander

1 tablespoon paprika

salt and freshly ground black pepper

For the dip

1 tablespoon olive oil

1 small onion, finely chopped

1 garlic clove, crushed

7-ounce can chopped tomatoes

1 fresh red chile, seeded and
   finely chopped

1 tablespoon balsamic vinegar

1 tablespoon chopped cilantro, plus extra
   to garnish

1 Preheat the oven to 400°F. Wash the potatoes. Cut them in half and then into 8 wedges.

2 Place the potato wedges in a saucepan of cold water. Bring to a boil, then lower the heat and simmer gently for 10 minutes, or until the potatoes have softened slightly. Drain well and pat dry on paper towels.

3 Mix the oil, garlic, allspice, coriander and paprika in a roasting pan. Season with salt and pepper. Add the potatoes and shake to coat thoroughly. Roast for 20 minutes, turning occasionally.

4 Meanwhile, make the chile dip. Heat the oil in a saucepan, add the onion and garlic and cook for 5–10 minutes, until soft and golden. Add the tomatoes with their juice and stir in the chile and vinegar.

5 Cook gently for 10 minutes, until the mixture has reduced and thickened. Season with salt and pepper. Stir in the cilantro and serve hot, with the potato wedges. Season with salt and freshly ground black pepper and garnish with cilantro.

Crisp Spring Rolls with Sweet Chili Dip

Dainty miniature spring rolls make delicious appetizers or perfect party finger food.

Makes 20–24

1 ounce rice vermicelli noodles

peanut oil

1 teaspoon finely grated fresh ginger root

2 scallions, finely shredded

2 ounces carrot, finely shredded

2 ounces snow peas, shredded

1 ounce young spinach leaves

2 ounces fresh bean sprouts

1 tablespoon fresh mint, finely chopped

1 tablespoon finely chopped cilantro

2 tablespoons light soy sauce

20–24 spring roll wrappers, each
    5 inches square

1 egg white, lightly beaten

For the dipping sauce

¼ cup sugar

¼ cup rice vinegar

2 fresh red chiles, seeded and
    finely chopped

1 First make the dipping sauce. Place the sugar and vinegar in a small saucepan with 2 tablespoons water. Heat gently, stirring until the sugar dissolves, then boil rapidly until it forms a light syrup. Stir in the chiles and let cool thoroughly.

2 Soak the noodles according to the package instructions. Rinse and drain well. Using scissors, snip the noodles into short lengths.

3 Heat a wok until hot. Add 1 tablespoon oil. Add the ginger and scallions and stir-fry for 15 seconds. Add the carrot and snow peas and stir-fry for 2–3 minutes. Add the spinach, bean sprouts, mint, cilantro, soy sauce and noodles and stir-fry for another minute. Set aside to cool.

4 Place a spring roll wrapper on the work surface. Put a spoonful of filling in the middle. Fold to encase the filling.

5 Fold in each side, then roll up tightly. Brush the end with beaten egg white to seal. Repeat until all the filling has been used.

6 Half-fill a wok with oil and heat to 350°F. Deep-fry the spring rolls in batches for 3–4 minutes, until golden and crisp. Drain on paper towels. Serve hot, with the sweet chile dipping sauce.

COOK'S TIP

You can cook the spring rolls 2–3 hours in advance. Then all you have to do is reheat them on a foil-lined baking sheet at 400°F for about 10 minutes, until they are ready to eat.

Potted Stilton with Herbs and Melba Toast

This appetizer is a great time-saver, as the potted Stilton can be made the day before, and the Melba toast will keep in an airtight container for up to two days.

INGREDIENTS

Serves 8

8 ounces (1 cup) Stilton or other
    blue cheese
4 ounces (½ cup) cream cheese
1 tablespoon port
1 tablespoon chopped fresh parsley
1 tablespoon snipped fresh chives, plus
    extra to garnish
½ cup finely chopped walnuts
salt and freshly ground black pepper

For the Melba toast
12 thin slices of white bread

1 Put the Stilton or other blue cheese, cream cheese and port in a blender or food processor and process until smooth.

2 Stir in the remaining ingredients and then season with salt and pepper.

3 Spoon into individual ramekins and level the tops. Cover with plastic wrap and chill until firm. Sprinkle with snipped chives just before serving.

4 To make the Melba toast, preheat the oven to 350°F. Toast the bread on both sides.

5 While the toast is still hot, cut off the crusts and cut each slice horizontally in two. While the bread is still warm, place it in a single layer on baking sheets and bake for 10–15 minutes, until golden brown and crisp. Continue with the remaining slices in the same way. Serve warm with the potted Stilton.

Mushroom and Bean Pâté

A light and tasty pâté, delicious served on whole-wheat bread or toast.

Serves 12

1 pound mushrooms, sliced

1 onion, chopped

2 garlic cloves, crushed

1 red bell pepper, seeded and diced

2 tablespoons vegetable stock

2 tablespoons dry white wine

14-ounce can red kidney beans, rinsed
    and drained

1 egg, beaten

1 cup fresh whole-wheat
    bread crumbs

1 tablespoon chopped fresh thyme

1 tablespoon chopped fresh rosemary

salt and freshly ground black pepper

lettuce and tomatoes, to garnish

1 Preheat the oven to 350°F. Lightly grease and line a nonstick 9 x 5 x 3-inch (8-cup) loaf pan. Put the mushrooms, onion, garlic, pepper, stock and wine in a saucepan. Cover and cook for about 10 minutes, stirring occasionally.

2 Set aside to cool slightly, then purée the mixture with the kidney beans in a blender or food processor until smooth.

3 Transfer the mixture to a bowl, add the egg, bread crumbs and herbs and mix thoroughly. Season with salt and pepper.

4 Spoon the mixture into the prepared pan and level the surface. Bake for 45–60 minutes, until lightly set and browned on top. Place on a wire rack and allow the pâté to cool completely in the pan. Once cool, cover and refrigerate for several hours. Turn out of the pan and serve in slices, garnished with lettuce and tomato.

Garlic Mushrooms with a Parsley Crust

These garlic mushrooms are perfect for dinner parties, or you could serve them in larger portions as a light supper dish with a green salad.

INGREDIENTS

Serves 4

12 ounces large mushrooms, stems
   removed

3 garlic cloves, crushed

12 tablespoons (1½ sticks) butter, softened

1 cup fresh white bread crumbs

1 cup chopped fresh parsley

1 egg, beaten

salt and cayenne pepper

8 cherry tomatoes, to garnish

1 Preheat the oven to 375°F. Arrange the mushrooms cup side up on a baking sheet. Mix together the garlic and butter in a small bowl and divide 8 tablespoons of the butter among the mushrooms.

2 Heat the remaining butter in a frying pan and lightly sauté the bread crumbs until golden brown. Place the chopped parsley in a bowl, add the bread crumbs, season with salt and cayenne pepper and mix well.

3 Stir in the egg and use the mixture to fill the mushroom caps. Bake for 10–15 minutes, until the topping has browned and the mushrooms have softened. Garnish with quartered cherry tomatoes.

COOK'S TIP

If you are planning ahead, stuffed mushrooms can be prepared up to 12 hours in advance and kept in the refrigerator before baking.

Asparagus Rolls with Herb Butter Sauce

For a taste sensation, try tender asparagus spears wrapped in crisp phyllo pastry. The buttery herb sauce makes the perfect accompaniment.

INGREDIENTS

Serves 2

4 sheets of phyllo pastry
4 tablespoons butter, melted
16 young asparagus spears, trimmed

For the sauce

2 shallots, finely chopped
1 bay leaf
⅔ cup dry white wine
12 tablespoons (1½ sticks) butter, softened
1 tablespoon chopped fresh herbs
salt and freshly ground black pepper
chopped chives, to garnish

1 Preheat the oven to 400°F. Cut the phyllo sheets in half. Brush a half sheet with melted butter. Fold one corner of the sheet down to the bottom edge to give a wedge shape.

2 Lay 4 asparagus spears on top at the longest edge, and roll up toward the shortest edge. Using the remaining phyllo and asparagus spears, make three more rolls in the same way.

3 Lay the rolls on a greased baking sheet. Brush with the remaining melted butter. Bake for 8 minutes, until golden brown.

4 Meanwhile, put the shallots, bay leaf and wine in a pan. Cover and cook over high heat until the wine is reduced to 3–4 tablespoons.

5 Strain the wine mixture into a bowl. Whisk in the butter a little at a time until the sauce is smooth and glossy.

6 Stir in the herbs and add salt and pepper to taste. Return to the pan and keep the sauce warm. Serve the rolls on individual plates with a salad garnish, if desired. Serve the sauce separately, sprinkled with chopped chives.

Fried Mozzarella

These crispy cheese slices make an unusual and tasty appetizer. They must be cooked just before serving.

INGREDIENTS

Serves 2–3

12 ounces mozzarella cheese

oil for deep-frying

2 eggs

flour seasoned with salt and freshly
    ground black pepper

plain dry bread crumbs

flat-leaf parsley, to garnish

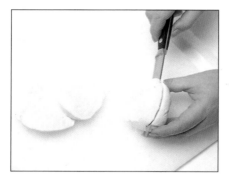

1 Cut the mozzarella into slices about ½ inch thick. Gently pat off any excess moisture with paper towels.

2 Heat the oil to 360°F, or until a small piece of bread sizzles as soon as it is dropped in. While the oil is heating, beat the eggs in a shallow bowl. Spread some seasoned flour on one plate and some bread crumbs on another.

3 Press the cheese slices into the flour, coating them evenly with a thin layer of flour. Shake off any excess. Dip them into the egg, then into the bread crumbs. Dip them once more into the egg, then again into the bread crumbs.

4 Fry immediately in the hot oil until golden brown. (You may have to do this in two batches, but do not let the breaded cheese wait for too long, or the bread crumb coating will separate from the cheese while it is being fried.) Drain on paper towels and serve hot, garnished with parsley.

Greek Cheese and Potato Patties

Delicious little fried morsels of potato and feta cheese, flavored with dill and lemon juice.

INGREDIENTS

Serves 4

1¼ pounds potatoes

4 ounces feta cheese

4 scallions, chopped

3 tablespoons chopped fresh dill

1 tablespoon lemon juice

1 egg, beaten

flour for dredging

3 tablespoons olive oil

salt and freshly ground black pepper

1 Boil the potatoes in their skins in lightly salted water until soft. Drain, then peel while still warm. Place in a bowl and mash. Crumble the feta cheese into the potatoes and add the scallions, dill, lemon juice and egg. Season with salt and pepper (the cheese is salty, so taste before you add salt). Stir well.

2 Cover the mixture and chill until firm. Divide the mixture into walnut-size balls, then flatten them slightly. Dredge in the flour. Heat the oil in a frying pan and fry the patties until golden brown on each side. Drain on paper towels and serve at once.

Cheese-Stuffed Pears

These pears, with their scrumptious creamy topping, make a sublime dish when served with a simple salad.

INGREDIENTS

Serves 4

¼ cup ricotta cheese

¼ cup dolcelatte (Gorgonzola dolce) cheese

1 tablespoon honey

½ celery rib, finely sliced

8 green olives, pitted and roughly chopped

4 dates, pitted and cut into thin strips

pinch of paprika

4 ripe pears

⅔ cup apple juice

1 Preheat the oven to 400°F. Place the ricotta in a bowl and crumble in the dolcelatte. Add the rest of the ingredients except for the pears and apple juice and mix well.

2 Halve the pears lengthwise and use a melon baller to remove the cores. Place in an ovenproof dish and divide the filling equally among them.

3 Pour the apple juice carefully into the dish and cover with foil. Bake for 20 minutes, or until the pears are tender.

4 Remove the foil and place the dish under a hot broiler for 3 minutes. Serve immediately.

COOK'S TIP

Choose ripe pears in season such as Bosc, Bartlett or Comice.

Mushroom Croustades

The rich mushroom flavor of this filling is heightened by the addition of mushroom ketchup.

INGREDIENTS

Serves 2–4

1 short French bread, about 10 inches

2 teaspoons olive oil

9 ounces portobello mushrooms, quartered

2 teaspoons mushroom ketchup

2 teaspoons lemon juice

2 tablespoons skim milk

2 tablespoons snipped fresh chives

salt and freshly ground black pepper

snipped fresh chives, to garnish

3 Place the mushrooms in a small saucepan with the mushroom ketchup, lemon juice and milk. Simmer for about 5 minutes, or until most of the liquid is evaporated.

4 Remove from the heat, then add the chives and season with salt and pepper. Spoon into the bread croustades and serve hot, garnished with snipped chives.

1 Preheat the oven to 400°F. Cut the French bread in half lengthwise. Cut a scoop out of the soft middle of each half, leaving a thick border all the way around.

2 Brush the bread with oil, place on a baking sheet and bake for 6–8 minutes, until golden and crisp.

Tomato Pesto Toasts

The flavor of pesto is so powerful that it can be used in very small amounts to good effect, as in these tasty snacks.

INGREDIENTS

Serves 2

2 thick slices crusty bread

3 tablespoons cream cheese or fromage frais

2 teaspoons red or green pesto

1 beefsteak tomato

1 red onion

salt and freshly ground black pepper

chopped basil, to garnish

1 Toast the bread slices until golden brown on both sides. Let cool.

2 Mix together the cheese and pesto in a small bowl until well blended, then spread thickly on the toasted bread.

3 Using a large, sharp knife, cut the tomato and red onion crosswise into thin slices.

4 Arrange the tomato and onion slices, overlapping, on the toast and season with salt and pepper. Transfer to a broiler rack and heat through under a hot broiler. Serve, garnished with chopped basil.

COOK'S TIP

Almost any type of crusty bread can be used for this recipe, but Italian olive oil bread and French bread will give the best flavor.

Asparagus with Eggs

The addition of fried eggs and grated Parmesan turns asparagus into something even more special.

INGREDIENTS

Serves 4

1 pound fresh asparagus

5 tablespoons butter

4 eggs

4 tablespoons grated fresh Parmesan
  cheese

salt and freshly ground black pepper

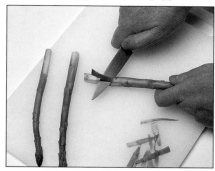

4 As soon as the asparagus is cooked, remove it from the water with two slotted spoons. Place it on a wire rack covered with a clean dish towel to drain. Divide the spears among warm individual serving plates. Place a fried egg on each and sprinkle with the grated Parmesan.

5 Melt the remaining butter in the frying pan. As soon as it is bubbling, but before it browns, pour it over the cheese and eggs on the asparagus. Season with salt and pepper and serve at once.

1 Cut off any woody ends from the asparagus. Peel the lower half of the spears by inserting a knife under the thick skin at the base and pulling up toward the tip. Wash the asparagus in cold water.

2 Bring a large pan of water to a boil. Boil the asparagus until just tender.

3 While the asparagus is cooking, melt a third of the butter in a frying pan. When bubbling, break in the eggs and cook them until the whites have set but the yolks are still soft.

Curried Eggs

Hard-boiled eggs are served on a bed of mild, creamy sauce with a hint of curry.

Serves 2

4 eggs

1 tablespoon sunflower oil

1 small onion, finely chopped

1-inch piece of fresh ginger root, peeled and grated

½ teaspoon ground cumin

½ teaspoon garam masala

1½ teaspoons tomato paste

2 teaspoons tandoori paste

2 teaspoons lemon juice

¼ cup light cream

1 tablespoon chopped cilantro

salt and freshly ground black pepper

cilantro sprigs, to garnish

1 Put the eggs in a pan of water. Bring to a boil, lower the heat and simmer for 10 minutes.

2 Meanwhile, heat the oil in a frying pan. Cook the onion for 2–3 minutes. Add the ginger and cook for 1 minute more.

3 Stir in the ground cumin, garam masala, tomato paste, tandoori paste, lemon juice and cream. Cook for 1–2 minutes, then stir in the cilantro. Season with salt and pepper.

4 Drain the eggs, remove the shells and cut each egg in half. Spoon the sauce into a serving bowl, top with the eggs and garnish with cilantro sprigs. Serve at once.

Roquefort Tartlets

These can be made in shallow muffin pans to serve hot as a first course. You could also make them in tiny tart pans, to serve warm as appetizing bite-size snacks with a drink before a meal.

INGREDIENTS

Makes 12

1½ cups all-purpose flour

large pinch of salt

8 tablespoons (1 stick) butter

1 egg yolk

2 tablespoons cold water

For the filling

1 tablespoon butter

2 tablespoons flour

⅔ cup milk

4 ounces Roquefort cheese, crumbled

⅔ cup heavy cream

½ teaspoon dried mixed herbs, such as tarragon, thyme and savory

3 egg yolks

salt and freshly ground black pepper

1 To make the pastry, sift the flour and salt into a bowl and rub the butter into the flour until it resembles bread crumbs. Mix the egg yolk with the water and stir into the flour to make a soft dough. Knead until smooth, wrap in plastic wrap and chill for 30 minutes. (You can also make the dough in a food processor.)

2 In a saucepan, melt the butter and stir in the flour and then the milk. Boil to thicken, stirring constantly. Off the heat, beat in the cheese and season with salt and pepper. Let cool. In another saucepan, bring the cream and herbs to a boil and cook until the liquid has reduced to 2 tablespoons. Beat into the cheese sauce with the eggs.

3 Preheat the oven to 375°F. On a lightly floured work surface, roll out the pastry to ⅛ inch thick. Stamp out rounds with a fluted cutter and use to line your chosen pans.

4 Divide the filling among the tartlets; they should be filled or two-thirds full. Stamp out smaller fluted rounds or star shapes for the tops and lay on top of each tartlet. Bake for 20–25 minutes, or until golden brown.

SALADS

Parmesan and Poached Egg Salad

Soft poached eggs, hot garlic croutons and cool, crisp salad greens make an unforgettable combination.

Serves 2

½ small loaf sandwich bread

5 tablespoons olive oil

2 eggs

4 ounces mixed salad greens

2 garlic cloves, crushed

½ tablespoon white wine vinegar

1 ounce Parmesan cheese

freshly ground black pepper (optional)

1 Remove the crusts from the bread. Cut the bread into 1-inch cubes.

2 Heat 2 tablespoons of the olive oil in a frying pan. Sauté the bread for about 5 minutes, tossing the cubes occasionally, until they are golden brown.

3 Meanwhile, bring a pan of water to a boil. Carefully slide in the shelled eggs, one at a time. Gently poach the eggs for 4 minutes, until lightly cooked.

5 Heat the remaining oil in the pan, add the garlic and vinegar and cook over high heat for 1 minute. Pour the warm dressing over each salad.

6 Place a poached egg on each salad. Sprinkle with shavings of Parmesan and freshly ground black pepper, if using.

4 Divide the salad greens between two plates. Remove the croutons from the pan and arrange them over the leaves. Wipe the pan clean with paper towels.

VARIATION

As an alternative to the poached eggs, you could add 1½ ounces /1½ cups of Greek black olives.

COOK'S TIP

Add a dash of vinegar to the water before poaching the eggs. This helps to keep the whites together. To make sure that a poached egg has a good shape, swirl the water with a spoon, whirlpool-fashion, before sliding in the egg.

Pear and Pecan Salad with Blue Cheese

Toasted pecans have a special affinity for crisp white pears. Their robust flavors combine especially well with a rich blue cheese dressing and make this a salad to remember.

Serves 4

½ cup shelled pecan halves

3 crisp pears

6 ounces young spinach, stems removed

1 head escarole or Boston lettuce

1 head radicchio

2 tablespoons blue cheese dressing

salt and freshly ground black pepper

crusty bread, to serve

1 Toast the pecans under a moderate broiler, to bring out their flavor.

2 Cut the pears into even slices, leaving the skin intact and discarding the cores.

3 Wash the salad greens and spin dry. Add the pears together with the toasted pecans, then toss with the dressing. Distribute among four large plates and season with salt and pepper. Serve with warm crusty bread.

VARIATION

If you want a lighter dressing, without cheese, combine 1 teaspoon of whole-grain mustard, ½ teaspoon of sugar, ¼ teaspoon of dried tarragon, 2 teaspoons of lemon juice and ¼ cup of olive oil in a jar and shake vigorously.

New Spring Vegetable Salad

This chunky salad makes a satisfying meal. Use other spring vegetables, if you like.

INGREDIENTS

Serves 4

1½ pounds small new potatoes, halved

14-ounce can fava beans, drained

4 ounces cherry tomatoes

½ cup walnut halves

2 tablespoons white wine vinegar

1 tablespoon whole-grain mustard

¼ cup olive oil

pinch of sugar

8 ounces young asparagus
spears, trimmed

6 scallions, trimmed

salt and freshly ground black pepper

baby spinach leaves, to serve

1 Put the potatoes in a saucepan. Cover with cold water and bring to a boil. Cook for 10–12 minutes, until tender. Meanwhile, put the fava beans in a bowl. Cut the tomatoes in half and add them to the bowl with the walnuts.

2 Put the white wine vinegar, mustard, olive oil and sugar into a screw-top jar. Season with salt and pepper. Close the jar tightly and shake well.

3 Add the asparagus to the potatoes and cook for 3 minutes more. Drain the cooked vegetables well. Cool under cold running water and drain again. Thickly slice the potatoes and cut the scallions in half.

4 Add the asparagus, potatoes and scallions to the bowl containing the fava bean mixture. Pour the dressing over the salad and toss well. Serve on a bed of baby spinach leaves.

Couscous Salad

This is a spicy variation on a classic lemon-flavored tabbouleh, which is traditionally made with bulgur rather than couscous.

Serves 4

3 tablespoons olive oil

5 scallions, chopped

1 garlic clove, crushed

1 teaspoon ground cumin

1½ cups vegetable stock

1 cup couscous

2 tomatoes, peeled and chopped

¼ cup chopped fresh parsley

¼ cup chopped fresh mint

1 fresh green chile, seeded and
    finely chopped

2 tablespoons lemon juice

salt and freshly ground black pepper

toasted pine nuts and grated lemon zest,
    to garnish

crisp lettuce leaves, to serve

1 Heat the oil in a saucepan. Add the scallions and garlic. Stir in the cumin and cook for 1 minute. Add the stock and bring to a boil.

2 Remove the pan from the heat, stir in the couscous, cover the pan and let it stand for 10 minutes, until the couscous has swelled and all the liquid has been absorbed. If you are using instant couscous, follow the package instructions.

3 Scrape the couscous into a bowl. Stir in the tomatoes, parsley, mint, chile and lemon juice. Season with salt and pepper. If possible, set aside for up to an hour, to allow the flavors to develop fully.

4 To serve, line a bowl with lettuce leaves and spoon the couscous salad over the top. Sprinkle the toasted pine nuts and grated lemon rind over the top, to garnish.

Brown Bean Salad

Brown beans are a smaller variety of the fava bean, sometimes called "ful." They are used in a classic Egyptian dish called "ful madames" and are occasionally seen in health food stores. Dried fava beans, black or kidney beans make a good substitute.

INGREDIENTS

Serves 6

12 ounces (1½ cups) dried brown beans

2 sprigs of fresh thyme

2 bay leaves

1 onion, halved

4 garlic cloves, crushed

1½ teaspoons cumin seeds, crushed

3 scallions, finely chopped

6 tablespoons chopped fresh parsley

4 teaspoons lemon juice

6 tablespoons olive oil

3 hard-boiled eggs, shelled and
    roughly chopped

1 pickled cucumber, roughly chopped

salt and freshly ground black pepper

1 Put the beans in a bowl with plenty of cold water and let soak overnight. Drain, transfer to a saucepan and cover with fresh water. Bring to a boil and boil rapidly for 10 minutes.

COOK'S TIP
~
The cooking time for dried beans can vary considerably. They may need only 45 minutes, or a lot longer.

2 Reduce the heat and add the thyme, bay leaves and onion. Simmer very gently for about 1 hour, until tender. Drain and discard the herbs and onion.

3 Mix together the garlic, cumin, scallions, parsley, lemon juice and oil. Season with salt and pepper. Pour over the beans and toss lightly together. Gently stir in the eggs and cucumber and serve at once.

Pepper and Wild Mushroom Pasta Salad

A combination of broiled peppers and wild mushrooms makes this pasta salad colorful as well as nutritious.

INGREDIENTS

Serves 6

1 red bell pepper, halved

1 yellow bell pepper, halved

1 green bell pepper, halved

12 ounces whole-wheat pasta shells
   or twists

2 tablespoons olive oil

3 tablespoons balsamic vinegar

5 tablespoons tomato juice

2 tablespoons chopped fresh basil

1 tablespoon chopped fresh thyme

6 ounces shiitake mushrooms, sliced

6 ounces oyster mushrooms, sliced

14-ounce can black-eyed peas, rinsed and
   drained

⅔ cup golden raisins

2 bunches scallions, finely chopped

salt and freshly ground black pepper

1 Preheat the broiler. Put the peppers cut side down on a broiler pan rack and place under the hot broiler for 10–15 minutes, until the skins are charred. Cover the peppers with a clean, damp dish towel and set aside to cool.

2 Meanwhile, cook the pasta in lightly salted boiling water for 10–12 minutes, until tender, then drain thoroughly.

3 Mix together the oil, vinegar, tomato juice, fresh basil and thyme. Add to the warm pasta and toss together.

4 Remove and discard the skins from the bell peppers. Seed and slice the peppers and add to the pasta with the mushrooms, black-eyed peas, golden raisins and scallions. Season with salt and pepper. Toss to mix and serve immediately or cover and chill in the refrigerator before serving.

Whole-Wheat Pasta Salad

This substantial salad is easily assembled from any combination of seasonal vegetables.

Serves 8

1 pound short whole-wheat pasta, such as fusilli or penne

3 tablespoons olive oil

2 medium carrots

1 small head broccoli

1 cup shelled peas, fresh or frozen

1 red or yellow bell pepper, seeded

2 celery ribs

4 scallions

1 large tomato

½ cup pitted olives

For the dressing

3 tablespoons wine or balsamic vinegar

¼ cup olive oil

1 tablespoon Dijon mustard

1 tablespoon sesame seeds

2 teaspoons chopped mixed fresh herbs such as parsley, thyme and basil

4 ounces (⅔ cup diced) Cheddar or mozzarella, or a combination of both

salt and freshly ground black pepper

cilantro, to garnish

1 Cook the pasta in a large pan of rapidly boiling salted water until it is tender. Drain and rinse under cold water to stop the cooking.

2 Drain well and turn into a large bowl. Toss with the 3 tablespoons of olive oil and set aside. Allow to cool completely before mixing with the other ingredients.

3 Lightly blanch the carrots, broccoli and peas in a large pan of boiling water. Refresh under cold water. Drain well.

4 Chop the carrots and broccoli into bite-size pieces and add to the pasta with the peas. Slice the pepper, celery, scallions and tomato into small pieces. Add them to the salad with the olives.

5 Make the dressing in a small bowl by combining the vinegar with the oil and mustard. Stir in the sesame seeds and herbs. Mix the dressing into the salad. Taste for seasoning; add salt and pepper or more oil and vinegar as necessary. Stir in the cheese. Allow the salad to stand for 15 minutes before serving. Garnish with cilantro.

Fruity Rice Salad

An appetizing and colorful rice salad combining many different flavors, ideal for a packed lunch.

INGREDIENTS

Serves 4–6

1 cup mixed brown and
    wild rice
1 yellow bell pepper, seeded and diced
1 bunch scallions, chopped
3 celery ribs, chopped
1 large beefsteak tomato, chopped
2 green-skinned eating apples, chopped
6 ounces (¾ cup) chopped dried apricots
4 ounces (½ cup) raisins
2 tablespoons unsweetened apple juice
2 tablespoons dry sherry
2 tablespoons light soy sauce
dash of Tabasco sauce
2 tablespoons chopped fresh parsley
1 tablespoon chopped fresh rosemary
salt and freshly ground black pepper

2 Place the pepper, scallions, celery, tomato, apples, apricots, raisins and the cooked rice in a serving bowl and mix well.

3 In a small bowl, mix together the apple juice, sherry, soy sauce, Tabasco sauce and herbs. Season with salt and pepper.

4 Pour the dressing over the rice mixture and toss the ingredients together to mix. Serve immediately or cover and chill in the refrigerator before serving.

1 Cook the rice in a large saucepan of lightly salted boiling water for about 30 minutes (or according to the package instructions), until tender. Rinse the cooked rice under cold running water to cool quickly, and drain thoroughly.

Marinated Cucumber Salad

Sprinkling the cucumber with salt draws out some of the liquid.

INGREDIENTS

Serves 4–6

2 medium cucumbers

1 tablespoon salt

½ cup sugar

¾ cup dry cider

1 tablespoon cider vinegar

3 tablespoons chopped fresh dill

pinch of freshly ground black pepper

sprig of dill, to garnish

1 Slice the cucumbers thinly and place them in a colander, sprinkling salt between each layer. Set the colander over a bowl and let drain for 1 hour.

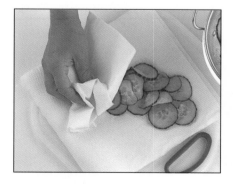

2 Thoroughly rinse the cucumber slices under cold running water to remove excess salt, then pat dry on absorbent paper towels.

3 Gently heat the sugar, cider and vinegar in a saucepan until the sugar has dissolved. Remove from the heat and let cool. Put the cucumber slices in a bowl, pour the cider mixture over them and let marinate for 2 hours.

4 Drain the cucumber and sprinkle with the dill and pepper to taste. Mix well and transfer to a serving dish. Garnish with a sprig of dill. Chill until ready to serve.

Classic Greek Salad

If you have ever visited Greece, you'll know that a Greek salad with a chunk of bread makes a delicious, filling meal.

Serves 4

1 head romaine lettuce

½ cucumber, halved lengthwise

4 tomatoes

8 scallions

⅓ cup Greek black olives

4 ounces feta cheese

6 tablespoons white wine vinegar

½ cup olive oil

salt and freshly ground black pepper

olives and bread, to serve (optional)

3 Slice the scallions. Add them to the bowl with the olives and toss well.

4 Cut the feta cheese into cubes and add to the salad.

5 Put the vinegar, olive oil and salt and pepper into a small bowl and whisk well. Pour the dressing over the salad and toss to combine. Serve at once, with olives and chunks of bread, if desired.

1 Tear the lettuce into pieces and place them in a large mixing bowl. Slice the cucumber and add to the bowl.

2 Cut the tomatoes into wedges and put them in the bowl.

COOK'S TIP

The salad can be assembled in advance and chilled, but add the lettuce and dressing just before serving. Keep the dressing at room temperature, as chilling deadens its flavor.

Fresh Spinach and Avocado Salad

Young, tender spinach leaves are delicious served with avocado, cherry tomatoes and radishes in a tofu sauce.

INGREDIENTS

Serves 2–3

1 large avocado

juice of 1 lime

8 ounces fresh baby spinach leaves

4 ounces cherry tomatoes

4 scallions, sliced

½ cucumber

2 ounces radishes, sliced

radish roses and herb sprigs, to garnish

For the dressing

4 ounces soft, silken tofu

3 tablespoons milk

2 teaspoons prepared mustard

½ teaspoon white wine vinegar

pinch of cayenne, plus extra to serve

salt and freshly ground black pepper

1 Cut the avocado in half, remove the pit, and strip off the skin. Cut the flesh into slices. Transfer to a plate, drizzle with the lime juice and set aside.

COOK'S TIP

Soft, silken tofu can be found in most supermarkets in long-life cartons.

2 Wash and dry the spinach leaves. Put them in a mixing bowl.

3 Cut the larger cherry tomatoes in half and add all the tomatoes to the mixing bowl, with the scallions. Cut the cucumber into chunks and add to the bowl with the sliced radishes.

4 Make the dressing. Put the tofu, milk, mustard, wine vinegar and cayenne in a food processor or blender. Add salt and pepper to taste. Process for 30 seconds, until smooth. Scrape the dressing into a bowl and add a little extra milk if you like a thinner dressing. Sprinkle with a little extra cayenne and garnish with radish roses and herb sprigs.

Sweet and Sour Peppers with Pasta Bows

A zesty dressing makes this simple pasta salad really special.

Serves 4–6

1 each red, yellow and orange bell pepper

1 garlic clove, crushed

2 tablespoons capers

2 tablespoons raisins

1 teaspoon whole-grain mustard

grated zest and juice of 1 lime

1 teaspoon honey

2 tablespoons chopped cilantro

8 ounces pasta bows

salt and freshly ground black pepper

shavings of Parmesan cheese, to
   serve (optional)

1 Quarter the peppers and remove the stalks and seeds. Place in boiling water and cook for 10–15 minutes, until tender. Drain and rinse under cold water. Peel away the skins and seeds and cut the flesh lengthwise into strips.

2 Put the garlic, capers, raisins, mustard, lime zest and juice, honey and cilantro into a bowl. Season with salt and pepper and whisk together.

3 Cook the pasta in a large pan of boiling salted water for 10–12 minutes, until tender. Drain thoroughly.

4 Return the pasta to the pan and add the peppers and dressing. Heat gently and toss to mix. Transfer to a warm serving bowl. Serve with a few shavings of Parmesan cheese, if you like.

Bulgur and Fava Bean Salad

This appetizing salad is ideal served with fresh crusty whole-wheat bread and homemade chutney or relish.

INGREDIENTS

Serves 6

2 cups bulgur

8 ounces frozen fava or lima beans

1 cup frozen petit pois (tiny peas)

8 ounces cherry tomatoes, halved

1 Spanish onion, chopped

1 red bell pepper, seeded and chopped

2 ounces snow peas, chopped

2 ounces watercress

1 tablespoon chopped fresh parsley

1 tablespoon chopped fresh basil

1 tablespoon chopped fresh thyme

French dressing

salt and freshly ground black pepper

3 Add the cherry tomatoes, onion, pepper, snow peas and watercress to the bulgur mixture. Toss together in the bowl until all the ingredients are well combined.

4 Add the chopped fresh parsley, basil, thyme and French dressing to taste. Season with salt and pepper and toss the ingredients together. Serve immediately or cover and chill in the refrigerator before serving.

1 Soak and cook the bulgur according to the package instructions. Drain thoroughly and put into a serving bowl.

2 Meanwhile, cook the beans and petit pois in boiling water for 3 minutes. Drain and add to the prepared bulgur.

COOK'S TIP

Use cooked couscous, boiled brown rice or whole-wheat pasta in place of the bulgur.

Sweet and Sour Artichoke Salad

Agrodolce is a sweet and sour sauce that works perfectly in this salad.

INGREDIENTS

Serves 4

6 small globe artichokes

juice of 1 lemon

2 tablespoons olive oil

2 medium onions, roughly chopped

6 ounces fresh or frozen fava beans, about 1 cup

6 ounces fresh or frozen peas, about 1½ cup

salt and freshly ground black pepper

fresh mint leaves, to garnish

For the salsa agrodolce

½ cup white wine vinegar

1 tablespoon sugar

handful of fresh mint leaves, roughly torn

1 Peel the outer leaves from the artichokes and cut into quarters. Place them in a bowl of water with the lemon juice.

2 Heat the oil in a large saucepan and cook the onions until golden. Add the beans and stir.

3 Drain the artichokes and add them to the pan. Pour in about 1¼ cups of water and cover. Simmer gently for 10–15 minutes.

4 Add the peas, season with salt and pepper and cook for another 5 minutes, stirring from time to time, until the vegetables are tender.

5 Drain the vegetables in a sieve and place them in a bowl. Let cool, then cover and chill in the refrigerator.

6 To make the salsa, mix all the ingredients in a pan. Heat gently until the sugar has dissolved. Simmer for 5 minutes. Let cool. Drizzle over the salad. Garnish with mint leaves.

Spanish Asparagus and Orange Salad

Complicated salad dressings are rarely found in Spain—they simply rely on the wonderful flavor of a good quality olive oil.

Serves 4

8 ounces asparagus, trimmed and cut into 2-inch pieces

2 large oranges

2 tomatoes, cut into eighths

3–4 romaine lettuce leaves, shredded (2 ounces)

2 tablespoons olive oil

½ teaspoon sherry vinegar

salt and freshly ground black pepper

1 Cook the asparagus in boiling salted water for 3–4 minutes, until just tender. Drain and refresh under cold water.

2 Grate the zest from half an orange and reserve. Peel both the oranges and cut into segments. Squeeze out the juice from the membrane and reserve the juice.

3 Put the asparagus, orange segments, tomatoes and lettuce into a salad bowl. Mix together the oil and vinegar and add 1 tablespoon of the reserved orange juice and 1 teaspoon of the zest. Season the dressing with salt and pepper. Just before serving, pour the dressing over the salad and mix gently to coat.

COOK'S TIP

Bibb lettuce can be used in place of romaine.

Grilled Goat Cheese Salad

*Here is the salad and cheese course
on one plate—or serve it as a quick
and satisfying appetizer or light
lunch. The fresh tangy flavor of goat
cheese contrasts with the mild
salad greens.*

INGREDIENTS

Serves 4

2 firm round whole goat cheeses, such as
Crottin de Chavignol
(2½–4 ounces each)

4 slices French bread

olive oil, for drizzling

6 ounces mixed salad greens, including
soft and bitter varieties

snipped fresh chives, to garnish

For the dressing

½ clove garlic

1 teaspoon Dijon mustard

1 teaspoon white wine vinegar

1 teaspoon dry white wine

3 tablespoons olive oil

salt and freshly ground black pepper

1 To make the dressing, rub a
large salad bowl with the cut
side of the garlic clove. Combine
the mustard, vinegar, wine, salt
and pepper in a bowl. Whisk in the
oil, 1 tablespoon at a time, to form
a thick vinaigrette.

2 Cut the goat cheeses in half
crosswise using a sharp knife.

3 Preheat the broiler to hot.
Arrange the bread slices on a
baking sheet and toast on one side.
Turn over and place a piece of
cheese, cut side up, on each slice.
Drizzle with oil and broil until the
cheese is lightly browned.

4 Place the greens and the
dressing in the salad bowl and
toss to coat the greens thoroughly.
Divide the salad among four plates,
top each with a goat cheese crouton
and serve, garnished with chives.

Tomato and Feta Cheese Salad

Sweet sun-ripened tomatoes are rarely more delicious than when served with feta cheese and olive oil. This salad, popular in Greece and Turkey, is enjoyed as a light meal with pieces of crisp bread.

INGREDIENTS

Serves 4

2 pounds tomatoes

7 ounces feta cheese

½ cup olive oil, preferably Greek

12 black olives

4 sprigs of fresh basil

freshly ground black pepper

1 Remove the tough cores from the tomatoes with a small, sharp knife.

2 Slice the tomatoes thickly and arrange in a shallow dish.

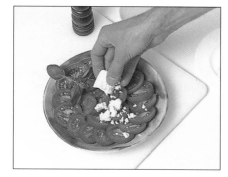

3 Crumble the cheese over the tomatoes, drizzle with olive oil, then sprinkle with olives and fresh basil. Season with black pepper and serve at room temperature.

Fennel, Orange and Arugula Salad

This light and refreshing salad is the ideal companion for spicy or rich foods.

INGREDIENTS

Serves 4

2 oranges
1 fennel bulb
4 ounces arugula leaves
⅓ cup black olives

For the dressing
2 tablespoons olive oil
1 tablespoon balsamic vinegar
1 small garlic clove, crushed
salt and freshly ground black pepper

1 With a vegetable peeler, cut strips of zest from the oranges, leaving the pith behind.

2 Cut the strips into thin julienne strips. Cook in boiling water for a few minutes. Drain.

3 Peel the oranges, removing all the white pith. Cut the orange flesh crosswise into thin rounds and discard any seeds.

4 Cut the fennel bulb in half lengthwise and slice across the bulb as thinly as possible. It is easier to do this with a food processor fitted with a slicing disk or using a mandoline.

5 Combine the oranges and fennel in a serving bowl and toss with the arugula leaves.

6 Mix together the oil, vinegar, garlic and seasoning and pour over the salad. Toss well and let stand for a few minutes. Sprinkle with the black olives and julienne strips of orange zest.

Eggplant, Lemon and Caper Salad

This cooked vegetable relish is delicious served with pasta or simply on its own with crusty bread.

INGREDIENTS

Serves 4

1 large eggplant, about 1½ pounds
1 teaspoon salt
4 tablespoons olive oil
grated zest and juice of 1 lemon
2 tablespoons capers, rinsed
12 pitted green olives
1 small garlic clove, chopped
2 tablespoons chopped fresh flat-leaf parsley
salt and freshly ground black pepper

1 Cut the eggplant into 1-inch cubes. Place the cubes in a colander and sprinkle with the salt. Set aside for 30 minutes, then rinse thoroughly under cold running water. Pat dry with paper towels.

2 Heat the olive oil in a large frying pan. Cook the eggplant cubes over medium heat for about 10 minutes, tossing regularly, until golden and softened. You may need to do this in two batches to ensure that all the eggplant cubes brown well. Drain on paper towels and season with a little salt.

COOK'S TIP

This will taste even better when made the day before. It will keep, covered, in the refrigerator for up to 4 days. To enrich this dish to serve on its own as a main course, add toasted pine nuts and shavings of Parmesan cheese. Serve with crusty bread.

3 Place the eggplant cubes in a large serving bowl and toss with the lemon zest and juice, capers, olives, garlic and chopped parsley.

4 Season with salt and pepper. Serve at room temperature.

Arugula, Pear and Parmesan Salad

For a sophisticated start to an elaborate meal, try this simple salad of honey-rich pears, fresh Parmesan and aromatic leaves of arugula.

INGREDIENTS

Serves 4

3 ripe pears, Bartlett or Comice

2 teaspoons lemon juice

3 tablespoons hazelnut or walnut oil

4 ounces arugula

3 ounces Parmesan cheese

freshly ground black pepper

open-textured bread, to serve

1 Peel and core the pears and slice thickly. Moisten with lemon juice to keep the flesh white.

2 Combine the nut oil with the pears. Add the arugula leaves and toss.

3 Turn the salad out onto four small plates and top with shavings of Parmesan cheese. Season with freshly ground black pepper and serve with open-textured bread.

COOK'S TIP

If you are unable to buy arugula easily, you can grow your own from early spring to late summer.

Tomato, Scallion and Cilantro Salad

Known as "cachumbar," this salad relish is most commonly served with Indian curries. There are many versions; this one will leave your mouth feeling cool and fresh after a spicy meal.

Serves 4

3 ripe tomatoes

2 scallions, chopped

¼ teaspoon sugar

3 tablespoons chopped cilantro

salt

2 Halve the tomatoes, remove the seeds and dice the flesh.

3 Combine the tomatoes with the scallions, sugar, chopped cilantro and salt. Serve at room temperature.

1 Remove the tough cores from the tomatoes with a small, sharp knife.

COOK'S TIP

This refreshing salad also makes a fine filler for pita bread with hummus.

SIDE DISHES

~

Sautéed Potatoes

These rosemary-scented, crisp golden potatoes are a favorite in French households.

INGREDIENTS

Serves 6

3 pounds baking potatoes

4–6 tablespoons oil or clarified butter

2 or 3 sprigs of fresh rosemary, leaves
   removed and chopped

salt and freshly ground black pepper

1 Peel the potatoes and cut them into 1-inch pieces. Place them in a bowl, cover with cold water and let soak for 10–15 minutes. Drain, rinse and drain again, then dry thoroughly in a dish towel.

2 Heat about 4 tablespoons of the oil or butter over medium-high heat until very hot but not smoking. Add the potatoes and cook for 2 minutes without stirring, so that they seal completely and brown on one side.

3 Shake the pan and toss the potatoes to brown on another side. Season with salt and pepper.

4 Add a little more oil or butter and continue cooking the potatoes over medium-low to low heat, stirring and shaking the pan frequently, for 20–25 minutes, until tender when pierced with a knife. About 5 minutes before the end of cooking, sprinkle the potatoes with the chopped rosemary.

Straw Potato Cake

These fried grated potatoes resemble straw, hence the name of the dish. You could make several small cakes instead of a large one, if you prefer—simply adjust the cooking time accordingly.

INGREDIENTS

Serves 4

1 pound baking potatoes

1½ tablespoons melted butter

1 tablespoon vegetable oil, plus more
   if needed

salt and freshly ground black pepper

1 Peel the potatoes and grate them coarsely, then immediately toss them with melted butter and season with salt and pepper.

2 Heat the oil in a large nonstick frying pan. Add the potato mixture and press down to form an even layer that covers the pan. Cook over medium heat for 7–10 minutes, until the bottom is well browned.

3 Loosen the potato cake by shaking the pan or running a thin spatula under it.

4 To turn the potato cake over, invert a large baking sheet over the frying pan and, holding it tightly against the pan, turn them both over together. Lift off the frying pan, return it to the heat and add a little oil if it looks dry. Slide the potato cake into the frying pan and continue cooking until crisp and browned on both sides. Serve hot.

Puffy Creamed Potatoes

This accompaniment consists of creamed potatoes incorporated into mini Yorkshire puddings. Serve them with a vegetable casserole or, for a meal on its own, serve two or three per person and accompany with salads.

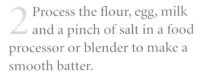

INGREDIENTS

Makes 6

10 ounces potatoes

creamy milk and butter for mashing

1 teaspoon chopped fresh parsley

1 teaspoon chopped fresh tarragon

⅔ cup all-purpose flour

1 egg

about ½ cup milk

oil or sunflower margarine, for baking

salt and freshly ground black pepper

1 Boil the potatoes until tender and mash with a little milk and butter. Stir in the chopped parsley and tarragon and season with salt and pepper. Preheat the oven to 400°F.

2 Process the flour, egg, milk and a pinch of salt in a food processor or blender to make a smooth batter.

3 Place about ½ teaspoon oil or a small pat of sunflower margarine in each of six ramekins and place in the oven on a baking sheet for 2–3 minutes, until the oil is very hot.

4 Working quickly, pour a small amount of batter (about 4 teaspoons) into each ramekin. Add a heaping tablespoon of mashed potatoes and then pour an equal amount of the remaining batter into each dish. Place in the oven and bake for 15–20 minutes, until the puddings are puffy and golden brown.

5 Using a thin spatula, carefully ease the puddings out of the ramekins and arrange on a large, warm serving dish. Serve at once.

Potatoes Dauphinois

Rich, creamy and satisfying, this is a comforting dish to serve when it's cold outside.

INGREDIENTS

Serves 4

1½ pounds potatoes, peeled and
   thinly sliced
1 garlic clove
2 tablespoons butter
1¼ cups light cream
¼ cup milk
salt and white pepper

1 Preheat the oven to 300°F. Place the potato slices in a bowl of cold water to remove the excess starch. Drain and pat dry with paper towels.

2 Cut the garlic in half and rub the cut side around the inside of a wide, shallow ovenproof dish. Butter the dish generously. Blend the cream and milk in a bowl.

3 Cover the bottom of the dish with a layer of potatoes. Dot a little butter over the potato layer, season with salt and pepper and then pour a little of the cream and milk mixture over the potatoes.

4 Continue making layers until all the ingredients have been used up, ending with a layer of cream. Bake for about 1¼ hours. If the dish browns too quickly, cover with a lid or with a piece of foil. The potatoes are ready when they are very soft and the top is golden brown.

Spicy Potatoes and Cauliflower

This dish is simplicity itself to make and can be eaten as a main course with Indian breads or rice, a raita such as cucumber and yogurt, and a fresh mint relish.

INGREDIENTS

Serves 2

8 ounces potatoes

5 tablespoons peanut oil

1 teaspoon ground cumin

1 teaspoon ground coriander

¼ teaspoon ground turmeric

¼ teaspoon cayenne pepper

1 fresh green chile, seeded and finely chopped

1 medium cauliflower, broken up into small florets

1 teaspoon cumin seeds

2 garlic cloves, cut into shreds

1–2 tablespoons cilantro, finely chopped

salt

1 Cook the potatoes in their skins in boiling salted water for about 20 minutes, until just tender. Drain and let cool. When cool enough to handle, peel and cut into 1-inch cubes.

2 Heat 3 tablespoons of the oil in a frying pan or wok. When hot, add the ground cumin, coriander, turmeric, cayenne pepper and chile. Let the spices sizzle for a few seconds.

3 Add the cauliflower and about ¼ cup water. Cook over medium heat, stirring constantly, for 6–8 minutes. Add the potatoes and stir-fry for 2–3 minutes. Season with salt, then remove from the heat.

4 Heat the remaining oil in a small frying pan. When hot, add the cumin seeds and garlic and cook until lightly browned. Pour the mixture over the vegetables. Sprinkle with the chopped cilantro and serve at once.

Garlic Mashed Potatoes

These creamy mashed potatoes have a wonderful aroma. Although two bulbs seems like a lot of garlic, the flavor is sweet and subtle when garlic is cooked in this way.

INGREDIENTS

Serves 6–8

2 garlic bulbs, separated into cloves, unpeeled

8 tablespoons (1 stick) unsalted butter

3 pounds baking potatoes

½–¾ cup milk

salt and white pepper

1 Bring a small saucepan of water to a boil over high heat. Add the garlic cloves and boil for 2 minutes, then drain and peel.

2 In a heavy frying pan, melt half of the butter over low heat. Add the blanched garlic cloves, then cover and cook gently for 20–25 minutes, until very tender and just golden, shaking the pan and stirring occasionally. Do not allow the garlic to scorch or brown.

3 Remove the pan from the heat and cool slightly. Spoon the garlic and any butter from the pan into a blender or food processor fitted with a metal blade and process until smooth. Transfer to a small bowl, press plastic wrap onto the surface to prevent a skin from forming and set aside.

4 Peel and quarter the potatoes, place in a large saucepan and add enough cold water to just cover them. Salt the water generously and bring to a boil over high heat.

5 Cook the potatoes until tender, then drain and work through a food mill or press through a sieve back into the saucepan. Return the pan to medium heat and, using a wooden spoon, stir the potatoes for 1–2 minutes to dry them out completely. Remove from the heat.

6 Warm the milk over medium-high heat until bubbles form around the edge. Gradually beat the milk, remaining butter and reserved garlic purée into the potatoes, then season with salt, if needed, and white pepper.

Roasted Potatoes, Peppers and Shallots

This popular dish from the Deep South is often served in elegant New Orleans restaurants.

INGREDIENTS

Serves 4

1¼ pounds waxy potatoes

12 shallots

2 yellow bell peppers

olive oil

2 sprigs of fresh rosemary

salt and freshly ground black pepper

1 Preheat the oven to 400°F. Wash the potatoes and blanch for 5 minutes in boiling water. Drain.

2 When the potatoes are cool enough to handle, peel them and halve lengthwise. Peel the shallots, allowing them to fall into their natural segments.

3 Cut each pepper lengthwise into 8 strips, discarding the seeds and pith.

4 Oil a shallow ovenproof dish thoroughly with olive oil.

5 Arrange the potatoes and peppers in alternating rows and stud with the shallots.

6 Cut the rosemary sprigs into 2-inch lengths and tuck among the vegetables. Season the dish generously with olive oil, salt and pepper and bake, uncovered, for 30–40 minutes, until all the vegetables are tender.

Baked Sweet Potatoes

Give sweet potatoes a Cajun flavor with salt, three different kinds of pepper and lavish quantities of butter. Serve half a potato per person as an accompaniment, or a whole one as a supper dish with a green salad peppered with watercress.

Serves 3–6

3 pink-skinned sweet potatoes, about
    1 pound each

6 tablespoons butter, sliced

black, white and cayenne peppers

salt

1 Wash the potatoes and leave the skins wet. Rub salt into the skins, prick them all over with a fork and place on the middle shelf of the oven. Turn on the oven to 400°F and bake for about an hour, until the flesh yields and feels soft when pressed.

COOK'S TIP

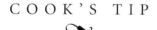

Sweet potatoes cook more quickly than ordinary ones, so there is no need to preheat the oven.

2 The potatoes can either be served in halves or whole. For halves, split each one lengthwise and make close crisscross cuts in the flesh of each half. Then spread with slices of butter and work the butter and seasonings roughly into the cuts with a knife point.

3 Alternatively, make an incision along the length of each potato if they are to be served whole. Open them slightly and put in butter slices along the length, seasoning with the peppers and a pinch of salt.

Thai Fragrant Rice

This lovely, soft, fluffy rice dish, perfumed with fresh lemongrass, is a classic Thai accompaniment to red and green curries.

INGREDIENTS

Serves 4

1 stalk of lemongrass

2 limes

1 cup brown basmati rice

1 tablespoon olive oil

1 onion, chopped

1-inch piece of fresh ginger root, peeled and finely chopped

1½ teaspoons coriander seeds

1½ teaspoons cumin seeds

3 cups vegetable stock

¼ cup chopped cilantro

lime wedges, to serve

1 Finely chop the lemongrass using a sharp knife.

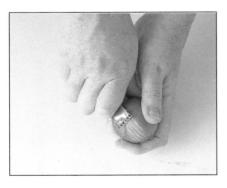

2 Remove the zest from the limes using a zester or fine grater. Avoid removing the pith with the zest.

3 Rinse the rice in plenty of cold water until the water runs clear. Drain through a sieve.

4 Heat the oil in a large pan and add the onion, ginger, spices, lemongrass and lime zest and cook gently for 2–3 minutes.

5 Add the rice and cook for another minute, then add the stock and bring to a boil. Reduce the heat to very low and cover the pan. Cook gently for 30 minutes, then check the rice. If it is still crunchy, cover the pan again and cook for 3–5 minutes more. Remove from the heat.

6 Stir in the chopped cilantro, fluff up the rice, cover and let sit for 10 minutes. Serve with lime wedges.

COOK'S TIP

Other varieties of rice, such as white basmati or long-grain, can be used for this dish, but you will need to adjust the cooking times accordingly.

Rice with Seeds and Spices

A change from plain rice and a colorful accompaniment to spicy curries. Basmati rice gives the best texture and flavor, but you can use ordinary long-grain rice, if you prefer.

INGREDIENTS

Serves 4

1 teaspoon sunflower oil

½ teaspoon ground turmeric

6 cardamom pods, lightly crushed

1 teaspoon coriander seeds, lightly crushed

1 garlic clove, crushed

1 cup basmati rice

1⅔ cups vegetable stock

½ cup plain yogurt

1 tablespoon toasted sunflower seeds

1 tablespoon toasted sesame seeds

salt and freshly ground black pepper

cilantro leaves, to garnish

1 Heat the oil in a nonstick frying pan and sauté the spices and garlic for about 1 minute, stirring all the time.

2 Add the rice and stock, bring to a boil, then cover and simmer for 15 minutes, or until just tender.

3 Stir in the yogurt and the toasted sunflower and sesame seeds. Season with salt and pepper and serve hot, garnished with cilantro leaves.

COOK'S TIP

Seeds are particularly rich in minerals, so they are a good addition to all kinds of dishes. Light toasting will improve their flavor.

Red Fried Rice

This vibrant rice dish owes its appeal as much to the bright colors of red onion, red bell pepper and tomatoes as it does to their flavors.

INGREDIENTS

Serves 2

¾ cup basmati rice

2 tablespoons peanut oil

1 small red onion, chopped

1 red bell pepper, seeded and chopped

8 ounces cherry tomatoes, halved

2 eggs, beaten

salt and freshly ground black pepper

1 Wash the rice several times under cold running water. Drain well. Bring a large pan of water to a boil. Add the rice and cook for 10–12 minutes.

2 Meanwhile, heat the oil in a wok until very hot. Add the onion and pepper and stir-fry for 2–3 minutes. Add the cherry tomatoes and continue stir-frying for 2 minutes more.

3 Pour in the beaten eggs all at once. Cook for 30 seconds without stirring, then stir to break up the egg as it sets.

4 Drain the cooked rice thoroughly. Add to the wok and toss it over the heat with the vegetable and egg mixture for 3 minutes. Season with salt and pepper and serve immediately.

Herbed Rice Pilaf

A quick and easy dish to make, this simple pilaf is delicious to eat. Serve with a selection of fresh seasonal vegetables, such as broccoli florets and carrots.

INGREDIENTS

Serves 4

8 ounces mixed brown basmati and
    wild rice

1 tablespoon olive oil

1 onion, chopped

1 garlic clove, crushed

1 teaspoon ground cumin

1 teaspoon ground turmeric

½ cup golden raisins

3 cups vegetable stock

2–3 tablespoons chopped fresh
    mixed herbs

salt and freshly ground black pepper

sprigs of fresh herbs and ¼ cup pistachio
    nuts, chopped, to garnish

1 Wash the rice under cold running water, then drain well. Heat the oil, add the onion and garlic and cook gently for 5 minutes, stirring occasionally.

2 Add the spices and rice and cook gently for 1 minute, stirring. Stir in the raisins and stock, bring to a boil, cover and simmer gently for 20–25 minutes, stirring occasionally.

3 Stir in the chopped mixed herbs and season with salt and pepper. Spoon the pilaf into a warmed serving dish and garnish with fresh herb sprigs and a sprinkling of chopped pistachio nuts. Serve immediately.

Cheese-Topped Roast Baby Vegetables

This is a simple way to bring out the flavor of baby vegetables.

INGREDIENTS

Serves 6

2¼ pounds mixed baby vegetables, such
    as eggplant, onions or shallots,
    zucchini, corn, button mushrooms

1 red bell pepper, seeded and cut into
    large chunks

1–2 garlic cloves, finely chopped

1–2 tablespoons olive oil

2 tablespoons chopped fresh
    mixed herbs

8 ounces cherry tomatoes

4 ounces mozzarella cheese, coarsely
    grated

salt and freshly ground black pepper

black olives, to garnish (optional)

1 Preheat the oven to 425°F. Cut the eggplant and onions or shallots in half lengthwise.

2 Place the baby vegetables, pepper and garlic in a shallow ovenproof dish. Season with salt and pepper, drizzle with the oil and toss the vegetables to coat. Bake for 20 minutes, until tinged brown at the edges, stirring once.

3 Stir in the herbs, scatter the tomatoes over the top and sprinkle with the mozzarella cheese. Bake for another 5–10 minutes, until the cheese has melted and is bubbling. Serve at once, garnished with black olives, if you like.

Chinese Brussels Sprouts

If you are bored with plain boiled Brussels sprouts, try pepping them up Chinese-style with this unusual stir-fried method.

INGREDIENTS

Serves 4

1 pound Brussels sprouts

1 teaspoon sesame or sunflower oil

2 scallions, sliced

½ teaspoon Chinese five-spice powder

1 tablespoon light soy sauce

1 Trim the Brussels sprouts, then shred them finely using a large, sharp knife or a food processor.

2 Heat the oil and add the sprouts and scallions. Stir-fry for about 2 minutes, without allowing the mixture to brown.

3 Stir in the five-spice powder and soy sauce, then cook, stirring, for another 2–3 minutes, until just tender. Serve hot with other Chinese dishes.

Festive Brussels Sprouts

This recipe originated in France, where it is a popular side dish at Christmastime.

INGREDIENTS

Serves 4–6

8 ounces chestnuts

½ cup milk

1¼ pounds (4 cups) small, tender
   Brussels sprouts

2 tablespoons butter

1 shallot, finely chopped

2–3 tablespoons dry white wine
   or water

1 Using a small knife, score a cross in the bottom of each chestnut. Bring a saucepan of water to a boil over medium-high heat, then drop in the chestnuts and boil for 6–8 minutes. Remove pan from the heat.

2 Using a slotted spoon, remove a few chestnuts from the pan, leaving the others immersed in the water until ready to peel. Before the chestnuts cool, remove the outer shell with a knife and then peel off the inner skin.

3 Rinse the pan, return the peeled chestnuts to it and add the milk. Add enough water to completely cover the chestnuts. Simmer over medium heat for 12–15 minutes, until the chestnuts are just tender. Drain and set aside.

4 Remove any wilted or yellow leaves from the Brussels sprouts. Trim the root ends but leave intact, or the leaves will separate. Using a small knife, score a cross in the bottom of each sprout so they cook evenly.

5 In a large, heavy frying pan, melt the butter over medium heat. Stir in the chopped shallot and cook for 1–2 minutes, until just softened, then add the Brussels sprouts and wine or water. Cook, covered, over medium heat for 6–8 minutes, shaking the pan and stirring occasionally, adding a little more water if necessary.

6 Add the poached chestnuts and toss gently to combine, then cover and cook for 3–5 minutes more, until the chestnuts and Brussels sprouts are tender.

Szechuan Eggplant

This medium-hot dish is also known as "fish fragrant eggplant" in China, because the eggplant is cooked with flavorings that are often used with fish.

INGREDIENTS

Serves 4

2 small eggplants

1 teaspoon salt

3 dried red chiles

peanut oil, for deep-frying

3–4 garlic cloves, finely chopped

½-inch piece of fresh ginger root, finely chopped

4 scallions, cut into 1-inch lengths (white and green parts separated)

1 tablespoon Chinese rice wine or medium-dry sherry

1 tablespoon light soy sauce

1 teaspoon sugar

¼ teaspoon ground roasted Szechuan peppercorns

1 tablespoon Chinese rice vinegar

1 teaspoon sesame oil

1 Trim the eggplant and cut into strips about 1½ inches wide and 3 inches long. Place the eggplant strips in a colander and sprinkle with the salt. Set aside for 30 minutes, then rinse thoroughly under cold running water. Pat dry with paper towels.

2 Meanwhile, soak the chiles in warm water for 15 minutes. Drain, then cut each chile into four pieces, discarding the seeds.

3 Half-fill a wok with oil and heat to 350°F. Deep-fry the eggplant until golden brown. Drain on paper towels. Pour off most of the oil from the wok. Reheat the oil and add the garlic, ginger and white scallion parts.

4 Stir-fry for 30 seconds. Add the eggplant and toss, then add the rice wine or sherry, soy sauce, sugar, ground peppercorns and rice vinegar. Stir-fry for 1–2 minutes. Sprinkle with the sesame oil and green scallion parts and serve immediately.

Bok Choy with Soy Sauce

In this recipe, Chinese greens are prepared in a very simple way— stir-fried and served with soy sauce. The combination makes a very simple, quickly prepared, tasty accompaniment.

INGREDIENTS

Serves 3-4
1 pound bok choy
2 tablespoons peanut oil
1–2 tablespoons plum sauce

2 Heat a wok until hot, add the oil and swirl it around.

3 Add the bok choy and stir-fry for 2–3 minutes, until the greens have wilted a little.

4 Add the plum sauce and continue to stir-fry for a few seconds more, until the greens are cooked but still slightly crisp. Serve immediately.

1 Trim the bok choy, removing any discolored leaves and damaged stems. Tear into manageable pieces.

VARIATION

You can replace the Chinese greens with Chinese flowering cabbage, which is also known by its Cantonese name, choy sam. It has green leaves and tiny yellow flowers, which are also eaten along with the leaves and stalks. It is available at Asian markets.

Sweet and Sour Onions

Cooked in this way, sweet pearl onions make an unusual and tasty side dish. This recipe originated in the Provence region of France.

INGREDIENTS

Serves 6

1 pound pearl onions, peeled

¼ cup wine vinegar

3 tablespoons olive oil

3 tablespoons sugar

3 tablespoons tomato paste

1 bay leaf

2 sprigs of fresh parsley

½ cup raisins

salt and freshly ground black pepper

1 Put all the ingredients in a saucepan with 1¼ cups water. Bring to a boil and simmer gently, uncovered, for 45 minutes, or until the onions are tender and most of the liquid has evaporated.

2 Remove the bay leaf and parsley, check the seasoning and transfer to a serving dish. Serve at room temperature.

Spinach with Raisins and Pine Nuts

Raisins and pine nuts are perfect partners. Here, tossed with wilted spinach and croutons, their contrasting textures make a delicious main-dish accompaniment.

INGREDIENTS

Serves 4

⅓ cup raisins

1 thick slice crusty white bread

3 tablespoons olive oil

⅓ cup pine nuts

1¼ pounds young spinach,
   stalks removed

2 garlic cloves, crushed

salt and freshly ground black pepper

1 Put the raisins in a small bowl with boiling water and let soak for 10 minutes. Drain.

2 Cut the bread into cubes and discard the crusts. Heat 2 tablespoons of the oil and sauté the bread until golden. Drain.

3 Heat the remaining oil in the pan. Sauté the pine nuts until they are beginning to color. Add the spinach and garlic and cook quickly, turning the spinach until it has just wilted.

4 Toss in the raisins and season with salt and pepper. Transfer to a warmed serving dish. Sprinkle with croutons and serve hot.

VARIATION

Use Swiss chard or beet greens instead of the spinach, and cook them a little longer.

Hot Parsnip Fritters on Baby Spinach

Deep-frying brings out the luscious sweetness of parsnips, and their flavor is perfectly complemented by walnut-dressed baby spinach leaves.

INGREDIENTS

Serves 4

2 large parsnips

1 cup all-purpose flour

1 egg, separated

½ cup milk

4 ounces baby spinach leaves, washed and dried

2 tablespoons olive oil

1 tablespoon walnut oil

1 tablespoon sherry vinegar

oil for deep-frying

1 tablespoon coarsely chopped walnuts

salt, freshly ground black pepper, and cayenne pepper

1 Peel the parsnips, bring to a boil in a pan of salted water and simmer for 10–15 minutes, until tender but not at all mushy. Drain, cool and cut diagonally into slices about 2 inches long and ¼–½ inch thick.

2 Put the flour in a bowl and make a well in the center. Put the egg yolk in the well and mix in with a fork. Add the milk while continuing to mix in the flour. Season with salt and black and cayenne peppers, and beat with a whisk until the batter is smooth.

3 Put the spinach leaves in a bowl. Mix the oils and vinegar. Season with salt and pepper.

4 When you are ready to serve, beat the egg white to soft peaks, fold in a little of the yolk batter, then fold the white into the batter. Heat the oil for frying.

5 Shake the dressing vigorously and toss with the salad. Arrange the salad on four plates and sprinkle with walnuts.

6 Dip the parsnip slices in batter and fry until puffy and golden. Drain on paper towels and keep warm. Arrange the fritters on top of the salad.

Parsnip and Chestnut Croquettes

The distinctive sweet, nutty taste of chestnuts blends perfectly with the sweet but earthy flavor of parsnips. Fresh chestnuts need to be peeled, but canned unsweetened chestnuts are nearly as good for this recipe.

INGREDIENTS

Makes 10–12

1 pound parsnips, cut roughly into
  small pieces
4 ounces shelled fresh or canned whole
  chestnuts
2 tablespoons butter
1 garlic clove, crushed
1 tablespoon chopped cilantro
1 egg, beaten
1½–2 ounces fresh white bread crumbs
vegetable oil, for frying
salt and freshly ground black pepper
sprig of cilantro, to garnish

1 Place the parsnips in a saucepan with enough water to cover. Bring to a boil, cover and simmer for 15–20 minutes.

2 Place the chestnuts in a pan of water, bring to a boil and simmer for 8–10 minutes. Drain, place in a bowl and mash roughly into a pulp.

3 Melt the butter in a saucepan and cook the garlic for 30 seconds. Drain the parsnips and mash with the garlic butter. Stir in the chestnuts and chopped cilantro. Season with salt and pepper.

4 Take about 1 tablespoon of the mixture at a time and form into small croquettes, about 3 inches long. Dip each croquette into the beaten egg and then roll in the bread crumbs.

5 Heat a little oil in a frying pan and fry each of the croquettes for 3–4 minutes, until crisp and golden, turning frequently so they brown evenly.

6 Drain the croquettes on sheets of paper towel, wiping away any excess oil, and serve at once, garnished with sprigs of cilantro.

Balti Baby Vegetables

There is a wide and wonderful selection of baby vegetables available in supermarkets these days, and this simple recipe does full justice to their delicate flavor and attractive appearance. Serve as part of a main meal or even as a light appetizer.

INGREDIENTS

Serves 4–6

10 new potatoes, halved

12–14 baby carrots

12–14 baby zucchini

2 tablespoons corn oil

15 pearl onions

2 tablespoons chili sauce

1 teaspoon garlic pulp

1 teaspoon ginger pulp

1 teaspoon salt

14-ounce can chickpeas, drained

10 cherry tomatoes

1 teaspoon crushed red pepper and
   2 tablespoons sesame seeds, to garnish

1 Bring a medium pan of salted water to a boil and add the new potatoes and baby carrots. After 12–15 minutes, add the zucchini and boil for another 5 minutes, or until all the vegetables are just tender.

2 Drain the vegetables well and set aside.

3 Heat the oil in a deep, round-bottomed frying pan or wok and add the onions. Cook until the onions turn golden brown. Lower the heat and add the chili sauce, garlic, ginger and salt, taking care not to burn the mixture.

4 Add the chickpeas and stir-fry over medium heat until the moisture has been absorbed.

5 Add the cooked vegetables and cherry tomatoes and continue cooking over medium heat, stirring with a slotted spoon, for about 2 minutes.

6 Garnish with crushed red pepper and sesame seeds and serve.

VARIATION

By varying the vegetables chosen and experimenting with different combinations, this recipe can form the basis for a variety of delicious vegetable accompaniments. Try different vegetables, such as baby corn, green beans, snow peas, okra, sugar snap peas and cauliflower florets.

Spring Vegetable Stir-Fry

A colorful, dazzling medley of fresh and sweet young vegetables.

INGREDIENTS

Serves 4

1 tablespoon peanut oil

1 garlic clove, sliced

1-inch piece of fresh ginger root, finely
   chopped

4 ounces baby carrots

4 ounces pattypan squash

4 ounces baby corn

4 ounces green beans, trimmed

4 ounces sugar snap peas, trimmed

4 ounces young asparagus, cut into
   3-inch pieces

8 scallions, trimmed and cut into
   2-inch pieces

4 ounces cherry tomatoes

For the dressing

juice of 2 limes

1 tablespoon honey

1 tablespoon soy sauce

1 teaspoon sesame oil

1 Heat the peanut oil in a wok or large frying pan.

2 Add the garlic and ginger and stir-fry over high heat for 1 minute.

3 Add the carrots, pattypan squash, baby corn and beans and stir-fry for another 3–4 minutes.

4 Add the sugar snap peas, asparagus, scallions and cherry tomatoes and stir-fry for another 1–2 minutes.

5 Mix the dressing ingredients together and add to the pan.

6 Stir well and then cover the pan. Cook for 2–3 minutes more, until the vegetables are just tender but still crisp.

COOK'S TIP

Stir-fries take only moments to cook, so prepare this dish at the last minute.

Fried Noodles, Bean Sprouts and Asparagus

Soft fried noodles contrast beautifully with crisp bean sprouts and
asparagus in this superquick recipe.

INGREDIENTS

Serves 2

4 ounces dried Chinese egg noodles

4 tablespoons vegetable oil

1 small onion, chopped

1-inch piece of fresh ginger root, peeled
   and grated

2 garlic cloves, crushed

6 ounces young asparagus
   spears, trimmed

4 ounces bean sprouts

4 scallions, sliced

3 tablespoons soy sauce

salt and freshly ground black pepper

1 Bring a pan of salted water
to a boil. Add the noodles and
cook for 2–3 minutes, until just
tender. Drain and toss with
2 tablespoons of the oil.

2 Heat the remaining oil in a
wok or frying pan until very
hot. Add the onion, ginger and
garlic and stir-fry for 2–3 minutes.
Add the asparagus and stir-fry for
2–3 minutes more.

3 Add the egg noodles and
bean sprouts and stir-fry for
2 minutes.

4 Stir in the scallions and soy
sauce. Season with salt and
pepper, adding salt sparingly, as
the soy sauce will probably supply
enough salt in itself. Stir-fry for
1 minute, then serve at once.

Deep-Fried Root Vegetables with Spiced Salt

All kinds of root vegetables may be finely sliced and deep-fried to make chips. Serve as an accompaniment to an Asian-style meal or simply by themselves as a snack.

INGREDIENTS

Serves 4–6

1 carrot

2 parsnips

2 raw beets

1 sweet potato

peanut oil, for deep-frying

¼ teaspoon cayenne pepper

1 teaspoon sea salt flakes

1 Peel all the vegetables, then slice the carrot and parsnips into long, thin ribbons and the beets and sweet potato into thin rounds. Pat dry all the vegetables on paper towels.

2 Half-fill a wok with oil and heat to 350°F. Add the vegetable slices in batches and deep-fry for 2–3 minutes, until golden and crisp. Remove and drain on paper towels.

3 Place the cayenne pepper and sea salt in a mortar and grind together to a coarse powder.

4 Pile up the vegetable chips on a serving plate and sprinkle with the spiced salt.

COOK'S TIP

To save time, you can slice the vegetables using a mandoline or a blender or food processor with a thin slicing disk attached.

Vegetables Provençal

The flavors of the Mediterranean shine through in this delicious side dish.

INGREDIENTS

Serves 6

1 onion, sliced

2 leeks, sliced

2 garlic cloves, crushed

1 red bell pepper, seeded and sliced

1 green bell pepper, seeded and sliced

1 yellow bell pepper, seeded and sliced

12 ounces zucchini, sliced

8 ounces mushrooms, sliced

14-ounce can chopped tomatoes

2 tablespoons ruby port

2 tablespoons tomato paste

1 tablespoon ketchup

14-ounce can chickpeas

1 cup pitted black olives

3 tablespoons chopped fresh mixed herbs

salt and freshly ground black pepper

chopped fresh mixed herbs, to garnish

1 Put the onion, leeks, garlic, peppers, zucchini and mushrooms in a large saucepan.

2 Add the tomatoes, port, tomato paste and ketchup and mix well.

3 Rinse and drain the chickpeas and add to the pan.

4 Cover, bring to a boil and simmer gently for 20–30 minutes, stirring occasionally, until the vegetables are cooked and tender but not overcooked.

5 Remove the lid and increase the heat slightly for the last 10 minutes of the cooking time, to thicken the sauce, if you like.

6 Stir in the olives and herbs and season with salt and pepper. Serve immediately, garnished with chopped mixed herbs.

COOK'S TIP
∾
This dish is also delicious served cold. It can be prepared in advance for a picnic, stored in the refrigerator, and served with plain yogurt or a refreshing tzatziki.

Spicy Chickpeas

Chickpeas are used and cooked in a variety of ways all over the Indian subcontinent. Tamarind gives this spicy dish a deliciously sharp, tangy flavor.

INGREDIENTS

Serves 4

1¼ cups dried chickpeas

2 ounces tamarind pulp

½ cup boiling water

3 tablespoons corn oil

½ teaspoon cumin seeds

1 onion, finely chopped

2 garlic cloves, crushed

1-inch piece of fresh ginger root, peeled and grated

1 fresh green chile, finely chopped

1 teaspoon ground cumin

1 teaspoon ground coriander

¼ teaspoon ground turmeric

½ teaspoon salt

8 ounces tomatoes, peeled and finely chopped

½ teaspoon garam masala

chopped fresh chiles and chopped onion, to garnish

1 Put the chickpeas in a large bowl and cover with plenty of cold water. Let soak overnight.

2 Drain the chickpeas and place in a large saucepan with double the volume of cold water. Bring to a boil and boil vigorously for 10 minutes. Skim off any scum. Cover and simmer for 1½–2 hours, or until the chickpeas are soft.

3 Meanwhile, break up the tamarind and soak in the boiling water for about 15 minutes. Rub the tamarind through a sieve into a bowl, discarding any seeds and fiber.

COOK'S TIP

To save time, make double the quantity of tamarind pulp and freeze in ice-cube trays. It will keep for up to 2 months.

4 Heat the oil in a large saucepan and sauté the cumin seeds for 2 minutes, until they splutter. Add the onion, garlic, ginger and chile and sauté for 5 minutes.

5 Add the cumin, coriander, turmeric and salt and sauté for 3–4 minutes. Add the tomatoes and tamarind pulp. Bring to a boil and simmer for 5 minutes.

6 Add the chickpeas and garam masala. Cover and simmer for about 45 minutes. Garnish with chopped chiles and onion.

Frijoles

A traditional Mexican bean dish that tastes great with tortillas and vegetable chili.

INGREDIENTS

Serves 6–8

1¼–1½ cups dried red kidney, pinto
   or black beans, picked over
   and rinsed

2 onions, finely chopped

2 garlic cloves, chopped

1 bay leaf

1 or more small fresh green chiles

2 tablespoons corn oil

2 tomatoes, peeled, seeded and chopped

salt

sprigs of fresh bay leaves, to garnish

1 Put the beans in a pan and add cold water to cover by 1 inch.

2 Add half the onion, half the garlic, the bay leaf and the chile or chiles. Bring to a boil and boil vigorously for about 10 minutes. Put the beans and liquid into an earthenware pot or large saucepan, cover and cook over low heat for 30 minutes. Add boiling water if the mixture starts to become dry.

3 When the beans begin to wrinkle, add 1 tablespoon of the corn oil and cook for another 30 minutes, or until the beans are tender. Add salt to taste and cook for 30 minutes more, but try to avoid adding any more water.

4 Remove the beans from the heat. Heat the remaining oil in a small frying pan and sauté the remaining onion and garlic together until the onion is soft. Add the tomatoes and cook for a few minutes more.

5 Spoon 3 tablespoons of the beans out of the pot or pan and add them to the tomato mixture. Mash to a paste. Stir into the beans to thicken the liquid. Cook for just long enough to heat through, if necessary. Serve the beans in small bowls and garnish with fresh bay leaves.

Peas with Pearl Onions and Cream

Ideally, use fresh peas and fresh pearl onions. Frozen peas are an acceptable substitute if fresh ones aren't available, but frozen onions tend to be insipid and are not worth using. Alternatively, use the white parts of scallions.

INGREDIENTS

Serves 4

6 ounces pearl onions

1 tablespoon butter

2 pounds fresh peas (about
   12 ounces shelled or frozen)

²⁄₃ cup heavy cream

2 tablespoons all-purpose flour

2 teaspoons chopped fresh parsley

1–2 tablespoons lemon juice (optional)

salt and freshly ground black pepper

1 Peel the onions and halve them if necessary. Melt the butter in a flameproof casserole and cook the onions for 5–6 minutes over moderate heat, until they begin to be flecked with brown.

2 Add the peas and stir-fry for a few minutes. Add ½ cup water and bring to a boil. Partially cover and simmer for about 10 minutes, until the peas and onions are tender. There should be a thin layer of water on the bottom of the pan—add a little more water if necessary or, if there is too much liquid, remove the lid and increase the heat until the liquid is reduced.

3 Using a small whisk, blend the cream with the flour. Remove the pan from the heat and stir in the combined cream and flour and the chopped parsley. Season with salt and pepper.

4 Cook over gentle heat for 3–4 minutes, until the sauce is thick. Taste and adjust the seasoning; add a little lemon juice to sharpen, if desired.

Red Cabbage in Port and Red Wine

A sweet and sour, spicy red cabbage dish, with the added crunch of pears and walnuts.

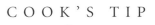

INGREDIENTS

Serves 6

1 tablespoon walnut oil
1 onion, sliced
2 whole star anise
1 teaspoon ground cinnamon
pinch of ground cloves
1 pound red cabbage, finely shredded
2 tablespoons dark brown sugar
3 tablespoons red wine vinegar
1¼ cups red wine
⅔ cup port
2 pears, cut into ½-inch cubes
½ cup raisins
½ cup walnut halves
salt and freshly ground black pepper

1 Heat the oil in a large pan. Add the onion and cook gently for about 5 minutes, until softened.

COOK'S TIP

You can braise this dish in a low oven for up to 1½ hours.

2 Add the star anise, cinnamon, cloves and cabbage and cook for about 3 minutes more.

3 Stir in the brown sugar, vinegar, red wine and port. Cover the pan; simmer gently for 10 minutes, stirring occasionally.

4 Stir in the cubed pears and raisins and cook for another 10 minutes, or until the cabbage is tender. Season with salt and pepper. Mix in the walnut halves and serve.

Beet and Celeriac Casserole

Beautiful ruby-red slices of beets and celeriac make a stunning light accompaniment to any main-course dish.

INGREDIENTS

Serves 6

12 ounces raw beets

12 ounces raw celeriac

4 sprigs of fresh thyme, chopped

6 juniper berries, crushed

½ cup fresh orange juice

½ cup vegetable stock

salt and freshly ground black pepper

1 Preheat the oven to 375°F. Peel and slice the beets very finely. Quarter and peel the celeriac and slice very finely.

2 Fill a 10-inch cast-iron ovenproof or flameproof frying pan with alternate layers of beet and celeriac slices, sprinkling with thyme, juniper and salt and pepper between each layer.

3 Mix the orange juice and stock together and pour over the gratin. Place over medium heat and bring to a boil. Boil for 2 minutes.

4 Cover with foil and place in the oven for 15–20 minutes. Remove the foil and raise the oven temperature to 400°F. Cook for another 10 minutes.

Runner Beans with Garlic

Delicate and fresh-tasting flageolet beans and sautéed garlic add a distinctly French flavor to this simple side dish.

Serves 4

1¼ cups flageolet beans

1 tablespoon olive oil

2 tablespoons butter

1 onion, finely chopped

1–2 garlic cloves, crushed

3–4 tomatoes, peeled and chopped

12 ounces runner beans, prepared and sliced

⅔ cup white wine

⅔ cup vegetable stock

2 tablespoons chopped fresh parsley

salt and freshly ground black pepper

1 Place the flageolet beans in a large saucepan of water, bring to a boil and simmer for ¾–1 hour, until tender.

2 Heat the olive oil and butter in a large frying pan and sauté the onion and garlic for 3–4 minutes, until soft.

3 Add the chopped tomatoes to the onions in the pan and continue cooking over gentle heat until they are soft.

4 Stir the flageolet beans into the onion and tomato mixture, then add the runner beans, wine, stock and a little salt. Stir. Cover and simmer for 5–10 minutes.

5 Increase the heat to reduce the liquid, then stir in the parsley, more salt, if necessary, and pepper.

Lima Beans in Chili Sauce

Try this fabulous dish of lima beans with a tomato and chile sauce for warming up on winter evenings.

Serves 4

1 pound lima or fava beans, thawed if frozen

2 tablespoons olive oil

1 onion, finely chopped

2 garlic cloves, chopped

12 ounces tomatoes, peeled, seeded and chopped

1 or 2 drained canned jalapeño chiles, seeded and chopped

salt

chopped cilantro, to garnish

1 Cook the beans in a saucepan of boiling water for 15–20 minutes, until tender. Drain and keep hot, to one side, in the covered saucepan.

2 Heat the olive oil in a frying pan and sauté the onion and garlic until the onion is soft but not brown. Add the tomatoes and cook until the mixture thickens.

3 Add the jalapeños and cook for 1–2 minutes. Season with salt.

4 Pour the mixture over the reserved beans and check that they are hot. If not, return everything to the frying pan and cook over low heat for just long enough to heat through. Place in a warmed serving dish, garnish with cilantro and serve.

Zucchini with Sun-Dried Tomatoes

Sun-dried tomatoes have a concentrated, sweet flavor that goes well with zucchini.

INGREDIENTS

Serves 6

10 sun-dried tomatoes, dry or preserved
    in oil and drained
¾ cup warm water
5 tablespoons olive oil
1 large onion, finely sliced
2 garlic cloves, finely chopped
2¼ pounds zucchini, cut into thin strips
salt and freshly ground black pepper

1 Slice the sun-dried tomatoes into thin strips. Place in a bowl with the warm water. Let stand for 20 minutes.

2 In a large frying pan or saucepan, heat the oil and stir in the onion. Cook over low to moderate heat until the onion softens but does not brown.

3 Stir in the garlic and zucchini strips. Cook for about 5 minutes, continuing to stir the mixture.

4 Stir in the tomatoes and their soaking liquid. Season with salt and pepper. Raise the heat slightly and cook until the zucchini are just tender. Adjust seasoning and serve hot or cold.

Tomato and Okra Stew

Okra is an unusual and delicious vegetable. It releases a sticky sap when cooked, which helps to thicken the stew.

Serves 6

1 tablespoon olive oil

1 onion, chopped

12-ounce jar pimientos, drained

2 x 14-ounce cans chopped tomatoes

10 ounces okra

2 tablespoons chopped fresh parsley

salt and freshly ground black pepper

1 Heat the oil in a heavy pan. Add the onion and cook for 2–3 minutes.

2 Coarsely chop the pimientos and add to the onion. Add the chopped tomatoes and mix well.

3 Cut the tops off the okra and cut into halves or quarters if large. Add to the tomato sauce in the pan. Season with plenty of salt and pepper.

4 Bring the stew to a boil. Lower the heat, cover the pan and simmer for 12 minutes, until the vegetables are tender and the sauce has thickened. Stir in the chopped parsley and serve at once.

Glazed Carrots with Cider

This dish is extremely simple to make. The carrots are cooked in the minimum of liquid to bring out the best of their flavor, and the cider adds a pleasant sharpness.

INGREDIENTS

Serves 4

1 pound young carrots

2 tablespoons butter

1 tablespoon brown sugar

½ cup cider

4 tablespoons vegetable stock or water

1 teaspoon Dijon mustard

1 tablespoon finely chopped fresh parsley

1 Trim the tops and bottoms of the carrots and peel them. Using a sharp knife, cut them into julienne strips.

COOK'S TIP

If the carrots are cooked before the liquid in the saucepan has reduced, transfer the carrots to a serving dish and rapidly boil the liquid until thick. Pour over the carrots and sprinkle with parsley.

2 Melt the butter in a frying pan, add the carrots and sauté for 4–5 minutes, stirring frequently. Sprinkle the brown sugar over the carrots and cook, stirring, for 1 minute, or until the sugar has dissolved.

3 Add the cider and stock or water, bring to a boil and stir in the mustard. Partially cover the pan and simmer for 10–12 minutes, until the carrots are just tender. Remove the lid and continue cooking until the liquid has reduced to a thick sauce.

4 Remove the saucepan from the heat, stir in the chopped fresh parsley and then spoon into a warmed serving dish.

Broccoli and Cauliflower Gratin

Broccoli and cauliflower make an attractive combination, and a yogurt and cheese sauce gives them extra piquant flavor.

INGREDIENTS

Serves 4

1 small cauliflower (about 9 ounces)

1 small head broccoli (about 9 ounces)

½ cup plain yogurt

1 cup grated Cheddar cheese

1 teaspoon whole-grain mustard

2 tablespoons whole-wheat bread crumbs

salt and freshly ground black pepper

1 Break the cauliflower and broccoli into florets and cook in lightly salted boiling water for 8–10 minutes, until just tender. Drain well and transfer to a flameproof dish.

COOK'S TIP

When preparing the cauliflower and broccoli, discard the tougher parts of the stalk, then break the florets into same-size pieces so they cook evenly.

2 Mix together the yogurt, grated cheese and mustard, then season the mixture with salt and pepper and spoon over the cauliflower and broccoli.

3 Preheat the broiler to moderately hot. Sprinkle the bread crumbs over the vegetables and broil until golden brown. Serve hot.

 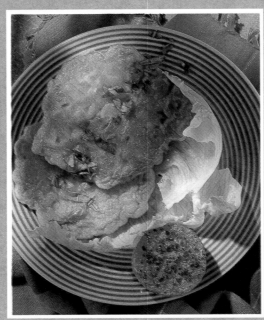 

LIGHT
LUNCHES

Summer Tomato Pasta

This is a deliciously light pasta dish, full of fresh flavors. Use buffalo-milk mozzarella if you can—the flavor is noticeably better.

Serves 4

2¼ cups dried penne

1 pound plum tomatoes

10 ounces mozzarella, drained

¼ cup olive oil

1 tablespoon balsamic vinegar

grated zest and juice of 1 lemon

15 fresh basil leaves, shredded

salt and freshly ground black pepper

fresh basil leaves, to garnish

3 Mix together the olive oil, balsamic vinegar, grated lemon zest, 1 tablespoon of the lemon juice and the basil. Season with salt and pepper. Add the tomatoes and mozzarella and let stand until the pasta is cooked.

4 Drain the pasta and toss with the tomato mixture. Serve immediately, garnished with fresh basil leaves.

1 Cook the pasta in boiling salted water, according to the package instructions, until just tender.

2 Quarter the tomatoes and remove the seeds, then chop the flesh into small cubes. Slice the mozzarella into similar-size pieces.

Pappardelle and Provençal Sauce

A classic French sauce of tomatoes and fresh vegetables adds color and robust flavor to pasta.

INGREDIENTS

Serves 4

2 small purple onions, peeled, root left intact

⅔ cup vegetable stock

1–2 garlic cloves, crushed

4 tablespoons red wine

2 zucchini, cut into short lengths

1 yellow bell pepper, seeded and sliced

14-ounce can whole peeled tomatoes

2 teaspoons chopped fresh thyme

1 teaspoon sugar

12 ounces pappardelle

salt and freshly ground black pepper

fresh thyme and 6 black olives, pitted and roughly chopped, to garnish

3 Cook the pasta in a large pan of boiling salted water, according to the instructions on the package, until tender. Drain the pasta thoroughly.

4 Transfer to a warmed serving dish and top with the vegetables. Garnish with fresh thyme and chopped black olives.

1 Cut each onion into eight wedges through the root end, to hold them together during cooking. Place in a saucepan with the stock and garlic. Bring to a boil, cover and simmer for 5 minutes, until tender.

2 Add the red wine, zucchini, pepper, tomatoes, thyme and sugar. Season with salt and pepper. Bring to a boil and cook gently for 5–7 minutes, shaking the pan occasionally to coat the vegetables with the sauce. (Do not overcook the vegetables, as they are much better if they are slightly crunchy.)

Fusilli with Peppers and Onions

Broiling the peppers for this simple pasta dish intensifies their natural sweetness and gives them a delicious smoky flavor.

INGREDIENTS

Serves 4

1 pound red and yellow bell peppers
   (about 2 large ones)
6 tablespoons olive oil
1 large red onion, thinly sliced
2 cloves garlic, crushed
14 ounces (4 cups) fusilli or other
   short pasta
3 tablespoons finely chopped fresh parsley
salt and freshly ground black pepper
freshly grated Parmesan cheese, to serve

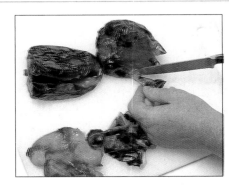

2 Peel the peppers. Cut them into quarters, remove the stems and seeds and slice the flesh into thin strips. Bring a large pan of water to a boil.

5 Meanwhile, add the peppers to the onions and mix together gently. Stir in about 3 tablespoons of the pasta cooking water. Season with salt and pepper. Stir in the chopped parsley.

3 Heat the olive oil in a large frying pan. Add the onion and cook over moderate heat until it is translucent, 5–8 minutes. Stir in the garlic and cook for 2 minutes more.

6 Drain the pasta. Transfer it to the pan with the vegetables and cook over moderate heat for 3–4 minutes, stirring constantly to mix the pasta into the sauce. Serve with the Parmesan passed separately.

1 Place the peppers under a hot broiler and turn occasionally until they are black and blistered on all sides. Remove, place in a paper bag and let sit for 5 minutes.

4 Add salt and the pasta to the boiling water and cook until the pasta is tender.

COOK'S TIP

Bell peppers were brought to Europe by Christopher Columbus, who discovered them in Haiti. The large red, yellow and orange peppers are ripe and therefore usually sweeter than green peppers, and have a fuller flavor.

Pasta Primavera

There's no better way to showcase the best of the spring season's young vegetables than in this delightful pasta dish.

Serves 4

8 ounces thin asparagus spears, cut in half

4 ounces snow peas, topped and tailed

4 ounces whole baby corn

8 ounces whole baby carrots

1 small red bell pepper, seeded and chopped

8 scallions, sliced

8 ounces torchietti or other pasta cuts

2/3 cup cottage cheese

2/3 cup low-fat yogurt

1 tablespoon lemon juice

1 tablespoon chopped fresh parsley

milk (optional)

1 tablespoon snipped chives

salt and freshly ground black pepper

sun-dried tomato bread, to serve

3 Cook the pasta in a large pan of boiling salted water until tender. Drain thoroughly. Put the cottage cheese, yogurt, lemon juice and parsley into a food processor or blender. Season with salt and pepper, then process until smooth. Thin the sauce with a little milk, if necessary.

4 Put the sauce in a large pan with the pasta and vegetables, heat gently and toss carefully. Transfer to a warmed serving plate, sprinkle the chives over the top and serve with sun-dried tomato bread.

1 Cook the asparagus spears in a pan of boiling salted water for 3–4 minutes. Add the snow peas halfway through the cooking time. Drain and rinse both under cold water.

2 Cook the baby corn, carrots, pepper and scallions in the same way until tender. Drain and rinse.

Penne with Fennel, Tomato and Blue Cheese

The anise flavor of the fennel makes it the perfect partner for tomato, especially when topped with blue cheese.

INGREDIENTS

INGREDIENTS

Serves 2

1 fennel bulb

8 ounces penne or other dried pasta shapes (about 2 cups)

2 tablespoons olive oil

1 shallot, finely chopped

1¼ cups passata or tomato sauce

pinch of sugar

1 teaspoon chopped fresh oregano

4 ounces blue cheese

salt and freshly ground black pepper

1 Cut the fennel bulb in half. Cut away the hard core and root. Slice the fennel thinly, then cut the slices into strips.

2 Bring a large pan of salted water to a boil. Add the pasta and cook for 10–12 minutes, until just tender.

3 Meanwhile, heat the oil in a small saucepan. Add the fennel and shallot and cook for 2–3 minutes over high heat, stirring occasionally.

4 Add the passata, sugar and oregano. Cover the pan and simmer gently for 10–12 minutes, until the fennel is tender. Season with salt and pepper. Drain the pasta and return it to the pan. Toss with the sauce. Serve with blue cheese crumbled over the top.

Peanut Noodles

Add any of your favorite vegetables to this quick lunch recipe—and increase the quantity of chile, if you can take the heat!

Serves 4

7 ounces medium Chinese egg noodles

2 tablespoons olive oil

2 garlic cloves, crushed

1 large onion, roughly chopped

1 red bell pepper, seeded and
    roughly chopped

1 yellow bell pepper, seeded and
    roughly chopped

12 ounces zucchini, roughly chopped

generous ¾ cup roasted unsalted peanuts,
    roughly chopped

For the dressing

¼ cup olive oil

grated zest and juice of 1 lemon

1 fresh red chile, seeded and finely
    chopped

3 tablespoons snipped fresh chives

1–2 tablespoons balsamic vinegar

salt and freshly ground black pepper

snipped fresh chives, to garnish

1 Cook the noodles according to the package instructions and drain well.

2 Meanwhile, heat the oil in a very large frying pan or wok and cook the garlic and onion for 3 minutes, or until beginning to soften. Add the peppers and zucchini and cook for another 15 minutes over medium heat, until beginning to soften and brown. Add the peanuts and cook for 1 minute more.

3 Whisk together the olive oil, grated lemon zest and 3 tablespoons of the lemon juice, the chile, chives and balsamic vinegar to taste. Season with salt and pepper.

4 Toss the noodles into the vegetables and stir-fry to heat through. Add the dressing, stir to coat and serve immediately, garnished with fresh chives.

Stir-Fried Vegetables with Cashew Nuts

Stir-frying is the perfect way to make a delicious, colorful and very speedy meal.

INGREDIENTS

Serves 4

2 pounds mixed vegetables (see Cook's Tip)

2–4 tablespoons sunflower or olive oil

2 garlic cloves, crushed

1 tablespoon grated fresh ginger root

½ cup cashew nuts or 4 tablespoons sunflower seeds, pumpkin seeds or sesame seeds

soy sauce

salt and freshly ground black pepper

1 Prepare the vegetables according to type. Carrots and cucumber should be cut into very fine matchsticks.

COOK'S TIP

Use a package of stir-fry vegetables or make up your own mixture. Choose from carrots, snow peas, baby corn, bok choy, cucumber, bean sprouts, mushrooms, bell peppers and scallions. Drained canned bamboo shoots and water chestnuts are delicious additions.

2 Heat a frying pan, then trickle the oil around the rim so that it runs down to coat the surface. When the oil is hot, add the garlic and ginger and cook for 2–3 minutes, stirring. Add the harder vegetables and toss over the heat for another 5 minutes, until they start to soften.

3 Add the softer vegetables and stir-fry everything over high heat for 3–4 minutes.

4 Stir in the cashew nuts or seeds. Season with soy sauce, salt and pepper. Serve at once.

Rice Noodles with Vegetable Chile Sauce

Fresh chile and cilantro combine to give this recipe quite a strong flavor kick.

INGREDIENTS

Serves 4

1 tablespoon sunflower oil
1 onion, chopped
2 garlic cloves, crushed
1 fresh red chile, seeded and
  finely chopped
1 red bell pepper, seeded and diced
2 carrots, finely chopped
6 ounces baby corn, halved
8-ounce can sliced bamboo shoots, rinsed
  and drained
14-ounce can red kidney beans, rinsed
  and drained
1¼ cups passata or tomato sauce
1 tablespoon soy sauce
1 teaspoon ground coriander
9 ounces rice noodles
2 tablespoons chopped cilantro
salt and freshly ground black pepper
fresh parsley sprigs, to garnish

3 Meanwhile, place the noodles in a bowl and cover with boiling water. Stir with a fork and let stand for 3–4 minutes, or according to the package instructions. Rinse and drain.

4 Stir the chopped cilantro into the sauce. Spoon the noodles onto warmed serving plates, top with the sauce, garnish with parsley and serve.

1 Heat the oil in a saucepan, add the onion, garlic, chile and pepper and cook gently for 5 minutes, stirring. Add the carrots, corn, bamboo shoots, kidney beans, passata, soy sauce and ground coriander and stir to mix.

2 Bring to a boil, then cover and simmer gently for 30 minutes, stirring occasionally, until the vegetables are tender. Season with salt and pepper.

Frittata with Sun-Dried Tomatoes

Adding just a few sun-dried tomatoes gives this frittata a distinctly Mediterranean flavor.

INGREDIENTS

Serves 3–4

6 sun-dried tomatoes, dry or packed in
   oil and drained
¼ cup olive oil
1 small onion, finely chopped
pinch of fresh thyme leaves
6 eggs
½ cup freshly grated Parmesan cheese
salt and freshly ground black pepper

1 Place the tomatoes in a small bowl and pour on enough hot water to just cover them. Soak for about 15 minutes. Lift the tomatoes out of the water and slice them into thin strips. Reserve the soaking water.

2 Heat the oil in a large nonstick or heavy frying pan. Stir in the onion and cook for 5–6 minutes, or until soft and golden. Add the tomatoes and thyme and continue to stir over moderate heat for 2–3 minutes. Season with salt and pepper.

3 Break the eggs into a bowl and beat lightly with a fork. Stir in 3–4 tablespoons of the tomato soaking water and the grated Parmesan cheese.

4 Raise the heat under the pan. When the oil is sizzling, pour in the eggs. Mix them quickly into the other ingredients and stop stirring. Lower the heat to moderate and cook for 4–5 minutes on the first side, or until the frittata is puffed and golden brown underneath.

5 Take a large plate, place it upside down over the pan and, holding it firmly with oven mitts, turn the pan and the frittata over onto it. Slide the frittata back into the pan and continue cooking until golden brown on the second side, 3–4 minutes more. Remove from the heat. The frittata can be served hot, at room temperature or cold. Cut it into wedges to serve.

Potato Gnocchi

Gnocchi are little dumplings made either with mashed potato and flour, as here, or with semolina. They should be light in texture, and must not be overworked while being made.

INGREDIENTS

Serves 4–6

2¼ pounds waxy potatoes, scrubbed

1 tablespoon salt

2–2½ cups all-purpose flour

1 egg

pinch of grated nutmeg

2 tablespoons butter

freshly grated Parmesan cheese, to serve

1 Place the unpeeled potatoes in a large pan of salted water. Bring to a boil and cook until the potatoes are tender but not falling apart. Drain. Peel as soon as possible, while the potatoes are still hot but cool enough to handle.

2 On a work surface, spread out a layer of flour. Mash the hot potatoes with a food mill, dropping them directly onto the flour. Sprinkle with about half of the remaining flour and mix very lightly into the potatoes.

3 Break the egg into the mixture, add the nutmeg and knead lightly, drawing in more flour as necessary. When the dough is light to the touch and no longer moist or sticky, it is ready to be rolled. Do not overwork, or the gnocchi will be heavy.

4 Divide the dough into four parts. On a lightly floured board form each part into a roll about ¾ inch in diameter, taking care not to overhandle the dough. Cut the rolls crosswise into pieces about ¾ inch long.

5 Hold an ordinary table fork with long tines sideways, leaning on the board. One by one, press and roll the gnocchi lightly along the tines of the fork toward the points, making ridges on one side and a depression with your thumb on the other.

6 Bring a large pan of water to a hard boil. Add salt and drop in about half the gnocchi.

7 When the gnocchi rise to the surface, after 3–4 minutes, they are done. Scoop them out, let drain and place in a warmed serving bowl. Dot with butter. Keep warm while the remaining gnocchi are boiling. As soon as they are cooked, toss the gnocchi with the butter or a heated sauce, sprinkle with grated Parmesan and serve.

VARIATION
~

Green gnocchi are made in exactly the same way as potato gnocchi, with the addition of fresh or frozen spinach. Use 1½ pounds fresh spinach or 14 ounces frozen leaf spinach. Mix with the potato and the flour in Step 2.

Almost any pasta sauce is suitable for serving with gnocchi; they are particularly good with a creamy Gorgonzola sauce, or simply drizzled with olive oil. Gnocchi can also be served in clear soup.

Vegetable Fajitas

*A colorful medley of mushrooms
and bell peppers in a spicy sauce,
wrapped in tortillas and served with
creamy guacamole.*

INGREDIENTS

Serves 2

1 onion
1 red bell pepper
1 green bell pepper
1 yellow bell pepper
1 garlic clove, crushed
8 ounces mushrooms
6 tablespoons vegetable oil
2 tablespoons medium chili powder
salt and freshly ground black pepper

For the guacamole
1 ripe avocado
1 shallot, coarsely chopped
1 fresh green chile, seeded and
   coarsely chopped
juice of 1 lime

To serve
4–6 flour tortillas, warmed
1 lime, cut into wedges
sprigs of cilantro

1 Slice the onion. Cut the peppers in half, remove the seeds and cut the flesh into strips. Combine the onion and peppers in a bowl. Add the crushed garlic and mix lightly.

2 Remove the mushroom stalks. Save for making stock, or discard. Slice the mushroom caps and add to the pepper mixture in the bowl. Mix the oil and chili powder in a cup, pour over the vegetable mixture and stir well. Set aside.

3 Make the guacamole. Cut the avocado in half and remove the pit and the peel. Put the flesh into a food processor or blender with the shallot, green chile and lime juice.

4 Process for 1 minute, until smooth. Scrape into a small bowl, cover tightly and put in the refrigerator to chill until required.

5 Heat a frying pan or wok until very hot. Add the marinated vegetables and stir-fry over high heat for 5–6 minutes, until the mushrooms and peppers are just tender. Season with salt and pepper. Spoon the filling onto each tortilla and roll up. Garnish with cilantro and serve with the guacamole and lime wedges.

Baked Eggs with Creamy Leeks

This is a traditional French way of enjoying eggs. You can vary the dish quite easily by experimenting with other vegetables, such as puréed spinach or ratatouille, as a base.

Serves 4

1 tablespoon butter, plus extra
   for greasing
8 ounces small leeks, thinly sliced
5–6 tablespoons whipping cream
freshly grated nutmeg
4 eggs
salt and freshly ground black pepper

1 Preheat the oven to 375°F. Generously butter the bottoms and sides of four ramekins or individual soufflé dishes.

3 Add 3 tablespoons of the cream and cook gently for about 5 minutes, until the leeks are very soft and the cream has thickened a little. Season with salt, pepper and nutmeg.

4 Arrange the ramekins in a small roasting pan and divide the leeks among them. Break an egg into each, spoon 1–2 teaspoons of the remaining cream over each egg and season lightly.

5 Pour boiling water into the roasting pan to come halfway up the side of the ramekins or soufflé dishes. Bake for about 10 minutes, until the whites are set and the yolks are still soft, or a little longer if you prefer them more well done.

2 Melt the butter in a small frying pan and cook the leeks over medium heat, stirring frequently, until softened but not browned.

VARIATION

Put 1 tablespoon of cream in each dish with some chopped herbs. Break in the eggs, add 1 tablespoon cream and a little grated cheese, then bake.

Chinese Garlic Mushrooms

High in protein and very low in fat, tofu is useful to keep handy for quick meals and snacks like this one.

INGREDIENTS

Serves 4

8 large portobello mushrooms

3 scallions, sliced

1 garlic clove, crushed

2 tablespoons mushroom sauce
  (a substitute for oyster sauce}

10-ounce package marinated tofu
  (bean curd), cut into small dice

7-ounce can corn, drained

2 teaspoons sesame oil

salt and freshly ground black pepper

1 Preheat the oven to 400°F. Finely chop the mushroom stalks and mix with the scallions, garlic and mushroom sauce.

2 Stir in the diced marinated tofu and corn, season with salt and pepper, then spoon the filling into the mushrooms.

3 Brush the edges of the mushrooms with the sesame oil. Arrange the stuffed mushrooms in a baking dish and bake for 12–15 minutes, until just tender. Serve at once.

COOK'S TIP

If you prefer, omit the mushroom sauce and use light soy sauce instead.

Savory Nut Loaf

This delicious nut loaf makes perfect picnic food.

INGREDIENTS

Serves 4

1 tablespoon olive oil, plus extra
    for greasing

1 onion, chopped

1 leek, chopped

2 celery ribs, finely chopped

8 ounces mushrooms, chopped

2 garlic cloves, crushed

15-ounce can lentils, rinsed and drained

1 cup mixed nuts, such as hazelnuts,
    cashews and almonds, finely chopped

½ cup all-purpose flour

½ cup grated aged Cheddar cheese

1 medium egg, beaten

3–4 tablespoons chopped fresh
    mixed herbs

salt and freshly ground black pepper

chives and sprigs of flat-leaf parsley,
    to garnish

1 Preheat the oven to 375°F. Lightly grease the bottom and sides of a 9 x 5 x 3-inch (8-cup) loaf pan and line with waxed paper.

2 Heat the oil in a large saucepan, add the chopped onion, leek, celery ribs and mushrooms and the crushed garlic, then cook gently for 10 minutes, until the vegetables have softened, stirring occasionally.

3 Add the lentils, mixed nuts, flour, grated cheese, egg and herbs. Season with salt and pepper and mix thoroughly.

4 Spoon the nut, vegetable and lentil mixture into the prepared loaf pan, making sure that it is pressed into the corners, and level the surface. Bake, uncovered, for 50–60 minutes, or until the nut loaf is lightly browned on top and firm to the touch.

5 Cool the loaf slightly in the pan, then turn out onto a serving plate. Serve hot or cold, cut into slices and garnished with chives and flat-leaf parsley.

Spicy Bean and Lentil Loaf

An appetizing, high-fiber savory loaf, ideal for brown-bag lunches.

INGREDIENTS

Serves 12

2 teaspoons olive oil

1 onion, finely chopped

1 garlic clove, crushed

2 celery ribs, finely chopped

14-ounce can red kidney beans

14-ounce can lentils

1 egg

1 carrot, coarsely grated

½ cup finely grated aged
   Cheddar cheese

1 cup fresh whole-wheat bread crumbs

1 tablespoon tomato paste

1 tablespoon ketchup

1 teaspoon each ground cumin, ground
   coriander and hot chili powder

salt and freshly ground
   black pepper

salad, to serve

1 Preheat the oven to 350°F. Lightly grease a 9 x 5 x 3-inch (8-cup) loaf pan.

2 Heat the oil in a saucepan, add the onion, garlic and celery and cook gently for 5 minutes, stirring occasionally. Remove the pan from the heat and cool slightly.

3 Rinse and drain the beans and lentils. Place in a blender or food processor with the onion mixture and egg and process until smooth.

4 Transfer the mixture to a bowl, add all the remaining ingredients and mix well. Season with salt and pepper.

5 Spoon the mixture into the prepared pan and level the surface. Bake for about 1 hour, then remove from the pan and serve hot or cold in slices, accompanied by a salad.

Stuffed Mushrooms

This is a classic mushroom dish, strongly flavored with garlic. Use portobello mushrooms or cremini mushrooms, which are sometimes available at farmers' markets.

Serves 4

1 pound portobello or cremini
   mushrooms
butter, for greasing
about 5 tablespoons olive oil
2 garlic cloves, crushed
3 tablespoons finely chopped parsley
¾–1 cup fresh white bread crumbs
salt and freshly ground black pepper
sprig of flat-leaf parsley, to garnish

1 Preheat the oven to 350°F.
Cut off the mushroom stalks
and reserve.

2 Arrange the mushroom caps in
a buttered shallow dish, gill
side up.

3 Heat 1 tablespoon of the oil in
a frying pan and sauté the
garlic briefly. Finely chop the
mushroom stalks and mix with the
parsley and bread crumbs. Add the
garlic and 1 tablespoon of the oil.
Season with salt and pepper. Pile a
little of the mixture into each
mushroom.

4 Add the remaining oil to the
dish and cover the mushrooms
with buttered waxed paper. Bake
for 15–20 minutes, removing the
paper for the last 5 minutes to
brown the tops. Garnish with a
sprig of flat-leaf parsley.

Baked Onions Stuffed with Feta

Serve these cheesy, nutty onions with warm olive bread for a fabulous lunch.

INGREDIENTS

Serves 4

4 large red onions

1 tablespoon olive oil

¼ cup pine nuts

4 ounces feta cheese, crumbled

½ cup fresh white bread crumbs

1 tablespoon chopped cilantro

salt and freshly ground black pepper

1 Preheat the oven to 350°F. Lightly grease a shallow ovenproof dish. Peel the onions and cut a thin slice from the top and bottom of each. Place the onions in a large saucepan of boiling water and cook for 10–12 minutes.

2 Remove the onions with a slotted spoon. Lay them out to drain on a sheet of paper towels and let cool slightly.

3 Using a small knife or your fingers, remove the inner sections of the onions, leaving about two or three outer rings. Finely chop the inner sections and place the outer shells in an ovenproof dish.

4 Heat the oil in a medium-size frying pan and sauté the chopped onions for 4–5 minutes, until golden, then add the pine nuts and stir-fry for a few minutes.

5 Place the feta cheese in a small bowl and stir in the onions, pine nuts, bread crumbs and cilantro. Season with a little salt and pepper.

6 Spoon the mixture into the onion shells. Cover loosely with foil and bake for about 30 minutes, removing the foil for the last 10 minutes to allow them to brown slightly. Serve hot.

Onion Tarts with Goat Cheese

A variation of the classic French Tarte à l'Oignon, this recipe uses young goat cheese as well as cream. The goat cheese is mild and creamy and complements the flavor of the onions.

INGREDIENTS

Serves 8

1½ cups all-purpose flour

5 tablespoons butter

1 ounce goat cheese or Cheddar
    cheese, grated

For the filling

1–1½ tablespoons olive or sunflower oil

3 onions, finely sliced

6 ounces young goat cheese

2 eggs, beaten

1 tablespoon light cream

2 ounces firm goat cheese or
    Cheddar cheese, grated

1 tablespoon chopped fresh tarragon

salt and freshly ground black pepper

1 To make the pastry, sift the flour into a bowl and rub in the butter until the mixture resembles fine bread crumbs. Stir in the cheese and enough cold water to make a dough. Knead lightly, put in a plastic bag and chill. Preheat the oven to 375°F.

2 Roll out the dough on a lightly floured surface, then cut into eight rounds using a 4½-inch pastry cutter, and line eight 4-inch tart pans. Prick the bottoms with a fork and bake for 10–15 minutes. Reduce the heat to 350°F.

3 Heat the oil in a large frying pan and cook the onions over low heat for 20–25 minutes, until they are a deep golden brown. Stir to prevent them from burning.

4 Beat the goat cheese with the eggs, cream, firm goat or Cheddar and tarragon. Season with salt and pepper and then stir in the onions.

5 Pour the mixture into the partially baked pastry shells and bake for 20–25 minutes, until golden. Serve warm or cold with a green salad.

Corn and Cheese Beggar's Purses

*These tasty pastries are simple to
make. Why not make double?
They'll go like hotcakes.*

INGREDIENTS

Makes 18–20

2 medium ears corn, or 9 ounces
    canned corn

4 ounces feta cheese

1 egg, beaten

2 tablespoons whipping cream

2 tablespoons freshly grated Parmesan

3 scallions, chopped

8–10 small sheets phyllo pastry

8 tablespoons butter, melted

freshly ground black pepper

1 Preheat the oven to 375°F.
Butter two muffin pans.

2 If using fresh corn, strip the
kernels from the cob using a
large sharp knife, cutting
downward from top to bottom of
the cob. Simmer in a little salted
water for 3–5 minutes, until
tender. For canned corn, drain
and rinse well under cold
running water.

3 Crumble the feta cheese into a
bowl and stir in the corn. Add
the egg, cream, Parmesan cheese,
scallions and ground black pepper
and stir well.

4 Take one sheet of pastry and
cut it in half to make a square.
(Keep the remaining pastry
covered with a damp cloth to
prevent it from drying out.) Brush
with melted butter and then fold
in four to make a smaller square
(about 3 inches).

5 Place a heaping teaspoon of
filling in the center of each
pastry square and then squeeze the
pastry around the filling to make a
"beggar's purse."

6 Continue making beggar's
purses until all the filling is
used up. Brush the outside of each
purse with any remaining butter,
put them in the prepared pans,
and bake for about 15 minutes,
until golden brown. Serve hot.

Cheese and Spinach Tart

This tart freezes well and can be reheated. It makes an excellent addition to a festive buffet.

Serves 8

8 tablespoons butter

2 cups all-purpose flour

½ teaspoon English mustard powder

½ teaspoon paprika

large pinch of salt

4 ounces Cheddar cheese, finely grated

1 egg, beaten, to glaze

For the filling

1 pound frozen spinach

1 onion, chopped

pinch of grated nutmeg

8 ounces (1 cup) cottage cheese

2 large eggs, beaten

½ cup freshly grated Parmesan cheese

⅔ cup light cream

salt and freshly ground black pepper

1 Rub the butter into the flour until it resembles fine bread crumbs. Stir in the mustard powder, paprika, salt and cheese. Blend to a dough with 3–4 tablespoons cold water. Knead until smooth, wrap and chill in the refrigerator for 30 minutes.

2 Put the spinach and onion in a pan, cover and cook slowly. Season with salt, pepper and nutmeg. Turn the spinach out into a bowl and cool slightly. Add the remaining filling ingredients.

3 Roll out two-thirds of the pastry on a lightly floured surface and use it to line a 9-inch tart pan. Press it well into the edges, removing excess pastry with a rolling pin. Spoon the filling into the pastry shell.

4 Preheat the oven to 400°F. Put a baking sheet in the oven to preheat.

5 Roll out the remaining pastry and cut it with a lattice pastry cutter. With the help of a rolling pin, lay it over the tart. Brush the seams with egg glaze. Press the edges together and trim off the excess pastry. Brush the pastry lattice with egg glaze and bake on the hot baking sheet for 35–40 minutes, or until golden brown. Serve hot or cold.

Gado Gado

The peanut sauce on this traditional Indonesian vegetable dish owes its flavor to galangal, an aromatic rhizome that resembles ginger.

INGREDIENTS

Serves 4

9 ounces white cabbage, shredded

4 carrots, cut into matchsticks

4 celery ribs, cut into matchsticks

9 ounces (4 cups) bean sprouts

½ cucumber, cut into matchsticks

fried onion, salted peanuts and sliced fresh chile, to garnish

For the peanut sauce

1 tablespoon oil

1 small onion, finely chopped

1 garlic clove, crushed

1 small piece galangal, peeled and grated

1 teaspoon ground cumin

¼ teaspoon chili powder

1 teaspoon tamarind paste or lime juice

4 tablespoons crunchy peanut butter

1 teaspoon light brown sugar

1 Steam the cabbage, carrots and celery for 3–4 minutes, until just tender. Let cool. Spread out the bean sprouts on a large serving dish. Arrange the cabbage, carrots, celery and cucumber on top.

2 To make the sauce, heat the oil in a saucepan, add the onion and garlic and cook gently for 5 minutes, until soft.

3 Stir in the galangal and spices and cook for 1 minute. Add the tamarind paste or lime juice, peanut butter and sugar. Mix well.

4 Heat the sauce gently, stirring occasionally and adding a little hot water if necessary, to make the sauce runny enough to coat the vegetables when poured.

5 Spoon a little of the sauce over the vegetables and toss lightly together. Garnish with fried onion, peanuts and sliced chile. Serve the rest of the sauce separately in a bowl.

COOK'S TIP

As long as the sauce remains the same, the vegetables can be altered at the whim of the cook and to reflect the contents of the vegetable bin.

Sliced Frittata with Tomato Sauce

This dish—cold frittata with a tomato sauce—is ideal for a light summer lunch.

Serves 3–4

6 eggs

2 tablespoons finely chopped fresh mixed
    herbs, such as basil, parsley, thyme
    and tarragon

¼ cup freshly grated
    Parmesan cheese

3 tablespoons olive oil

salt and freshly ground black pepper

For the tomato sauce

2 tablespoons olive oil

1 small onion, finely chopped

12 ounces fresh tomatoes, chopped, or
    14-ounce can chopped tomatoes

1 garlic clove, chopped

salt and freshly ground black pepper

1 To make the frittata, break the eggs into a bowl and beat them lightly with a fork. Beat in the herbs and Parmesan. Season with salt and pepper. Heat the oil in a large nonstick or heavy frying pan until hot but not smoking.

2 Pour in the seasoned egg mixture. Cook, without stirring, until the frittata is puffed and golden brown underneath.

3 Take a large plate, place it upside down over the pan and, holding it firmly with oven mitts, turn the pan and the frittata over onto it. Slide the frittata back into the pan and continue cooking for 3–4 minutes more, until it is golden brown on the second side. Remove from the heat and let cool completely.

4 To make the tomato sauce, heat the oil in a medium-heavy saucepan. Add the onion and cook slowly until it is soft. Add the tomatoes, garlic and ¼ cup water and season with salt and pepper. Cover the pan and cook over moderate heat for about 15 minutes.

5 Remove from the heat and let cool slightly before pressing the sauce through a food mill or sieve. Let cool completely.

6 To assemble the salad, cut the frittata into thin slices. Place them in a serving bowl and toss lightly with the sauce. Serve at room temperature or chilled.

Ratatouille

A classic vegetable stew, packed full of fresh vegetables and herbs and absolutely bursting with wonderful flavor.

INGREDIENTS

Serves 4

2 large eggplant, roughly chopped

4 zucchini, roughly chopped

⅔ cup olive oil

2 onions, sliced

2 garlic cloves, chopped

1 large red bell pepper, seeded and
    roughly chopped

2 large yellow bell peppers, seeded and
    roughly chopped

sprig of fresh rosemary

sprig of fresh thyme

1 teaspoon coriander seeds, crushed

3 plum tomatoes, peeled, seeded
    and chopped

8 basil leaves, torn

salt and freshly ground black pepper

sprigs of fresh parsley or basil, to garnish

1 Sprinkle the eggplant and zucchini with salt, then put them in a colander with a plate and a weight on top to extract the bitter juices. Let sit for about 30 minutes.

2 Heat the olive oil in a large saucepan. Add the onions and cook gently for 6–7 minutes, until just softened. Add the garlic and cook for another 2 minutes.

3 Rinse the eggplant and zucchini and pat dry with a clean dish towel. Add to the pan with the peppers, increase the heat and sauté until the peppers are just turning brown.

4 Add the herbs and coriander seeds, then cover the pan and cook gently for about 40 minutes.

5 Add the tomatoes and season with salt and pepper. Cook gently for another 10 minutes, until the vegetables are soft but not too mushy. Remove the sprigs of herbs. Stir in the torn basil leaves and check the seasoning. Let cool slightly and serve warm or cold, garnished with sprigs of parsley or basil.

Corn Cakes with Grilled Tomatoes

Crisp corn fritters are simple to make and guaranteed to become a midday favorite.

INGREDIENTS

Serves 4

1 large ear of fresh corn

¾ cup all-purpose flour

1 egg

a little milk

2 large, firm tomatoes

1 garlic clove, crushed

1 teaspoon dried oregano

2–3 tablespoons olive oil, plus extra for shallow-frying

salt and freshly ground black pepper

8 cupped iceberg lettuce leaves, to serve

shredded fresh basil leaves, to garnish

1 Pull the husks and silk away from the corn, then hold the ear upright on a board and cut downward with a heavy knife to strip off the kernels. Put the kernels in a pan of boiling water and cook for 3 minutes after the water has returned to a boil, then drain and rinse under cold running water to cool quickly.

2 Put the flour in a bowl, make a well in the center and break the egg into it. Start stirring with a fork, adding a little milk to make a soft dropping consistency. Stir in the drained corn and season with salt and pepper.

3 Preheat the broiler. Halve the tomatoes horizontally and make two or three crisscross slashes across the cut side of each half. Rub in the crushed garlic and the oregano and season with salt and pepper. Drizzle with oil and broil until lightly browned.

4 While the tomatoes broil, heat some oil in a wide frying pan and drop a tablespoon of batter into the center. Cook the fritters one at a time over low heat, turning each one as soon as the top is set. Drain on paper towels and keep warm while cooking the remaining fritters. The mixture should make at least eight corn cakes.

5 For each serving, put two corn cakes on lettuce leaves, garnish with basil and serve with a broiled tomato half.

Fresh Cèpes with a Parsley Dressing

To capture the just-picked flavor of mushrooms, try this delicious salad enriched with an egg yolk and walnut oil dressing. Choose small cèpes or portobellos for a firm texture and a fine flavor.

INGREDIENTS

Serves 4

12 ounces fresh cèpes or portobellos

6 ounces mixed salad greens, such as young spinach and frisée

½ cup broken walnut pieces, toasted

2 ounces Parmesan cheese

salt and freshly ground black pepper

For the dressing

2 egg yolks

½ teaspoon Dijon mustard

5 tablespoons peanut oil

3 tablespoons walnut oil

2 tablespoons lemon juice

2 tablespoons chopped fresh parsley

pinch of sugar

1 For the dressing, place the egg yolks in a screw-top jar with the mustard, oils, lemon juice, parsley and sugar. Shake well.

2 Slice the mushrooms thinly using a sharp knife.

3 Place the mushrooms in a large salad bowl and combine with the dressing. Let stand for 10–15 minutes for the flavors to mingle.

4 Wash and spin the salad greens, then toss with the mushrooms.

5 Turn out onto four large plates, season with salt and pepper, then sprinkle with toasted walnut pieces and shavings of Parmesan cheese.

COOK'S TIP

The dressing for this salad uses raw egg yolks. Be sure to use only the freshest eggs from a reputable supplier. Pregnant women, young children and the elderly are advised not to eat raw egg yolks. If this presents a problem, the dressing can be made without the egg yolks.

Sun-Dried Tomato and Parmesan Carbonara

The ingredients for this recipe can easily be doubled to serve four. Why not try it with plenty of garlic bread and a big green salad?

INGREDIENTS

Serves 2

6 ounces tagliatelle

10 sun-dried tomatoes in olive oil, drained

2 eggs, beaten

2/3 cup heavy cream

1 tablespoon whole-grain mustard

2/3 cup freshly grated Parmesan cheese

12 fresh basil leaves, shredded

salt and pepper

fresh basil leaves, to garnish

crusty bread, to serve

1 Cook the pasta in boiling salted water until it is just tender but still retains a little bite (al dente).

2 Meanwhile, cut the sun-dried tomatoes into small pieces.

3 Beat together the eggs, cream and mustard in a bowl, adding plenty of salt and pepper, until they are well combined and smooth. Do not allow the mixture to become frothy.

4 Drain the pasta and immediately return to the hot saucepan with the cream mixture, sun-dried tomatoes, Parmesan cheese and shredded fresh basil. Return to very low heat for 1 minute, stirring gently, until the mixture thickens slightly. Adjust the seasoning and serve immediately, garnished with basil leaves. Serve with plenty of crusty bread.

Omelet with Beans

Every good cook should have a few omelets in his or her repertoire. This version includes soft white beans and is finished with a layer of toasted sesame seeds.

INGREDIENTS

Serves 4

2 tablespoons olive oil

1 teaspoon sesame oil

1 Spanish onion, chopped

1 small red bell pepper, seeded and diced

2 celery ribs, chopped

14-ounce can soft white beans,
    such as cannellini, drained

8 eggs

3 tablespoons sesame seeds

salt and freshly ground black pepper

green salad, to serve

3 In a medium bowl, beat the eggs with a fork and season with salt and pepper, then pour over the ingredients in the pan.

4 Stir the egg mixture with a flat wooden spoon until it begins to stiffen, then allow to firm over low heat for 6–8 minutes.

5 Preheat the broiler to moderate. Sprinkle the omelet with sesame seeds and brown evenly under the broiler.

6 Cut the omelet into thick wedges and serve warm with a green salad.

1 Heat the olive and sesame oils in a 12-inch flameproof frying pan. Add the onion, pepper and celery and cook to soften without coloring.

2 Add the beans and continue to cook for several minutes to heat through.

VARIATION

You can also use sliced cooked potatoes, any seasonal vegetables, baby artichoke hearts and chickpeas in this omelet.

Mushroom Hunter's Omelet

Perfect for Sunday brunch, this omelet is simplicity itself to make.

INGREDIENTS

Serves 1

2 tablespoons unsalted butter, plus extra for cooking

4 ounces assorted wild and cultivated mushrooms such as young cèpes, chanterelles, cremini, portobellos, and oyster mushrooms, trimmed and sliced

3 eggs, at room temperature

salt and freshly ground black pepper

1 Melt the butter in a small omelet pan, add the mushrooms and cook until the juices run. Season with salt and pepper, remove from pan and set aside. Wipe the pan.

2 Break the eggs into a bowl, season and beat with a fork. Heat the pan over high heat, add a pat of butter and let it begin to brown. Pour in the beaten egg and stir briskly with the back of a fork.

3 When the eggs are two-thirds set, add the mushrooms and let the omelet finish cooking for 10–15 seconds.

4 Tap the handle of the omelet pan sharply with your fist to loosen the omelet from the pan, then fold and turn out onto a plate. Serve with warm crusty bread and a simple green salad.

SUPPERS

Vegetable Pilaf

A popular vegetable rice dish that makes a tasty light supper.

INGREDIENTS

Serves 4–6

1 cup basmati rice
2 tablespoons oil
½ teaspoon cumin seeds
2 bay leaves
4 green cardamom pods
4 cloves
1 onion, finely chopped
1 carrot, finely diced
⅓ cup thawed frozen peas
⅓ cup thawed frozen corn
¼ cup cashew nuts, lightly fried
¼ teaspoon ground cumin
salt

1 Wash the rice in several changes of cold water. Put in a bowl and cover with water. Let soak for about 30 minutes.

2 Heat the oil in a large frying pan and sauté the cumin seeds for 2 minutes. Add the bay leaves, cardamom and cloves and sauté for another 2 minutes.

3 Add the onion and cook for 5 minutes, until softened and lightly browned.

4 Stir in the carrot and cook for 3–4 minutes.

5 Drain the rice and add to the pan together with the peas, corn and cashew nuts. Cook for 4–5 minutes.

6 Add 2 cups water, ground cumin and salt. Bring to a boil, cover and simmer for 15 minutes over low heat, until all the water is absorbed. Let stand, covered, for 10 minutes before serving.

Red Pepper Risotto

The character of this delicious risotto depends on the type of rice you use. With arborio rice, the risotto should be moist and creamy. If you use brown rice, reduce the amount of liquid for a drier dish with a nutty flavor.

Serves 6

3 large red bell peppers

2 tablespoons olive oil

3 large garlic cloves, thinly sliced

1½ x 14-ounce cans chopped tomatoes

2 bay leaves

5–6¼ cups vegetable stock

2½ cups arborio rice or
    brown rice

6 fresh basil leaves, snipped

salt and freshly ground black pepper

1 Preheat the broiler. Put the peppers in a broiler pan and broil until the skins are blackened and blistered all over. Put the peppers in a bowl, cover with several layers of damp paper towels and set aside for 10 minutes. Peel off the skins, then slice the peppers, discarding the cores and seeds.

2 Heat the oil in a wide, shallow pan. Add the garlic and tomatoes and cook over gentle heat for 5 minutes, then add the pepper slices and bay leaves. Stir well and cook for 15 minutes more, still over gentle heat.

3 Pour the stock into a large, heavy saucepan and heat it to simmering point. Stir the rice into the vegetable mixture and cook for about 2 minutes, then add two or three ladlefuls of the hot stock. Cook, stirring occasionally, until all the stock has been absorbed into the rice.

4 Continue to add stock in this way, making sure each addition has been absorbed before pouring in the next. When the rice is tender, season with salt and pepper. Remove the pan from the heat, cover and let stand for 10 minutes before stirring in the basil and serving.

Risotto with Mushrooms

The addition of wild mushrooms gives this risotto a wonderfully authentic woody flavor.

INGREDIENTS

Serves 3–4

⅓ cup dried wild mushrooms, preferably porcini

6 ounces fresh cultivated mushrooms

juice of ½ lemon

6 tablespoons butter

2 tablespoons finely chopped parsley

3¾ cups vegetable stock

2 tablespoons olive oil

1 small onion, finely chopped

1½ cups medium-grain risotto rice, such as arborio

½ cup dry white wine

3 tablespoons freshly grated Parmesan cheese

salt and freshly ground black pepper

sprig of flat-leaf parsley, to garnish

1 Place the dried mushrooms in a small bowl with about 1½ cups warm water. Soak for at least 40 minutes. Rinse the mushrooms thoroughly. Filter the soaking water through a sieve lined with paper towels, and reserve.

2 Wipe the fresh mushrooms with a damp cloth and slice finely. Place in a bowl and toss with the lemon juice.

3 In a large, heavy frying pan or casserole, melt a third of the butter. Stir in the fresh sliced mushrooms and cook over moderate heat until they release their juices and begin to brown. Stir in the parsley, cook for 30 seconds more and remove to a side dish.

4 Place the stock in a saucepan and add the mushroom water. Heat broth to a simmer.

5 Heat another third of the butter with the olive oil in the same pan the mushrooms were cooked in. Stir in the onion and cook until it is soft and golden. Add the rice, stirring for 1–2 minutes to coat it with the oils in the pan. Add the soaked and sautéed mushrooms and mix well.

6 Pour in the wine, raise the heat slightly, and cook over moderate heat until it evaporates.

7 Add one small ladleful of the hot broth. Over moderate heat, cook until the broth is absorbed or evaporates, stirring the rice with a wooden spoon to prevent it from sticking to the pan. Add a little more broth and stir until the rice dries out again. Continue stirring and adding the liquid a little at a time. After about 20 minutes, taste the rice. Add salt and pepper.

8 Continue cooking, stirring and adding the liquid until the rice is al dente, or tender but still firm to the bite. The total cooking time of the risotto may be 20–35 minutes. If you run out of broth, use hot water.

9 Remove the risotto pan from the heat. Stir in the remaining butter and the Parmesan. Grind in a little black pepper and taste again for salt. Allow the risotto to rest for 3–4 minutes before serving, garnished with a sprig of flat-leaf parsley.

Parsnip, Eggplant and Cashew Biryani

Full of the flavors of India, this hearty supper dish is great for chilly winter evenings.

INGREDIENTS

Serves 4–6
1 small eggplant, sliced
10 ounces basmati rice
3 parsnips
3 onions
2 garlic cloves
1-inch piece of fresh ginger root, peeled
about 4 tablespoons vegetable oil
6 ounces (¾ cup) unsalted cashew nuts
¼ cup golden raisins
1 red bell pepper, seeded and sliced
1 teaspoon ground cumin
1 teaspoon ground coriander
½ teaspoon chili powder
½ cup plain yogurt
1¼ cups vegetable stock
2 tablespoons butter
salt and freshly ground black pepper
2 hard-boiled eggs, quartered, and sprigs of cilantro, to garnish

1 Sprinkle the eggplant with salt and set aside for 30 minutes. Rinse, pat dry and cut into bite-size pieces.

2 Soak the rice in a bowl of cold water for 40 minutes. Peel and core the parsnips. Cut into ½-inch pieces. Process 1 onion, the garlic and ginger in a food processor. Add 2–3 tablespoons water and process to a paste.

3 Finely slice the remaining onions. Heat 3 tablespoons of the oil in a large flameproof casserole and sauté the onions gently for 10–15 minutes, until they are soft and deep golden brown. Remove and drain.

4 Add ¼ cup of the cashew nuts to the pan and stir-fry for 2 minutes, checking that they do not burn. Add the raisins and cook until they swell. Remove and drain on paper towels.

5 Add the eggplant and sliced pepper to the pan and stir-fry for 4–5 minutes. Drain on paper towels. Cook the parsnips for 4–5 minutes. Stir in the remaining cashew nuts and cook for 1 minute. Transfer to the plate with the eggplant and set aside.

6 Add the remaining 1 tablespoon of oil to the pan. Add the onion paste. Cook, stirring, over moderate heat for 4–5 minutes, until the mixture turns golden. Stir in the cumin, coriander and chili powder. Cook, stirring, for 1 minute, then reduce the heat and add the yogurt.

7 Bring the mixture slowly to a boil and stir in the stock, parsnips, eggplant and bell pepper. Season with salt and pepper, cover and simmer for 30–40 minutes, until the parsnips are tender. Transfer to an ovenproof casserole.

8 Preheat the oven to 300°F. Drain the rice and add to 1¼ cups salted boiling water. Cook gently for 5–6 minutes, until the rice is tender but slightly undercooked.

9 Drain the rice and pile it in a mound on top of the parsnip mixture. Make a hole from the top to the bottom using the handle of a wooden spoon. Sprinkle the reserved fried onions, cashew nuts and raisins over the rice and dot with butter. Cover with a double layer of foil and secure it in place with a lid.

10 Bake for 35–40 minutes. To serve, spoon the mixture onto a warmed serving dish and garnish with quartered eggs and sprigs of cilantro.

Leek, Mushroom and Lemon Risotto

A delicious risotto, packed full of flavor, this is a great recipe for an informal supper with friends.

INGREDIENTS

Serves 4

8 ounces trimmed leeks

8 ounces cremini mushrooms

2 tablespoons olive oil

3 garlic cloves, crushed

6 tablespoons butter

1 large onion, roughly chopped

scant 1¾ cups arborio rice

5 cups hot vegetable stock

grated zest and juice of 1 lemon

⅔ cup freshly grated
    Parmesan cheese

¼ cup mixed chopped fresh chives and
    flat-leaf parsley

salt and freshly ground black pepper

lemon wedges and sprigs of flat-leaf
    parsley, to serve

1 Wash the leeks well. Slice in half lengthwise and roughly chop. Wipe the mushrooms with paper towels and roughly chop.

VARIATION

For a tangier taste, you could substitute a lime for the lemon in this recipe.

2 Heat the oil in a large saucepan and cook the garlic for 1 minute. Add the leeks, mushrooms and plenty of seasoning and cook over medium heat for about 10 minutes, or until softened and browned. Remove from the pan and set aside.

3 Add 2 tablespoons of the butter to the pan and cook the onion over medium heat for about 5 minutes.

4 Stir in the rice and cook for 1 minute. Add a ladleful of stock to the pan and cook gently, stirring occasionally, until all the liquid is absorbed.

5 Stir in more liquid as each ladleful is absorbed; this should take 20–25 minutes. The risotto will turn thick and creamy, and the rice should be tender but not sticky.

6 Just before serving, stir in the leeks, mushrooms, remaining butter, grated lemon zest and 3 tablespoons of the juice, half the Parmesan and the herbs. Adjust the seasoning and serve, sprinkled with the remaining Parmesan and herbs. Serve with lemon wedges and sprigs of flat-leaf parsley.

Risotto alla Milanese

This traditional Italian risotto is rich and creamy, and deliciously flavored with garlic, shavings of Parmesan and fresh parsley.

Serves 4

2 garlic cloves, crushed

4 tablespoons chopped fresh parsley

finely grated zest of 1 lemon

For the risotto

1 teaspoon saffron strands

2 tablespoons butter

1 large onion, finely chopped

1½ cups arborio rice

⅔ cup dry white wine

4 cups vegetable stock

Parmesan cheese shavings, to serve

salt and freshly ground black pepper

1 Mix together the garlic, parsley and lemon zest in a bowl. Reserve and set aside.

2 Put the saffron in a small bowl with 1 tablespoon boiling water and let stand while the saffron is infused. Melt the butter in a heavy frying pan and gently cook the onion for 5 minutes, until softened and golden.

3 Stir in the rice and cook for about 2 minutes, until it becomes translucent. Add the wine and saffron mixture and cook for several minutes, until all the wine is absorbed.

4 Add 2½ cups of the stock to pan and simmer gently until the stock is absorbed, stirring frequently.

5 Gradually add more stock, a ladleful at a time, until the rice is tender. (The rice might be tender and creamy before you've added all the stock, so add it slowly toward the end of the cooking time.)

6 Season the risotto with salt and pepper and transfer to a serving dish. Sprinkle lavishly with shavings of Parmesan cheese and the garlic and parsley mixture.

Vegetable Chili

This alternative to traditional chili con carne is delicious served with brown rice.

INGREDIENTS

Serves 4

2 onions, chopped

1 garlic clove, crushed

3 celery ribs, chopped

1 green bell pepper, seeded and diced

8 ounces mushrooms, sliced

2 zucchini, sliced

14-ounce can red kidney beans, rinsed
    and drained

14-ounce can chopped tomatoes

⅔ cup passata or tomato sauce

2 tablespoons tomato paste

1 tablespoon ketchup

1 teaspoon each hot chili powder, ground
    cumin and ground coriander

salt and freshly ground black pepper

plain yogurt and cayenne pepper,
    to serve

sprigs of cilantro, to garnish

2 Add the kidney beans, tomatoes, passata, tomato paste and ketchup.

3 Add the spices, season with salt and pepper and mix well.

4 Cover, bring to a boil and simmer for 20–30 minutes, stirring occasionally, until the vegetables are tender. Serve with plain yogurt, sprinkled with cayenne pepper. Garnish with cilantro sprigs.

1 Put the onions, garlic, celery, pepper, mushrooms and zucchini in a large saucepan and mix together.

Whole-Wheat Pasta with Caraway Cabbage

Crunchy cabbage and Brussels sprouts are the perfect partners for pasta in this healthy dish.

INGREDIENTS

Serves 6

6 tablespoons olive oil or sunflower oil

3 onions, roughly chopped

12-ounce round white cabbage, roughly chopped

12 ounces Brussels sprouts, trimmed and halved

2 teaspoons caraway seeds

1 tablespoon chopped fresh dill

1⅔ cups vegetable stock

7 ounces (1¼ cups) fresh or dried whole-wheat pasta spirals

salt and freshly ground black pepper

fresh dill sprigs, to garnish

1 Heat the oil in a large saucepan and sauté the onions over low heat for 10 minutes, until softened.

2 Add the cabbage and Brussels sprouts and cook for 2–3 minutes, then stir in the caraway seeds and dill. Pour in the stock and season with salt and pepper. Cover and simmer for 5–10 minutes, until the cabbage and sprouts are crisp-tender.

3 Meanwhile, cook the pasta in a pan of lightly salted boiling water, following the package instructions, until just tender.

4 Drain the pasta, pour it into a bowl and add the cabbage mixture. Toss lightly, adjust the seasoning, garnish with dill and serve immediately.

Cauliflower and Broccoli with Tomato Sauce

The addition of broccoli to the cauliflower gives extra color and texture to this dish.

INGREDIENTS

Serves 6

1 onion, finely chopped

14-ounce can chopped tomatoes

3 tablespoons tomato paste

3 tablespoons whole-wheat flour

1¼ cups skim milk

1¼ cups water

2½ pounds (6 cups) mixed cauliflower and broccoli florets

salt and freshly ground black pepper

1 Mix the onion, tomatoes and tomato paste in a small saucepan. Bring to a boil, lower the heat and simmer gently for 15–20 minutes.

2 Mix the flour to a paste with a little of the milk. Stir the paste into the tomato mixture, then gradually add the remaining milk and water.

3 Stir the mixture constantly until it boils and thickens. Season with salt and pepper. Keep the sauce hot.

4 Steam the cauliflower and broccoli over boiling water for 5–7 minutes, or until the florets are just tender. Transfer the vegetables to a dish, pour the tomato sauce over them and serve with extra pepper sprinkled over the top, if you like.

Mushroom Bolognese

A quick—and exceedingly tasty—vegetarian version of the classic Italian dish. This dish is easy to prepare and makes a very satisfying meal.

Serves 4

1 pound mushrooms
1 tablespoon olive oil
1 onion, chopped
1 garlic clove, crushed
1 tablespoon tomato paste
14-ounce can chopped tomatoes
3 tablespoons chopped fresh oregano
1 pound fresh pasta
salt and freshly ground black pepper
Parmesan cheese, to serve

1 Trim the mushroom stems neatly, then cut each mushroom into quarters.

COOK'S TIP

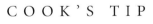

If you prefer to use dried pasta, make this the first thing that you cook. It will take 10–12 minutes, during which time you can make the mushroom mixture. Use 12 ounces dried pasta.

2 Heat the oil in a large pan. Add the chopped onion and garlic and cook for 2–3 minutes.

3 Add the mushrooms to the pan and cook over high heat for 3–4 minutes, stirring occasionally.

4 Stir in the tomato paste, chopped tomatoes and 1 tablespoon of the oregano. Lower the heat, cover and cook for about 5 minutes.

5 Meanwhile, bring a large pan of salted water to a boil. Cook the pasta for 2–3 minutes, until just tender.

6 Season the bolognese sauce with salt and pepper. Drain the pasta, pour it into a bowl and add the mushroom mixture. Toss to mix well. Serve in individual bowls, topped with shavings of fresh Parmesan and the remaining chopped fresh oregano.

Broccoli and Ricotta Cannelloni

A fabulous pasta dish that looks very impressive but is actually quite quick and simple to prepare and tastes wonderful.

INGREDIENTS

Serves 4

2 teaspoons olive oil

12 dried cannelloni tubes, 3 inches long

4 cups broccoli florets

1½ cups fresh bread crumbs

⅔ cup milk

4 tablespoons olive oil, plus extra for brushing

1 cup ricotta cheese

pinch of grated nutmeg

6 tablespoons grated Parmesan or Pecorino cheese

2 tablespoons pine nuts

salt and freshly ground black pepper

For the tomato sauce

2 tablespoons olive oil

1 onion, finely chopped

1 garlic clove, crushed

2 x 14-ounce cans chopped tomatoes

1 tablespoon tomato paste

4 black olives, pitted and chopped

1 teaspoon dried thyme

1 Preheat the oven to 375°F. Lightly grease four ovenproof dishes with olive oil.

2 Bring a large saucepan of water to a boil, add the olive oil to the water to prevent the pasta from sticking together and simmer the cannelloni, uncovered, for 6–7 minutes, or until it is nearly cooked.

3 Meanwhile, steam or boil the broccoli for 10 minutes, until tender. Drain the pasta, rinse under cold water and set aside. Drain the broccoli and let it cool, then place in a food processor or blender and process until smooth. Set aside.

4 Place the bread crumbs in a bowl, add the milk and oil and stir until softened. Add the ricotta, broccoli purée, nutmeg and 4 tablespoons of the Parmesan or Pecorino cheese. Season with salt and pepper, then set aside.

5 To make the sauce, heat the oil in a frying pan and add the onions and garlic. Cook for 5–6 minutes, until softened, then stir in the tomatoes, tomato paste, black olives and thyme. Season with salt and pepper. Boil rapidly for 2–3 minutes, then pour into the four ovenproof dishes.

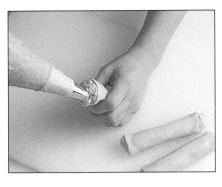

6 Spoon the cheese mixture into a pastry bag fitted with a ½-inch nozzle. Carefully open the cannelloni tubes. Standing each one upright on a board, pipe the filling into each tube. Divide the tubes equally among the four dishes and lay them in rows in the tomato sauce.

7 Brush the tops of the cannelloni with a little olive oil and sprinkle with the remaining Parmesan or Pecorino cheese and pine nuts. Bake for 25–30 minutes, until golden.

COOK'S TIP

If you don't have cannelloni tubes, you can cook lasagne sheets until al dente, spoon the mixture along one short edge of the sheet and roll it up to encase the filling.

Spiced Tofu Stir-Fry

The colors in this aromatic stir-fry are as pleasing to the eye as the flavors are to the palate. Serve with noodles or egg-fried rice.

INGREDIENTS

Serves 4

2 teaspoons ground cumin

1 tablespoon paprika

1 teaspoon ground ginger

good pinch of cayenne pepper

1 tablespoon sugar

10 ounces tofu (bean curd)

4 tablespoons oil

2 garlic cloves, crushed

1 bunch scallions, sliced

1 red bell pepper, seeded and sliced

1 yellow bell seeded and sliced

8 ounces (generous 3 cups) cremini
    mushrooms, halved or quartered
    if necessary

1 large zucchini, sliced

4 ounces haricots verts, halved

scant ½ cup pine nuts

1 tablespoon lime juice

1 tablespoon honey

salt and pepper

1 Mix together the cumin, paprika, ginger, cayenne and sugar with plenty of seasoning. Cut the tofu into cubes and coat them in the spice mixture.

2 Heat some of the oil in a wok or large frying pan. Cook the tofu over high heat for 3–4 minutes, turning occasionally (take care not to break up the tofu too much). Remove with a slotted spoon. Wipe out the pan with paper towels.

3 Add the remaining oil to the pan and cook the garlic and scallions for 3 minutes. Add the remaining vegetables and cook over medium heat for 6 minutes, or until beginning to soften and turn golden. Season well.

4 Return the tofu to the pan with the pine nuts, lime juice and honey. Heat through and serve immediately.

Butternut Squash and Sage Pizza

The combination of sweet butternut squash, sage and sharp goat cheese works wonderfully on this pizza.

Serves 4

½ teaspoon active dry yeast

pinch of sugar

4 cups white bread flour

1 teaspoon salt

2 tablespoons olive oil

1 tablespoon butter

2 tablespoons olive oil

2 shallots, finely chopped

1 butternut squash, peeled, seeded and
    cubed, about 1 pound prepared weight

16 sage leaves

2 x 14-ounce cans chunky tomato sauce

4 ounces mozzarella cheese, sliced

4 ounces firm goat cheese

salt and freshly ground black pepper

1 Put 1¼ cups warm water in a measuring cup. Add the yeast and sugar and let sit 5–10 minutes, until mixture is frothy.

2 Sift the flour and salt into a large bowl and make a well in the center. Gradually pour in the yeast mixture and the olive oil. Mix to make a smooth dough. Knead on a lightly floured surface for about 10 minutes, until smooth, springy and elastic. Place the dough in a floured bowl, cover and let rise in a warm place for 1½ hours.

3 Preheat the oven to 400°F. Oil four baking sheets. Put the butter and oil in a roasting pan and heat in the oven for a few minutes. Add the shallots, squash and half the sage leaves. Toss to coat. Roast for 15–20 minutes, until tender.

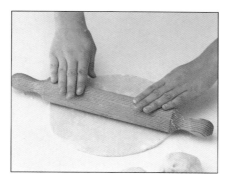

4 Raise the oven temperature to 425°F. Divide the dough into four equal pieces and roll out each piece on a floured surface to a 10-inch round.

5 Transfer each round to a baking sheet and spread with tomato sauce, leaving a ½-inch border all around. Spoon the squash and shallot mixture over the top.

6 Arrange the mozzarella over the squash mixture and crumble the goat cheese on top. Sprinkle with the remaining sage leaves and season with plenty of salt and pepper. Bake for 15–20 minutes, until the cheese has melted and the crusts are golden.

Eggplant, Shallot and Tomato Calzone

Eggplant, shallots and sun-dried tomatoes make an unusual filling for calzone. Add more or less crushed red pepper, depending on how fiery you like your food.

INGREDIENTS

Serves 2

¼ teaspoon active dry yeast

pinch of sugar

2 cups white bread flour

1 teaspoon salt

¼ cup olive oil

4 baby eggplant

3 shallots, chopped

1 garlic clove, chopped

10 sun-dried tomatoes in oil,
     drained and chopped

¼ teaspoon crushed red pepper

2 teaspoons chopped fresh thyme

3 ounces mozzarella cheese, cubed

salt and freshly ground black pepper

1–2 tablespoons freshly grated Parmesan
     cheese, to serve

1 To make the dough, put ⅔ cup warm water in a measuring cup. Add the yeast and sugar and let sit for 5–10 minutes, until frothy.

2 Sift the flour and salt into a large bowl and make a well in the center. Gradually pour in the yeast mixture and 1 tablespoon oil. Mix to make a smooth dough. Knead the dough on a lightly floured surface for 10 minutes, until smooth. The dough should be springy and elastic.

3 Place the dough in a floured bowl, cover and let rise in a warm place for 1½ hours. Preheat the oven to 425°F. Trim the eggplant, then cut into small cubes.

4 Heat 1 tablespoon of the oil in a frying pan and cook the shallots until soft. Add the eggplant, garlic, sun-dried tomatoes, crushed red pepper, thyme and seasoning. Cook for 4–5 minutes, stirring frequently, until the eggplant is beginning to soften.

5 Divide the dough in half and roll out each piece on a lightly floured surface to a 7-inch circle.

6 Spread the eggplant mixture over half of each round, leaving a 1-inch border, then top with the mozzarella cubes.

7 Dampen the edges with water, then fold over the other half of dough to enclose the filling. Press the edges firmly together to seal. Place the calzones on two greased baking sheets.

8 Brush with half the remaining olive oil and make a small hole in the top of each to allow the steam to escape. Bake for 15–20 minutes, until golden. Remove from the oven and brush with the remaining oil. Sprinkle with the Parmesan cheese and serve immediately.

Ravioli with Ricotta and Spinach

Homemade ravioli are fun to make, and can be stuffed with different cheese or vegetable fillings. This filling is particularly easy to make.

INGREDIENTS

Serves 4

14 ounces fresh spinach or 6 ounces
    frozen spinach

¾ cup ricotta cheese

1 egg

½ cup grated Parmesan cheese

pinch of grated nutmeg

salt and freshly ground black pepper

For the pasta

1½ cups flour

3 eggs

For the sauce

6 tablespoons butter

5–6 sprigs of fresh sage

1 Wash the fresh spinach well in several changes of water. Place in a saucepan, cover and cook until tender, about 5 minutes. Drain. Cook frozen spinach according to the package instructions. When cool, squeeze out as much moisture as possible. Chop finely.

2 Combine the chopped spinach with the ricotta, egg, Parmesan and nutmeg. Season with salt and pepper. Cover and set aside.

3 To make the pasta, place the flour in the center of a clean smooth work surface. Make a well in the middle. Break the eggs into the well. Add a pinch of salt.

4 Start beating the eggs with a fork, gradually drawing the flour from the inside walls of the well. As the paste thickens, continue mixing with your hands.

5 Incorporate as much flour as possible until the mixture forms a mass. It will still be lumpy. If it still sticks to your hands, add a little more flour. Set the dough aside. Scrape off the dough from the work surface until it is smooth.

6 Lightly flour the work surface. Knead the dough. Work for about 10 minutes, or until the dough is smooth and elastic.

7 Divide the dough in half. Flour the rolling pin and the work surface. Pat the dough into a disk and begin rolling out into a flat circle. Roll until it is about ⅛ inch thick. Do the same with the second half of the dough.

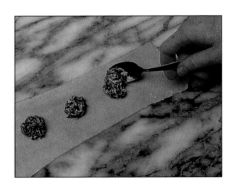

8 Cut the dough into sheets. Place small teaspoons of filling along the pasta in rows 2 inches apart. Cover with another sheet of pasta, pressing down gently to expel any air pockets.

9 Use a fluted pastry wheel to cut between the rows to form small squares with filling in the center of each. If the edges do not stick well, moisten with milk or water and press together.

10 Place the ravioli on a lightly floured surface and allow to dry for at least 30 minutes. Turn occasionally so they are completely dry on both sides. Bring a large pan of salted water to a boil.

11 Heat the butter and sage together over very low heat, taking care that the butter melts but does not darken.

12 Drop the ravioli into the boiling water. Stir gently to prevent them from sticking together. They will be cooked in very little time, 4–5 minutes. Drain carefully and arrange in individual serving dishes. Spoon on the sauce and serve at once.

Cilantro Ravioli with Pumpkin Filling

A stunning pasta that combines fresh herbs with a superb creamy pumpkin and roast garlic filling.

INGREDIENTS

Serves 4–6

scant 1 cup unbleached bread flour

2 eggs

pinch of salt

3 tablespoons chopped cilantro

sprigs of cilantro, to garnish

For the filling

4 garlic cloves in their skins

1 pound pumpkin, peeled and
    seeds removed

½ cup ricotta cheese

4 sun-dried tomatoes in olive oil,
    drained and finely chopped
    (reserve 2 tablespoons of the oil)

freshly ground black pepper

1 Place the flour, eggs, salt and cilantro in a food processor. Pulse until combined.

2 Knead the dough on a lightly floured board until smooth.

3 Wrap the dough in plastic wrap and let rest in the refrigerator for 20–30 minutes.

4 Preheat the oven to 400°F. Place the garlic cloves on a baking sheet and bake for 10 minutes, until softened. Steam the pumpkin for 5–8 minutes, until tender, and drain well.

5 Peel the garlic cloves and mash into the pumpkin together with the ricotta and sun-dried tomatoes. Season with plenty of black pepper.

6 Divide the pasta into four pieces and flatten slightly. Using a pasta machine on its thinnest setting, roll out each piece. Lay the sheets of pasta on a clean dish towel until slightly dried.

7 Using a 3-inch crinkle-edged round cutter, stamp out 36 rounds.

8 Top 18 of the rounds with a teaspoonful of the pumpkin mixture, brush the edges with water and place another round of pasta on top. Press firmly around the edges to seal. Bring a large pan of water to a boil, add the ravioli and cook for 3–4 minutes. Drain well and toss with the reserved tomato oil. Add pepper and serve garnished with cilantro sprigs.

VARIATION

For an alternative filling you could replace the ricotta cheese with 1 ounce grated Parmesan cheese mixed with 4 ounces cottage cheese. Serve with shavings of Parmesan.

Purée of Lentils with Baked Eggs

This unusual dish makes an excellent supper. For a nutty flavor you could add a 14-ounce can of unsweetened chestnut purée to the lentil mixture.

INGREDIENTS

Serves 4

2 cups washed brown lentils

3 leeks, thinly sliced

2 teaspoons coriander seeds, crushed

1 tablespoon chopped cilantro

2 tablespoons chopped fresh mint

1 tablespoon red wine vinegar

4 cups vegetable stock

4 eggs

salt and freshly ground black pepper

generous handful of chopped
   parsley to garnish

1 Put the lentils in a deep saucepan. Add the leeks, coriander seeds, cilantro, mint, vinegar and stock. Bring to a boil, then lower the heat and simmer for 30–40 minutes, until the lentils are cooked and have absorbed all the liquid.

2 Preheat the oven to 350°F.

3 Season the lentils with salt and pepper and mix well. Spread out in four lightly greased baking dishes about 6 inches in diameter and 2 inches deep.

4 Using the back of a spoon, make a hollow in the lentil mixture in each dish. Break an egg into each hollow. Cover the dishes with foil and bake for 15–20 minutes, or until the whites are set and the yolks are still soft. Sprinkle with plenty of parsley and serve at once.

Harvest Vegetable and Lentil Casserole

Take advantage of root vegetables in season to produce a hearty dish that's not only full of natural goodness but delicious, too.

INGREDIENTS

Serves 6

1 tablespoon sunflower oil

2 leeks, sliced

1 garlic clove, crushed

4 celery ribs, chopped

2 carrots, sliced

2 parsnips, diced

1 sweet potato, diced

8 ounces rutabaga, diced

6 ounces whole brown or green lentils

1 pound tomatoes, peeled, seeded and chopped

1 tablespoon chopped fresh thyme

1 tablespoon chopped fresh marjoram

3¾ cups vegetable stock

1 tablespoon cornstarch

salt and freshly ground black pepper

sprigs of fresh thyme, to garnish

1 Preheat the oven to 350°F. Heat the oil in a flameproof casserole over moderate heat. Add the leeks, garlic and celery and cook gently for 3 minutes.

2 Add the carrots, parsnips, sweet potato, rutabaga, lentils, tomatoes, herbs, stock and seasoning. Stir well. Bring to a boil, stirring occasionally.

3 Cover and bake for about 50 minutes, until the vegetables and the lentils are cooked and tender. While it is cooking, remove the casserole from the oven and stir the vegetable mixture once or twice so that it is evenly cooked.

4 Remove the casserole from the oven. Blend the cornstarch with 3 tablespoons cold water in a bowl. Stir into the casserole and heat, stirring constantly, until the mixture comes to a boil and thickens. Simmer gently for 2 minutes.

5 Spoon the vegetable mixture into bowls and serve garnished with thyme sprigs.

Vegetable Lasagne

This recipe uses fresh vegetables and herbs to create a delicious version of the favorite classic.

INGREDIENTS

Serves 8

15–18 fresh or precooked lasagne sheets
2 tablespoons olive oil
1 medium onion, very finely chopped
1¼ pounds tomatoes, fresh or
    canned, chopped
1½ pounds cultivated or wild
    mushrooms, or a combination of both
6 tablespoons butter
2 garlic cloves, finely chopped
juice of ½ lemon
4 cups béchamel sauce
1½ cups freshly grated Parmesan
    or Cheddar cheese, or a
    combination of both
salt and freshly ground black pepper

1 Butter a large, shallow, ovenproof baking dish, preferably rectangular or square.

2 Heat the oil in a small frying pan and sauté the onion until translucent. Add the chopped tomatoes and cook for 6–8 minutes, stirring often. Season with salt and pepper and set aside.

3 Wipe the mushrooms carefully with a damp cloth. Slice finely. Heat half the butter in a frying pan and, when it is bubbling, add the mushrooms. Cook until the mushrooms start to exude their juice. Add the garlic and lemon juice and season with salt and pepper.

4 Cook the mushroom mixture until nearly all the liquids have evaporated and the mushrooms are starting to brown. Set aside.

5 Preheat the oven to 400°F. Bring a pan of water to a boil and place a bowl of cold water near the stove. Add salt to the rapidly boiling water.

6 Drop in 3 or 4 of the lasagne sheets. Cook for about 30 seconds. Remove them from the pan and drop them into the cold water for 30 seconds. Remove and lay out to dry. Continue with the remaining pasta. If using pre-cooked lasagne, skip this step.

7 To assemble the lasagne, have all the elements at hand: the baking dish, fillings, pasta, cheeses and butter. Spread one large spoonful of the béchamel sauce over the bottom of the dish. Arrange a layer of pasta in the dish, cutting it with a sharp knife so that it fits well. Cover the pasta with a thin layer of mushrooms, then one of béchamel sauce. Sprinkle with a little cheese.

8 Make another layer of pasta and spread with a thin layer of tomatoes, then one of béchamel. Sprinkle with cheese.

9 Repeat the layers in the same order, ending with a layer of pasta and béchamel. Do not make more than about 6 layers. Use the pasta trimmings to patch any gaps in the pasta. Sprinkle with cheese and dot with the remaining butter.

10 Bake for 20 minutes. Remove from the oven and let stand for 5 minutes.

COOK'S TIP

Fresh pasta is not necessarily better than dried, but it takes much less time to cook, as it still contains moisture. Fresh pasta should always be stored in the refrigerator or freezer until ready for cooking.

Chile, Tomato and Spinach Pizza

This richly flavored topping with a hint of spice makes a colorful and satisfying pizza.

INGREDIENTS

Serves 3

1–2 fresh red chiles

3 tablespoons tomato oil (from jar of sun-dried tomatoes)

1 onion, chopped

2 garlic cloves, chopped

10 sun-dried tomatoes in oil, drained

14-ounce can chopped tomatoes

1 tablespoon tomato paste

6 ounces fresh spinach

1 pizza crust, 10–12 inches in diameter

3 ounces firm smoked cheese, grated

3 ounces aged Cheddar, grated

salt and freshly ground black pepper

1 Seed and finely chop the chiles.

2 Heat 2 tablespoons of the tomato oil in a saucepan, add the onion, garlic and chiles and cook gently for about 5 minutes, until they are soft.

3 Roughly chop the sun-dried tomatoes. Add to the pan with the chopped tomatoes and tomato paste. Season with salt and pepper. Simmer, uncovered, stirring occasionally, for 15 minutes.

4 Remove the stalks from the spinach and wash the leaves in plenty of cold water. Drain well and pat dry with paper towels. Roughly chop the spinach.

5 Stir the spinach into the sauce. Cook, stirring, for another 5–10 minutes, until the spinach has wilted and no excess moisture remains. Let cool.

6 Meanwhile, preheat the oven to 425°F. Brush the pizza crust with the remaining tomato oil, then spoon the sauce over it. Sprinkle with the grated cheeses and bake for 15–20 minutes, until crisp and golden. Serve immediately.

COOK'S TIP

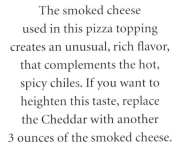

The smoked cheese used in this pizza topping creates an unusual, rich flavor, that complements the hot, spicy chiles. If you want to heighten this taste, replace the Cheddar with another 3 ounces of the smoked cheese.

Tagliatelle with Spinach Gnocchi

*Gnocchi are extremely smooth
and light and make a delicious
accompaniment to this pasta dish.*

INGREDIENTS

Serves 4–6

1 pound mixed flavored tagliatelle
shavings of Parmesan cheese, to garnish

For the spinach gnocchi

1 pound frozen chopped spinach
1 small onion, finely chopped
1 garlic clove, crushed
¼ teaspoon ground nutmeg
14 ounces low-fat cottage cheese
4 ounces dried white bread crumbs
¾ cup semolina or all-purpose flour
½ cup grated Parmesan cheese
3 egg whites

For the tomato sauce

1 onion, finely chopped
1 celery rib, finely chopped
1 red bell pepper, seeded and diced
1 garlic clove, crushed
⅔ cup vegetable stock
14-ounce can whole peeled tomatoes
1 tablespoon tomato paste
2 teaspoons sugar
1 teaspoon dried oregano
salt and freshly ground black pepper

1 To make the tomato sauce, put
the chopped onion, celery,
pepper and garlic in a nonstick
pan. Add the stock, bring to a
boil and cook for 5 minutes, or
until tender.

2 Add the tomatoes, tomato
paste, sugar and oregano.
Season to taste, bring to a boil and
simmer, stirring occasionally, for
30 minutes, until thick.

3 Put the spinach, onion and
garlic in a saucepan, cover and
cook until the spinach is defrosted.
Remove the lid and increase the
heat. Season with salt, pepper and
nutmeg. Cool in a bowl. Mix in the
remaining ingredients. Shape into
about 24 ovals and refrigerate for
30 minutes.

4 Cook the gnocchi in boiling
salted water for about
5 minutes. Remove with a slotted
spoon and drain. Cook the
tagliatelle in a pan of boiling salted
water until al dente. Drain.
Transfer to serving plates and top
with gnocchi, the tomato sauce
and shavings of Parmesan cheese.

Pizza with Fresh Vegetables

This pizza can be made with any combination of fresh vegetables. Most will benefit from being blanched or sautéed before being baked on the pizza.

INGREDIENTS

Serves 4

14 ounces peeled plum tomatoes, fresh
    or canned, weighed whole, without
    extra juice
2 medium broccoli spears
8 ounces fresh asparagus
2 small zucchini
5 tablespoons olive oil
⅓ cup shelled peas, fresh
    or frozen
4 scallions, sliced
1 pizza crust, 10–12 inches in diameter
3 ounces mozzarella cheese, cut into
    small dice (about ⅓ cup)
10 leaves fresh basil, torn into pieces
2 cloves garlic, finely chopped
salt and freshly ground black pepper

1 Preheat the oven to 475°F for at least 20 minutes before baking the pizza. Strain the tomatoes through the medium disk of a food mill, scraping in all the pulp.

2 Peel the broccoli stems and asparagus and blanch with the zucchini in boiling water for 4–5 minutes. Drain. Cut the broccoli and asparagus into bite-size pieces and slice the zucchini lengthwise.

3 Heat 2 tablespoons of the olive oil in a small saucepan. Stir in the peas and scallions and cook for 5–6 minutes, stirring often. Remove from the heat.

4 Spread the puréed tomatoes over the pizza crust, leaving the rim uncovered. Add the other vegetables, spreading them evenly over the tomatoes.

5 Sprinkle with the mozzarella, basil, garlic, salt and pepper and remaining olive oil. Immediately place the pizza in the oven. Bake for about 20 minutes, or until the crust is golden brown and the cheese has melted.

Ricotta and Fontina Pizza

The earthy flavors of the mixed mushrooms perfectly complement the two creamy cheeses in this delectable recipe.

INGREDIENTS

Serves 4

½ teaspoon active dry yeast

pinch of sugar

4 cups white bread flour

1 teaspoon salt

2 tablespoons olive oil

For the tomato sauce

14-ounce can chopped tomatoes

⅔ cup passata or tomato sauce

1 large garlic clove, finely chopped

1 teaspoon dried oregano

1 bay leaf

2 teaspoons malt vinegar

salt and freshly ground black pepper

For the topping

2 tablespoons olive oil

1 garlic clove, finely chopped

12 ounces mixed mushrooms (cremini, portobello or button), sliced

2 tablespoons chopped fresh oregano, plus whole leaves, to garnish

generous 1 cup ricotta cheese

8 ounces Fontina cheese, sliced

1 To make the dough, put 1¼ cups warm water in a measuring cup. Add the yeast and sugar and let sit for 5–10 minutes, until frothy.

2 Sift the flour and salt into a large bowl and make a well in the center. Gradually pour in the yeast mixture and the olive oil. Mix to make a smooth dough. Knead on a lightly floured surface for about 10 minutes, until dough is smooth, springy and elastic. Place the dough in a floured bowl, cover and let rise in a warm place for 1½ hours.

3 Meanwhile, make the tomato sauce. Put all the ingredients in a saucepan, cover and bring to a boil. Lower the heat, remove the lid and simmer for 20 minutes, stirring occasionally, until reduced.

4 To make the topping, heat the oil in a frying pan. Add the garlic and mushrooms and season with salt and pepper. Cook, stirring, for about 5 minutes, or until the mushrooms are tender and golden. Set aside.

5 Preheat the oven to 425°F. Brush four baking sheets with oil. Knead the dough for 2 minutes, then divide into four equal pieces. Roll out each piece to a 10-inch round and place on a baking sheet.

6 Spoon the tomato sauce over each dough round. Brush the edge with a little olive oil. Add the mushrooms, oregano and cheeses. Season to taste. Bake for about 15 minutes, until golden brown and crisp. Garnish with oregano leaves.

COOK'S TIP

To freeze, allow to cool to room temperature after baking. Wrap in foil and freeze. Thaw completely and heat in a warm oven before serving.

Red Cabbage and Apple Casserole

The brilliant color and pungent flavor make this an excellent winter dish. Serve it with plenty of rye bread.

INGREDIENTS

Serves 6

1½ pounds red cabbage

3 onions, chopped

2 fennel bulbs, roughly chopped

2 tablespoons caraway seeds

3 large, tart eating apples or 1 large
    cooking apple

1¼ cups plain yogurt

1 tablespoon creamed horseradish

salt and freshly ground black pepper

crusty rye bread, to serve

1 Preheat the oven to 300°F. Shred the cabbage finely, discarding any tough stalks. Mix with the onions, fennel and caraway seeds in a large bowl. Peel, core and chop the apples, then stir them into the cabbage mixture. Transfer the mixture to a casserole dish.

2 Mix the yogurt with the creamed horseradish. Stir the yogurt and horseradish mixture into the casserole, season with salt and pepper and cover tightly.

3 Bake for 1½ hours, stirring once or twice during cooking. Serve hot, with rye bread.

Mixed Vegetables with Artichokes

Baking a vegetable medley in the oven is a wonderfully easy way of producing a quick and simple, wholesome midweek meal.

INGREDIENTS

Serves 4

2 tablespoons olive oil

1½ pounds frozen fava or lima beans

4 turnips, peeled and sliced

4 leeks, sliced

1 red bell pepper, seeded and sliced

7 ounces fresh spinach leaves or
    4 ounces frozen spinach

2 x 14-ounce cans artichoke
    hearts, drained

¼ cup pumpkin seeds

soy sauce

salt and freshly ground black pepper

2 Cover the casserole and bake the vegetables for 30–40 minutes, or until the turnips are slightly soft.

1 Preheat the oven to 350°F. Pour the olive oil into a casserole. Cook the beans in a saucepan of boiling lightly salted water for about 10 minutes. Drain the beans and place them in the casserole with the turnips, leeks, pepper, spinach and canned artichoke hearts.

3 Stir in the pumpkin seeds and soy sauce to taste. Season with salt and pepper to taste and serve immediately.

Vegetable Moussaka

This is a really flavorful main-course dish. It can be served with warm fresh bread for a hearty, satisfying meal.

INGREDIENTS

Serves 6

1 pound eggplant, sliced

4 ounces whole green lentils

2½ cups vegetable stock

1 bay leaf

3 tablespoons olive oil

1 onion, sliced

1 garlic clove, crushed

8 ounces mushrooms, sliced

14-ounce can chickpeas, rinsed
   and drained

14-ounce can chopped tomatoes

2 tablespoons tomato paste

2 teaspoons dried herbes de Provence

1¼ cups plain yogurt

3 eggs

½ cup grated aged Cheddar cheese

salt and freshly ground black pepper

sprigs of fresh flat-leaf parsley,
   to garnish

1 Sprinkle the eggplant slices with salt and place in a colander. Cover and place a weight on top. Let sit for at least 30 minutes, to allow the bitter juices to be extracted.

2 Meanwhile, place the lentils, stock and bay leaf in a saucepan, cover, bring to a boil and simmer for about 20 minutes, until the lentils are just tender but not mushy. Drain thoroughly and keep warm.

3 Heat 1 tablespoon of the oil in a large saucepan, add the onion and garlic and cook, stirring, for 5 minutes. Stir in the lentils, mushrooms, chickpeas, tomatoes, tomato paste, herbs and 3 table-spoons water. Bring to a boil, cover and simmer gently for 10 minutes, stirring occasionally.

4 Preheat the oven to 350°F. Rinse the eggplant slices, drain and pat dry. Heat the remaining oil in a frying pan and cook the slices in batches for 3–4 minutes, turning once so both sides are browned.

5 Season the lentil mixture with salt and pepper. Arrange a layer of eggplant slices in the bottom of a large, shallow, ovenproof dish or roasting pan, then spoon a layer of the lentil mixture on top. Continue the layers until all the eggplant slices and lentil mixture are used up.

6 Beat the yogurt, eggs and salt and pepper together and pour the mixture over the vegetables. Sprinkle generously with the grated Cheddar cheese and bake for about 45 minutes, until the topping is golden brown and bubbling. Serve immediately, garnished with the flat-leaf parsley.

VARIATION
~

Sliced and sautéed zucchini or potatoes can be used instead of the eggplant in this dish.

Eggplant Curry

A simple and delicious way of cooking eggplant that retains their full flavor.

Serves 4

2 large eggplant, about 1 pound each

3 tablespoons oil

½ teaspoon black mustard seeds

1 bunch scallions, finely chopped

4 ounces button mushrooms, halved

2 garlic cloves, crushed

1 fresh red chile, finely chopped

½ teaspoon chili powder

1 teaspoon ground cumin

1 teaspoon ground coriander

¼ teaspoon ground turmeric

1 teaspoon salt

14-ounce can chopped tomatoes

1 tablespoon chopped cilantro

sprigs of cilantro, to garnish

1 Preheat the oven to 400°F. Brush both of the eggplant with 1 tablespoon of the oil and prick with a fork. Bake for 30–35 minutes, until soft.

2 Meanwhile, heat the remaining oil in a saucepan and sauté the mustard seeds for 2 minutes, until they being to splutter.

3 Add the scallions, mushrooms, garlic and chile and cook for 5 minutes. Stir in the chili powder, cumin, coriander, turmeric and salt and cook for 3–4 minutes. Add the tomatoes and simmer for 5 minutes.

4 Cut each eggplant in half lengthwise and scoop out the soft flesh into a bowl. Mash the flesh briefly.

5 Add the mashed eggplant and chopped cilantro to the saucepan. Bring to a boil and simmer for 5 minutes, or until the sauce thickens. Serve garnished with cilantro sprigs.

COOK'S TIP

If you want to omit some of the oil, wrap the eggplants in foil and bake them for 1 hour.

Vegetable Korma

The blending of spices produces a subtle, aromatic curry.

Serves 4

4 tablespoons (½ stick) butter

2 onions, sliced

2 garlic cloves, crushed

1-inch piece of fresh
   ginger root, grated

1 teaspoon ground cumin

1 tablespoon ground coriander

6 cardamom pods

2-inch cinnamon stick

1 teaspoon ground turmeric

1 fresh red chile, seeded and
   finely chopped

1 potato, peeled and cut into
   1-inch cubes

1 small eggplant, chopped

4 ounces mushrooms, thickly sliced

1 cup green beans, cut into 1-inch lengths

¼ cup plain yogurt

⅔ cup heavy cream

1 teaspoon garam masala

salt and freshly ground black pepper

sprigs of cilantro, to garnish

pappadams, to serve

1 Melt the butter in a heavy saucepan. Add the onions and cook for 5 minutes, until soft. Add the garlic and ginger and cook for 2 minutes, then stir in the cumin, coriander, cardamom, cinnamon stick, turmeric and chile. Cook, stirring, for 30 seconds.

2 Add the potato, eggplant and mushrooms and about ¾ cup water. Cover the pan, bring to a boil, then lower the heat and simmer for 15 minutes. Add the green beans and cook, uncovered, for 5 minutes.

VARIATION

Any combination of vegetables can be used for this korma, including carrots, cauliflower, broccoli, peas and chickpeas.

3 With a slotted spoon, remove the vegetables to a warmed serving dish and keep hot. Allow the cooking liquid to bubble up until it reduces a little. Season with salt and pepper, then stir in the yogurt, cream and garam masala. Pour the sauce over the vegetables and garnish with cilantro. Serve with pappadams.

Mushroom and Okra Curry

*This simple but delicious curry with
its fresh gingery mango relish is best
served with plain basmati rice.*

Serves 4

4 garlic cloves, roughly chopped
1-inch piece of fresh ginger root, peeled
   and roughly chopped
1–2 fresh red chiles, seeded and chopped
¾ cup cold water
1 tablespoon sunflower oil
1 teaspoon coriander seeds
1 teaspoon cumin seeds
1 teaspoon ground cumin
2 green cardamom pods, seeds removed
   and ground
pinch of ground turmeric
14-ounce can chopped tomatoes
1 pound mushrooms, quartered if large
8 ounces okra, trimmed and cut into
   ½-inch slices
2 tablespoons chopped cilantro

For the mango relish
1 large ripe mango, about 1¼ pounds
1 small garlic clove, crushed
1 onion, finely chopped
2 teaspoons grated fresh ginger root
1 fresh red chile, seeded and
   finely chopped
pinch of salt and sugar

1 To make the mango relish, peel
the mango and cut off the flesh
from the pit.

2 In a bowl, mash the mango
flesh with a fork, or process in
a food processor or blender. Mix in
the rest of the relish ingredients.
Set aside.

3 Place the garlic, ginger, chiles
and 3 tablespoons of the water
in a blender or food processor and
process until smooth.

4 Heat the sunflower oil in a
large saucepan. Add the whole
coriander and cumin seeds and
allow them to sizzle for a few
seconds. Add the ground cumin,
cardamom and turmeric and cook
for about 1 minute more.

5 Add the garlic paste, tomatoes
and remaining water. Stir to
mix well, then add the mushrooms
and okra. Stir again, then bring to
a boil. Reduce the heat, cover and
simmer for 5 minutes.

6 Remove the cover, turn up
the heat slightly and cook for
another 5–10 minutes, until the
okra is tender but not too soft.

7 Stir in the chopped cilantro
and serve with the mango
relish and rice.

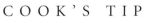

COOK'S TIP

When buying okra, choose firm,
brightly colored pods that are
less than 4 inches long.

Provençal Stuffed Peppers

Stuffed peppers are easy to make for a light and healthy supper.

Serves 4

1 tablespoon olive oil

1 red onion, sliced

1 zucchini, diced

4 ounces mushrooms, sliced

1 garlic clove, crushed

14-ounce can chopped tomatoes

1 tablespoon tomato paste

scant ⅓ cup pine nuts

2 tablespoons chopped fresh basil

4 large yellow bell peppers

½ cup red Leicester or Cheddar cheese, finely grated

salt and freshly ground black pepper

fresh basil leaves, to garnish

2 Stir in the tomatoes and tomato paste, then bring to a boil and simmer, uncovered, for 10–15 minutes, stirring occasionally, until thickened slightly. Remove from the heat and stir in the pine nuts, basil and seasoning.

3 Cut the peppers in half lengthwise and seed them. Blanch in a pan of boiling water for about 3 minutes. Drain.

4 Place the peppers in a shallow ovenproof dish and fill them with the vegetable mixture.

5 Cover the dish with foil and bake for 20 minutes. Uncover, sprinkle each pepper with grated cheese and bake for another 5–10 minutes, until the cheese is melted and bubbling. Garnish with basil leaves and serve.

1 Preheat the oven to 350°F. Heat the oil in a saucepan, add the onion, zucchini, mushrooms and garlic and cook gently for 3 minutes, stirring occasionally.

VARIATION

Use the vegetable filling to stuff other vegetables, such as zucchini or eggplant, in place of the bell peppers.

Spicy Chickpea and Eggplant Stew

This is a Lebanese dish that's full of the spicy flavors of the Middle East.

Serves 4

3 large eggplant, cubed

1 cup chickpeas,
   soaked overnight

¼ cup olive oil

3 garlic cloves, chopped

2 large onions, chopped

½ teaspoon ground cumin

½ teaspoon ground cinnamon

½ teaspoon ground coriander

3 x 14-ounce cans chopped tomatoes

salt and freshly ground black pepper

For the garnish

2 tablespoons olive oil

1 onion, sliced

1 garlic clove, sliced

sprigs of cilantro

1 Place the eggplant in a colander and sprinkle with salt. Set the colander in a bowl and let sit for 30 minutes to allow the bitter juices to escape. Rinse the eggplant with cold water and dry on paper towels.

2 Drain the chickpeas and put in a saucepan with enough water to cover. Bring to a boil and simmer for 1–1½ hours, or until tender. Drain.

3 Heat the oil in a large saucepan. Add the garlic and onion and cook until soft. Add the spices and cook, stirring, for a few seconds. Stir in the eggplant and cook for 5 minutes. Add the tomatoes and chickpeas and season with salt and pepper. Cover and simmer for 20 minutes.

4 To make the garnish, heat the oil in a frying pan and, when very hot, add the sliced onion and garlic. Fry until golden and crisp. Serve the stew with rice, topped with the onion and garlic and garnished with cilantro.

Vegetable Hot Pot with Cheese Triangles

Use a selection of your favorite vegetables, as long as the overall weight remains the same. Firm vegetables may need a little longer cooking time.

Serves 6

2 tablespoons oil

2 garlic cloves, crushed

1 onion, roughly chopped

1 teaspoon mild chili powder

1 pound potatoes, peeled and
    roughly chopped

1 pound celeriac, peeled and
    roughly chopped

12 ounces carrots, roughly chopped

12 ounces trimmed leeks, roughly
    chopped

8 ounces cremini mushrooms, halved

¼ cup all-purpose flour

2½ cups vegetable stock

14-ounce can chopped tomatoes

1 tablespoon tomato paste

2 tablespoons chopped fresh thyme

14-ounce can kidney beans, drained
    and rinsed

salt and freshly ground black pepper

sprigs of fresh thyme, to garnish
    (optional)

For the topping

8 tablespoons (1 stick) butter

2 cups self-rising flour

4 ounces Cheddar cheese, grated

2 tablespoons snipped fresh chives

about 5 tablespoons milk

1 Preheat the oven to 350°F. Heat the oil in a large, flame-proof casserole and sauté the garlic and onion for 5 minutes, or until beginning to brown. Stir in the chili powder and cook for 1 minute more.

2 Add the potatoes, celeriac, carrots, leeks and mushrooms. Cook for 3–4 minutes. Stir in the flour and cook for 1 minute.

3 Gradually stir in the stock with the tomatoes, tomato paste and thyme and season with plenty of salt and pepper. Bring to a boil, stirring. Cover and bake for 30 minutes.

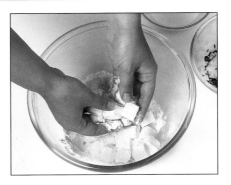

4 Meanwhile, make the topping. Rub the butter into the flour, then stir in half the cheese with the chives and plenty of salt and pepper. Add just enough milk to make a smooth dough.

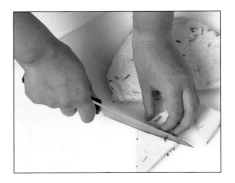

5 Roll out the dough until it is 1 inch thick. Cut into 12 triangles and brush with milk.

6 Remove the casserole from the oven, add the beans and stir to combine. Place the triangles on top and sprinkle with the remaining cheese. Return to the oven, uncovered, and bake for 20–25 minutes. Serve garnished with fresh thyme sprigs, if using.

Sweet and Sour Mixed Bean Hot Pot

An appetizing mixture of beans and vegetables in a tasty sweet and sour sauce, topped with potato.

Serves 6

1 pound unpeeled potatoes

1 tablespoon olive oil

3 tablespoons butter

⅓ cup whole-wheat flour

1¼ cups passata or tomato sauce

⅔ cup unsweetened apple juice

¼ cup each light brown sugar,
    ketchup, dry sherry, cider vinegar and
    light soy sauce

14-ounce can lima beans

14-ounce can flageolet beans

14-ounce can chickpeas

6 ounces green beans, chopped
    and blanched

8 ounces shallots, sliced and blanched

8 ounces mushrooms, sliced

1 tablespoon each chopped fresh thyme
    and marjoram

salt and freshly ground black pepper

sprigs of fresh herbs, to garnish

2 Place the butter, flour, passata, apple juice, sugar, ketchup, sherry, vinegar and soy sauce in a saucepan. Heat gently, whisking constantly, until the sauce comes to a boil and thickens. Simmer gently for 3 minutes, stirring.

3 Rinse and drain the beans and chickpeas and add to the sauce with all the remaining ingredients except the herb garnish. Mix well.

1 Preheat the oven to 400°F. Thinly slice the potatoes and parboil them for 4 minutes. Drain the potatoes thoroughly, toss them in the oil so they are lightly coated all over and set aside.

4 Spoon the bean mixture into a casserole.

5 Arrange the potato slices over the top, overlapping them slightly and completely covering the bean mixture.

6 Cover the casserole with foil and bake for about 1 hour, until the potatoes are cooked and tender. Remove the foil for the last 20 minutes of the cooking time, to lightly brown the potatoes. Serve garnished with fresh herb sprigs.

COOK'S TIP

Vary the proportions of beans used in this recipe, depending on what ingredients you have in your pantry.

Spicy Baked Potatoes

Simple baked potatoes take on an exciting new character with the addition of a few herbs and spices.

INGREDIENTS

Serves 2–4

2 large baking potatoes
1 teaspoon sunflower oil
1 small onion, finely chopped
1-inch piece fresh ginger root, grated
1 teaspoon ground cumin
1 teaspoon ground coriander
½ teaspoon ground turmeric
garlic salt
plain yogurt and sprigs of cilantro,
   to serve

1 Preheat the oven to 375°F. Prick the potatoes with a fork. Bake for 1 hour, or until soft.

2 Cut the potatoes in half, scoop out the flesh and set aside. Heat the oil in a nonstick frying pan and fry the onion for a few minutes to soften. Stir in the ginger, cumin, coriander and turmeric.

3 Stir over low heat for about 2 minutes, then add the potato flesh and garlic salt to taste.

4 Cook the potato mixture for another 2 minutes, stirring occasionally. Spoon the mixture back into the potato shells and top each with a spoonful of plain yogurt and a sprig or two of cilantro. Serve hot.

Baked Leeks with Cheese and Yogurt

Like all vegetables, the fresher leeks are, the better their flavor, and the freshest leeks available should be used for this dish. Small, young leeks are around at the beginning of the season and are perfect to use here.

INGREDIENTS

Serves 4

2 tablespoons butter

8 small leeks, about 1½ pounds

2 small eggs or 1 large one, beaten

5 ounces fresh goat cheese

⅓ cup plain yogurt

½ cup grated Parmesan cheese

½ cup fresh white or brown bread crumbs

salt and freshly ground black pepper

1 Preheat the oven to 350°F. Butter a shallow ovenproof dish. Trim the leeks, cut a slit from top to bottom and rinse well under cold water.

2 Place the leeks in a saucepan of water, bring to a boil and simmer gently for 6–8 minutes, until just tender. Remove and drain well using a slotted spoon. Arrange in the prepared dish.

3 Beat the eggs with the goat cheese, yogurt and half the Parmesan cheese. Season well with salt and pepper.

4 Pour the cheese and yogurt mixture over the leeks. Mix the bread crumbs and remaining Parmesan cheese together and sprinkle over the sauce. Bake for 35–40 minutes, until the top is crisp and golden brown.

Tofu Stir-Fry with Egg Noodles

Sweet and delicately flavored, this is the perfect supper for lovers of Chinese food.

INGREDIENTS

Serves 4

8 ounces firm smoked tofu (bean curd)

2 tablespoons sherry or vermouth

3 tablespoons dark soy sauce

3 leeks, thinly sliced

1-inch piece fresh ginger root, peeled and finely grated

1–2 fresh red chiles, seeded and sliced in rings

1 small red bell pepper, seeded and sliced thinly

²⁄₃ cup vegetable stock

2 teaspoons honey

2 teaspoons cornstarch

8 ounces medium Chinese egg noodles

salt and freshly ground black pepper

1 Cut the tofu into ³⁄₄-inch cubes. Put it in a bowl with the sherry or vermouth and the soy sauce. Toss to coat each piece and then let marinate for about 30 minutes.

2 Put the leeks, ginger, chiles, pepper and stock in a frying pan. Bring to a boil and cook quickly over high heat for 2–3 minutes, until all the ingredients are just soft.

3 Strain the tofu, reserving the marinade, and set the tofu aside. Mix the honey and cornstarch into the marinade.

4 Put the egg noodles into a large pan of boiling water. Remove from the heat and let stand for about 6 minutes, until cooked (or follow the package instructions).

5 Heat a nonstick frying pan and quickly sauté the tofu until lightly golden brown on all sides.

6 Place the vegetable mixture and the tofu in a saucepan with the marinade and stir well until the liquid is thick and glossy. Spoon onto the egg noodles and serve at once.

VARIATION

Tofu absorbs flavors readily when marinated. If you are not a great fan of tofu, you could substitute any type of firm smoked cheese and omit Step 5.

Beet, Wild Mushroom and Potato Casserole

This inexpensive dish captures the spirit of some traditional Polish autumn menus.

INGREDIENTS

Serves 4

2 tablespoons vegetable oil

1 medium onion, chopped

3 tablespoons all-purpose flour

1¼ cups vegetable stock

1½ pounds cooked beets, peeled
     and chopped

5 tablespoons light cream

2 tablespoons creamed horseradish

1 teaspoon hot mustard

1 tablespoon wine vinegar

1 teaspoon caraway seeds

2 tablespoons butter

1 shallot, chopped

8 ounces assorted wild and cultivated
     mushrooms, trimmed and sliced

3 tablespoons chopped fresh parsley

For the potato border

2 pounds floury potatoes, peeled

⅔ cup milk

1 tablespoon chopped fresh dill (optional)

salt and freshly ground black pepper

1 Preheat the oven to 375°F. Lightly oil a 9-inch round baking dish. Heat the oil in a large saucepan, add the onion and cook until soft, without coloring. Stir in the flour, remove from the heat and gradually add the stock, stirring until well blended.

2 Return to the heat, stir and simmer to thicken, then add the beets, cream, creamed horseradish, mustard, vinegar and caraway seeds.

3 To make the potato border, bring the potatoes to a boil in salted water and cook for 20 minutes. Drain well and mash with the milk. Add the dill, if using, and season with salt and pepper.

4 Spoon the potatoes into the prepared dish and make a well in the center. Spoon the beet mixture into the well and set aside.

5 Melt the butter in a large nonstick frying pan and cook the shallot until soft, without browning. Add the mushrooms and cook over moderate heat until their juices begin to run. Increase the heat and boil off the moisture. When quite dry, season with salt and pepper and stir in most of the chopped parsley.

6 Spread the mushrooms over the beet mixture, cover and bake for about 30 minutes. Serve at once, garnished with the reserved parsley.

COOK'S TIP

If you are planning ahead, this entire dish can be made in advance and heated when needed. Allow 50 minutes baking time from room temperature.

SPECIAL
OCCASIONS

Breaded Eggplant with Hot Vinaigrette

Crisp on the outside, beautifully tender within, these eggplant slices taste wonderful with a spicy dressing flavored with chiles and capers.

INGREDIENTS

Serves 2

1 large eggplant
½ cup all-purpose flour
2 eggs, beaten
2 cups fresh white bread crumbs
vegetable oil, for frying
1 head of radicchio
salt and freshly ground black pepper

For the dressing

2 tablespoons olive oil
1 garlic clove, crushed
1 tablespoon drained capers
1 tablespoon white wine vinegar
1 tablespoon chili oil

1 Remove the ends from the eggplant. Cut it into ½-inch slices. Set aside.

COOK'S TIP

It is a good idea to salt the eggplant slices before frying in order to draw out some of their moisture. This will also reduce the amount of oil they absorb.

2 Season the flour with a generous amount of salt and pepper. Spread out in a shallow dish. Pour the beaten eggs into a second dish. Spread out the bread crumbs in a third.

3 Dip the eggplant slices in the flour, then in the beaten egg and finally in the bread crumbs, patting them on top to make an even coating.

4 Pour vegetable oil into a large frying pan to a depth of about ¼ inch. Heat the oil, then fry the eggplant slices for 3–4 minutes, turning once. Drain well on paper towels.

5 To make the dressing, heat the olive oil in a small pan. Add the garlic and capers and cook over gentle heat for 1 minute. Increase the heat, add the vinegar and cook for 30 seconds. Stir in the chili oil and remove the pan from the heat.

6 Arrange the radicchio leaves on two plates. Top with the hot eggplant slices. Drizzle with the vinaigrette and serve.

Broccoli Timbales

This elegant but easy-to-make dish can be made with almost any puréed vegetable, such as carrot or celeriac. To avoid last-minute fuss, make the timbales a few hours ahead and cook while the first course is being eaten. Or serve them on their own as an appetizer with a little white wine butter sauce.

INGREDIENTS

Serves 4

1 tablespoon butter

12 ounces broccoli florets

3 tablespoons crème fraîche or
   whipping cream

1 egg, plus one egg yolk

1 tablespoon chopped scallion

pinch of freshly grated nutmeg

salt and freshly ground black pepper

white wine butter sauce, to serve
   (optional)

fresh chives, to garnish (optional)

1 Preheat the oven to 375°F. Lightly butter four ¾-cup ramekins. Line the bottoms with waxed paper and butter the paper.

2 Steam the broccoli in the top of a covered steamer over boiling water for 8–10 minutes, until very tender.

3 Put the broccoli in a food processor fitted with the metal blade and process with the cream, egg and egg yolk until smooth.

4 Add the scallion and season with salt, pepper and nutmeg. Pulse to mix.

5 Spoon the purée into the ramekins and place in a roasting pan. Add boiling water to come halfway up the sides. Bake for 25 minutes, until just set. Invert onto warmed plates and peel off the paper. If serving as an appetizer, pour sauce around each timbale and garnish with chives.

Fonduta with Steamed Vegetables

Fonduta is a creamy cheese sauce from Italy. Traditionally, it is garnished with slices of white truffles and eaten with toasted bread rounds.

Serves 4

assorted vegetables, such as fennel, broccoli, carrots, cauliflower and zucchini

8 tablespoons (1 stick) butter

12–16 rounds of Italian bread or French baguette

For the fonduta

11 ounces Fontina cheese

1 tablespoon flour

milk, as required

4 tablespoons butter

½ cup freshly grated Parmesan cheese

pinch of grated nutmeg

2 egg yolks, at room temperature

a few slivers of white truffle (optional)

salt and freshly ground black pepper

1 About 6 hours before you want to serve the fonduta, cut the Fontina into chunks and place in a bowl. Sprinkle with the flour. Pour in enough milk to barely cover the cheese and set aside in a cool place. The cheese should be at room temperature before being cooked.

2 Just before preparing the fonduta, steam the vegetables until tender. Cut into pieces. Place on a serving platter, dot with butter and keep warm.

3 Butter the bread and toast lightly in the oven or under the broiler. Pass the egg yolks through a sieve and set aside.

4 For the fonduta, melt the butter in a bowl set over a pan of simmering water, or in a double boiler. Strain the Fontina and add it with 3–4 tablespoons of its soaking milk. Cook, stirring, until the cheese melts. When it is hot and has formed a homogeneous mass, add the Parmesan and stir until melted. Season with nutmeg, salt and pepper.

5 Remove from the heat and immediately beat in the sieved egg yolks. Spoon into warmed individual serving bowls, garnish with white truffle slivers, if using, and serve with the vegetables and toasted bread.

Red Pepper and Watercress Phyllo Parcels

Peppery watercress combines well with sweet red pepper in these crisp little parcels.

Makes 8

3 red bell peppers

6 ounces watercress

1 cup ricotta cheese

¼ cup blanched almonds, toasted and chopped

8 sheets phyllo pastry

2 tablespoons olive oil

salt and freshly ground black pepper

green salad, to serve

3 Gradually mix in the ricotta and almonds, and season with salt and pepper.

4 Working with 1 sheet of phyllo pastry at a time, cut out 2 x 7-inch rectangles and 2 x 2-inch squares from each sheet. Brush 1 of the large pieces with a little olive oil and place the second large piece at an angle of 90° to form a star shape.

5 Carefully place one of the squares in the center of the star shape. Brush lightly with olive oil and top with the second square.

6 Top with one-eighth of the red pepper mixture. Bring the edges of the pastry together to form a purse shape and twist to seal. Place on a lightly greased baking sheet and cook for 25–30 minutes, until crisp and golden. Serve with green salad.

1 Preheat the oven to 375°F. Place the peppers under a hot broiler until blistered and charred. Place in a paper bag. When cool enough to handle, peel, seed and pat dry on paper towels.

2 Place the peppers and water-cress in a food processor and pulse until coarsely chopped. Spoon into a bowl.

COOK'S TIP

Keep phyllo pastry refrigerated until you need to use it. When working with the pastry, try to handle it as little as possible, and keep the work area cool.

Buckwheat Blinis with Mushroom Caviar

These little Russian pancakes are traditionally served with fish roe caviar and sour cream. The term caviar is also given to fine vegetable mixtures called "ikry." This wild mushroom caviar has a rich and silky texture.

INGREDIENTS

Serves 4

1 cup white bread flour

⅓ cup buckwheat flour

½ teaspoon salt

1¼ cups milk

1 teaspoon active dry yeast

2 eggs, separated

1 cup sour cream or crème fraîche,
   to serve

For the caviar

12 ounces assorted wild mushrooms, such
   as cremini, porcini, oyster and
   portobello mushrooms

1 teaspoon celery salt

2 tablespoons walnut oil

1 tablespoon lemon juice

3 tablespoons chopped fresh parsley

freshly ground black pepper

1 To make the caviar, trim and chop the mushrooms and place them in a glass bowl. Toss with the celery salt and cover with a weighted plate.

2 Let the mushrooms sit for 2 hours, until the juices have run out into the bottom of the bowl. Rinse them thoroughly to remove the salt.

3 Drain the mushrooms and press out as much iiquid as you can with the back of a spoon. Return them to the bowl and toss with the walnut oil, lemon juice and parsley. Season with pepper and chill until ready to serve.

4 For the blinis, sift the two flours together with the salt in a large mixing bowl. Warm the milk to lukewarm. Add the yeast to the milk, stirring until dissolved, then pour into the flour. Add the egg yolks and stir to make a smooth batter. Cover with a damp cloth and let sit in a warm place to rise for about 30 minutes.

5 Beat the egg whites in a clean bowl until stiff, then fold into the risen batter.

6 Heat a cast-iron pan to moderate. Moisten with oil, then drop spoonfuls of the batter onto the surface, turn them over and cook briefly on the other side. Spoon the mushroom caviar on top and serve with the sour cream.

Greek Phyllo Twists

Spinach and feta cheese make up the secret filling hidden inside these pretty phyllo parcels.

Serves 4

1 tablespoon olive oil

1 small onion, finely chopped

10 ounces fresh spinach, stalks removed

4 tablespoons butter, melted

4 sheets phyllo pastry (each about
   18 x 10 inches)

1 egg

pinch of grated nutmeg

¼ cup crumbled feta cheese

1 tablespoon freshly grated Parmesan
   cheese

salt and freshly ground black pepper

1 Preheat the oven to 375°F. Heat the oil in a pan, add the onion and cook gently for 5–6 minutes, until softened.

2 Add the spinach leaves and cook, stirring, until the spinach has wilted and some of the liquid has evaporated. Let cool.

3 Brush four 4-inch-diameter removable-bottomed tartlet pans with a little melted butter. Take two sheets of the phyllo pastry and cut each into eight 4½-inch squares. Keep the remaining sheets covered.

4 Brush four squares at a time with melted butter. Line the first tartlet tin with one square, gently easing it into the bottom and up the sides. Leave the edges overhanging.

5 Lay the remaining three buttered squares on top of the first, turning them so the corners form a star shape. Repeat for the remaining tartlet pans.

6 Beat the egg with the nutmeg and season with salt and pepper. Stir in the cheeses and spinach. Divide the mixture among the pans and smooth the tops. Fold the overhanging pastry back over the filling.

7 Cut one of the remaining sheets of pastry into eight 4-inch rounds. Brush with butter and place two on top of each tartlet. Press around the edges to seal. Brush the remaining sheet of pastry with butter and cut into strips. Twist each strip and lay on top of the tartlets. Let stand for 5 minutes, then bake for 30–35 minutes. Serve hot or cold.

Grilled Vegetable Terrine

Impress your guests with a colorful layered terrine using a mixture of Mediterranean vegetables.

Serves 6

2 large red bell peppers, quartered, cored
   and seeded
2 large yellow bell peppers, quartered,
   cored and seeded
1 large eggplant, sliced lengthwise
2 large zucchini, sliced lengthwise
6 tablespoons olive oil
1 large red onion, thinly sliced
½ cup raisins
1 tablespoon tomato paste
1 tablespoon red wine vinegar
1⅔ cups tomato juice
2 tablespoons agar-agar
fresh basil leaves, to garnish

For the dressing
6 tablespoons olive oil
2 tablespoons red wine vinegar
salt and freshly ground black pepper

1 Place the peppers skin side up under a hot broiler until blackened. Put in a bowl. Cover.

2 Arrange the eggplant and zucchini slices on separate baking sheets. Brush them with oil and cook under the broiler.

3 Heat the remaining olive oil in a frying pan. Add the onion, raisins, tomato paste and red wine vinegar. Cook until soft.

4 Line a 7½-cup terrine with plastic wrap.

5 Pour half the tomato juice into a saucepan. Sprinkle with the agar-agar. Dissolve over low heat.

6 Layer the red peppers in the terrine and cover with some of the tomato juice and agar-agar. Add the eggplant, zucchini, yellow peppers and onion mixture.

7 Pour tomato juice over each layer of vegetables and finish with another layer of red peppers.

8 Add the remaining tomato juice to any left in the pan and pour into the terrine. Give the terrine a sharp tap to disperse the juice. Cover and chill in the refrigerator until set.

9 To make the dressing, whisk together the oil and vinegar. Season with salt and pepper.

10 Turn out the terrine and remove the plastic wrap. Serve in thick slices, drizzled with dressing. Garnish with basil leaves.

Leek Soufflé

Soufflés are a great way to impress guests at a dinner party. This one is simple to make but it looks very sophisticated.

Serves 2–3

4 tablespoons (½ stick) butter

1 tablespoon sunflower oil

2 leeks, thinly sliced

about 1¼ cups milk

¼ cup all-purpose flour

4 eggs, separated

3 ounces Gruyère or Emmenthal
    cheese, grated

salt and freshly ground black pepper

1 Preheat the oven to 350°F. Grease a large soufflé dish with 1 tablespoon of the butter. Heat the sunflower oil and 1 tablespoon butter in a small saucepan or flameproof casserole and cook the leeks over gentle heat for 4–5 minutes, until soft but not brown.

2 Stir in the milk and bring to a boil. Cover and simmer for 4–5 minutes, until the leeks are tender. Strain the liquid through a sieve into a measuring cup.

3 Melt the remaining butter, stir in the flour and cook for 1 minute. Remove from the heat.

4 Add enough milk to the reserved liquid to make 1¼ cups. Gradually stir the milk into the flour mixture to make a smooth sauce. Return to the heat and bring to a boil, stirring. When thickened, remove from the heat. Cool slightly and beat in the egg yolks, cheese and leeks.

5 Beat the egg whites until stiff and, using a large metal spoon, fold into the leek and egg mixture. Pour into the prepared soufflé dish and bake for about 30 minutes, until puffed and golden brown. Serve immediately.

Broccoli and Chestnut Terrine

Served hot or cold, this versatile terrine is equally suitable for a dinner party or for a picnic. A light salad makes an ideal accompaniment.

INGREDIENTS

Serves 4–6

1 pound broccoli, cut into small florets

8 ounces cooked chestnuts, roughly chopped

1 cup fresh whole-wheat bread crumbs

¼ cup plain yogurt

2 tablespoons finely grated Parmesan cheese

2 eggs, beaten

pinch of grated nutmeg

salt and freshly ground black pepper

new potatoes, to serve

For the salad and dressing (optional)

¼ cup olive oil

1 tablespoon lemon juice

½ teaspoon sugar

salt and freshly ground black pepper

1 tablespoon chopped fresh thyme or dill

9 ounces mixed salad greens

1 Preheat the oven to 350°F. Line a 9 x 5 x 3-inch (8-cup) loaf pan with baking parchment.

2 Blanch or steam the broccoli for 3–4 minutes, until just tender. Drain well. Reserve one-fourth of the smallest florets and chop the rest finely.

3 Mix together the chestnuts, bread crumbs, yogurt and Parmesan. Season with salt, pepper and nutmeg.

4 Gradually fold in the chopped broccoli, reserved florets and the beaten eggs.

5 Spoon the broccoli mixture into the prepared pan.

6 Place in a roasting pan and pour in boiling water to come halfway up the sides of the loaf pan. Bake for 20–25 minutes.

7 Meanwhile, to make the salad dressing, if using, mix together the olive oil, lemon juice and sugar. Season with salt and pepper and stir in the thyme or dill. Arrange the salad greens on a plate. Pour the dressing over the salad.

8 Remove the roasting pan from the oven and turn the terrine out onto a plate. Cut into even slices and serve with new potatoes.

Goat Cheese Soufflé

Make sure everyone is seated before the soufflé comes out of the oven, because it will begin to deflate almost immediately. This recipe works equally well with strong blue cheeses, such as Roquefort.

INGREDIENTS

Serves 4–6

3 tablespoons butter

¼ cup all-purpose flour

¾ cup milk

1 bay leaf

freshly grated nutmeg

grated Parmesan cheese, for sprinkling

1½ ounces herb and garlic soft cheese

5 ounces firm goat cheese, diced

6 egg whites, at room temperature

¼ teaspoon cream of tartar

salt and freshly ground black pepper

1 Melt 2 tablespoons butter in a heavy saucepan over medium heat. Add the flour and cook until golden, stirring occasionally.

2 Pour in half the milk, stirring vigorously until smooth. Stir in the remaining milk and add the bay leaf. Season with a pinch of salt and plenty of pepper and nutmeg. Reduce the heat to medium low, cover and simmer gently for about 5 minutes, stirring occasionally.

3 Preheat the oven to 375°F. Generously butter a 6¼-cup soufflé dish and sprinkle with Parmesan cheese.

4 Remove the sauce from the heat and discard the bay leaf. Stir in both cheeses.

5 In a clean, grease-free bowl, using an electric mixer or balloon whisk, beat the egg whites slowly until they become frothy. Add the cream of tartar, increase the speed and continue beating until they form soft peaks, then stiffer peaks that just flop over a little at the top.

6 Stir a spoonful of beaten egg whites into the cheese sauce to lighten it, then pour the cheese sauce over the remaining whites. Using a large metal spoon, gently fold the sauce into the whites until the mixtures are just combined.

7 Pour the soufflé mixture into the prepared dish and bake for 25–30 minutes, until puffed and golden brown. Serve at once.

Celeriac and Blue Cheese Roulade

Celeriac adds a delicate and subtle flavor to this attractive dish.

INGREDIENTS

Serves 6

1 tablespoon butter

8 ounces cooked spinach, drained and chopped

⅔ cup light cream

4 large eggs, separated

2 tablespoons grated Parmesan cheese

pinch of nutmeg

salt and freshly ground black pepper

For the filling

8 ounces celeriac

lemon juice

3 ounces Gorgonzola cheese

4 ounces fromage frais

1 Preheat the oven to 400°F. Line a 13 x 9-inch jelly roll pan with baking parchment.

2 Melt the butter in a saucepan and add the spinach. Cook until all the liquid has evaporated. Remove the pan from the heat. Stir in the cream, egg yolks, Parmesan and nutmeg. Season.

3 Beat the egg whites until stiff, fold them gently into the spinach mixture and then spoon into the prepared pan. Spread the mixture evenly and use an icing spatula to smooth the surface.

4 Bake for 10–15 minutes, until the roulade is firm to the touch. Turn out onto a sheet of waxed paper and peel away the lining paper. Roll up the roulade with the waxed paper inside and let cool slightly.

5 To make the filling, peel the celeriac and grate it into a bowl. Sprinkle with lemon juice to taste. Blend the Gorgonzola cheese and fromage frais together and mix with the celeriac and a little black pepper.

6 Unroll the roulade, spread with the filling and roll up again, this time without the paper. Serve at once or wrap loosely and chill.

Spinach and Wild Mushroom Soufflé

Wild mushrooms combine especially well with eggs and spinach in this sensational soufflé. Almost any combination of mushrooms can be used for this recipe, although the firmer varieties provide the best texture for the dish.

INGREDIENTS

Serves 4

8 ounces fresh spinach, washed, or
    4 ounces frozen chopped spinach
4 tablespoons (½ stick) unsalted butter,
    plus extra for greasing
1 garlic clove, crushed
6 ounces assorted wild mushrooms such
    as porcini, cremini, oyster and
    portobello mushrooms
1 cup milk
3 tablespoons all-purpose flour
6 eggs, separated
pinch of grated nutmeg
¼ cup grated Parmesan cheese
salt and freshly ground black pepper

1 Preheat the oven to 375°F. Steam the spinach over moderate heat for 3–4 minutes. Cool under running water, then drain. Press out as much liquid as you can with the back of a large spoon and chop finely. If using frozen spinach, defrost and prepare following the package instructions. Squeeze dry in the same way.

2 Melt the butter in a saucepan and cook the garlic and mushrooms over low heat until softened. Turn up the heat and evaporate the juices. When dry, add the spinach and transfer to a bowl. Cover and keep warm.

3 Measure 3 tablespoons of the milk into a bowl. Bring the remainder to a boil. Stir the flour and egg yolks into the cold milk in the bowl and blend well. Stir the boiling milk into the egg and flour mixture, return to the pan and simmer to thicken. Add the spinach mixture to the pan. Season with salt, pepper and nutmeg.

4 Butter a 4-cup soufflé dish, paying particular attention to the sides. Sprinkle with a little of the Parmesan. Set aside.

5 Beat the egg whites until stiff. Bring the spinach mixture back to a boil. Stir in a spoonful of beaten egg white, then fold the mixture into the remaining egg white.

6 Turn the mixture into the soufflé dish, spread level, sprinkle with the remaining cheese and bake in the oven for about 25 minutes, until puffed and golden brown. Serve immediately, before the soufflé has a chance to deflate.

COOK'S TIP

The soufflé base can be prepared up to 12 hours in advance and reheated before the beaten egg whites are folded in.

Sweet Potato Roulade

Sweet potato works particularly well as the base for this roulade. Serve in thin slices for a truly impressive dinner party dish.

Serves 6

1 cup low-fat cream cheese

5 tablespoons plain yogurt

6–8 scallions, finely chopped

2 tablespoons chopped Brazil nuts, roasted

1 pound sweet potatoes, peeled and cubed

12 allspice berries, crushed

4 eggs, separated

¼ cup finely grated Edam cheese

1 tablespoon sesame seeds

salt and freshly ground black pepper

green salad, to serve

1 Preheat the oven to 400°F. Grease and line a 13 x 10-inch jelly roll pan with baking parchment, snipping the corners with scissors to fit.

2 In a small bowl, mix together the cheese, yogurt, scallions and Brazil nuts. Set aside.

3 Boil or steam the sweet potatoes until tender. Drain well. Place in a food processor with the allspice and blend until smooth. Spoon into a bowl and stir in the egg yolks and Edam. Season with salt and pepper.

4 Beat the egg whites until stiff but not dry. Fold one-third of the egg whites into the sweet potatoes to lighten the mixture before gently folding in the rest.

5 Pour into the prepared pan, tipping it to get the mixture into the corners. Smooth gently with a spatula and bake for 10–15 minutes.

6 Meanwhile, lay a large sheet of waxed paper on a clean dish towel and sprinkle with the sesame seeds. When the roulade is cooked, turn it out onto the paper, trim the edges and roll it up. Let cool. When cool, carefully unroll, spread with the cheese filling and roll up again. Cut into slices and serve with a green salad.

COOK'S TIP

Choose the orange-fleshed variety of sweet potato for the most striking color.

Asparagus Tart with Ricotta

A delightful tart filled with the delicate flavors of mixed cheeses and fresh asparagus.

Serves 4

6 tablespoons (¾ stick) butter

1½ cups all-purpose flour

pinch of salt

For the filling

8 ounces asparagus

2 eggs, beaten

1 cup ricotta cheese

2 tablespoons strained plain yogurt

6 tablespoons grated Parmesan cheese

salt and freshly ground black pepper

1 Preheat the oven to 400°F. Rub the butter into the flour and salt. Stir in enough cold water to form a smooth dough and knead lightly on a floured surface.

2 Roll out the pastry and line a 9-inch tart pan. Press firmly into the pan and prick all over with a fork. Bake for about 10 minutes, until the pastry is firm but still pale. Remove from the oven and reduce the temperature to 350°F.

3 Trim the asparagus if necessary. Cut 2 inches from the tops and chop the remaining stalks into 1-inch pieces. Bring a pan of water to a boil.

4 Add the asparagus stalks, then the tips, to the boiling water. Simmer for 4–5 minutes. Drain.

5 Beat together the eggs, ricotta, yogurt and Parmesan. Season, stir in the asparagus stalks and pour into the pastry shell. Place the tips on top. Bake for 35–40 minutes, until golden. Serve warm or cold.

Asparagus with Tarragon Hollandaise

This is the perfect appetizer for an early summer dinner party, when the new season's asparagus is just in and at its best. Making hollandaise sauce in a blender or food processor is incredibly easy and virtually foolproof!

Serves 4

1¼ pounds fresh asparagus

For the hollandaise sauce

2 egg yolks

1 tablespoon lemon juice

8 tablespoons (1 stick) butter

2 teaspoons finely chopped fresh tarragon

salt and freshly ground black pepper

1 Prepare the asparagus, lay it in a steamer or in an asparagus steamer and place over a saucepan of rapidly boiling water. Cover and steam for 6–10 minutes, until tender (the cooking time will depend on the thickness of the asparagus stems).

2 To make the hollandaise sauce, place the egg yolks and lemon juice in a blender or food processor. Season with salt and pepper and process briefly. Melt the butter in a small pan until foaming and then, with the blender or food processor running, pour it onto the egg mixture in a slow and steady stream.

3 Stir in the tarragon by hand or process it (for a sauce speckled with green or a pale green sauce, respectively).

4 Arrange the asparagus on small plates, pour some of the hollandaise sauce on top and sprinkle with pepper. Serve the remaining sauce in a pitcher.

Spring Vegetable Boxes with Pernod Sauce

Pernod is the perfect companion for the tender taste of early vegetables in crisp pastry shells. This is a very impressive dish for a dinner party, and it tastes as good as it looks.

INGREDIENTS

Serves 4

8 ounces puff pastry, thawed
   if frozen
1 tablespoon freshly grated
   Parmesan cheese
1 tablespoon chopped fresh parsley
beaten egg to glaze
6 ounces shelled fava beans
4 ounces baby carrots, scraped
4 baby leeks, cleaned
generous ½ cup peas,
   thawed if frozen
2 ounces snow peas, trimmed
salt and freshly ground black pepper
sprigs of fresh dill, to garnish

For the sauce

7-ounce can chopped tomatoes
2 tablespoons butter
2 tablespoons all-purpose flour
pinch of sugar
3 tablespoons chopped fresh dill
1¼ cups water
1 tablespoon Pernod

1 Preheat the oven to 425°F. Lightly grease a baking sheet.

2 Roll out the pastry very thinly. Sprinkle the grated cheese and parsley over the surface of the pastry sheets, fold and roll once more, so that the cheese and parsley are mixed into the pastry. Cut into four 3 x 4-inch rectangles.

3 Lift the rectangles onto the baking sheet. With a sharp knife, score an inner rectangle about ½ inch from the edge of each rectangle, cutting halfway through. (This will be removed once the boxes are cooked.) Score crisscross lines on the inner rectangles, brush with egg and bake for 12–15 minutes, until golden.

4 Meanwhile, make the sauce. Press the tomatoes through a sieve into a pan, add the remaining ingredients and bring to a boil, stirring all the time. Lower the heat and simmer until required. Season with salt and pepper.

5 Cook the fava beans in a pan of lightly salted boiling water for about 8 minutes. Add the carrots, leeks and peas and cook for another 5 minutes. Add the snow peas and cook for 1 minute more. Drain all the vegetables thoroughly.

6 Using a knife, remove the notched inner rectangles from the pastry boxes. Set them aside to use as lids. Spoon the vegetables into the pastry boxes, pour the sauce over them, put the pastry lids on top and serve garnished with dill.

COOK'S TIP

❧

If there is time, chill the pastry boxes for 20 minutes before baking.

Vegetable Kashmiri

This is a delicious vegetable curry, in which a variety of fresh mixed vegetables are cooked in a spicy, aromatic yogurt sauce.

INGREDIENTS

Serves 4

2 teaspoons cumin seeds

8 black peppercorns

2 green cardamom pods, seeds only

2-inch cinnamon stick

½ teaspoon grated nutmeg

3 tablespoons oil

1 fresh green chile, chopped

1-inch piece of fresh
    ginger root, grated

1 teaspoon chili powder

½ teaspoon salt

2 large potatoes, cut into
    1-inch chunks

8 ounces cauliflower, broken into florets

8 ounces okra, thickly sliced

⅔ cup plain yogurt

⅔ cup vegetable stock

toasted sliced almonds and sprigs of
    cilantro, to garnish

1 Grind the cumin seeds, peppercorns, cardamom seeds, cinnamon stick and nutmeg to a fine powder using a blender or a mortar and pestle.

2 Heat the oil in a large saucepan and cook the chile and ginger for 2 minutes, stirring all the time.

3 Add the chili powder, salt and ground spice mixture and cook for 2–3 minutes, stirring all the time to prevent the spices from sticking.

4 Stir in the potatoes, cover and cook for 10 minutes over low heat, stirring occasionally.

5 Add the cauliflower and okra and cook for 5 minutes.

6 Add the yogurt and stock. Bring to a boil, then reduce the heat. Cover and simmer for 20 minutes, or until all the vegetables are tender. Garnish with toasted almonds and cilantro sprigs.

COOK'S TIP

This curry tastes good using most vegetables. Try to choose vegetables that have contrasting colors and textures.

Phyllo Vegetable Pie

This is a memorable main course.

INGREDIENTS

Serves 6-8

8 ounces leeks

11 tablespoons
   (1 stick plus 3 tablespoons) butter

8 ounces carrots, cubed

8 ounces mushrooms, sliced

8 ounces Brussels sprouts, quartered

2 garlic cloves, crushed

4 ounces (½ cup) cream cheese

4 ounces Roquefort or Stilton cheese

⅔ cup heavy cream

2 eggs, beaten

8 ounces cooking apples

8 ounces (1 cup) cashew nuts or
   pine nuts, toasted

12 ounces frozen phyllo pastry, thawed

salt and freshly ground black pepper

1 Preheat the oven to 350°F. Cut the leeks in half through the root and wash them to remove any soil, separating the layers slightly to check that they are clean. Slice into ½-inch pieces, drain and dry on paper towels.

2 Heat 3 tablespoons of the butter in a large pan and cook the leeks and carrots over medium heat for 5 minutes. Add the mushrooms, Brussels sprouts and garlic and cook for another 2 minutes. Turn the vegetables out into a bowl and let them cool.

3 Whisk the cream cheese, blue cheese, cream and eggs in a bowl. Season with salt and pepper. Pour over the vegetables.

4 Peel and core the apples and cut into ½-inch cubes. Add them to the vegetables with the toasted nuts.

5 Melt the remaining butter in a pan. Brush the inside of a 9-inch springform pan with melted butter. Brush two-thirds of the pastry sheets with butter, one at a time, and use them to line the bottom and sides of the pan, overlapping the layers so that there are no gaps.

6 Spoon in the vegetable mixture and fold the excess phyllo pastry over toward the center to cover the filling.

7 Brush the remaining phyllo sheets with butter and cut them into 1-inch strips. Cover the surface of the pie with the strips, arranging them decoratively in a rough mound.

8 Bake for 35–40 minutes, until golden brown and crisp all over. Let stand for 5 minutes to cool, then carefully remove the pan and transfer the pie to a serving plate.

COOK'S TIP

For a firmer crust on the pastry, brush the top of the pie with beaten egg just before baking.

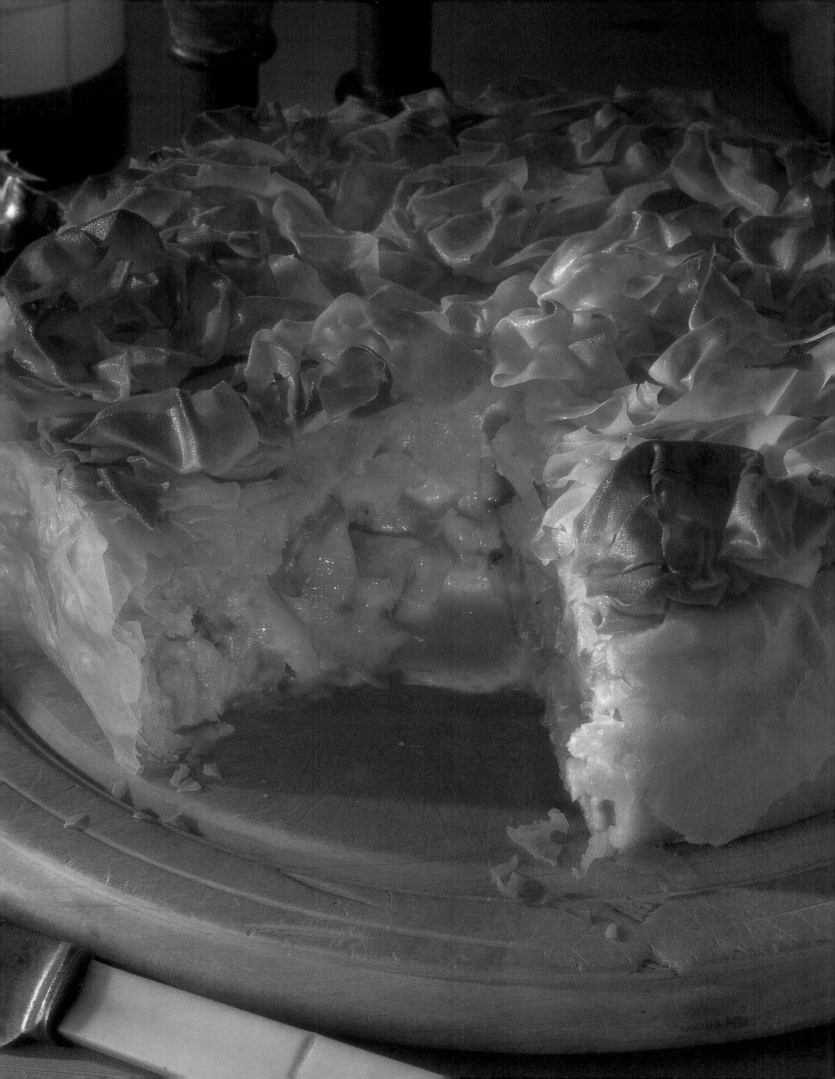

Cauliflower and Mushroom Gougère

This puffy, golden brown, cheese-flavored pastry shell filled with lovely fresh vegetables is a wonderful dinner party dish.

INGREDIENTS

Serves 4–6

8 tablespoons (1 stick) butter

1¼ cups all-purpose flour

4 eggs

4 ounces Gruyère or Cheddar cheese, finely diced

1 teaspoon Dijon mustard

salt and freshly ground black pepper

For the filling

1 small head cauliflower

7-ounce can tomatoes

1 tablespoon sunflower oil

1 tablespoon butter

1 onion, chopped

4 ounces button mushrooms, halved if large

sprig of fresh thyme

1 Preheat the oven to 400°F. Butter a large ovenproof dish. Place 1¼ cups water and the butter together in a large saucepan and heat until the butter has melted. Remove from the heat and add all the flour at once. Beat well with a wooden spoon for about 30 seconds, until smooth. Allow to cool slightly.

2 Beat in the eggs, one at a time, and continue beating until the mixture is thick and glossy. Stir in the cheese and mustard and season with salt and pepper. Spread the mixture around the sides of the ovenproof dish, leaving a hollow in the center for the filling.

3 To make the filling, cut the cauliflower into florets, discarding the woody, hard stalk.

4 Purée the tomatoes in a blender or food processor, then pour into a measuring cup. Add enough water to make 1¼ cups of liquid.

5 Heat the oil and butter in a nonstick frying pan. Sauté the onion for 3–4 minutes. Add the mushrooms and cook for 2–3 minutes. Add the cauliflower and stir-fry for 1 minute. Add the tomato liquid and thyme. Season. Cook over low heat for 5 minutes.

6 Spoon into the hollow in the ovenproof dish. Bake for 40 minutes, until the pastry has risen.

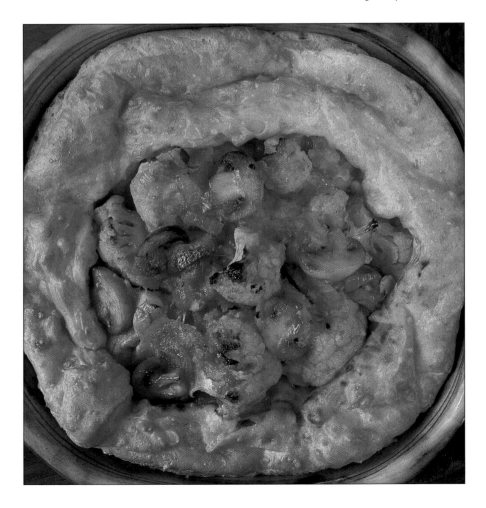

Potato, Spinach and Pine Nut Gratin

Pine nuts add a satisfying crunch to this gratin of wafer-thin potato slices and spinach in a creamy cheese sauce. Serve with a simple lettuce and tomato salad.

INGREDIENTS

Serves 2

1 pound potatoes

1 garlic clove, crushed

3 scallions, thinly sliced

⅔ cup light cream

1 cup milk

8 ounces frozen chopped spinach, thawed

1 cup grated Cheddar cheese

scant ¼ cup pine nuts

salt and freshly ground black pepper

lettuce and tomato salad, to serve

1 Peel the potatoes and cut them carefully into wafer-thin slices. Spread them out in a large, heavy nonstick frying pan.

2 Sprinkle the crushed garlic and sliced scallions evenly over the potatoes.

3 Pour the cream and milk over the potatoes. Place the pan over gentle heat, cover and cook for 8 minutes, or until the potatoes are tender.

4 Using your hands, squeeze the spinach dry. Add the spinach to the potatoes, mixing lightly. Cover the pan and cook for 2 minutes more.

5 Season with salt and pepper, then spoon the mixture into a shallow flameproof casserole. Preheat the broiler.

6 Sprinkle the grated cheese and pine nuts over the spinach mixture. Heat under the broiler for 2–3 minutes, until the topping begins to turn golden. Serve with a lettuce and tomato salad.

Spinach and Ricotta Conchiglie

Large pasta shells are designed to hold a variety of delicious stuffings. Few are more pleasing than this mixture of chopped spinach and ricotta cheese.

INGREDIENTS

Serves 4

12 ounces large conchiglie

scant 2 cups passata or tomato pulp

10 ounces frozen chopped spinach, thawed

2 slices crustless white bread, crumbled

½ cup milk

¼ cup olive oil

2¼ cups ricotta cheese

pinch of grated nutmeg

1 garlic clove, crushed

½ teaspoon black olive paste (optional)

¼ cup freshly grated Parmesan cheese

2 tablespoons pine nuts

salt and freshly ground black pepper

1 Preheat the oven to 350°F. Bring a large saucepan of salted water to a boil. Add the pasta and cook according to the package instructions. Refresh under cold water, drain and reserve until needed.

2 Pour the passata or tomato pulp into a nylon sieve over a bowl and strain to thicken. Place the spinach in another sieve and press out any excess liquid with the back of a spoon.

3 Place the bread, milk and 3 tablespoons of the oil in a food processor and process. Add the spinach and ricotta and season with salt, pepper and nutmeg. Process briefly to combine.

4 Mix together the sieved passata or tomato pulp, garlic, remaining oil and olive paste, if using. Spread the sauce evenly over the bottom of a flameproof dish.

5 Spoon the spinach mixture into a pastry bag fitted with a large plain nozzle and fill the pasta shells (alternatively, fill with a spoon). Arrange the pasta shells over the sauce.

6 Heat the pasta in the oven for 15 minutes. Preheat the broiler to moderate. Sprinkle pasta with Parmesan cheese and pine nuts and finish under the broiler to brown the cheese.

COOK'S TIP

Choose a large saucepan when cooking pasta, and give an occasional stir to prevent the shapes from sticking together. If passata is not available, use a can of chopped tomatoes, sieved and puréed.

Index

Acknowledgments

*The publishers would like to thank the following for their
contributions to this book:*

RECIPE CONTRIBUTORS

Michelle Berridale-Johnson, Angela Boggiano, Carla Capalbo,
Jacqueline Clark, Carole Clements, Matthew Drennan, Sarah
Edmonds, Joanna Farrow, Christine France, Silvana Franco,
Sarah Gates, Shirley Gill, Shehzaid Husain, Christine Ingram,
Peter Jordan, Manisha Kanani, Elizabeth Lambert Ortiz, Ruby
Le Bois, Lesley Mackley, Sue Maggs, Sallie Morris, Annie
Nichols, Anne Sheasby, Stephen Wheeler, Kate Whiteman,
Elizabeth Wolf-Cohen, Jenni Wright.

PHOTOGRAPHERS

Karl Adamson, William Adams-Lingwood, Edward Allwright,
Steve Baxter, James Duncan, Michelle Garrett, Amanda
Heywood, Janine Hosegood, David Jordan, Patrick McLeavey,
Thomas Odulate, Peter Reilly.

STYLISTS

Madeleine Brehaut, Michelle Garrett, Amanda Heywood,
Clare Hunt, Marian Price, Kirsty Rawlings, Judy Williams.

HOME ECONOMISTS

Hilary Guy, Jane Hartshorn, Wendy Lee, Lucy McKelvie,
Jane Stevenson, Stephen Wheeler.

THE COMPLETE BOOK OF
MAIN COURSES

THE COMPLETE BOOK OF
MAIN COURSES

THE WORLD'S MOST POPULAR RECIPES: OVER 180 TIMELESS DISHES WITH
STEP-BY-STEP INSTRUCTIONS AND OVER 800 FABULOUS PHOTOGRAPHS

Jenni Fleetwood

HERMES
HOUSE

This edition is published by Hermes House

Hermes House is an imprint of Anness Publishing Ltd
Hermes House, 88–89 Blackfriars Road, London SE1 8HA
tel. 020 7401 2077; fax 020 7633 9499; info@anness.com

A CIP catalogue record for this book is available from the British Library.

Previously published as part of a larger compendium, *The Ultimate Book of Main Course Dishes*

Publisher: Joanna Lorenz
Editorial Director: Helen Sudell
Editor: Joy Wotton
Production Controller: Pedro Nelson
Designers: Nigel Partridge, Steers McGillan Ltd and Sarah Williams
Recipes: Alex Barker, Carla Capalbo, Lesley Chamberlain, Jacqueline Clark, Roz Denny,
Patrizia Diemling, Matthew Drennan, Joanna Farrow, Valerie Ferguson, Jenni Fleetwood,
Silvano Franco, Yasuko Fukuoka, Shirley Gill, Brian Glover, Nicola Graimes, Juliet Harbutt,
Deh-Ta Hsiung, Christine Ingram, Manisha Kanani, Emi Kasuko, Lucy Knox, Gilly Love,
Lesley Mackley, Norma MacMillan, Jane Milton, Sallie Morris, Keith Richmond, Anne Sheasby,
Marlena Spieler, Linda Tubby, Laura Washburn, Kate Whiteman
Photographers: Nicki Dowey, Michelle Garrett, Amanda Heywood, Janine Hosegood, David Jordan,
Dave King, William Lingwood, Thomas Odulate, Craig Robertson and Sam Stowell

3 5 7 9 10 8 6 4 2

NOTES
All nutritional information is given per portion unless otherwise stated.

Bracketed terms are intended for American readers.

For all recipes, quantities are given in both metric and imperial measures and, where
appropriate, measures are also given in standard cups and spoons. Follow one set, but not a
mixture, because they are not interchangeable.

Standard spoon and cup measures are level.
1 tsp = 5ml, 1 tbsp = 15ml, 1 cup = 250ml/8fl oz

Australian standard tablespoons are 20ml. Australian readers should use 3 tsp in place of 1 tbsp
for measuring small quantities of flour, salt etc.

Medium (US large) eggs are used unless otherwise stated.

CONTENTS

INTRODUCTION

Fifty years ago, main dishes were just that – the most important part of any meal and the course around which all others revolved. Most cookbooks of that era focused on the roast, the casserole or the mixed grill, paying scant attention to any other dishes. Then came the food revolution. People started eating out more and, as they dwelt on the delights of appetizers and desserts, main dishes started to take second place. In some restaurants, main courses disappeared entirely. Now it appears as though the pendulum has swung again. Nostalgia, coupled with nutritional advice that stresses the importance of eating small amounts of protein with plenty of vegetables, has put the main course back where it rightfully belongs – as the pivotal part of every meal.

However, the main course still has something of an image problem. Appetizers and desserts are seen as enticing and exciting, but main courses seem to have earned adjectives like "comforting", "robust", "satisfying" and "rib-sticking". When it comes to planning a special occasion meal, most of us have no difficulty in deciding what to serve for the first and final courses – it's what comes between the first and the last that proves to be the most problematic.

That's where this book comes in. With over 185 recipes you need never struggle for inspiration again. In fact, the difficulty will lie in deciding what to choose from this superb collection, whether it be a colourful healthy salad, a stunning soufflé, a pasta dish or the full works in the form of a meat or chicken roast or a hearty casserole.

BREAKING THE RULES

The days of the marathon meal – with an appetizer or soup leading to the fish course, followed by a main dish, a sorbet (sherbet), dessert, crackers and cheese and, finally, coffee – have largely disappeared. And today it is perfectly acceptable simply to serve guests a satisfying stew with lots of deliciously crusty bread for mopping up the juices, a beautiful baked fish with a pile of buttery new potatoes or a home-baked pie with a crisp salad. The rule is that there are virtually no rules, so that when you are entertaining at home, you can dispense with soups and appetizers altogether, if you like, or you can simply offer guests canapés with their drinks as they arrive.

The classic meat-and-two-veg theme has also vanished as more people have either become vegetarians or simply chosen to limit the amount of meat they eat. Today, a main course can be a roulade, a pie, a risotto, a substantial soup – or anything else you choose to serve. A curry with a cooling raita and plump Peshwari naan would go down well, as would a home-made pizza with a stylish marinara topping. It is even perfectly acceptable to serve sausages and mash and, if you prop the sausages on a mound of spicy mashed sweet potato and surround them with caramelized onions, you'll be recreating a fashionable restaurant dish that will delight your guests.

You don't necessarily have to serve vegetables alongside your chosen main dish either. Instead, they can star in the appetizer or appear in a salad, served French-style as a separate course. When serving vegetables, consider a fresh medley of steamed batons of carrots, leeks and celery, for instance, or a mixture of roast vegetables. That way you cut down on last-minute cooking, and avoid the flurry in the kitchen when your guests have just arrived. You'll have time to make them welcome.

Although the rules may have been relaxed somewhat, some of the old suggestions remain intact, simply because they make good sense. Whatever you choose to serve, the

Left: A filling risotto made with fresh seafood is an elegant and delicious alternative to a traditional meat-and-three-vegetable main meal.

meal should always be balanced in terms of flavours, colours and textures. For example, it wouldn't be a good idea to serve a creamy mousse as a main course then follow it with a silky-smooth dessert, or to serve a juicy Thai stew or curry after a soup. If the main course is quite dry, for example a

country meat loaf, it should be accompanied by a succulent side dish, such as creamed leeks or mushrooms. It also makes good sense to try and avoid using the same ingredients in successive courses as repeatedly encountering the same flavours and textures can be boring.

THE FINER DETAILS

The appearance of the food on the plate has become just as important as the actual dish itself, so do give some thought to the colours and shapes of the ingredients used in the dish. Although the ubiquitous sprig of parsley seems to have been consigned to the great herb garden in the sky, more interesting garnishes, such as tiny bunches of redcurrants, braided chives or cucumber ribbons can add colour and shape to any plate. Just make sure

Left: Casseroles and curries are best served as a main course when they are not preceded by soups.

Above: Beautifully presented and elegantly garnished food will create a sophisticated look.

the garnish is appropriate – try lemon wedges with a fish dish, a fresh sprig of herbs on a vegetable stew, or spring onion curls with an Asian curry.

STRESS-FREE COOKING

When planning any meal, make life easy for yourself by preparing or cooking as much as possible ahead of time. Ease a heavy workload by using kitchen appliances such as the microwave oven, food processor and any other time-saving appliances you may have. Make use of your fridge and freezer – many dishes are even better when made ahead of time and reheated.

Most importantly, enjoy yourself – cooking and sharing good food with friends and family is one of life's greatest pleasures, so master these main dishes and you'll have many wonderful meals in store.

PREPARING AND COOKING AHEAD

The marvellous thing about many main dishes is that they can be prepared in advance and cooked when required. Not only does this keep stress levels low but it also ensures that success levels remain high. Slow-cooked dishes, such as casseroles and stews, are also a boon as they need little attention and reward the cook by quietly gaining in flavour as they simmer in the oven. At the other end of the spectrum are dishes such as stir-fries and salads, which need little or no cooking. This time, careful preparation is the key. Salad leaves can be washed and dried, then bagged and put in the refrigerator. Not only will they be ready to toss together at the last minute, but they will also become crisper on standing. Stir-fry vegetables should all be cut to a similar size. Although it is not a good idea to do this too far ahead, because valuable nutrients will be lost, such advance preparation is helpful when you know you will be in a hurry later.

COOKING IN ADVANCE

Dishes such as stews, curries and casseroles often benefit from being made the day before they are to be served. This allows time for the flavours of the different ingredients to meld. If it is more convenient, you can cook dishes like this even further ahead,

Right: The components of a salad can be prepared in advance, ready for last-minute assembly when required.

freeze them and defrost them when you need to. The food must be cold before being placed in the freezer. Let it cool for a little, then place the dish or pot in a sink of very cold or iced water to accelerate the chilling process. Some china is designed to withstand extremes of temperature and can be used in both the oven and the freezer, but it is not recommended that you switch between the two without either allowing the hot food to cool, or the frozen food to thaw completely. It is best to thaw dishes overnight in the refrigerator. If you use a microwave for thawing, always follow the instructions in your handbook, and stir the stew or casserole frequently as it thaws, to make sure the item thaws evenly. When thawing a large block of frozen food in the microwave, it is a good idea to defrost it in short bursts, with a resting time between each, so that the heat that is generated spreads throughout the defrosting food and is not concentrated only in certain areas.

Rather than tie up a favourite straight-sided casserole or gratin dish by transferring it to the freezer for several weeks, tip the contents into a pan or dish, then wash the casserole or

dish and line it with microwave-proof film (wrap). Return the casserole or stew to the dish, and place it in the freezer. Lift out the contents when frozen, then double wrap and label the block and return it to the freezer. When you want to serve the food, just unwrap the block and return it to the original dish for thawing and reheating.

LEFTOVERS

As with freshly cooked food intended for the freezer, leftovers should be cooled quickly if they are to be kept for another meal. Leaving leftovers in their original dishes to cool slowly in a warm kitchen could encourage harmful bacteria to multiply in the food, causing illness. So transfer leftovers to clean, cold dishes and as soon as they have cooled, cover them and place them in the refrigerator. Use the next day and reheat thoroughly.

Leftovers can also be recycled, and the remains of dishes such as chicken, game or meat casseroles, can be used as a filling for a pie. A simple fish pie, topped with mashed potato, can easily be transformed into hot, crisp fish cakes. However, you should not rework ingredients more than once.

Left: Cooking casseroles and stews a day ahead is not only convenient, but also improves the flavour of the dish.

FREEZING TIPS AND TECHNIQUES

• Cool food rapidly, then wrap securely and label – with a description, the date and number of servings. If you are freezing several items at the same time, use the fast-freeze facility on your freezer.

• Hearty soups and stews freeze well, unless they contain chopped potatoes, rice, barley or pasta, which lose texture and become mushy on freezing. If these ingredients are included in the recipe, add them after thawing, then simmer the soup or stew until these ingredients are fully cooked.

• Stews and casseroles freeze well, but leave a little head room in the container to allow the liquid to expand during the freezing process.

• Blot the surface of a stew to remove surplus fat before freezing or chill so that fat solidifies and can be lifted off. Fat can become rancid, especially if a dish is frozen for a long time. Omit bacon unless you are freezing a composite dish for just a few weeks.

• Make sure that any pieces of meat or poultry in a dish that includes a sauce or gravy are fully submerged in the liquid, to reduce the risk of their drying out in the freezer.

• Although fish in sauce can be frozen, the thawed and reheated dish will not taste so good as when it was originally made, so it is better to cook such dishes on the day you serve them.

• Small items, such as meatballs, burgers and fish cakes, freeze well. Open-freeze them on trays, then wrap individually so that you can remove just as many as you need at any time.

Rice advice

Although rice can be cooked ahead of time and frozen or chilled for reheating, it is essential that it is cooled quickly and thoroughly before being stored. It should be reheated until it is very hot and served immediately. Never keep cooked rice warm for long periods. These precautions are necessary to avoid food poisoning.

STORAGE TIMES

• Meat casseroles and stews improve in taste if they are cooked ahead, but they should not be kept in the refrigerator for more than 2 days before being reheated and served.

• Soups can be frozen for a period of up to 3 months. Leave adequate space when wrapping the container to allow for expansion on freezing.

• Casseroles or stews containing bacon, pork or ham should not be frozen for more than 6 weeks. If these ingredients are not present, optimum freezing time is 2 months.

• Minced (ground) beef dishes, such as chilli con carne, freeze well. These can be stored for up to 2 months.

• Curries freeze well for up to 3 months, but the flavour of the spices deteriorates after this.

• Cooked pasta dishes, such as lasagne and cannelloni, can be frozen for up to 3 months.

• Cooked fish dishes in sauce can be frozen for up to 1 month only. Frozen fish cakes should be used within 2 months.

Above: Make the most of your freezer by batch-cooking suitable dishes, such as stews, casseroles and chilli con carne.

REHEATING

It is important always to make sure that a dish has thawed completely before reheating. Food should be piping hot all the way through before being served, especially if it contains meat on the bone. Timing will depend on the specific ingredients and the quantities being used, but as a guide, a chicken casserole that has been thawed to room temperature should be reheated for 45–60 minutes in an oven preheated to 200°C/400°F/Gas 6. Stir the casserole and check its temperature occasionally. Such delicate foods as fish should not be reheated for so long that their flavour and texture is spoiled. If you reheat foods in a pan on top of the stove, stir them frequently to prevent them from sticking to the base of the pan. If you use the microwave to reheat food, then follow the instructions in your handbook for the precise cooking time.

CHOOSING ACCOMPANIMENTS

The decision about what side-dishes to serve with your chosen main dish will depend very much on whatever else is on the menu. You don't have to serve a vast array of vegetable accompaniments, especially if you've started the meal with a salad or a fruit appetizer, such as grapefruit cocktail or a slice of melon. It is, however, traditional (and sound nutritional sense) to offer a carbohydrate of some sort alongside the main dish. Obvious choices would be rice, potatoes, pasta and bread, but you could also choose grains such as couscous, polenta and lentils or even quinoa (pronounced keen-wa), an extremely nutritious and tasty South American grain, that is cooked in a similar way to rice.

RICE

If you choose rice, make sure that it complements the main course. Basmati rice, with its slightly nutty flavour, is perfect for Indian dishes, whereas Thai fragrant rice is the first choice for a green or red curry from that country. Try to experiment with the more unusual rices, too, such as the red rice from the Camargue and California. Brown rice makes a good accompaniment to vegetable casseroles and stews, or it can be cooked, cooled and made into a salad to serve with kebabs and grilled meat.

POTATOES

Mashed or creamed potato tastes great with creamy fish dishes, fried liver and sausages and pork casserole. The modern trend is to flavour the mash with garlic, mustard or herbs. You could try a mixture of mashed potato and celeriac, or mashed potato and swede (rutabaga). Sweet potato mash tastes great, too – for extra interest, stir in a few spoonfuls of a hot Mexican tomato salsa. For smooth results, use a ricer, potato masher or fork.

Roast potatoes and baked layered potatoes are great served with roasts, baked fish or pot roasts, while potato chips (French fries) or fried potatoes are often partnered with steak.

Baked potatoes, split and topped with butter, cream cheese, Stilton or crème fraîche are delicious with grills (broils). When the first new potatoes arrive in the shops, they are a special treat, especially if you toss the boiled or steamed potatoes with butter and chopped fresh parsley or finely grated lemon rind. For flap-free main courses, consider potato dishes that don't require any last-minute attention.

GRAINS AND PULSES

Couscous is an excellent partner for Moroccan tagines and similar dishes that have quite a lot of liquid. It is readily available from supermarkets and the latest pre-cooked forms of couscous are exceptionally quick and easy to prepare. Polenta is an Italian staple and is a very good alternative to mashed potato. Soft polenta can be served with stews and casseroles and when polenta is grilled, it is an excellent alternative to bread. Quinoa, which is available from health food stores, is a nutty-flavoured grain that goes well with vegetable stews, such as ratatouille, and bean pots. Although lentils are usually included as an ingredient in a recipe, Puy lentils are a classic French accompaniment. Serve them hot with braised meat and game.

Left: Mashed potato is a versatile accompaniment, whether served plain or flavoured with herbs or mustard.

Above: Serve piping-hot garlic bread with baked pasta dishes.

PASTA

There are many different forms of pasta, from Italian spaghetti and tagliatelle to the wide range of Asian egg and rice noodles. Choose the type that suits your dish, not just in terms of its origin, but also to reap maximum value from the shape. Slim or flat noodles are not only great with thin, creamy sauces, they also go well with stir-fried vegetables, while penne and rigatoni are sturdy enough for chunky sauces.

BREAD

If you are serving a rich casserole or stew that has plenty of gravy or sauce, a rustic loaf or a supply of freshly baked wholemeal (whole-wheat) rolls will not only suit the mood of the meal, but also give guests an excuse to mop up every last drop of gravy. There are dozens of delicious loaves available, so try some unusual varieties. Soda bread is perfect with an Irish stew, while lavash, a large flat bread that is torn into pieces at the table, is great with Middle Eastern dishes. Italian breads, such as focaccia, are ideal with hearty casseroles such as osso bucco. Garlic bread is delicious with fish brochettes, grilled (broiled) pork chops or lamb steaks cooked on the barbecue. For a change, make your own garlic butter and transform rolls into individual garlic and herb breads.

SALADS

Although substantial salads, such as Insalata di Mare or Salad Niçoise, make perfect main course dishes in their own right, those salads that are less elaborate and substantial are better served as accompaniments to main meals. Use really fresh ingredients as these have a far superior flavour and crisp texture.

Salads don't work particularly well with meat or chicken stews or very creamy dishes, but they are perfect partners for pizzas, cold pies, baked pasta dishes such as lasagne, roulades, fajitas and grilled (broiled) fish and meat dishes. A simple green salad tossed with fresh herbs picked from the garden or window box is ideal and not overly time-consuming to make. Salads based on tomatoes, with added ingredients such as red onion or orange segments, are not only versatile but also simple to prepare.

Salad dressings should be kept simple so as not to compete with the other flavours in the bowl. A mixture of lemon juice, olive oil, fresh herbs, salt and freshly ground black pepper proves ideal for most salads and takes minutes to prepare, and any dressing that you don't use can be stored in the refrigerator until needed.

Below: A crisp salad is easy to prepare and goes well with main courses that don't contain a lot of sauce.

VEGETABLES

The choice of which vegetables to serve as accompaniments depends on what is part of the main dish. A main dish that includes a selection of vegetables, such as escalopes of chicken with baby vegetables, would be good on its own, or with potatoes or a similar starch vegetable. However, you might wish to offer a selection of three or four different vegetables with roast lamb or pork. Try to balance crisp vegetables such as roast potatoes, lightly cooked broccoli and crunchy cabbage with creamy offerings such as puréed celeriac, carrot or parsnip.

Always imagine what the food will look like on the plate and aim to have a mixture of colours and textures. For example, baby carrots, puréed spinach and fried potatoes would add colour as well as texture to a main course, whereas mashed potato, cauliflower and braised celery would look – and taste – rather plain and dreary.

CONDIMENTS AND SAUCES

Many dishes are enhanced if they are served with a complementary relish or sauce. Roasts are traditionally served with rich-flavoured sauces: cranberry sauce with turkey, mint sauce with lamb and horseradish cream with beef. Spicy

Below: Braised leeks make a wonderful accompaniment when teamed with sweet carrots.

food is best with a cooling condiment. Curry, for instance, is complemented by a cucumber raita. When serving chilli dishes, piquant relishes and tomato salsas are perfect, adding colour and texture to the meal. Classic Italian salsa verde is a natural partner for sautéed fish or grilled steak, while a rich onion gravy goes well with sausages, liver, pork chops or toad-in-the-hole. Dark rich gravies are also good with mounds of creamy mashed potato.

Classic vegetable companions

Some vegetables seem to go particularly well with specific meat, poultry or fish dishes.

• The slightly tart flavour of braised red cabbage with apples is excellent with roast pork or baked ham.

• Fennel, with its delicate, almost aniseedy flavour, is the perfect partner for fish or chicken.

• Sweet-tasting corn and smoked haddock go well together, but it is better to use naturally-coloured haddock to avoid overdoing the yellow theme.

• Mashed swede (rutabaga) is the classic accompaniment for haggis, but also tastes great with herbed sausages or spicy minced (ground) beef patties.

• Spinach is classically served with veal dishes and it also goes well with fish dishes.

• Sweet potatoes, especially when candied, are simply superb with baked ham. They are also the classic accompaniment for Thanksgiving turkey.

• Green beans frequently partner tomato-based stews, but they are also very good with grilled meats and fish.

• Roast vegetables, such as aubergines (eggplant), red onion, courgettes (zucchini) and celery, make a colourful bed for baked chicken breast portions or pork chops, and are also excellent with roast meats of all types.

HEARTY SOUPS

Whether you're cooking for the family, or having friends around for a casual supper, nothing beats a bowl of steaming soup on a chilly day. Soup spells comfort as well as flavour, and when the soup is a substantial one, such as Clam Chowder or Chunky Lamb and Chickpea Broth, there's no need for elaborate accompaniments. A little freshly grated Parmesan, if appropriate, some warm bread rolls, the salt cellar and pepper mill – and the meal is served. For a sophisticated occasion, serve Seafood Laksa or Bouillabaisse. The preparation may take a little longer, but the ease of serving will be just the same.

SPINACH AND RICE SOUP

USE VERY YOUNG SPINACH LEAVES TO PREPARE THIS LIGHT AND FRESH-TASTING SOUP.

SERVES FOUR

INGREDIENTS
675g/1½lb fresh spinach
  leaves, washed
45ml/3 tbsp extra virgin olive oil
1 small onion, finely chopped
2 garlic cloves, finely chopped
1 small fresh red chilli, seeded and
  finely chopped
225g/8oz/generous 1 cup risotto rice
1.2 litres/2 pints/5 cups
  vegetable stock
salt and freshly ground black pepper
shavings of pared Parmesan or
  Pecorino cheese, to serve

1 Place the spinach in a large pan with just the water that clings to its leaves after washing. Add a large pinch of salt. Heat gently until the spinach has wilted, then remove from the heat and drain, reserving any liquid.

2 Either chop the spinach finely using a large kitchen knife or place in a food processor and process the leaves to a fairly coarse purée.

VARIATION
You can substitute Swiss chard for the spinach, if you like.

COOK'S TIP
Buy Parmesan or Pecorino cheese in the piece from a reputable supplier, and it will be full of flavour and easy to grate or shave with a vegetable peeler.

3 Heat the oil in a large pan. Add the onion, garlic and chilli and cook gently for 4–5 minutes, until softened. Stir in the rice until well coated, then pour in the stock and reserved spinach liquid. Bring to the boil, lower the heat and simmer for 10 minutes.

4 Add the spinach and season with salt and pepper to taste. Cook the soup for a further 5–7 minutes, until the rice is tender. Taste and adjust the seasoning, if necessary. Ladle into heated bowls, top with the shavings of Parmesan or Pecorino and serve immediately.

Per portion: Energy 340Kcal/1431kJ; Protein 9.2g; Carbohydrate 52.3g, of which sugars 3.4g; Fat 11.9g, of which saturates 1.9g; Cholesterol 0mg; Calcium 320mg; Fibre 4g; Sodium 449mg.

LOBSTER BISQUE

BISQUE IS A LUXURIOUS, VELVETY SOUP, WHICH CAN BE MADE WITH ANY CRUSTACEANS.

<u>SERVES SIX</u>

INGREDIENTS
    500g/1¼lb fresh lobster
    75g/3oz/6 tbsp butter
    1 onion, chopped
    1 carrot, diced
    1 celery stick, diced
    45ml/3 tbsp brandy, plus extra for
        serving (optional)
    250ml/8fl oz/1 cup dry white wine
    1 litre/1¾ pints/4 cups fish stock
    15ml/1 tbsp tomato purée (paste)
    75g/3oz/scant ½ cup long grain rice
    1 fresh bouquet garni
    150ml/¼ pint/⅔ cup double (heavy)
        cream, plus extra to garnish
    salt, ground white pepper and
        cayenne pepper

1 Cut the lobster into pieces. Melt half the butter in a large pan, add the vegetables and cook over a low heat until soft. Put in the lobster and stir until the shell on each piece turns red.

2 Pour over the brandy and set it alight. When the flames die down, add the wine and boil until reduced by half. Pour in the fish stock and simmer for 2–3 minutes. Remove the lobster.

3 Stir in the tomato purée and rice, add the bouquet garni and cook until the rice is tender. Meanwhile, remove the lobster meat from the shell and return the shells to the pan. Dice the lobster meat and set it aside.

COOK'S TIP
It is best to buy a live lobster, chilling it in the freezer until it is comatose and then killing it just before cooking. If you can't face the procedure, use a cooked lobster; take care not to over-cook the flesh. Stir for only 30–60 seconds.

4 When the rice is cooked, discard all the larger pieces of shell. Tip the mixture into a blender or food processor and process to a purée. Press the purée through a fine sieve placed over the clean pan. Stir the mixture, then heat until almost boiling. Season with salt, pepper and cayenne, then lower the heat and stir in the cream. Dice the remaining butter and whisk it into the bisque. Add the diced lobster meat and serve immediately. If you like, pour a small spoonful of brandy into each soup bowl and swirl in a little extra cream.

Per portion: Energy 406Kcal/1684kJ; Protein 20.3g; Carbohydrate 13.7g, of which sugars 3.1g; Fat 25.2g, of which saturates 15g; Cholesterol 153mg; Calcium 84mg; Fibre 0.7g; Sodium 365mg.

CLAM CHOWDER

IF FRESH CLAMS ARE HARD TO FIND, USE FROZEN OR CANNED CLAMS FOR THIS CLASSIC RECIPE FROM NEW ENGLAND. LARGE CLAMS SHOULD BE CUT INTO CHUNKY PIECES. RESERVE A FEW CLAMS IN THEIR SHELLS FOR GARNISH, IF YOU LIKE. TRADITIONALLY, THE SOUP IS SERVED WITH SAVOURY BISCUITS CALLED SALTINE CRACKERS. YOU SHOULD BE ABLE TO FIND THESE IN ANY GOOD DELICATESSEN.

SERVES FOUR

INGREDIENTS
100g/3¾oz salt pork or thinly sliced
   unsmoked bacon, diced
1 large onion, chopped
2 potatoes, peeled and cut into
   1cm/½in cubes
1 bay leaf
1 fresh thyme sprig
300ml/½ pint/1¼ cups milk
400g/14oz cooked clams, cooking
   liquid reserved
150ml/¼ pint/⅔ cup double
   (heavy) cream
salt, ground white pepper and
   cayenne pepper
finely chopped fresh parsley, to garnish

1 Put the salt pork or unsmoked bacon in a pan, and heat gently, stirring frequently, until the fat runs and the meat is starting to brown. Add the chopped onion and cook over a low heat, stirring occasionally, until softened but not browned.

2 Add the cubed potatoes, the bay leaf and thyme sprig, stir well to coat with fat, then pour in the milk and reserved clam liquid and bring to the boil. Lower the heat and simmer for about 10 minutes, until the potatoes are tender but still firm. Lift out the bay leaf and thyme sprig and discard.

3 Remove the shells from most of the clams. Add all the clams to the pan and season to taste with salt, pepper and cayenne. Simmer gently for 5 minutes more, then stir in the cream. Heat until the soup is very hot, but do not allow it to boil. Pour into a warmed tureen, garnish with the chopped fresh parsley and serve immediately.

CHINESE CRAB AND CORN SOUP

FROZEN WHITE CRAB MEAT WORKS AS WELL AS FRESH IN THIS DELICATELY FLAVOURED SOUP.

SERVES FOUR

INGREDIENTS
600ml/1 pint/2½ cups fish or
   chicken stock
2.5cm/1in fresh root ginger, very
   thinly sliced
400g/14oz can creamed corn
150g/5oz cooked white crab meat
15ml/1 tbsp arrowroot or
   cornflour (cornstarch)
15ml/1 tbsp Chinese rice wine or
   dry sherry
15–30ml/1–2 tbsp light soy sauce
1 egg white
salt and ground white pepper
shredded spring onions (scallions),
   to garnish

COOK'S TIP
This soup is sometimes made with whole kernel corn, but creamed corn gives a better texture. If you can't find it in a can, use thawed frozen creamed corn instead; the result will be just as good.

1 Put the stock and ginger in a large, heavy pan and bring to the boil over a medium heat. Stir in the creamed corn and bring back to the boil.

2 Turn off the heat and add the crab meat. Put the arrowroot or cornflour in a cup and stir in the rice wine or sherry to make a smooth paste, then stir this into the soup. Cook over a low heat for about 3 minutes, until the soup has thickened and is slightly glutinous in consistency. Add light soy sauce, salt and white pepper to taste.

3 In a bowl, whisk the egg white to a stiff foam. Gradually fold it into the soup. Ladle the soup into heated bowls, garnish each portion with spring onions and serve immediately.

VARIATION
To make prawn (shrimp) and corn soup, substitute 150g/5oz cooked peeled and deveined prawns for the crab meat. Chop the peeled prawns coarsely and add to the soup at the beginning of step 2.

Top per portion: Energy 439Kcal/1829kJ; Protein 25.6g; Carbohydrate 25.9g, of which sugars 8.8g; Fat 26.6g, of which saturates 15.2g; Cholesterol 136mg; Calcium 204mg; Fibre 1.8g; Sodium 1638mg.
Below per portion: Energy 201Kcal/852kJ; Protein 11.3g; Carbohydrate 33.8g, of which sugars 9.9g; Fat 3.2g, of which saturates 0.5g; Cholesterol 27mg; Calcium 17mg; Fibre 1.4g; Sodium 695mg.

MATELOTE

TRADITIONALLY THIS FISHERMEN'S SOUP IS MADE FROM FRESHWATER FISH, INCLUDING EEL, ALTHOUGH IN NORMANDY, THEY USE SEA FISH AND CONGER EEL. ANY FIRM FISH CAN BE USED, BUT TRY TO INCLUDE AT LEAST SOME EEL, AND USE A ROBUST DRY WHITE OR RED WINE FOR EXTRA FLAVOUR.

SERVES SIX

INGREDIENTS

   1kg/2¼lb mixed fish, including
     450g/1lb conger eel if possible
   50g/2oz/¼ cup butter
   1 onion, thickly sliced
   2 celery sticks, thickly sliced
   2 carrots, thickly sliced
   1 bottle dry white or red wine
   1 fresh bouquet garni containing
     parsley, bay leaf and chervil
   2 cloves
   6 black peppercorns
   beurre manié for thickening
     (see Cook's Tip)
   salt and cayenne pepper
For the garnish
   25g/1oz/2 tbsp butter
   12 baby (pearl) onions, peeled
   12 button (white) mushrooms
   chopped flat leaf parsley

1 Cut all the fish into thick slices, removing any obvious bones. Melt the butter in a large pan, add the fish and sliced vegetables and stir over a medium heat until lightly browned. Pour in the wine and enough cold water to cover. Add the bouquet garni and spices and season. Bring to the boil, lower the heat and simmer gently for 20–30 minutes, until the fish is tender, skimming the surface occasionally.

2 Meanwhile, prepare the garnish. Heat the butter in a deep frying pan and sauté the baby onions until golden and tender. Add the mushrooms and cook until golden. Season and keep hot.

3 Strain the soup through a large sieve placed over a clean pan. Discard the herbs and spices in the sieve, then divide the fish among deep soup plates (you can skin the fish if you wish, but this is not essential) and keep hot.

4 Reheat the soup until it boils. Lower the heat and whisk in the *beurre manié* little by little until the soup thickens. Season to taste with salt and pepper and pour over the fish. Garnish each portion with the sautéed baby onions and mushrooms and sprinkle with chopped parsley. Serve immediately.

COOK'S TIP
To make the *beurre manié* for thickening, mix 15g/½oz/1 tbsp softened butter with 15ml/1 tbsp plain (all-purpose) flour. Add to the boiling soup, a pinch at a time, whisking constantly.

Per portion: Energy 305Kcal/1275kJ; Protein 32.1g; Carbohydrate 5.7g, of which sugars 4.6g; Fat 8.4g, of which saturates 4.6g; Cholesterol 94mg; Calcium 49mg; Fibre 1.6g; Sodium 169mg.

PROVENÇAL FISH SOUP

THE RICE MAKES THIS A SUBSTANTIAL MAIN MEAL SOUP. BASMATI OR THAI RICE HAS THE BEST FLAVOUR, BUT ANY LONG GRAIN RICE COULD BE USED. IF USING A QUICK-COOK RICE, COOK THE VEGETABLES FOR LONGER BEFORE ADDING THE RICE.

SERVES FOUR TO SIX

INGREDIENTS
450g/1lb fresh mussels
about 250ml/8fl oz/1 cup white wine
675–900g/1½–2lb mixed white fish
   fillets such as monkfish, plaice,
   flounder, cod or haddock
6 large scallops
30ml/2 tbsp olive oil
3 leeks, chopped
1 garlic clove, crushed
1 red (bell) pepper, seeded and cut
   into 2.5cm/1in pieces
1 yellow (bell) pepper, seeded and
   cut into 2.5cm/1in pieces
175g/6oz fennel, cut into
   4cm/1½in pieces
400g/14oz can chopped tomatoes
about 1.2 litres/2 pints/5 cups
   well-flavoured fish stock
generous pinch of saffron threads,
   soaked in 15ml/1 tbsp hot water
175g/6oz/scant 1 cup basmati
   rice, soaked
8 large raw prawns (shrimp), peeled
   and deveined
salt and ground black pepper
30–45ml/2–3 tbsp fresh dill,
   to garnish
crusty bread, to serve (optional)

1 Scrub the mussels and pull off the beards, discarding any shellfish that do not close when tapped with a knife. Place them in a heavy pan. Add 90ml/6 tbsp of the wine, cover tightly, bring to the boil over a high heat and cook, shaking the pan occasionally, for about 3 minutes or until all the mussels have opened. Strain, reserving the liquid. Set aside half the mussels in their shells for the garnish; shell the rest and put them in a bowl. Discard any mussels that have not opened.

2 Cut the fish into 2.5cm/1in cubes. Detach the corals from the scallops and slice the white flesh into three or four pieces. Add the scallops to the fish and the corals to the mussels.

3 Heat the olive oil in a pan and cook the leeks and garlic for 3–4 minutes, until softened. Add the peppers and fennel and cook for 2 minutes more.

4 Add the tomatoes, stock, saffron water, reserved mussel liquid and the remaining wine. Season well and cook for 5 minutes. Drain the rice, stir it into the mixture, cover and simmer for 10 minutes, until it is just tender.

5 Carefully stir in the white fish and cook over a low heat for 5 minutes. Add the prawns and cook for a further 2 minutes, then add the scallop corals and mussels and cook for 2–3 minutes more, until all the fish is tender. If the soup seems dry, add a little extra white wine or stock, or a little of both. Spoon into warmed soup dishes, top with the mussels in their shells and sprinkle with the dill. Serve with fresh crusty bread, if you like.

COOK'S TIP

To make your own fish stock, place about 450g/1lb white fish trimmings – bones, heads, but not gills – in a large pan. Add a chopped onion, carrot, bay leaf, fresh parsley sprig, 6 peppercorns and a 5cm/2in piece of pared lemon rind. Pour in 1.2 litres/2 pints/5 cups water, bring to the boil and simmer for 25–30 minutes. Strain through muslin (cheesecloth).

Per portion: Energy 544Kcal/2283kJ; Protein 55.9g; Carbohydrate 49.2g, of which sugars 11.7g; Fat 9.3g, of which saturates 1.4g; Cholesterol 143mg; Calcium 177mg; Fibre 5.6g; Sodium 325mg.

SEAFOOD LAKSA

A LAKSA IS A MALAYSIAN STEW OF FISH, POULTRY, MEAT OR VEGETABLES WITH NOODLES. AUTHENTIC LAKSAS ARE OFTEN VERY HOT, AND COOLED BY THE COCONUT MILK AND THE NOODLES. IF YOU WOULD PREFER A SPICY VERSION, ADD A LITTLE CHILLI POWDER INSTEAD OF SOME OF THE PAPRIKA.

SERVES FOUR TO FIVE

INGREDIENTS
  3 medium-hot fresh red
    chillies, seeded
  4–5 garlic cloves
  5ml/1 tsp mild paprika
  10ml/2 tsp fermented shrimp paste
  25ml/1½ tbsp chopped fresh root
    ginger or galangal
  250g/9oz small red shallots
  25g/1oz fresh coriander (cilantro),
    preferably with roots
  45ml/3 tbsp groundnut (peanut) oil
  5ml/1 tsp fennel seeds, crushed
  2 fennel bulbs, cut into thin wedges
  600ml/1 pint/2½ cups fish stock
  300g/11oz thin vermicelli
    rice noodles
  450ml/¾ pint/scant 2 cups
    coconut milk
  juice of 1–2 limes
  30–45ml/2–3 tbsp Thai fish sauce
  450g/1lb firm white fish fillet, such
    as monkfish, halibut or snapper
  450g/1lb large raw prawns (shrimp)
    (about 20), peeled and deveined
  small bunch of fresh holy basil or
    ordinary basil
  2 spring onions (scallions),
    thinly sliced

1 Put the chillies, garlic, paprika, shrimp paste, ginger or galangal and 2 shallots in a food processor, blender or spice grinder and process to a paste. Remove the roots and stems from the coriander and add them to the paste; chop and reserve the coriander leaves. Add 15ml/1 tbsp of the oil to the paste and process again until fairly smooth.

2 Heat the remaining oil in a large pan. Add the remaining shallots, the fennel seeds and fennel wedges. Cook over a medium heat, stirring occasionally, until lightly browned, then add 45ml/3 tbsp of the spice paste and stir-fry for about 1–2 minutes. Pour in the fish stock and bring to the boil. Reduce the heat and simmer for 8–10 minutes.

3 Meanwhile, cook the vermicelli rice noodles according to the packet instructions. Drain and set aside.

4 Add the coconut milk and the juice of 1 lime to the pan of shallots. Stir in 30ml/2 tbsp of the fish sauce. Bring to a simmer and taste, adding a little more spice paste, lime juice or fish sauce as necessary.

5 Cut the fish into chunks and add to the pan. Cook for 2–3 minutes, then add the prawns and cook until they turn pink. Chop most of the basil and add to the pan with the reserved coriander.

6 Divide the noodles among wide bowls, then ladle in the soup. Sprinkle with spring onions and the remaining whole basil leaves. Serve immediately.

Per portion: Energy 524Kcal/2199kJ; Protein 43.1g; Carbohydrate 65.1g, of which sugars 6.3g; Fat 10.1g, of which saturates 2g; Cholesterol 233mg; Calcium 162mg; Fibre 1.9g; Sodium 356mg.

BOUILLABAISSE

AUTHENTIC BOUILLABAISSE COMES FROM THE SOUTH OF FRANCE AND INCLUDES RASCASSE (SCORPION FISH) AS AN ESSENTIAL INGREDIENT. IT IS, HOWEVER, PERFECTLY POSSIBLE TO MAKE THIS WONDERFUL MAIN-COURSE SOUP WITHOUT IT. USE AS LARGE A VARIETY OF FISH AS YOU CAN.

SERVES FOUR

INGREDIENTS
    45ml/3 tbsp olive oil
    2 onions, chopped
    2 leeks, white parts only, chopped
    4 garlic cloves, chopped
    450g/1lb ripe tomatoes, peeled
      and chopped
    3 litres/5 pints/12 cups boiling fish
      stock or water
    15ml/1 tbsp tomato purée (paste)
    large pinch of saffron threads
    1 fresh bouquet garni, containing
      2 thyme sprigs, 2 bay leaves and
      2 fennel sprigs
    3kg/6½lb mixed fish, cleaned and
      cut into large chunks
    4 potatoes, peeled and
      thickly sliced
    salt, pepper and cayenne pepper
    a bowl of Rouille and a bowl of
      Aioli, to serve
For the garnish
    16 slices of French bread, toasted
      and rubbed with garlic
    30ml/2 tbsp chopped fresh parsley

2 Simmer the soup for 5–8 minutes, removing each type of fish as it becomes cooked. Continue to cook until the potatoes are very tender. Season well with salt, pepper and cayenne.

3 Divide the fish and potatoes among individual soup plates. Strain the soup and ladle it over the fish. Garnish with toasted French bread and parsley. Serve with rouille and aioli.

1 Heat the oil in a large pan. Add the onions, leeks, garlic and tomatoes. Cook until slightly softened. Stir in the stock or water, tomato purée and saffron. Add the bouquet garni and boil until the oil is amalgamated. Lower the heat; add the fish and potatoes.

COOK'S TIP
Suitable fish for Bouillabaisse include rascasse, conger eel, monkfish, red gurnard and John Dory.

Per portion: Energy 814Kcal/3426kJ; Protein 142.3g; Carbohydrate 28.1g, of which sugars 10.8g; Fat 15.1g, of which saturates 2.2g; Cholesterol 345mg; Calcium 121mg; Fibre 4.9g; Sodium 895mg.

MEDITERRANEAN LEEK AND FISH SOUP WITH TOMATOES

THIS CHUNKY SOUP, WHICH IS ALMOST A STEW, MAKES A ROBUST AND WONDERFULLY AROMATIC MEAL IN A BOWL. SERVE IT WITH CRISP-BAKED CROÛTES SPREAD WITH A SPICY GARLIC MAYONNAISE.

SERVES FOUR

INGREDIENTS

30ml/2 tbsp olive oil
2 large thick leeks, white and green
  parts separated, both thinly sliced
5ml/1 tsp crushed coriander seeds
good pinch of dried red chilli flakes
300g/11oz salad potatoes, sliced
200g/7oz can Italian peeled
  chopped plum tomatoes
600ml/1 pint/2½ cups fish stock
150ml/¼ pint/⅔ cup fruity white wine
1 fresh bay leaf
1 star anise
strip of pared orange rind
good pinch of saffron threads
450g/1lb white fish fillets, such as
  monkfish, sea bass, cod or haddock
450g/1lb small squid, cleaned
250g/9oz uncooked peeled
  prawns (shrimp)
30–45ml/2–3 tbsp chopped parsley
salt and ground black pepper
To serve
  1 short French loaf, sliced and toasted
  spicy garlic mayonnaise

1 Gently heat the oil in a pan, then add the green part of the leeks, the coriander and chilli and cook for 5 minutes.

2 Add the potatoes and tomatoes and pour in the stock and wine. Add the bay leaf, star anise, orange rind and saffron.

3 Bring to the boil, reduce the heat and part-cover the pan. Simmer for 20 minutes, or until the potatoes are tender. Taste and adjust the seasoning.

4 Cut the fish into chunks. Cut the squid sacs into rectangles and score a criss-cross pattern into them without cutting right through.

5 Add the fish to the soup and cook gently for 4 minutes. Add the prawns and cook for 1 minute. Add the squid and the shredded white part of the leek and cook, stirring occasionally, for 2 minutes.

6 Stir in the chopped parsley and serve with toasted French bread and spicy garlic mayonnaise.

Per portion: Energy 326Kcal/1379kJ; Protein 49.7g; Carbohydrate 17.5g, of which sugars 4.4g; Fat 4.2g, of which saturates 0.9g; Cholesterol 421mg; Calcium 106mg; Fibre 2.9g; Sodium 333mg.

FISH SOUP WITH ROUILLE

MAKING THIS SOUP IS SIMPLICITY ITSELF, ALTHOUGH THE EXQUISITE FLAVOUR SUGGESTS IT IS THE PRODUCT OF PAINSTAKING PREPARATION AND COOKING.

SERVES SIX

INGREDIENTS
1kg/2¼lb mixed fish
30ml/2 tbsp olive oil
1 onion, chopped
1 carrot, chopped
1 leek, chopped
2 large ripe tomatoes, chopped
1 red (bell) pepper, seeded
    and chopped
2 garlic cloves, peeled
150g/5oz/⅔ cup tomato
    purée (paste)
1 large fresh bouquet garni,
    containing 3 parsley sprigs, 3 celery
    sticks and 3 bay leaves
300ml/½ pint/1¼ cups white wine
salt and ground black pepper
For the rouille
2 garlic cloves, coarsely chopped
5ml/1 tsp coarse salt
1 thick slice of white bread, crust
    removed, soaked in water and
    squeezed dry
1 fresh red chilli, seeded and
    coarsely chopped
45ml/3 tbsp olive oil
salt and cayenne pepper
For the garnish
12 slices of baguette, toasted in
    the oven
50g/2oz/½ cup grated Gruyère cheese

1 Cut the fish into 7.5cm/3in chunks, removing any obvious bones. Heat the oil in a large, heavy pan, then add the fish, onion, carrot, leek, tomatoes and red pepper. Cook over a medium heat, stirring occasionally, until the vegetables begin to colour.

2 Add all the other soup ingredients, then pour in just enough cold water to cover the mixture. Season well and bring to just below boiling point, then lower the heat to a bare simmer, cover and cook for 1 hour.

3 Meanwhile, make the rouille. Put the garlic and coarse salt in a mortar and crush to a paste with a pestle. Add the soaked bread and chilli and pound until smooth, or purée in a food processor. Whisk in the olive oil, a drop at a time, to make a smooth, shiny sauce that resembles mayonnaise. Season with salt and add a pinch of cayenne if you like a fiery taste. Set the rouille aside.

4 Lift out and discard the bouquet garni from the soup. Purée the soup in batches in a food processor, then strain through a fine sieve placed over a clean pan, pushing the solids through with the back of a ladle.

5 Reheat the soup without letting it boil. Check the seasoning and ladle into individual bowls. Top each serving with two slices of toasted baguette, a spoonful of rouille and some grated Gruyère.

COOK'S TIP
Any firm fish can be used for this recipe. If you use whole fish, include the heads, which enhance the flavour of the soup.

Per portion: Energy 513Kcal/2159kJ; Protein 41.3g; Carbohydrate 48.2g, of which sugars 11.7g; Fat 14.8g, of which saturates 3.6g; Cholesterol 85mg; Calcium 192mg; Fibre 4.4g; Sodium 642mg.

PUMPKIN, RICE AND CHICKEN SOUP

THIS IS A WARM, COMFORTING CHICKEN SOUP WHOSE SPICE AND ORANGE RIND GARNISH WILL BRIGHTEN THE DULLEST WINTER DAY. FOR AN EVEN MORE SUBSTANTIAL MEAL, ADD A LITTLE MORE RICE AND MAKE SURE YOU USE ALL THE CHICKEN FROM THE STOCK.

SERVES FOUR

INGREDIENTS

1 wedge of pumpkin, about 450g/1lb
15ml/1 tbsp sunflower oil
25g/1oz/2 tbsp butter
6 green cardamom pods
2 leeks, chopped
115g/4oz/generous ½ cup basmati
   rice, soaked
350ml/12fl oz/1½ cups milk
salt and freshly ground black pepper
generous strips of pared orange rind,
   to garnish

For the chicken stock
2 chicken quarters
1 onion, quartered
2 carrots, chopped
1 celery stalk, chopped
6–8 peppercorns
900ml/1½ pints/3¾ cups water

1 First make the chicken stock. Place the chicken quarters, onion, carrots, celery and peppercorns in a large, heavy pan. Pour in the water and bring to the boil over a low heat. Skim off any scum on the surface if necessary, then lower the heat, cover and simmer gently for 1 hour.

2 Strain the chicken stock into a clean, large bowl, discarding the vegetables. Skin and bone one or both chicken pieces and cut the flesh into strips. (If not using both chicken pieces for the soup, reserve the other piece for another recipe.)

3 Peel the pumpkin and remove all the seeds and pith, so that you have about 350g/12oz flesh. Cut the flesh into 2.5cm/1in cubes.

4 Heat the oil and butter in a pan, add the cardamom pods and cook for about 2–3 minutes, until slightly swollen. Add the leeks and pumpkin. Cook, stirring, for 3–4 minutes over a medium heat, then lower the heat, cover and sweat for 5 minutes more, or until the pumpkin is quite soft, stirring once or twice.

5 Measure out 600ml/1 pint/2½ cups of the stock and add to the pumpkin mixture. Bring to the boil, then lower the heat, cover and simmer gently for 10–15 minutes, until the pumpkin is soft.

6 Pour the remaining stock into a measuring jug (cup) and make up with water to 300ml/½ pint/1¼ cups. Drain the rice and put it into a pan. Pour in the stock, bring to the boil, then simmer for about 10 minutes, until the rice is tender. Add seasoning to taste.

7 Remove and discard the cardamom pods, then process the soup in a blender or food processor until smooth. Pour it back into a clean saucepan and stir in the milk, chicken and rice (with any stock that has not been absorbed). Heat until simmering. Ladle into warm bowls, garnish with the strips of pared orange rind and freshly ground black pepper and serve immediately with wholemeal (whole-wheat) bread.

Per portion: Energy 336Kcal/1406kJ; Protein 25.4g; Carbohydrate 33.9g, of which sugars 7.8g; Fat 11g, of which saturates 5g; Cholesterol 71mg; Calcium 168mg; Fibre 2.9g; Sodium 122mg.

CHICKEN AND LEEK SOUP WITH PRUNES AND BARLEY

THIS RECIPE IS BASED ON THE TRADITIONAL SCOTTISH SOUP, COCK-A-LEEKIE. THE UNUSUAL COMBINATION OF LEEKS AND PRUNES IS SURPRISINGLY DELICIOUS.

SERVES SIX

INGREDIENTS
    1 chicken, weighing about 2kg/4¼lb
    900g/2lb leeks
    1 fresh bay leaf
    a few each fresh parsley stalks and
        thyme sprigs
    1 large carrot, thickly sliced
    2.4 litres/4 pints/10 cups chicken or
        beef stock
    115g/4oz/generous ½ cup
        pearl barley
    400g/14oz ready-to-eat prunes
    salt and ground black pepper
    chopped fresh parsley, to garnish

1 Cut the breast portions off the chicken and set aside. Place the remaining carcass in a large pan. Cut half the leeks into 5cm/2in lengths and add them to the pan. Tie the bay leaf, parsley and thyme into a bouquet garni and add to the pan with the carrot and the stock. Bring to the boil, then reduce the heat and cover. Simmer gently for 1 hour. Skim off any scum when the water first boils and during simmering.

2 Add the chicken breast portions and cook for another 30 minutes, until they are just cooked. Leave until cool enough to handle, then strain the stock into a bowl. Reserve all the chicken meat. Discard all the skin, bones, cooked vegetables and herbs. Skim as much fat as you can from the stock, then return it to the pan.

3 Meanwhile, rinse the pearl barley thoroughly in a sieve under cold running water, then cook it in a large pan of boiling water over a medium heat for about 10 minutes. Drain, rinse well again and drain thoroughly.

4 Add the pearl barley to the stock. Bring to the boil over a medium heat, then lower the heat and cook very gently for 15–20 minutes, until the barley is just cooked and tender. Season the soup with 5ml/1 tsp salt and black pepper to taste.

5 Add the prunes. Slice the remaining leeks and add them to the pan. Bring to the boil, then simmer for 10 minutes, or until the leeks are just cooked.

6 Slice the chicken breast portions and add them to the soup with the remaining chicken meat, sliced or cut into neat pieces. Reheat if necessary, then ladle the soup into deep plates and sprinkle with chopped parsley.

Per portion: Energy 606Kcal/2533kJ; Protein 44.9g; Carbohydrate 40g, of which sugars 23.9g; Fat 30.8g, of which saturates 8.4g; Cholesterol 220mg; Calcium 45mg; Fibre 4.2g; Sodium 405mg.

POT-COOKED UDON IN MISO SOUP

UDON IS A WHITE WHEAT NOODLE, MORE POPULAR IN THE SOUTH AND WEST OF JAPAN THAN THE NORTH. IT IS EATEN WITH VARIOUS HOT AND COLD SAUCES AND SOUPS. HERE, IN THIS DISH KNOWN AS MISO NIKOMI UDON, THE NOODLES ARE COOKED IN A CLAY POT WITH A RICH MISO SOUP.

SERVES FOUR

INGREDIENTS

200g/7oz skinless, boneless chicken
   breast portions
10ml/2 tsp sake
2 abura-age (thin deep fried tofu)
900ml/1½ pints/3¾ cups dashi
   stock, or the same amount
   of water and 7.5ml/1½ tsp
   dashi-no-moto
6 large fresh shiitake mushrooms,
   stalks removed, quartered
4 spring onions (scallions), trimmed
   and chopped into 3mm/⅛in lengths
30ml/2 tbsp mirin
about 90g/3½oz aka miso or
   hatcho miso
300g/11oz dried udon noodles
4 eggs
seven spice powder (optional)

1 Cut the chicken into bitesize pieces and place in a shallow dish. Sprinkle with sake and leave to marinate in a cool place for 15 minutes.

2 Put the abura-age in a sieve and thoroughly rinse with hot water from the kettle to wash off the oil. Drain on kitchen paper and cut each abura-age into four squares.

3 To make the soup, heat the dashi stock in a large pan. When it has come to the boil, add the chicken pieces, shiitake mushrooms and abura-age and cook for 5 minutes over a medium heat. Remove the pan from the heat and add the spring onions.

4 Put the mirin and miso paste into a small bowl. Scoop 30ml/2 tbsp soup from the pan and mix this in well.

5 To cook the udon, boil at least 2 litres/ 3½ pints/9 cups water in a large pan. The water should not come higher than two-thirds the depth of the pan. Cook the udon for 6 minutes and drain.

6 Put the udon in one large flameproof clay pot or casserole (or divide among four small pots). Mix the miso paste into the soup and check the taste. Add more miso if required. Ladle in enough soup to cover the udon, and arrange the soup ingredients on top of the udon.

7 Put the soup on a medium heat and break the eggs on top. When the soup bubbles, wait for 1 minute, then cover and remove from the heat. Leave to stand for 2 minutes. Serve with seven spice powder, if you like.

Per portion: Energy 666Kcal/2781kJ; Protein 49.6g; Carbohydrate 61.9g, of which sugars 1.8g; Fat 24.4g, of which saturates 1.8g; Cholesterol 225mg; Calcium 1536mg; Fibre 0.7g; Sodium 655mg.

HOT AND SOUR SOUP

ONE OF CHINA'S MOST POPULAR SOUPS, THIS IS FAMED FOR ITS CLEVER BALANCE OF FLAVOURS. THE "HOT" COMES FROM PEPPER; THE "SOUR" FROM VINEGAR. SIMILAR SOUPS ARE FOUND THROUGHOUT ASIA, SOME RELYING ON CHILLIES AND LIME JUICE TO PROVIDE THE ESSENTIAL FLAVOUR CONTRAST.

SERVES SIX

INGREDIENTS

4–6 dried shiitake mushrooms
2–3 small pieces of wood ear (dried Chinese mushroom) and a few golden needles (lily buds) (optional)
115g/4oz pork fillet (tenderloin), cut into fine strips
45ml/3 tbsp cornflour (cornstarch)
150ml/¼ pint/⅔ cup water
15–30ml/1–2 tbsp sunflower oil
1 small onion, finely chopped
1.5 litres/2½ pints/6¼ cups beef or chicken stock, or 2 × 300g/11oz cans consommé made up to the full quantity with water
150g/5oz drained fresh firm tofu, diced
60ml/4 tbsp rice vinegar
15ml/1 tbsp light soy sauce
1 egg, beaten
5 ml/1 tsp sesame oil
salt and ground white or black pepper
2–3 spring onions (scallions), shredded, to garnish

1 Place the shiitake mushrooms in a bowl, with the pieces of wood ear and the golden needles, if using. Add sufficient warm water to cover and leave to soak for about 30 minutes. Drain the mushrooms, reserving the soaking water. Cut off and discard the mushroom stems and slice the caps finely. Trim away any tough stem from the wood ears, then chop them finely. Using kitchen string, tie the golden needles into a bundle.

2 Lightly dust the strips of pork fillet with some of the cornflour. Mix the remaining cornflour to a smooth paste with the measured water.

3 Heat the oil in a wok or pan and cook the onion until soft. Increase the heat and cook the pork until it changes colour. Add the stock or consommé, mushrooms, soaking water, and wood ears and golden needles, if using. Bring to the boil, then simmer for 15 minutes.

4 Discard the golden needles, lower the heat and stir in the cornflour paste to thicken. Add the tofu, vinegar, soy sauce, and salt and pepper.

5 Bring the soup to just below boiling point, then drizzle in the beaten egg by letting it drop from a whisk (or to be authentic, the fingertips) so that it forms threads in the soup. Stir in the sesame oil and serve at once, garnished with spring onion shreds.

Per portion: Energy 169Kcal/709kJ; Protein 7.6g; Carbohydrate 19.7g, of which sugars 0.8g; Fat 7.2g, of which saturates 1.2g; Cholesterol 44mg; Calcium 141mg; Fibre 0.2g; Sodium 351mg.

MISO SOUP WITH PORK AND VEGETABLES

THIS IS QUITE A RICH AND FILLING SOUP. ITS JAPANESE NAME, TANUKI JIRU, MEANS RACCOON SOUP FOR HUNTERS, BUT AS RACCOONS ARE NOT EATEN NOWADAYS, PORK IS NOW USED.

SERVES FOUR

INGREDIENTS
  200g/7oz lean boneless pork
  15cm/6in piece gobo or 1 parsnip
  50g/2oz mooli (daikon)
  4 fresh shiitake mushrooms
  ½ konnyaku or ½ × 225–285g/
    8–10¼oz packet tofu
  a little sesame oil, for stir-frying
  600ml/1 pint/2½ cups dashi stock, or
    the same amount of water and
    10ml/2 tsp dashi-no-moto
  70ml/4½ tbsp miso
  2 spring onions (scallions), chopped
  5ml/1 tsp sesame seeds

1 Press the meat down on a chopping board using the palm of your hand and slice horizontally into very thin long strips, then cut the strips crossways into small pieces. Set the pork aside.

2 Peel the gobo using a potato peeler, then cut diagonally into 1cm/½in thick slices. Quickly plunge the slices into a bowl of cold water to stop them discolouring. If you are using parsnip, peel, cut it in half lengthways, then cut it into 1cm/½in thick half-moon-shaped slices.

3 Peel and slice the mooli into 1.5cm/⅔in thick discs. Cut the discs into 1.5cm/⅔in cubes. Remove the shiitake stalks and cut the caps into quarters.

4 Place the konnyaku in a pan of boiling water and cook for 1 minute. Drain and cool. Cut in quarters lengthways, then crossways into 3mm/⅛in thick pieces.

5 Heat a little sesame oil in a heavy cast-iron or enamelled pan until purple smoke rises. Stir-fry the pork, then add the tofu, if using, the konnyaku and all the vegetables except for the spring onions. When the colour of the meat has changed, add the stock.

6 Bring to the boil over a medium heat, and skim off the foam until the soup looks fairly clear. Reduce the heat, cover, and simmer for 15 minutes.

7 Put the miso in a small bowl, and mix with 60ml/4 tbsp hot stock to make a smooth paste. Stir one-third of the miso into the soup. Taste and add a little more miso if required. Add the spring onion and remove from the heat. Serve very hot in individual soup bowls and sprinkle with sesame seeds.

Per portion: Energy 114Kcal/475kJ; Protein 15.8g; Carbohydrate 1g, of which sugars 0.8g; Fat 5.2g, of which saturates 1.1g; Cholesterol 32mg; Calcium 306mg; Fibre 0.4g; Sodium 41mg.

CHUNKY LAMB AND CHICKPEA BROTH

THIS JEWISH DISH OF SAVOURY MEATS AND BEANS IS BAKED IN A VERY LOW OVEN FOR SEVERAL HOURS. A PARCEL OF RICE IS OFTEN ADDED TO THE BROTH PART-WAY THROUGH COOKING, WHICH PRODUCES A LIGHTLY PRESSED RICE WITH A SLIGHTLY CHEWY TEXTURE.

SERVES EIGHT

INGREDIENTS

250g/9oz/1 cup chickpeas,
   soaked overnight
45ml/3 tbsp olive oil
1 onion, chopped
10 garlic cloves, chopped
1 parsnip, sliced
3 carrots, sliced
5–10ml/1–2 tsp ground cumin
2.5ml/½ tsp ground turmeric
15ml/1 tbsp chopped fresh root ginger
2 litres/3½ pints/8 cups beef stock
1 potato, peeled and cut into chunks
½ marrow (large zucchini), sliced or
   cut into chunks
400g/14oz fresh or canned
   tomatoes, diced
45–60ml/3–4 tbsp brown or
   green lentils
2 bay leaves
250g/9oz salted meat such as
   salt (corned) beef (or double the
   quantity of lamb)
250g/9oz piece of lamb
½ large bunch fresh coriander
   (cilantro), chopped
200g/7oz/1 cup long grain rice
1 lemon, cut into wedges and a spicy
   sauce or fresh chillies, finely
   chopped, to serve

1 Preheat the oven to 120°C/250°F/ Gas ½. Drain the chickpeas.

2 Heat the oil in a large flameproof casserole, add the onion, garlic, parsnip, carrots, cumin, turmeric and ginger and cook for 2–3 minutes. Add the chickpeas, stock, potato, marrow, tomatoes, lentils, bay leaves, salted meat, lamb and coriander. Cover and cook in the oven for about 3 hours.

COOK'S TIP

Add 1–2 pinches of bicarbonate of soda (baking soda) to the soaking chickpeas to make them tender, but do not add too much as it can make them mushy.

3 Put the rice on a double thickness of muslin (cheesecloth) and tie together at the corners, leaving enough room for the rice to expand while it is cooking.

4 Two hours before the end of cooking, remove the casserole from the oven. Place the rice parcel in the casserole, anchoring the edge of the muslin parcel under the lid so that the parcel is held above the soup and allowed to steam. Return the casserole to the oven and continue cooking for a further 2 hours.

5 Carefully remove the lid and the rice. Skim any fat off the top of the soup and ladle the soup into warm bowls with a scoop of the rice and one or two pieces of meat. Serve with lemon wedges and a spoonful of hot sauce or chopped fresh chillies.

Per portion: Energy 384Kcal/1619kJ; Protein 22.1g; Carbohydrate 46.8g, of which sugars 5.6g; Fat 13.4g, of which saturates 3.9g; Cholesterol 43mg; Calcium 95mg; Fibre 5.4g; Sodium 88mg.

FRAGRANT BEETROOT AND VEGETABLE SOUP WITH SPICED LAMB KUBBEH

THE JEWISH COMMUNITY FROM COCHIN IN INDIA IS SCATTERED NOW BUT THEY ARE STILL FAMOUS FOR THEIR CUISINE. THIS TANGY SOUP IS SERVED WITH DUMPLINGS MADE OF BRIGHT YELLOW PASTA WRAPPED AROUND A SPICY LAMB FILLING AND A SPOONFUL OF FRAGRANT GREEN HERB PASTE.

SERVES SIX TO EIGHT

INGREDIENTS
15ml/1 tbsp vegetable oil
½ onion, finely chopped
6 garlic cloves
1 carrot, diced
1 courgette (zucchini), diced
½ celery stick, diced (optional)
4–5 cardamom pods
2.5ml/½ tsp curry powder
4 vacuum-packed beetroot (beets)
   (cooked not pickled), finely diced
   and juice reserved
1 litre/1¾ pints/4 cups
   vegetable stock
400g/14oz can chopped tomatoes
45–60ml/3–4 tbsp chopped fresh
   coriander (cilantro) leaves
2 bay leaves
15ml/1 tbsp sugar
salt and ground black pepper
15–30ml/1–2 tbsp white wine
   vinegar, to serve
For the kubbeh
2 large pinches of saffron threads
15ml/1 tbsp hot water
15ml/1 tbsp vegetable oil
1 large onion, chopped
250g/9oz lean minced (ground) lamb
5ml/1 tsp vinegar
½ bunch fresh mint, chopped
115g/4oz/1 cup plain (all-purpose) flour
2–3 pinches of salt
2.5–5ml/½–1 tsp ground turmeric
45–60ml/3–4 tbsp cold water
For the ginger and coriander paste
4 garlic cloves, chopped
15–25ml/1–1½ tbsp chopped
   fresh root ginger
½–4 fresh mild chillies
½ large bunch of fresh
   coriander (cilantro)
30ml/2 tbsp white wine vinegar
extra virgin olive oil

COOK'S TIP
Serve any leftover paste with meatballs
or spread on sandwiches.

1 To make the paste, put the garlic, ginger and chillies in a food processor and process. Add the coriander, vinegar, oil and salt and process to a purée. Set aside.

2 To make the kubbeh filling, place the saffron and hot water in a small bowl and leave to infuse (steep). Meanwhile, heat the oil in a pan and cook the onion until softened. Put the onion and saffron water in a food processor and blend. Add the lamb, season and blend. Add the vinegar and mint, then chill.

3 To make the kubbeh dough, put the flour, salt and ground turmeric in a food processor, then gradually add the water, processing until it forms a sticky dough. Knead on a floured surface for 5 minutes, wrap in a plastic bag and leave to stand for 30 minutes.

4 Divide the dough into 10–15 pieces. Roll each into a ball, then, using a pasta machine, roll into very thin rounds.

5 Lay the rounds on a well-floured surface. Place a spoonful of filling in the middle of each. Dampen the edges of the dough, then bring them together and seal. Set aside on a floured surface.

6 To make the soup, heat the oil in a pan, add the onion and cook for about 10 minutes, or until softened but not browned. Add half the garlic, the carrot, courgette, celery, if using, cardamom pods and curry powder and cook for 2–3 minutes.

7 Add three of the diced beetroot, the stock, tomatoes, coriander, bay leaves and sugar to the pan. Bring to the boil, then reduce the heat and simmer for about 20 minutes.

8 Add the remaining beetroot, beetroot juice and garlic to the soup. Season with salt and pepper to taste and set aside until ready to serve.

9 To serve, reheat the soup and poach the dumplings in a large pan of salted boiling water for about 4 minutes. Using a slotted spoon, remove the dumplings from the water as they are cooked and place on a plate to keep warm.

10 Ladle the soup into bowls, adding a dash of vinegar to each bowl, then add two or three dumplings and a small spoonful of the ginger and coriander paste to each. Serve immediately.

Per portion: Energy 253Kcal/1061kJ; Protein 12.2g; Carbohydrate 26.6g, of which sugars 10.8g; Fat 11.6g, of which saturates 3.4g; Cholesterol 32mg; Calcium 73mg; Fibre 2.8g; Sodium 90mg.

EGG AND
CHEESE DISHES

Although eggs and cheese feature in every one of the recipes that follow, they are not always principal ingredients. In this eclectic collection, Sea Trout Mousse rubs shoulders with Classic Cheese Soufflé and a very up-market omelette that was invented in honour of the novelist Arnold Bennett. Roulades make very good main courses, and this chapter includes a delectable combination of leek roulade with cheese walnut and sweet pepper filling. Many recipes are ideal for vegetarians — if cheese is included, choose a variety made without rennet.

POTATO AND RED PEPPER FRITTATA

A FRITTATA IS LIKE A LARGE OMELETTE. THIS TASTY VERSION IS FILLED WITH POTATOES AND PLENTY OF HERBS. DO USE FRESH MINT IN PREFERENCE TO DRIED IF YOU CAN FIND IT.

2 Whisk together the eggs, mint and seasoning in a bowl, then set aside. Heat the oil in a large frying pan.

3 Add the onion, garlic, peppers and potatoes to the pan and cook, stirring occasionally, for 5 minutes.

4 Pour the egg mixture over the vegetables in the frying pan and stir gently over a low heat.

5 Push the mixture towards the centre of the pan as it cooks to allow the liquid egg to run on to the base. Meanwhile preheat the grill (broiler).

6 When the frittata is lightly set, place the pan under the hot grill for 2–3 minutes until the top is a light golden brown colour.

7 Serve hot or cold, cut into wedges piled high on a serving dish and garnished with sprigs of mint.

SERVES THREE TO FOUR

INGREDIENTS
    450g/1lb small new or
        salad potatoes
    6 eggs
    30ml/2 tbsp chopped
        fresh mint
    30ml/2 tbsp olive oil
    1 onion, chopped
    2 garlic cloves, crushed
    2 red (bell) peppers, seeded and
        coarsely chopped
    salt and ground black pepper
    fresh mint sprigs,
        to garnish

1 Cook the potatoes in their skins in lightly salted, boiling water until just tender. Drain and leave to cool slightly, then cut into thick slices.

Per portion: Energy 374Kcal/1563kJ; Protein 16.7g; Carbohydrate 34.9g, of which sugars 11.3g; Fat 19.4g, of which saturates 4.5g; Cholesterol 381mg; Calcium 87mg; Fibre 3.9g; Sodium 162mg.

FRITTATA WITH LEEK, RED PEPPER AND SPINACH

ALTHOUGH ITALIAN FRITTATA IS GENERALLY SLIGHTLY SOFTER IN TEXTURE, IT IS NOT HUGELY DIFFERENT FROM SPANISH TORTILLA. THIS COMBINATION OF SWEET LEEK, RED PEPPER AND SPINACH IS WONDERFULLY DELICIOUS WITH THE EGG.

SERVES THREE TO FOUR

INGREDIENTS
30ml/2 tbsp olive oil
1 red (bell) pepper, seeded and diced
2.5–5ml/½–1 tsp ground
  toasted cumin
3 leeks (about 450g/1lb),
  thinly sliced
150g/5oz small spinach leaves
45ml/3 tbsp pine nuts, toasted
5 large (US extra large) eggs
15ml/1 tbsp chopped fresh basil
15ml/1 tbsp chopped fresh flat
  leaf parsley
salt and ground black pepper
watercress, to garnish
50g/2oz/⅔ cup grated Parmesan
  cheese, to serve (optional)

1 Heat a frying pan and add the oil. Add the red pepper and cook over a medium heat, stirring occasionally, for 6–8 minutes, until soft and beginning to brown. Add 2.5ml/½ tsp of the cumin and cook for another 1–2 minutes.

2 Stir in the leeks, then part-cover the pan and cook gently for about 5 minutes, until the leeks have softened and collapsed. Season with salt and ground black pepper.

3 Add the spinach and cover. Leave the spinach to wilt in the steam for 3–4 minutes, then stir to mix it into the vegetables, adding the pine nuts.

4 Beat the eggs with salt, pepper, the remaining cumin, basil and parsley. Add to the pan and cook over a gentle heat until the bottom of the omelette sets and turns golden brown. Pull the edges of the omelette away from the sides of the pan as it cooks and tilt the pan so that the uncooked egg runs underneath.

5 Preheat the grill (broiler). Flash the frittata under the hot grill to set the egg on top, but do not let it become too brown. Cut the frittata into wedges and serve warm, garnished with watercress and sprinkled with Parmesan, if using.

VARIATION
A delicious way to serve frittata is to pack it into a slightly hollowed-out crusty loaf and then drizzle it with a little extra virgin olive oil. Wrap tightly in clear film (plastic wrap) and leave to stand for 1–2 hours before cutting into thick slices. It is ideal picnic fare.

Per portion: Energy 268Kcal/1115kJ; Protein 15.5g; Carbohydrate 9.3g, of which sugars 8g; Fat 19g, of which saturates 2g; Cholesterol 0mg; Calcium 132mg; Fibre 5.5g; Sodium 265mg.

LEEK ROULADE WITH CHEESE, WALNUT AND SWEET PEPPER FILLING

THIS ROULADE IS SURPRISINGLY EASY TO PREPARE, AND IT MAKES A GOOD MAIN COURSE WHEN SERVED WITH HOME-MADE TOMATO SAUCE. IT IS ALSO EXCELLENT AS PART OF A BUFFET.

SERVES FOUR TO SIX

INGREDIENTS
    butter or oil, for greasing
    30ml/2 tbsp fine dry
        white breadcrumbs
    75g/3oz/1 cup finely grated
        Parmesan cheese
    50g/2oz/¼ cup butter
    2 leeks, thinly sliced
    40g/1½oz/⅓ cup plain (all-
        purpose) flour
    250ml/8fl oz/1 cup milk
    5ml/1 tsp Dijon mustard
    1.5ml/¼ tsp freshly grated nutmeg
    2 large (US extra large) eggs,
        separated, plus 1 egg white
    2.5ml/½ tsp cream of tartar
    salt and ground black pepper
    rocket (arugula) and balsamic
        dressing, to serve
For the filling
    2 large red (bell) peppers
    350g/12oz/1½ cups ricotta cheese,
    90g/3½oz/scant 1 cup
        chopped walnuts
    4 spring onions (scallions), chopped
    15g/½oz/½ cup fresh basil leaves

1 Grease and line a 30 × 23cm/ 12 × 9in Swiss roll tin (jelly roll pan) with baking parchment, then sprinkle with the breadcrumbs and 30ml/2 tbsp of the grated Parmesan. Preheat the oven to 190°C/375°F/Gas 5.

2 Melt the butter in a pan and cook the leeks for 5 minutes, until softened.

3 Stir in the flour and cook over a low heat, stirring constantly, for 2 minutes, then gradually stir in the milk. Cook for 3–4 minutes, stirring constantly to make a thick sauce.

4 Stir in the mustard and nutmeg and season with salt and plenty of pepper. Reserve 30–45ml/2–3 tbsp of the remaining Parmesan, then stir the rest into the sauce. Cool slightly.

5 Beat the egg yolks into the sauce. In a scrupulously clean bowl, whisk the egg whites and cream of tartar until stiff. Stir 2–3 spoonfuls of the egg white into the leek mixture, then carefully fold in the remaining egg white.

6 Pour the mixture into the tin and gently level it out using a spatula. Bake for 15–18 minutes, until risen and just firm to a light touch in the centre. If the roulade is to be served hot, increase the oven temperature to 200°C/400°F/Gas 6 after removing the roulade.

7 Meanwhile, heat the grill (broiler). Halve and seed the peppers, then grill (broil) them, skin sides uppermost, until black. Place in a bowl, cover and leave for 10 minutes. Peel and cut into strips.

8 Beat the cheese with the walnuts and spring onions. Chop half the basil and beat it into the mixture. Season to taste.

9 Place a large sheet of baking parchment on the work surface and sprinkle with the remaining Parmesan. Turn out the roulade on to it. Strip off the lining paper and allow the roulade to cool slightly. Spread the cheese mixture over it and top with the red pepper strips. Tear the remaining basil leaves and sprinkle them over the top.

10 Using the parchment as a guide, roll up the roulade and roll it on to a serving platter. If serving hot, roll the roulade on to a baking sheet, cover with a tent of foil and bake for 15–20 minutes. Serve with rocket and drizzle with dressing.

Per portion: Energy 602Kcal/2500kJ; Protein 32.9g; Carbohydrate 22.3g, of which sugars 13.7g; Fat 44.1g, of which saturates 18g; Cholesterol 184mg; Calcium 486mg; Fibre 4.3g; Sodium 740mg.

SOFT TACOS WITH SPICED OMELETTE

SERVED HOT, WARM OR COLD, THESE TACOS MAKE EASY FOOD ON THE MOVE FOR YOUNGER MEMBERS OF THE FAMILY, WHEN THEY NEED SOMETHING NOURISHING TO TAKE ON A PICNIC, HIKE OR CYCLE RIDE.

SERVES FOUR

INGREDIENTS
    30ml/2 tbsp sunflower oil
    50g/2oz/1 cup beansprouts
    50g/2oz carrots, cut into
       thin sticks
    25g/1oz Chinese cabbage, chopped
    15ml/1 tbsp light soy sauce
    4 eggs
    1 small spring onion (scallion),
       thinly sliced
    5ml/1 tsp Cajun seasoning
    25g/1oz/2 tbsp butter
    4 soft flour tortillas, warmed in
       the oven or microwave
    salt and ground black pepper

COOK'S TIP
You can buy fresh soft tortillas in large
supermarkets. They freeze well, so keep
a packet or two in the freezer.

1 Heat the oil in a small frying pan and
stir-fry the beansprouts, carrot sticks
and chopped cabbage until they begin
to soften. Add the soy sauce, stir to
combine and set aside.

2 Place the eggs, sliced spring onion,
Cajun seasoning, salt and ground black
pepper in a bowl, and beat together.
Melt the butter in a small pan until it
sizzles. Add the beaten eggs and cook
over a gentle heat, stirring constantly,
until almost firm.

3 Divide the vegetables and scrambled
egg evenly among the tortillas, fold up
into cones or parcels and serve. For
travelling, the tacos can be wrapped in
kitchen paper and foil.

VARIATION
Fill warm pitta breads with this spicy
omelette mixture. Mini pitta breads are
perfect for younger children who may
find the folded tacos difficult to handle.

FRENCH COUNTRY-STYLE EGGS

THIS VARIATION ON AN OMELETTE COOKS THE "FILLING" IN THE OMELETTE MIXTURE ITSELF. YOU CAN INCORPORATE LOTS OF DIFFERENT INGREDIENTS, SUCH AS LEFTOVER VEGETABLES.

SERVES TWO

INGREDIENTS
    45–75ml/3–5 tbsp sunflower oil
    50g/2oz thick bacon rashers (strips)
       or pieces, rinds removed
       and chopped
    2 thick slices of bread,
       cut into small cubes
    1 small onion, chopped
    1–2 celery sticks, thinly sliced
    115g/4oz cooked potato, diced
    5 eggs, beaten
    2 garlic cloves, crushed
    handful of young spinach or sorrel
       leaves, stalks removed,
       torn into pieces
    few fresh parsley sprigs, chopped
    salt and ground black pepper

1 Heat the oil in a large heavy frying
pan, and cook the bacon and bread
cubes until they are crisp and turning
golden. Add the chopped onion, celery
and diced potato, and continue cooking
over a low heat, stirring frequently until
all the vegetables have softened and are
beginning to turn golden brown.

2 Beat the eggs with the garlic and
seasoning, and pour over the vegetables.
When the underside is beginning to set,
add the spinach or sorrel. Cook until they
have wilted and the omelette is only just
soft in the middle. Fold the omelette in
half and slide it out of the pan. Serve
topped with the parsley, if you like.

Top per portion: Energy 280Kcal/1168kJ; Protein 9.5g; Carbohydrate 24.2g, of which sugars 2g; Fat 16.7g, of which saturates 5.5g; Cholesterol 204mg; Calcium 80mg; Fibre 1.5g; Sodium 217mg.
Below per portion: Energy 488Kcal/2034kJ; Protein 23.7g; Carbohydrate 26.2g, of which sugars 3.4g; Fat 32.7g, of which saturates 6.7g; Cholesterol 483mg; Calcium 130mg; Fibre 2.1g; Sodium 649mg.

CLASSIC CHEESE SOUFFLÉ

A LIGHT, DELICATE, MELT-IN-THE-MOUTH CHEESE SOUFFLÉ MAKES ONE OF THE MOST DELIGHTFUL BRUNCHES IMAGINABLE. ALL YOU NEED TO GO WITH IT IS SALAD, A GLASS OF GOOD WINE AND PLENTY OF TIME TO RELAX AND ENJOY A LAZY WEEKEND.

SERVES TWO TO THREE

INGREDIENTS
50g/2oz/¼ cup butter
30–45ml/2–3 tbsp dried breadcrumbs
200ml/7fl oz/scant 1 cup milk
30g/1¼oz/3 tbsp plain (all-purpose) flour
pinch of cayenne pepper
2.5ml/½ tsp mustard powder
50g/2oz/½ cup mature (sharp) grated Cheddar cheese
25g/1oz/⅓ cup freshly grated Parmesan cheese
4 eggs, separated, plus 1 egg white
salt and ground black pepper

2 Heat the milk in a large pan. Add the remaining butter, flour and cayenne, with the mustard powder. Bring to the boil over a low heat, whisking steadily until the mixture thickens to a smooth sauce.

5 Add a few spoonfuls of the beaten egg whites to the sauce to lighten it. Beat well, then tip the rest of the whites into the pan and, with a large metal spoon, gently fold in the egg whites, using a figure-of-eight movement to combine the mixtures.

1 Preheat the oven to 190°C/375°F/Gas 5. Melt 15ml/1 tbsp of the butter and use to grease a 1.2 litre/2 pint/5 cup soufflé dish thoroughly. Coat the inside of the dish with breadcrumbs. Shake out any excess.

3 Simmer the sauce for a minute or two, then turn off the heat and whisk in all the Cheddar and half the Parmesan. Cool a little, then beat in the egg yolks. Check the seasoning; the mixture should be well seasoned. Set aside.

6 Pour the mixture into the prepared soufflé dish, level the top and, to help the soufflé rise evenly, run your finger around the inside rim of the dish.

7 Place the dish on a baking sheet. Sprinkle the remaining Parmesan over the top of the soufflé mixture and bake for about 25 minutes, until risen and golden brown. Serve immediately.

VARIATIONS
• Crumbled blue cheese, such as Stilton, Shropshire Blue or Fourme d'Ambert, will produce a soufflé with a much stronger, sharper flavour.
• This soufflé can also be served as a more substantial main meal by adding a few extra ingredients. Try putting a layer of chopped vegetables, such as ratatouille or sautéed mushrooms, at the base of the dish before adding the cheese mixture. Bake as above.

4 Whisk the egg whites in a large grease-free bowl until they form soft, glossy peaks. Do not overbeat or the whites will become grainy and difficult to fold in.

COOK'S TIP
It is important to serve soufflé the moment it is cooked and taken from the oven. Otherwise, the wonderful puffed top may sink before it reaches the expectantly waiting diners.

Per portion: Energy 654Kcal/2721kJ; Protein 31.9g; Carbohydrate 28.2g, of which sugars 5.5g; Fat 46.1g, of which saturates 25.3g; Cholesterol 476mg; Calcium 558mg; Fibre 0.8g; Sodium 797mg.

SOUFFLÉ OMELETTE WITH MUSHROOMS

A LIGHT-AS-AIR OMELETTE MAKES AN IDEAL MEAL FOR ONE, ESPECIALLY WITH THIS DELICIOUS FILLING. USE A COMBINATION OF DIFFERENT MUSHROOMS IF YOU LIKE.

SERVES ONE

INGREDIENTS
    2 eggs, separated
    15g/½oz/1 tbsp butter
    flat leaf parsley or coriander
        (cilantro) leaves, to garnish
For the mushroom sauce
    15g/½oz/1 tbsp butter
    75g/3oz/generous 1 cup button
        (white) mushrooms, thinly sliced
    15ml/1 tbsp plain (all-purpose) flour
    85–120ml/3–4fl oz/⅓–½ cup milk
    5ml/1 tsp chopped fresh
        parsley (optional)
    salt and ground black pepper

1 To make the mushroom sauce, melt the butter in a pan or frying pan and add the sliced mushrooms. Cook gently for 4–5 minutes, stirring occasionally, until tender and golden.

2 Stir in the flour, then gradually add the milk, stirring constantly. Cook until boiling and thickened. Add the parsley, if using, and season to taste with salt and pepper. Keep warm.

3 Beat the egg yolks with 15ml/1 tbsp water and season with a little salt and pepper. Whisk the egg whites until stiff, then fold into the egg yolks using a metal spoon. Preheat the grill (broiler).

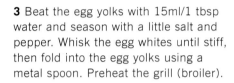

4 Melt the butter in a large frying pan and pour the egg mixture into the pan. Cook over a gentle heat for 2–4 minutes. Place the frying pan under the grill and cook for a further 3–4 minutes until the top is golden brown.

5 Slide the omelette on to a warmed serving plate, pour the mushroom sauce over the top and fold the omelette in half. Serve, garnished with parsley or coriander leaves.

COOK'S TIP
For extra flavour, add a few drops of Worcestershire sauce to the mushrooms as they are cooking.

Per portion: Energy 566Kcal/2348kJ; Protein 18.9g; Carbohydrate 20.1g, of which sugars 4.7g; Fat 46.1g, of which saturates 25g; Cholesterol 471mg; Calcium 199mg; Fibre 1.4g; Sodium 423mg.

OMELETTE ARNOLD BENNETT

CREATED FOR THE AUTHOR ARNOLD BENNETT, WHO FREQUENTLY DINED AT THE SAVOY HOTEL IN LONDON, THIS CREAMY, SMOKED HADDOCK SOUFFLÉ OMELETTE IS NOW SERVED ALL OVER THE WORLD.

SERVES TWO

INGREDIENTS

175g/6oz smoked haddock fillet, poached and drained
50g/2oz/4 tbsp butter, diced
175ml/6fl oz/¾ cup whipping or double (heavy) cream
4 eggs, separated
40g/1½oz/⅓ cup grated mature (sharp) Cheddar cheese
ground black pepper
watercress, to garnish

COOK'S TIP
Try to buy traditional cold-smoked haddock that does not contain artificial colouring for this recipe. Besides being better for you, it gives the omelette a lighter, more attractive colour.

1 Remove the skin and any bones from the haddock fillet and discard. Carefully flake the flesh using a fork.

2 Melt half the butter with 60ml/4 tbsp of the cream in a fairly small non-stick pan, then add the flaked fish and stir together gently. Cover the pan with a lid, remove it from the heat and set aside to cool completely.

3 Mix the egg yolks with 15ml/1 tbsp cream. Add pepper, then stir into the fish. In a separate bowl, mix the cheese and the remaining cream. Stiffly whisk the egg whites, then fold into the fish mixture. Heat the remaining butter in an omelette pan, add the fish mixture and cook until browned underneath. Pour the cheese mixture over and grill (broil) until bubbling. Garnish and serve.

Per portion: Energy 821Kcal/3396kJ; Protein 36.1g; Carbohydrate 2.6g, of which sugars 2.6g; Fat 74g, of which saturates 42.6g; Cholesterol 577mg; Calcium 280mg; Fibre 0g; Sodium 1123mg.

PRAWN, EGG AND AVOCADO MOUSSES

LIGHT AND CREAMY, WITH LOTS OF TEXTURE AND A DELICIOUS COMBINATION OF FLAVOURS, THESE LITTLE MOUSSES ARE BEST SERVED AS A LIGHT LUNCH ON THE DAY YOU MAKE THEM.

SERVES SIX

INGREDIENTS
olive oil, for greasing
11g/¼oz sachet (envelope) gelatine
juice and rind of 1 lemon
60ml/4 tbsp good mayonnaise
60ml/4 tbsp chopped fresh dill
5ml/1 tsp anchovy essence (extract)
5ml/1 tsp Worcestershire sauce
4 eggs, hard-boiled, shelled
 and chopped
175g/6oz/1 cup cooked, peeled
 prawns (shrimp), chopped if large
1 large ripe but just firm avocado,
 peeled, stoned (pitted) and diced
250ml/8fl oz/1 cup double (heavy) or
 whipping cream, lightly whipped
2 egg whites
salt and ground black pepper
fresh dill sprigs, to garnish
hot bread or toast, to serve

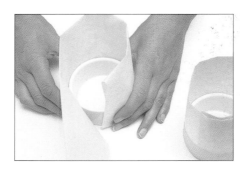

1 Lightly grease six small ramekins, then wrap a piece of greaseproof (waxed) paper tightly around each of the dishes to form a collar. Make sure that the paper comes well above the top of the dish, allowing plenty of room for the mousse to stand above the top of the dish. Secure firmly with tape so that the paper will support the mousse as it sets. If you prefer, prepare one small soufflé dish rather than individual ramekins.

2 Place the gelatine, lemon juice and 15ml/1 tbsp hot water in a small bowl, and place over a pan of hot water. Stir until the mixture becomes clear. Cool slightly, then blend in the lemon rind, mayonnaise, dill and sauces.

3 Mix the chopped hard-boiled eggs, prawns and avocado in a medium bowl. Stir in the gelatine mixture, then fold in the whipped cream. Whisk the egg whites until holding soft peaks and fold into the mixture with seasoning to taste. Spoon into the ramekins and chill for about 4 hours. Garnish with dill and serve with hot bread or toast.

COOK'S TIP
Other fish or shellfish can make a good alternative to prawns. Try substituting the same quantity of smoked trout or cooked crab meat.

Per portion: Energy 431Kcal/1778kJ; Protein 7.5g; Carbohydrate 1.7g, of which sugars 1.2g; Fat 43.9g, of which saturates 17.5g; Cholesterol 131mg; Calcium 50mg; Fibre 0.8g; Sodium 195mg.

SMOKED FISH AND ASPARAGUS MOUSSE

THIS ELEGANT MOUSSE LOOKS VERY SPECIAL WITH ITS STUDDING OF ASPARAGUS AND SMOKED SALMON.
SERVE A MUSTARD AND DILL DRESSING SEPARATELY IF YOU LIKE.

<u>SERVES EIGHT</u>

INGREDIENTS
    15ml/1 tbsp powdered gelatine
    juice of 1 lemon
    105ml/7 tbsp fish stock
    50g/2oz/¼ cup butter, plus extra
      for greasing
    2 shallots, finely chopped
    225g/8oz smoked trout fillets
    105ml/7 tbsp sour cream
    225g/8oz/1 cup low-fat cream cheese
      or cottage cheese
    1 egg white
    12 spinach leaves, blanched
    12 fresh asparagus spears,
      lightly cooked
    115g/4oz smoked salmon, cut into
      long strips
    salt
    shredded beetroot (beet) and leaves,
      to garnish

4 Grease a 1 litre/1¾ pint/4 cup loaf tin (pan) or terrine with butter, then line it with the spinach leaves. Carefully spread half the trout mousse over the spinach-covered base, arrange the asparagus spears on top, then cover with the remaining trout mousse.

5 Arrange the smoked salmon strips lengthways on the mousse and fold over the overhanging spinach leaves. Cover with clear film (plastic wrap) and chill for 4 hours, until set. To serve, remove the clear film, turn out on to a serving dish and garnish.

1 Sprinkle the gelatine over the lemon juice and leave until spongy. In a small pan, heat the fish stock, then add the soaked gelatine and stir to dissolve completely. Set aside. Melt the butter in a small pan, add the shallots and cook gently until softened but not coloured.

2 Break up the smoked trout fillets and put them in a food processor with the shallots, sour cream, stock mixture and cream or cottage cheese. Process until smooth, then spoon into a bowl.

3 In a clean bowl, beat the egg white with a pinch of salt to soft peaks. Fold into the fish. Cover the bowl and chill for 30 minutes, or until starting to set.

Per portion: Energy 174Kcal/723kJ; Protein 15.8g; Carbohydrate 2.8g, of which sugars 2.6g; Fat 11g, of which saturates 6g; Cholesterol 58mg; Calcium 75mg; Fibre 0.8g; Sodium 432mg.

STRIPED FISH TERRINE

SERVE THIS ATTRACTIVE TERRINE COLD OR JUST WARM, WITH A HOLLANDAISE SAUCE IF YOU LIKE. IT IS IDEAL FOR A SUMMER LUNCHEON OR BUFFET.

SERVES EIGHT

INGREDIENTS
  15ml/1 tbsp sunflower oil
  450g/1lb salmon fillet, skinned
  450g/1lb sole fillets, skinned
  3 egg whites
  105ml/7 tbsp double (heavy) cream
  15ml/1 tbsp finely chopped
    fresh chives
  juice of 1 lemon
  115g/4oz/1 cup fresh or frozen
    peas, cooked
  5ml/1 tsp chopped fresh mint leaves
  salt, ground white pepper and
    grated nutmeg
  thinly sliced cucumber, salad cress
    and chives, to garnish

1 Grease a 1 litre/1¾ pint/4 cup loaf tin (pan) or terrine with the oil. Slice the salmon thinly, then cut it and the sole into long strips, 2.5cm/1in wide. Preheat the oven to 200°C/400°F/Gas 6.

2 Line the terrine neatly with alternate slices of salmon and sole, leaving the ends overhanging the edge. You should be left with about a third of the salmon and half the sole.

3 In a grease-free bowl, beat the egg whites with a pinch of salt until they form soft peaks. Purée the remaining sole in a food processor. Spoon into a mixing bowl, season, then fold in two-thirds of the egg whites, followed by two-thirds of the cream. Put half the mixture into a second bowl; stir in the chives. Add nutmeg to the first bowl.

4 Purée the remaining salmon, scrape it into a bowl; add the lemon juice. Fold in the remaining whites, then the cream.

5 Process the peas and mint. Season the mixture and spread it over the base of the terrine, smoothing the surface with a spatula. Spoon over the sole with chives mixture and spread evenly.

6 Add the salmon mixture, then finish with the plain sole mixture. Cover with the overhanging fish fillets and make a lid of oiled foil. Stand the terrine in a roasting pan and pour in enough boiling water to come halfway up the sides.

7 Bake for 15–20 minutes, until the top fillets are just cooked and the mousse feels springy. Remove the foil, lay a wire rack over the top of the terrine and invert both rack and terrine on to a lipped baking sheet to catch the cooking juices that drain out. Keep these to make fish stock or soup.

8 Leaving the tin in place, let the terrine stand for about 15 minutes, then turn the terrine over again. Invert it on to a serving dish and lift off the tin carefully. Serve warm, or chill in the refrigerator first and serve cold. Garnish with thinly sliced cucumber, salad cress and chives before serving.

COOK'S TIPS
• Pop the salmon into the freezer about an hour before slicing it. If it is almost frozen, it will be much easier to slice.
• You can line the tin or terrine with oven-safe clear film (plastic wrap) after greasing and before adding the salmon and sole strips. This makes it a little easier to turn out the terrine but is not strictly necessary.

Per portion: Energy 245Kcal/1019kJ; Protein 23.8g; Carbohydrate 1.9g, of which sugars 0.6g; Fat 15.8g, of which saturates 5.7g; Cholesterol 74mg; Calcium 38mg; Fibre 0.7g; Sodium 107mg.

QUENELLES OF SOLE

Traditionally, these light fish "dumplings" are made with pike, but they are even better made with sole or other white fish. If you are feeling extravagant, serve them with a creamy shellfish sauce studded with crayfish tails or prawns.

SERVES SIX

INGREDIENTS
   450g/1lb sole fillets, skinned and cut
      into large pieces
   4 egg whites
   600ml/1 pint/2½ cups double
      (heavy) cream
   salt, ground white pepper and
      grated nutmeg
For the sauce
   1 small shallot, finely chopped
   60ml/4 tbsp dry vermouth
   120ml/4fl oz/½ cup fish stock
   150ml/¼ pint/⅔ cup double
      (heavy) cream
   50g/2oz/¼ cup butter, diced
   chopped fresh parsley, to garnish

1 Check the sole for stray bones, then put the pieces in a blender or food processor. Add a generous pinch of salt and a grinding of pepper. Switch on and, with the motor running, add the egg whites one at a time through the feeder tube to make a smooth purée. Press the purée through a metal sieve placed over a bowl. Stand the bowl of purée in a larger bowl and surround it with plenty of crushed ice or ice cubes.

2 Whip the cream until very thick and floppy, but not stiff. Gradually fold it into the fish mousse, making sure each spoonful has been absorbed completely before adding the next. Season with salt and pepper, then stir in nutmeg to taste. Cover the bowl of mousse and transfer it, still in its bowl of ice, to the refrigerator. Chill for several hours.

3 To make the sauce, combine the shallot, vermouth and fish stock in a small pan. Bring to the boil and cook until reduced by half. Add the cream and boil again until the sauce has the consistency of single (light) cream. Strain, return to the pan and whisk in the butter, one piece at a time, until the sauce is very creamy. Season and keep hot, but do not let it boil.

4 Bring a wide shallow pan of lightly salted water to the boil, then reduce the heat so that the water surface barely trembles. Using two tablespoons dipped in hot water, shape the fish mousse into ovals. As each quenelle is shaped, slip it into the simmering water.

5 Poach the quenelles, in batches, for 8–10 minutes, until they feel just firm to the touch, but are still slightly creamy inside. As each is cooked, lift it out on a slotted spoon, drain on kitchen paper and keep hot. When all the quenelles are cooked, arrange them on heated plates. Pour the sauce around. Serve garnished with parsley.

COOK'S TIP
Keep the heat low when poaching, as quenelles disintegrate in boiling water.

Per portion: Energy 767Kcal/3165kJ; Protein 17.6g; Carbohydrate 2.5g, of which sugars 2.5g; Fat 75.3g, of which saturates 46.1g; Cholesterol 227mg; Calcium 86mg; Fibre 0g; Sodium 195mg.

SEA TROUT MOUSSE

THIS DELICIOUSLY CREAMY MOUSSE MAKES A LITTLE SEA TROUT GO A LONG WAY. IT IS EQUALLY GOOD MADE WITH FRESH SALMON FILLETS IF SEA TROUT IS UNAVAILABLE.

SERVES SIX

INGREDIENTS
250g/9oz sea trout fillet
120ml/4fl oz/½ cup fish stock
2 gelatine leaves, or 15ml/1 tbsp
   powdered gelatine
juice of ½ lemon
30ml/2 tbsp dry sherry or
   dry vermouth
30ml/2 tbsp freshly grated Parmesan
300ml/½ pint/1¼ cups
   whipping cream
2 egg whites
15ml/1 tbsp sunflower oil
salt and ground white pepper
For the garnish
5cm/2in piece of cucumber, with
   peel, thinly sliced and halved
fresh dill or chervil

1 Put the sea trout in a shallow pan. Pour in the fish stock and heat to simmering point. Poach the fish for 3–4 minutes, until it is lightly cooked. Strain the stock into a jug (pitcher) and leave the trout to cool slightly.

2 Add the gelatine to the hot stock and stir until it has dissolved completely. Set aside until required.

COOK'S TIP
Serve the mousse with Melba toast, if you like. Toast thin slices of bread on both sides under the grill (broiler), then cut off the crusts and carefully slice each piece of toast in half horizontally. Return to the grill pan, untoasted sides up, and grill (broil) again. The thin slices will swiftly brown and curl.

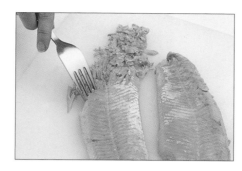

3 When the trout is cool enough to handle, remove the skin and flake the flesh. Pour the stock into a food processor or blender. Process briefly, then gradually add the flaked trout, lemon juice, sherry or vermouth and Parmesan through the feeder tube, continuing to process the mixture until it is smooth. Scrape into a large bowl and leave to cool completely.

4 Lightly whip the cream in a bowl; fold it into the cold trout mixture. Season to taste, then cover with clear film (plastic wrap) and chill until the mousse is just beginning to set. It should have the consistency of mayonnaise.

5 In a grease-free bowl, beat the egg whites with a pinch of salt until softly peaking. Using a large metal spoon, stir one-third into the trout mixture to slacken it, then fold in the rest.

6 Lightly grease six ramekins with the sunflower oil. Divide the mousse among the ramekins and level the surface. Place in the refrigerator for 2–3 hours, until set. Just before serving, arrange a few slices of cucumber and a small herb sprig on each mousse and add a little chopped dill or chervil.

Per portion: Energy 286Kcal/1181kJ; Protein 12g; Carbohydrate 1.5g, of which sugars 1.5g; Fat 25.2g, of which saturates 13.9g; Cholesterol 58mg; Calcium 94mg; Fibre 0g; Sodium 111mg.

SALADS

These are salads in a starring role — main course dishes that can be served solo or used as the main attractions on a buffet table. For a summer lunch, Chicken and Mango Salad would be an excellent choice, or you might like to celebrate a special occasion with a magnificent Insalata di Mare. As the weather cools, introduce a hint of warmth with a Warm Dressed Salad with Poached Eggs or Seared Swordfish with Citrus Dressing. For a picnic or packed lunch, Bean Salad with Tuna and Red Onion would be the ideal choice. Pack the dressing separately and add it about half an hour before serving.

PERUVIAN SALAD

THIS REALLY IS A SPECTACULAR-LOOKING SALAD. IT COULD BE SERVED AS A SIDE DISH OR WOULD MAKE A DELICIOUS LIGHT LUNCH. IN PERU, WHITE RICE WOULD BE USED, BUT BROWN RICE ADDS AN INTERESTING TEXTURE AND FLAVOUR.

SERVES FOUR

INGREDIENTS

225g/8oz/2 cups cooked long grain brown or white rice
15ml/1 tbsp chopped fresh parsley
1 red (bell) pepper
1 small onion, sliced
olive oil, for sprinkling
115g/4oz green beans, halved
50g/2oz/½ cup baby corn
4 quail's eggs, hard-boiled
25–50g/1–2oz Spanish ham, cut into thin slices (optional)
1 small avocado
lemon juice, for sprinkling
75g/3oz mixed salad leaves
15ml/1 tbsp capers
about 10 stuffed olives, halved

For the dressing

1 garlic clove, crushed
60ml/4 tbsp olive oil
45ml/3 tbsp sunflower oil
30ml/2 tbsp lemon juice
45ml/3 tbsp natural (plain) yogurt
2.5ml/½ tsp mustard
2.5ml/½ tsp sugar
salt and freshly ground black pepper

1 Make the dressing by placing all the ingredients in a bowl and whisking with a fork until smooth. Alternatively, shake the ingredients together in a jam jar.

2 Put the cooked rice into a large, glass salad bowl and spoon in about half the dressing. Add the chopped parsley, stir well to mix and set aside in a cool place.

3 Cut the pepper in half, remove the seeds and pith, then place the halves, cut side down, in a small roasting pan. Add the onion rings. Sprinkle the onion with a little olive oil, place the pan under a hot grill (broiler) and cook for 5–6 minutes, until the pepper blackens and blisters and the onion turns golden. You may need to stir the onion once or twice so that it grills (broils) evenly.

4 Stir the onion in with the rice. Put the pepper in a plastic bag and knot the bag. When the steam has loosened the skin on the pepper halves and they are cool enough to handle, peel them and cut the flesh into thin strips.

COOK'S TIP
This dish looks particularly attractive if served in a deep, glass salad bowl. Guests can then see the various layers, starting with the white rice, then the green salad leaves, topped by the bright colours of peppers, corn, eggs and olives.

5 Cook the green beans in boiling water for 2 minutes, then add the corn and cook for 1–2 minutes more, until tender. Drain both vegetables, refresh them under cold water, then drain again. Place in a large mixing bowl and add the red pepper strips, quails' eggs and ham, if using.

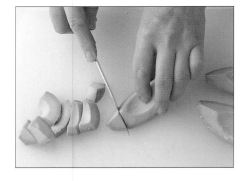

6 Peel the avocado, remove the stone (pit), and cut the flesh into slices or chunks. Sprinkle with the lemon juice to prevent discoloration. Put the salad leaves in a separate mixing bowl, add the avocado and mix lightly. Arrange the salad on top of the rice.

7 Stir about 45ml/3 tbsp of the remaining dressing into the green bean and pepper mixture. Pile this on top of the salad.

8 Sprinkle the capers and stuffed olives on top and serve the salad with the remaining dressing.

Per portion: Energy 404Kcal/1675kJ; Protein 6.3g; Carbohydrate 25.6g, of which sugars 6.9g; Fat 31.3g, of which saturates 5.2g; Cholesterol 58mg; Calcium 75mg; Fibre 3.7g; Sodium 598mg.

CAESAR SALAD

THIS MUCH-ENJOYED SALAD WAS CREATED BY CAESAR CORDONI IN TIJUANA IN 1924. BE SURE TO USE CRISP LETTUCE AND ADD THE SOFT EGGS AND GARLIC CROÚTONS AT THE LAST MINUTE.

3 Add the remaining olive oil to the salad leaves and season with salt and pepper. Toss to coat well.

4 Break the soft-boiled eggs on top. Sprinkle with the lemon juice and toss to combine the ingredients.

5 Add the grated Parmesan cheese and anchovies, if using, then toss again.

6 Sprinkle the croûtons on top of the salad and serve immediately.

COOK'S TIPS

To make a tangier dressing, mix the olive oil with 30ml/2 tbsp white wine vinegar, 2.5ml/½ tsp mustard, 5ml/1 tsp sugar, and salt and pepper.

SERVES SIX

INGREDIENTS
175ml/6fl oz/¾ cup salad oil,
  preferably olive oil
115g/4oz/2 cups French or
  Italian bread, cut in 2.5cm/
  1in cubes
1 large garlic clove, crushed with
  the flat side of a knife
1 cos or romaine lettuce
2 eggs, boiled for 1 minute
120ml/4fl oz/½ cup
  lemon juice
50g/2oz/⅔ cup freshly grated
  Parmesan cheese
6 anchovy fillets, drained and
  finely chopped (optional)
salt and ground black pepper

1 Heat 50ml/2fl oz/¼ cup of the oil in a frying pan. Add the bread and garlic and cook, stirring constantly, until the cubes are golden brown. Drain on kitchen paper and discard the garlic.

2 Tear large lettuce leaves into smaller pieces. Put all the lettuce in a bowl.

Per portion: Energy 307Kcal/1272kJ; Protein 8g; Carbohydrate 11.7g, of which sugars 1.4g; Fat 25.7g, of which saturates 5.4g; Cholesterol 84mg; Calcium 149mg; Fibre 0.7g; Sodium 230mg.

WARM DRESSED SALAD <u>WITH</u> POACHED EGGS

SOFT POACHED EGGS, CHILLI, HOT CROÛTONS AND COOL, CRISP SALAD LEAVES MAKE A LIVELY AND UNUSUAL COMBINATION. THIS DELICIOUS SALAD IS PERFECT FOR A SUMMER LUNCH.

SERVES TWO

INGREDIENTS
½ small loaf Granary (whole-wheat) bread
45ml/3 tbsp chilli oil
2 eggs
115g/4oz mixed salad leaves
45ml/3 tbsp extra virgin olive oil
2 garlic cloves, crushed
15ml/1 tbsp balsamic vinegar
50g/2oz Parmesan cheese, shaved
ground black pepper (optional)

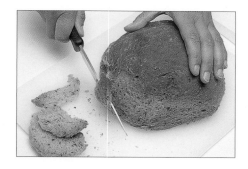

1 Carefully cut the crust from the Granary loaf and discard. Cut the bread into 2.5cm/1in cubes.

2 Heat the chilli oil in a large frying pan. Add the bread cubes and cook for about 5 minutes, tossing the cubes occasionally, until they are crisp and golden brown all over.

COOK'S TIP
If you are very sensitive to spicy flavours, cook the croûtons in olive oil or a nut oil, such as walnut or hazelnut, rather than using chilli oil.

3 Meanwhile, bring a pan of water to the boil. Break each egg into a jug (pitcher) and carefully slide into the water, one at a time. Gently poach the eggs for about 4 minutes until cooked.

4 Divide the salad leaves between two plates. Remove the croûtons from the pan and arrange them over the leaves.

5 Wipe the pan clean with kitchen paper. Then heat the olive oil in the pan, add the garlic and vinegar and cook over high heat for 1 minute. Pour the warm dressing over the salads.

6 Place a poached egg on each salad. Top with thin Parmesan shavings and a little ground black pepper, if you like.

Per portion: Energy 730Kcal/3042kJ; Protein 26.2g; Carbohydrate 48.4g, of which sugars 3.9g; Fat 49.3g, of which saturates 12.1g; Cholesterol 215mg; Calcium 556mg; Fibre 3.8g; Sodium 890mg.

THAI PRAWN SALAD WITH GARLIC DRESSING AND FRIZZLED SHALLOTS

IN THIS INTENSELY FLAVOURED SALAD, PRAWNS AND MANGO ARE PARTNERED WITH A SWEET-SOUR GARLIC DRESSING HEIGHTENED WITH THE HOT TASTE OF CHILLI. THE CRISP FRIZZLED SHALLOTS ARE A TRADITIONAL ADDITION TO THAI SALADS.

SERVES FOUR TO SIX

INGREDIENTS
- 675g/1½lb raw prawns (shrimp), peeled and deveined with tails on
- finely shredded rind of 1 lime
- ½ fresh red chilli, seeded and finely chopped
- 30ml/2 tbsp olive oil, plus extra for brushing
- 1 ripe but firm mango
- 2 carrots, cut into long thin shreds
- 10cm/4in piece cucumber, sliced
- 1 small red onion, halved and thinly sliced
- a few fresh coriander (cilantro) sprigs
- a few fresh mint sprigs
- 45ml/3 tbsp roasted peanuts, coarsely chopped
- 4 large shallots, thinly sliced and fried until crisp in 30ml/2 tbsp groundnut (peanut) oil
- salt and ground black pepper

For the dressing
- 1 large garlic clove, chopped
- 10–15ml/2–3 tsp caster (superfine) sugar
- juice of 2 limes
- 15–30ml/1–2 tbsp Thai fish sauce
- 1 fresh red chilli, seeded
- 5–10ml/1–2 tsp light rice vinegar

1 Place the prawns in a glass or china dish and add the lime rind and chilli. Season with salt and pepper and spoon the oil over them. Toss to mix and leave to marinate for 30–40 minutes.

2 For the dressing, place the garlic in a mortar with 10ml/2 tsp caster sugar and pound until smooth, then work in the juice of 1½ limes and 15ml/1 tbsp of the Thai fish sauce.

3 Transfer the dressing to a jug (pitcher). Finely chop half the chilli. and add it to the dressing. Taste and add more sugar, lime juice, fish sauce and the rice vinegar to taste.

COOK'S TIP
To devein prawns, make a shallow cut down the back of the prawn using a small, sharp knife. Using the tip of the knife, lift out the thin, black vein, then rinse the prawn thoroughly under cold, running water.

4 Peel and stone (pit) the mango, then cut it into very fine strips.

5 Toss together the mango, carrots, cucumber and onion, and half the dressing. Arrange the salad on individual plates or in bowls.

6 Heat a ridged, cast-iron griddle pan or heavy frying pan until very hot. Brush with a little olive oil, then sear the prawns for 2–3 minutes on each side, until they turn pink and are patched with brown on the outside. Arrange the prawns on the salads.

7 Sprinkle the remaining dressing over the salads and top with the sprigs of coriander and mint. Finely shred the remaining chilli and sprinkle it over the salads with the peanuts and crisp-fried shallots. Serve immediately.

Per portion: Energy 349Kcal/1458kJ; Protein 33.5g; Carbohydrate 15.4g, of which sugars 13.7g; Fat 17.4g, of which saturates 3g; Cholesterol 329mg; Calcium 162mg; Fibre 2.8g; Sodium 596mg.

PRAWN SALAD

IN MEXICO, THIS SALAD WOULD FORM THE FISH COURSE IN A FORMAL MEAL, BUT IT IS SO GOOD THAT YOU'LL WANT TO SERVE IT ON ALL SORTS OF OCCASIONS. IT IS PERFECT FOR A BUFFET LUNCH.

SERVES FOUR

INGREDIENTS

450g/1lb cooked peeled
  prawns (shrimp)
juice of 1 lime
3 tomatoes
1 ripe but firm avocado
30ml/2 tbsp hot chilli sauce
5ml/1 tsp sugar
150ml/¼ pint/⅔ cup sour cream
2 Little Gem (Bibb) lettuces
salt and ground black pepper
fresh basil leaves and strips of green
  (bell) pepper to garnish

1 Put the prawns in a large bowl, add the lime juice and salt and pepper. Toss lightly, then leave to marinate.

2 Cut a cross in the base of each tomato. Place them in a heatproof bowl and pour over boiling water to cover.

3 After 3 minutes, lift the tomatoes out on a slotted spoon and plunge them into a bowl of cold water. Drain. The skins will have begun to peel back easily from the crosses.

4 Peel the tomatoes completely, then cut them in half and squeeze out the seeds. Chop the flesh into 1cm/½in cubes and add it to the prawns.

5 Cut the avocado in half, remove the skin and stone (pit), then slice the flesh into 1cm/½in chunks. Add it to the prawn and tomato mixture.

6 Mix the hot chilli sauce, sugar and sour cream in a bowl. Fold into the prawn mixture. Line a bowl with the lettuce leaves, then top with the prawn mixture. Cover and chill for at least 1 hour, then garnish with fresh basil and strips of green pepper. Crusty bread makes a perfect accompaniment.

Per portion: Energy 284Kcal/1185kJ; Protein 28.1g; Carbohydrate 5g, of which sugars 4.4g; Fat 16.9g, of which saturates 6.7g; Cholesterol 114mg; Calcium 226mg; Fibre 2.3g; Sodium 1814mg.

INSALATA DI MARE

YOU CAN VARY THE SEAFOOD IN THIS ITALIAN SALAD ACCORDING TO WHAT IS AVAILABLE, BUT TRY TO INCLUDE AT LEAST TWO KINDS OF SHELLFISH AND SOME SQUID. THE SALAD IS GOOD WARM OR COLD.

SERVES FOUR

INGREDIENTS
    450g/1lb live mussels, scrubbed
      and bearded
    450g/1lb small clams, scrubbed
    105ml/7 tbsp dry white wine
    225g/8oz squid, cleaned
    4 large scallops, with their corals
    30ml/2 tbsp olive oil
    2 garlic cloves, finely chopped
    1 small dried red chilli, crumbled
    225g/8oz whole cooked prawns
      (shrimp), in the shell
    6–8 large chicory (Belgian
      endive) leaves
    6–8 radicchio leaves
    15ml/1 tbsp chopped fresh flat leaf
      parsley, to garnish
For the dressing
    5ml/1 tsp Dijon mustard
    30ml/2 tbsp white
      wine vinegar
    5ml/1 tsp lemon juice
    120ml/4fl oz/½ cup extra virgin
      olive oil
    salt and ground black pepper

1 Put the mussels and clams in a large pan with the white wine. Cover and cook over a high heat, shaking the pan occasionally, for about 4 minutes, until they have opened. Discard any that remain closed. Use a slotted spoon to transfer the shellfish to a bowl, then strain and reserve the cooking liquid and set it aside.

2 Cut the squid into thin rings; chop the tentacles. Leave small squid whole. Halve the scallops horizontally.

3 Heat the oil in a frying pan, add the garlic, chilli, squid, scallops and corals, and sauté for about 2 minutes, until just cooked and tender. Lift the squid and scallops out of the pan; reserve the oil.

4 When the shellfish are cool enough to handle, shell them, keeping a dozen of each in the shell. Peel all but 6–8 of the prawns. Pour the shellfish cooking liquid into a small pan, set over a high heat and reduce by half. Mix all the shelled and unshelled mussels and clams with the squid and scallops, then add the prawns.

5 To make the dressing, whisk the mustard with the vinegar and lemon juice together and season to taste. Add the olive oil, whisk vigorously, then whisk in the reserved cooking liquid and the oil from the frying pan. Pour the dressing over the seafood mixture and toss lightly to coat well.

6 Arrange the chicory and radicchio leaves around the edge of a large serving dish and pile the mixed seafood salad into the centre. Sprinkle with the chopped flat leaf parsley and serve immediately or chill first.

Per portion: Energy 445Kcal/1861kJ; Protein 41.1g; Carbohydrate 3.8g, of which sugars 1g; Fat 27.9g, of which saturates 4.3g; Cholesterol 241mg; Calcium 219mg; Fibre 0.5g; Sodium 585mg.

WHITEFISH SALAD

SMOKED WHITEFISH IS ONE OF THE GLORIES OF DELI FOOD AND, MADE INTO A SALAD WITH MAYONNAISE AND SOUR CREAM, IT BECOMES INDISPENSABLE AS A BRUNCH DISH. EAT IT WITH A STACK OF BAGELS, PUMPERNICKEL OR RYE BREAD. IF YOU CAN'T FIND SMOKED WHITEFISH, USE ANY OTHER SMOKED FIRM WHITE FISH, SUCH AS HALIBUT OR COD.

SERVES FOUR TO SIX

INGREDIENTS
 1 smoked whitefish, skinned
  and boned
 2 celery sticks, chopped
 ½ red, white or yellow onion
  or 3–5 spring onions
  (scallions), chopped
 45ml/3 tbsp mayonnaise
 45ml/3 tbsp sour cream or Greek
  (US strained plain) yogurt
 juice of ½–1 lemon
 1 round lettuce
 ground black pepper
 5–10ml/1–2 tsp chopped fresh
  parsley, to garnish

1 Break the smoked fish into bitesize pieces. In a bowl, combine the chopped celery, onion or spring onion, mayonnaise, and sour cream or yogurt, and add lemon juice to taste.

2 Fold the fish into the mixture and season with pepper. Arrange the lettuce leaves on serving plates, then spoon the whitefish salad on top. Serve chilled, sprinkled with parsley.

Per portion: Energy 172Kcal/719kJ; Protein 16g; Carbohydrate 4.3g, of which sugars 3.4g; Fat 10.4g, of which saturates 2g; Cholesterol 35mg; Calcium 62mg; Fibre 1.1g; Sodium 640mg.

SALAD NIÇOISE

MADE WITH THE FRESHEST OF INGREDIENTS, THIS CLASSIC PROVENÇAL SALAD MAKES A SIMPLE YET UNBEATABLE SUMMER DISH. SERVE WITH COUNTRY-STYLE BREAD AND CHILLED WHITE WINE.

SERVES FOUR

INGREDIENTS
115g/4oz green beans, trimmed
   and cut in half
115g/4oz mixed salad leaves
½ small cucumber, thinly sliced
4 ripe tomatoes, quartered
50g/2oz can anchovies, drained
4 eggs, hard-boiled
1 tuna steak, about 175g/6oz
olive oil, for brushing
½ bunch of small radishes, trimmed
50g/2oz/½ cup small
   black olives
salt and ground black pepper
For the dressing
90ml/6 tbsp extra virgin olive oil
2 garlic cloves, crushed
15ml/1 tbsp white wine vinegar

4 Preheat the grill (broiler). Brush the tuna with olive oil and sprinkle with salt and black pepper. Grill (broil) for 3–4 minutes on each side until cooked through. Cool, then flake with a fork.

5 Sprinkle the flaked tuna, sliced anchovies, quartered eggs, radishes and olives over the salad. Pour over the dressing and toss together lightly to combine. Serve immediately.

1 To make the dressing, whisk together the oil, garlic and vinegar in a bowl and season to taste with salt and pepper. Alternatively, shake together in a screw-top jar. Set aside.

2 Cook the green beans in a pan of boiling water for 2 minutes, until just tender, then drain.

3 Mix together the salad leaves, sliced cucumber, tomatoes and green beans in a large, shallow bowl. Halve the anchovies lengthways and shell and quarter the eggs.

VARIATION

Opinions vary on whether Salad Niçoise should include potatoes but, if you like, include a few small cooked new potatoes.

Per portion: Energy 378Kcal/1569kJ; Protein 23g; Carbohydrate 5.1g, of which sugars 4.7g; Fat 29.6g, of which saturates 5.2g; Cholesterol 241mg; Calcium 122mg; Fibre 2.5g; Sodium 889mg.

BEAN SALAD WITH TUNA AND RED ONION

THIS MAKES A GREAT, SUMMERY MAIN MEAL IF SERVED WITH A GREEN SALAD, SOME GARLIC MAYONNAISE AND PLENTY OF WARM, CRUSTY BREAD.

SERVES FOUR

INGREDIENTS
  250g/9oz/1⅓ cups dried haricot
    (navy) or cannellini beans, soaked
    overnight in cold water
  1 bay leaf
  200–250g/7–9oz fine green
    beans, trimmed
  1 large red onion, very thinly sliced
  45ml/3 tbsp chopped fresh flat
    leaf parsley
  200–250g/7–9oz good-quality canned
    tuna in olive oil, drained
  200g/7oz cherry tomatoes, halved
  salt and ground black pepper
  a few onion rings, to garnish
For the dressing
  90ml/6 tbsp extra virgin olive oil
  15ml/1 tbsp tarragon vinegar
  5ml/1 tsp tarragon mustard
  1 garlic clove, finely chopped
  5ml/1 tsp grated lemon rind
  a little lemon juice
  pinch of caster (superfine)
    sugar (optional)

1 Drain the beans and bring them to the boil in fresh water with the bay leaf added. Boil rapidly for 10 minutes, then reduce the heat and boil steadily for 1–1½ hours, until tender. Drain well. Discard the bay leaf.

2 Meanwhile, place all the dressing ingredients apart from the lemon juice and sugar in a jug (pitcher) and whisk until mixed. Season to taste with salt, pepper, lemon juice and a pinch of caster sugar, if you like. Leave to stand.

3 Blanch the green beans in plenty of boiling water for 3–4 minutes. Drain, refresh under cold water and drain thoroughly again.

4 Place both types of beans in a bowl. Add half the dressing and toss to mix. Stir in the onion and half the chopped parsley, then season to taste with salt and pepper.

5 Flake the tuna into large chunks with a knife and toss it into the beans with the tomato halves.

6 Arrange the salad on four individual plates. Drizzle the remaining dressing over the salad and sprinkle the remaining chopped parsley on top. Garnish with a few onion rings and serve immediately, at room temperature.

Per portion: Energy 443Kcal/1857kJ; Protein 29.1g; Carbohydrate 33.7g, of which sugars 6.4g; Fat 22.3g, of which saturates 3.3g; Cholesterol 25mg; Calcium 100mg; Fibre 12g; Sodium 162mg.

SEARED SWORDFISH WITH CITRUS DRESSING

THIS CONTEMPORARY JAPANESE DISH TAKES CONVENTIONAL SALAD INGREDIENTS AND MIXES THEM WITH SHOYU, DASHI AND SESAME OIL FOR A BRIGHT, NEW TASTE. FRESH FISH IS SLICED THINLY AND SEARED OR MARINATED, THEN SERVED WITH SALAD LEAVES AND VEGETABLES.

SERVES FOUR

INGREDIENTS
    75g/3oz mooli (daikon), peeled
    50g/2oz carrot, peeled
    1 Japanese or salad cucumber
    10ml/2 tsp vegetable oil
    300g/11oz skinned fresh swordfish
      steak, cut against the grain
    2 cartons salad cress
    15ml/1 tbsp toasted
      sesame seeds
For the dressing
    105ml/7 tbsp shoyu
    105ml/7 tbsp second dashi stock,
      or the same amount of water and
      5ml/1 tsp dashi-no-moto
    30ml/2 tbsp toasted sesame oil
    juice of ½ lime
    rind of ½ lime, shredded into
      thin strips

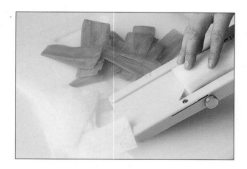

1 Make the vegetable garnishes first. Use a very sharp knife, mandolin or vegetable slicer with a julienne blade to make very thin (about 4cm/1½in long) strands of mooli, carrot and cucumber. Soak the mooli and carrot in ice-cold water for 5 minutes, then drain well and keep in the refrigerator.

2 Mix together all the ingredients for the dressing and stir well, then chill.

3 Heat the oil in a small frying pan until smoking hot. Sear the fish for 30 seconds on all sides. Plunge it into cold water in a bowl to stop the cooking. Dry on kitchen paper and wipe off as much oil as possible.

4 Cut the swordfish steak in half lengthways before slicing it into 5mm/¼in thick pieces in the other direction, against the grain.

5 Arrange the fish slices in a ring on individual plates. Mix the vegetable strands, salad cress and sesame seeds. Fluff up with your hands, then shape them into a sphere. Gently place it in the centre of the plate, on the swordfish. Pour the dressing around the plate's edge and serve immediately.

COOK'S TIP
This dish is traditionally made with fillet cut with the grain. To prepare, cut it in half lengthways, then slice against the grain by holding a knife horizontally to the chopping board.

Per portion: Energy 192Kcal/799kJ; Protein 15.6g; Carbohydrate 4.1g, of which sugars 3.7g; Fat 12.7g, of which saturates 2g; Cholesterol 31mg; Calcium 53mg; Fibre 1.1g; Sodium 1887mg.

WARM CHICKEN AND TOMATO SALAD WITH HAZELNUT DRESSING

This simple, warm salad combines pan-fried chicken and spinach with a light, nutty dressing. Serve it for lunch on an autumn day.

SERVES FOUR

INGREDIENTS
 45ml/3 tbsp olive oil
 30ml/2 tbsp hazelnut oil
 15ml/1 tbsp white wine vinegar
 1 garlic clove, crushed
 15ml/1 tbsp chopped fresh mixed herbs
 225g/8oz baby spinach leaves
 250g/9oz cherry tomatoes, halved
 1 bunch of spring onions
 (scallions), chopped
 2 skinless, chicken breast fillets, cut
 into thin strips
 salt and ground black pepper

VARIATIONS
• Use other meat or fish, such as steak, pork fillet (tenderloin) or salmon fillet, in place of the chicken.
• Any salad leaves can be used instead of the baby spinach.

1 First make the dressing: place 30ml/2 tbsp of the olive oil, the hazelnut oil, vinegar, garlic and chopped herbs in a small bowl or jug (pitcher) and whisk together until mixed. Set aside.

2 Trim any long stalks from the spinach leaves, then place in a large serving bowl with the tomatoes and spring onions, and toss together to mix.

3 Heat the remaining olive oil in a frying pan, and stir-fry the chicken over a high heat for 7–10 minutes, until it is cooked, tender and lightly browned.

4 Arrange the cooked chicken pieces over the salad. Give the dressing a quick whisk to blend, then drizzle it over the salad. Add salt and pepper to taste, toss lightly and serve immediately.

Per portion: Energy 234Kcal/973kJ; Protein 20.5g; Carbohydrate 3.6g, of which sugars 3.5g; Fat 15.3g, of which saturates 2.4g; Cholesterol 53mg; Calcium 114mg; Fibre 2.2g; Sodium 131mg.

CHICKEN AND MANGO SALAD WITH ORANGE RICE

THIS FRESH AND DELICIOUS RECIPE DRAWS ITS INSPIRATION FROM ALL OVER THE WORLD.

SERVES FOUR

INGREDIENTS
 15ml/1 tbsp sunflower oil
 1 onion, chopped
 1 garlic clove, crushed
 30ml/2 tbsp red curry paste
 10ml/2 tsp apricot jam
 30ml/2 tbsp chicken stock
 about 450g/1lb cooked chicken, cut
  into small pieces
 150ml/¼ pint/⅔ cup natural
  (plain) yogurt
 60–75ml/4–5 tbsp mayonnaise
 1 large mango, peeled, stoned
  (pitted) and cut into 1cm/½in dice
 fresh flat leaf parsley sprigs,
  to garnish
 poppadums, to serve
For the orange rice
 175g/6oz/scant 1 cup white long
  grain rice
 225g/8oz carrots, grated
  (about 1⅓ cups)
 1 large orange, cut
  into segments
 40g/1½oz/⅓ cup roasted flaked
  (sliced) almonds
For the dressing
 45ml/3 tbsp olive oil
 60ml/4 tbsp sunflower oil
 45ml/3 tbsp lemon juice
 1 garlic clove, crushed
 15ml/1 tbsp chopped mixed fresh
  herbs, such as tarragon, parsley,
  chives
 salt and freshly ground black pepper

1 Heat the oil in a frying pan. Add the onion and garlic and cook over a medium heat, stirring occasionally, for 3–4 minutes, until soft.

2 Stir in the curry paste and cook for about 1 minute, stirring constantly, then lower the heat and stir in the apricot jam and chicken stock. Mix well, then add the chopped chicken and stir until it is thoroughly coated in the paste. Spoon into a bowl, cover with clear film (plastic wrap) and leave to cool.

3 Meanwhile, boil the rice in plenty of lightly salted water until just tender. Drain, rinse under cold water and drain again. When cool, stir into the grated carrots and add the orange segments and flaked almonds.

4 Make the dressing by whisking all the ingredients together in a bowl.

5 When the chicken mixture is cool, stir in the yogurt and mayonnaise, then add the mango, stirring it in carefully so as not to break the flesh. Chill for about 30 minutes.

6 When ready to serve, pour the dressing into the rice salad and mix well. Spoon on to a platter and mound the cold curried chicken on top. Garnish with flat leaf parsley and serve with poppadums.

COOK'S TIP
A simple way of dicing a mango is to take two thick slices from either side of the large flat stone (pit) without peeling the fruit. Make criss-cross cuts in the flesh on each slice and then turn inside out. The cubes of flesh will stand proud of the skin and can be easily cut off.

Per portion: Energy 776Kcal/3245kJ; Protein 35.9g; Carbohydrate 60.2g, of which sugars 21.1g; Fat 45.3g, of which saturates 6.4g; Cholesterol 93mg; Calcium 172mg; Fibre 4.5g; Sodium 206mg.

WARM SALAD OF BAYONNE HAM AND NEW POTATOES

WITH A LIGHTLY SPICED NUTTY DRESSING, THIS WARM SALAD IS AS DELICIOUS AS IT IS FASHIONABLE, AND AN EXCELLENT CHOICE FOR INFORMAL ENTERTAINING.

SERVES FOUR

INGREDIENTS
    225g/8oz new potatoes, halved
      if large
    50g/2oz green beans
    115g/4oz young spinach leaves
    2 spring onions (scallions), sliced
    4 eggs, hard-boiled and quartered
    50g/2oz Bayonne ham, cut
      into strips
    juice of ½ lemon
    salt and ground black pepper
For the dressing
    60ml/4 tbsp olive oil
    5ml/1 tsp ground turmeric
    5ml/1 tsp ground cumin
    50g/2oz/½ cup shelled hazelnuts

1 Cook the potatoes in salted, boiling water for 10–15 minutes, or until tender, then drain. Cook the beans in salted, boiling water for 2 minutes, then drain.

2 Toss the potatoes and beans with the spinach and spring onions in a bowl.

3 Arrange the hard-boiled egg quarters on the salad and sprinkle the strips of ham over the top. Sprinkle with the lemon juice and season with plenty of salt and pepper.

4 Heat the dressing ingredients in a large frying pan and continue to cook, stirring frequently, until the nuts turn golden. Pour the hot, nutty dressing over the salad and serve immediately.

VARIATION
Replace the potatoes with a 400g/14oz can mixed beans and pulses. Drain and rinse the beans and pulses, then drain again. Toss lightly with the green beans and spring onions.

Per portion: Energy 323Kcal/1341kJ; Protein 12.4g; Carbohydrate 10.9g, of which sugars 2.2g; Fat 25.8g, of which saturates 4.2g; Cholesterol 199mg; Calcium 105mg; Fibre 2.3g; Sodium 270mg.

WARM SALAD WITH HAM, EGG AND ASPARAGUS

WHEN YOU THINK IT'S TOO HOT FOR PASTA, TRY SERVING IT IN A WARM SALAD. HERE IT IS COMBINED WITH HAM, EGGS AND ASPARAGUS. A MUSTARD DRESSING MADE FROM THE ASPARAGUS STEMS CREATES A RICH AND TANGY ACCOMPANIMENT.

SERVES FOUR

INGREDIENTS
450g/1lb asparagus
450g/1lb dried tagliatelle
225g/8oz cooked ham, in 5mm/¼in thick slices, cut into sticks
2 eggs, hard-boiled and sliced
50g/2oz Parmesan cheese, shaved
salt and ground black pepper

For the dressing
50g/2oz cooked potato
75ml/5 tbsp olive oil, preferably Sicilian
15ml/1 tbsp lemon juice
10ml/2 tsp Dijon mustard
120ml/4fl oz/½ cup vegetable stock

VARIATIONS
Use sliced chicken instead of the ham or thin slices of softer Italian cheese, such as Fontina or asiago.

1 Trim and discard the tough woody part of the asparagus. Cut the spears in half and cook the thicker halves in boiling salted water for 12 minutes. After 6 minutes add the tips. Drain, then refresh under cold water until warm.

2 Finely chop 150g/5oz of the thick asparagus pieces. Place in a food processor with the dressing ingredients and process until smooth.

3 Cook the pasta in a large pan of salted water according to the packet instructions, until tender. Refresh under cold water until warm, and drain.

4 To serve, toss the pasta with the asparagus sauce and divide among four plates. Top with the ham, hard-boiled eggs and asparagus tips. Serve immediately with a sprinkling of Parmesan cheese shavings.

Per portion: Energy 707Kcal/2975kJ; Protein 36g; Carbohydrate 88.4g, of which sugars 6.6g; Fat 25.8g, of which saturates 6.4g; Cholesterol 159mg; Calcium 230mg; Fibre 5.3g; Sodium 859mg.

BEEF AND GRILLED SWEET POTATO SALAD WITH SHALLOT AND HERB DRESSING

THIS SALAD MAKES A GOOD MAIN DISH FOR A SUMMER BUFFET, ESPECIALLY IF THE BEEF HAS BEEN CUT INTO FORK-SIZE STRIPS. IT IS ABSOLUTELY DELICIOUS WITH A SIMPLE POTATO SALAD AND SOME PEPPERY LEAVES, SUCH AS WATERCRESS, MIZUNA OR ROCKET.

SERVES SIX TO EIGHT

INGREDIENTS

800g/1¾lb fillet (tenderloin) of beef
5ml/1 tsp black peppercorns, crushed
10ml/2 tsp chopped fresh thyme
60ml/4 tbsp olive oil
450g/1lb orange-fleshed sweet
  potato, peeled
salt and ground black pepper
For the dressing
1 garlic clove, chopped
15g/½oz/½ cup flat leaf parsley
30ml/2 tbsp chopped fresh
  coriander (cilantro)
15ml/1 tbsp salted capers, rinsed
½–1 fresh green chilli, seeded
  and chopped
10ml/2 tsp Dijon mustard
10–15ml/2–3 tsp white wine vinegar
75ml/5 tbsp extra virgin olive oil
2 shallots, finely chopped

1 Roll the beef fillet in the crushed peppercorns and thyme, then set aside to marinate for a few hours. Preheat the oven to 200°C/400°F/Gas 6.

2 Heat half the olive oil in a heavy frying pan. Add the beef and brown it all over, turning frequently, to seal it. Place on a baking tray and cook in the oven for 10–15 minutes.

3 Remove the beef from the oven, and cover with foil, then leave to rest for 10–15 minutes.

4 Meanwhile, preheat the grill (broiler). Cut the sweet potatoes into 1cm/½in slices. Brush with the remaining olive oil, season to taste with salt and pepper, and grill (broil) for about 5–6 minutes on each side, until tender and browned. Cut the sweet potato slices into strips and place them in a bowl.

5 Cut the beef into slices or strips and toss with the sweet potato, then set the bowl aside.

6 For the dressing, process the garlic, parsley, coriander, capers, chilli, mustard and 10ml/2 tsp of the vinegar in a food processor or blender until chopped. With the motor still running, gradually pour in the oil to make a smooth dressing. Season the dressing with salt and pepper and add more vinegar, to taste. Stir in the shallots.

7 Toss the dressing into the sweet potatoes and beef and leave to stand for up to 2 hours before serving.

COOK'S TIP
Not only do orange-fleshed sweet potatoes look more appetizing than white ones, but they are also better for you, as they contain antioxidant vitamins that help protect against disease.

Per portion: Energy 400Kcal/1670kJ; Protein 29.2g; Carbohydrate 16g, of which sugars 4.3g; Fat 24.9g, of which saturates 6.2g; Cholesterol 81mg; Calcium 23mg; Fibre 1.8g; Sodium 89mg.

THAI BEEF SALAD

ALL THE INGREDIENTS FOR THIS TRADITIONAL THAI DISH — KNOWN AS YAM NUA YANG — ARE WIDELY AVAILABLE IN LARGER SUPERMARKETS.

SERVES FOUR

INGREDIENTS
675g/1½lb fillet steak
  (beef tenderloin)
30ml/2 tbsp olive oil
2 small mild red chillies, seeded
  and sliced
225g/8oz/3¼ cups shiitake
  mushrooms, sliced
For the dressing
3 spring onions (scallions), chopped
2 garlic cloves, finely chopped
juice of 1 lime
15–30ml/1–2 tbsp fish or oyster
  sauce, to taste
5ml/1 tsp soft light brown sugar
30ml/2 tbsp chopped fresh
  coriander (cilantro)
To serve
1 cos or romaine lettuce, torn
  into strips
175g/6oz cherry tomatoes, halved
5cm/2in piece cucumber, peeled,
  halved and thinly sliced
45ml/3 tbsp toasted sesame seeds

1 Preheat the grill (broiler), then cook the steak for 2–4 minutes on each side depending on how well done you like steak. Leave to cool for at least 15 minutes.

2 Use a very sharp knife to slice the meat as thinly as possible and place the slices in a bowl.

VARIATION
If you can find them, yellow chillies make a colourful addition to this dish. Substitute one for one of the red chillies.

3 Heat the olive oil in a small frying pan. Add the seeded and sliced red chillies and the sliced mushrooms and cook for 5 minutes, stirring occasionally. Turn off the heat and add the grilled (broiled) steak slices to the pan, then stir well to coat the slices in the chilli and mushroom mixture.

4 Stir all the ingredients for the dressing together, then pour it over the meat mixture and toss gently.

5 Arrange the salad ingredients on a serving plate. Spoon the warm steak mixture into the centre and sprinkle the sesame seeds over, then serve.

Per portion: Energy 381Kcal/1591kJ; Protein 39.8g; Carbohydrate 4.1g, of which sugars 3.8g; Fat 23g, of which saturates 6.6g; Cholesterol 103mg; Calcium 105mg; Fibre 2.5g; Sodium 352mg.

RICE AND RISOTTO

If you're the sort of person who finds cooking relaxing and loves chatting to friends while preparing a meal, rustle up a tasty risotto. You need to stand at the stove and stir the rice for twenty minutes just before serving, but the action is both soothing and satisfying and the results are inevitably delicious. Chicken and Prawn Jambalaya is another wonderful dish for entertaining. Like Seafood Paella, it is full of flavour and the combination of ingredients means that every mouthful brings a taste of the delightfully unexpected.

STUFFED VEGETABLES

COLOURFUL, EASY TO PREPARE AND UTTERLY DELICIOUS, THIS MAKES A POPULAR SUPPER DISH, AND WITH A CHOICE OF VEGETABLES INCLUDED IN THE RECIPE, THERE'S BOUND TO BE SOMETHING TO APPEAL TO EVERY MEMBER OF THE FAMILY.

SERVES FOUR

INGREDIENTS

1 aubergine (eggplant)
1 green (bell) pepper
2 beefsteak tomatoes
45ml/3 tbsp olive oil
1 onion, chopped
2 garlic cloves, crushed
115g/4oz/1–1½ cups button (white)
  mushrooms, chopped
1 carrot, grated
225g/8oz/2 cups cooked white long
  grain rice
15ml/1 tbsp chopped fresh dill
90g/3½oz/scant ½ cup crumbled feta
  cheese
75g/3oz/¾ cup pine nuts,
  lightly toasted
30ml/2 tbsp currants
salt and ground black pepper

1 Preheat the oven to 190°C/375°F/ Gas 5. Lightly grease a shallow ovenproof dish. Cut the aubergine in half, through the stalk, and scoop out the flesh from each half, taking care not to pierce the skin, to leave two hollow "boats". Dice the aubergine flesh. Cut the pepper in half lengthways and remove the cores and seeds.

2 Cut off the tops from the tomatoes and hollow out the centres with a spoon. Chop the flesh and add it to the diced aubergine. Place the tomatoes upside down on kitchen paper to drain.

3 Bring a pan of water to the boil, add the aubergine halves and blanch for 3 minutes. Add the pepper halves to the boiling water and blanch for 3 minutes more. Drain the vegetables, then place, hollow side up, in the baking dish.

4 Heat 30ml/2 tbsp oil in a pan and cook the onion and garlic for about 5 minutes. Stir in the diced aubergine and tomato mixture with the mushrooms and carrot. Cover, cook for 5 minutes until softened, then mix in the rice, dill, feta, pine nuts and currants. Season to taste.

5 Divide the mixture among the vegetable shells, sprinkle with the remaining olive oil and bake for 20 minutes, until the topping has browned. Serve hot or cold.

Per portion: Energy 544Kcal/2265kJ; Protein 12.9g; Carbohydrate 63.3g, of which sugars 17.2g; Fat 26.8g, of which saturates 5.3g; Cholesterol 16mg; Calcium 134mg; Fibre 4.1g; Sodium 343mg.

ROASTED SQUASH

GEM SQUASH HAS A SWEET, SUBTLE FLAVOUR THAT CONTRASTS WELL WITH OLIVES AND SUN-DRIED TOMATOES IN THIS RECIPE. THE RICE ADDS SUBSTANCE WITHOUT CHANGING ANY OF THE FLAVOURS.

2 Mix the rice, tomatoes, olives, cheese, half the olive oil and basil in a bowl.

3 Oil a shallow ovenproof dish with the remaining oil, just large enough to hold the squash side by side. Divide the rice mixture among the squash and place them in the dish.

SERVES FOUR

INGREDIENTS

4 whole gem squashes
225g/8oz/2 cups cooked white
  long grain rice
75g/3oz/1½ cups sun-dried
  tomatoes in oil, drained
  and chopped
50g/2oz/½ cup pitted black
  olives, chopped
60ml/4 tbsp soft goat's cheese
30ml/2 tbsp olive oil
15ml/1 tbsp chopped fresh basil
  leaves, plus fresh basil sprigs,
  to serve
yogurt and mint dressing
  or green salad,
  to serve (optional)

1 Preheat the oven to 180°C/350°F/ Gas 4. Using a sharp knife, trim away the base of each gem squash and then slice off the tops. Using a spoon, scoop out and discard the seeds.

4 Cover with foil and bake for about 45–50 minutes, until the squash is tender when pierced with the point of a sharp knife or skewer. Garnish with basil sprigs and serve with a yogurt and mint dressing or with a green salad if you like.

Per portion: Energy 280Kcal/1170kJ; Protein 8.7g; Carbohydrate 23.6g, of which sugars 5g; Fat 17.4g, of which saturates 6.3g; Cholesterol 23mg; Calcium 125mg; Fibre 3.1g; Sodium 434mg.

BASMATI AND NUT PILAFF

VEGETARIANS WILL LOVE THIS SIMPLE PILAFF. ADD WILD OR CULTIVATED MUSHROOMS, IF YOU LIKE.

SERVES FOUR

INGREDIENTS

15–30ml/1–2 tbsp sunflower oil
1 onion, chopped
1 garlic clove, crushed
1 large carrot, coarsely grated
225g/8oz/generous 1 cup basmati
   rice, soaked
5ml/1 tsp cumin seeds
10ml/2 tsp ground coriander
10ml/2 tsp black mustard
   seeds (optional)
4 green cardamom pods
450ml/¾ pint/scant 2 cups vegetable
   stock or water
1 bay leaf
75g/3oz/¾ cup unsalted walnuts and
   cashew nuts
salt and ground black pepper
fresh parsley or coriander (cilantro)
   sprigs, to garnish

1 Heat the oil in a large, shallow frying pan. Add the onion, garlic and carrot and cook over a low heat, stirring occasionally, for 3–4 minutes, until softened. Thoroughly drain the rice and then add to the pan with the cumin seeds, ground coriander, black mustard seeds and cardamom pods. Cook for 1–2 minutes more, stirring constantly to coat the grains in oil.

2 Pour in the stock or water, add the bay leaf and season well. Bring to the boil, lower the heat, cover and simmer very gently for 10–12 minutes.

3 Remove the pan from the heat without lifting the lid. Leave to stand for about 5 minutes, then check the rice. If it is cooked, there will be small steam holes on the surface of the rice. Remove and discard the bay leaf and the cardamom pods.

4 Stir in the nuts, taste and adjust the seasoning if necessary. Spoon on to a warm platter, garnish with the parsley or coriander and serve.

COOK'S TIP
Use whichever nuts you prefer in this dish – even unsalted peanuts taste good, although almonds, cashew nuts or pistachios are more exotic.

Per portion: Energy 376Kcal/1562kJ; Protein 7.5g; Carbohydrate 50g, of which sugars 4g; Fat 16g, of which saturates 1.4g; Cholesterol 0mg; Calcium 43mg; Fibre 1.6g; Sodium 7mg.

MUSHROOM PILAFF

THIS DISH IS SIMPLICITY ITSELF, YET IT IS FULL OF DELICIOUS INDIAN FLAVOURS.

SERVES FOUR

INGREDIENTS
    30ml/2 tbsp vegetable oil
    2 shallots, finely chopped
    1 garlic clove, crushed
    3 green cardamom pods
    25g/1oz/2 tbsp ghee or butter
    175g/6oz/2½ cups button (white)
      mushrooms, sliced
    225g/8oz/generous 1 cup basmati
      rice, soaked
    5ml/1 tsp grated fresh root ginger
    good pinch of garam masala
    15ml/1 tbsp chopped fresh
      coriander (cilantro)
    salt

1 Heat the oil in a flameproof casserole and cook the shallots, garlic and cardamom pods over a medium heat for 3–4 minutes, until the shallots have softened and are beginning to brown.

2 Add the ghee or butter. When it has melted, add the mushrooms and cook for 2–3 minutes more.

3 Add the rice, ginger and garam masala. Stir-fry over a low heat for 2–3 minutes, then stir in 450ml/¾ pint/ scant 2 cups water and a little salt. Bring to the boil, then cover tightly and simmer over a low heat for 10 minutes.

4 Remove the casserole from the heat. Leave to stand, still covered, for 5 minutes. Add the chopped coriander and gently fork it through the rice. Spoon into a warm serving bowl and serve immediately.

Per portion: Energy 309Kcal/1286kJ; Protein 5.2g; Carbohydrate 46.3g, of which sugars 1g; Fat 11.2g, of which saturates 4g; Cholesterol 13mg; Calcium 18mg; Fibre 0.7g; Sodium 41mg.

ROASTED PEPPER RISOTTO

THIS MAKES AN EXCELLENT AND COLOURFUL VEGETARIAN LUNCH OR SUPPER DISH.

SERVES THREE TO FOUR

INGREDIENTS
    1 red (bell) pepper
    1 yellow (bell) pepper
    15ml/1 tbsp olive oil
    25g/1oz/2 tbsp butter
    1 onion, chopped
    2 garlic cloves, crushed
    275g/10oz/1½ cups risotto rice
    1 litre/1¾ pints/4 cups simmering
      vegetable stock
    50g/2oz/⅔ cup freshly grated
      Parmesan cheese
salt and ground black pepper
freshly grated Parmesan cheese, to
    serve (optional)

1 Preheat the grill (broiler). Cut the peppers in half, remove the seeds and pith and arrange, cut side down, on a baking sheet. Place under the grill for 5–6 minutes until the skin is charred. Put the peppers in a plastic bag, tie the ends and leave for 4–5 minutes.

2 Peel the peppers when they are cool enough to handle and the steam has loosened the skin. Cut into thin strips.

3 Heat the oil and butter in a pan and cook the onion and garlic for 4–5 minutes over a low heat until the onion begins to soften. Add the peppers and cook the mixture for 3–4 minutes more, stirring occasionally.

4 Stir in the rice. Cook over a medium heat for 3–4 minutes, stirring all the time, until the rice is evenly coated in oil and the outer part of each grain has become translucent.

5 Add a ladleful of stock. Cook, stirring, until all the liquid has been absorbed. Continue to add the stock, a ladleful at a time, making sure each quantity has been absorbed before adding the next.

6 When the rice is tender but retains a little "bite", stir in the Parmesan, and add seasoning to taste. Cover and leave to stand for 3–4 minutes, then serve, with extra Parmesan, if using.

Per portion: Energy 555Kcal/2312kJ; Protein 16.1g; Carbohydrate 80.1g, of which sugars 10g; Fat 18g, of which saturates 8.4g; Cholesterol 34mg; Calcium 238mg; Fibre 2.6g; Sodium 241mg.

RISOTTO WITH FOUR VEGETABLES

THIS IS ONE OF THE PRETTIEST RISOTTOS, ESPECIALLY WHEN MADE WITH ACORN SQUASH.

SERVES THREE TO FOUR

INGREDIENTS
115g/4oz/1 cup shelled fresh peas
115g/4oz/1 cup green beans, cut
    into short lengths
30ml/2 tbsp olive oil
75g/3oz/6 tbsp butter
1 acorn squash, skin and seeds
    removed, flesh cut into batons
1 onion, finely chopped
275g/10oz/1½ cups risotto rice
120ml/4fl oz/½ cup Italian dry
    white vermouth
1 litre/1¾ pints/4 cups boiling
    chicken stock
75g/3oz/1 cup freshly grated
    Parmesan cheese
salt and ground black pepper

1 Bring a pan of lightly salted water to the boil, add the peas and beans and cook for 2–3 minutes, until the vegetables are just tender. Drain, refresh under cold running water, drain again and set aside.

2 Heat the oil with 25g/1oz/2 tbsp of the butter in a medium pan until foaming. Add the squash and cook gently for 2–3 minutes, or until just softened. Remove with a slotted spoon and set aside. Add the onion to the pan and cook gently for about 3 minutes, stirring frequently, until softened.

3 Stir in the rice until the grains start to swell and burst, then add the vermouth. Stir until the vermouth stops sizzling and most of it has been absorbed by the rice, then add a few ladlefuls of the stock, with salt and pepper to taste. Stir over a low heat until the stock has been absorbed.

4 Gradually add the remaining stock, a few ladlefuls at a time, allowing the rice to absorb the liquid before adding more, and stirring all the time.

VARIATIONS
Shelled broad (fava) beans can be used instead of the peas, and asparagus tips instead of the green beans. Use courgettes (zucchini) if acorn squash is not available.

5 After about 20 minutes, when all the stock has been absorbed and the rice is cooked and creamy but still has a "bite", gently stir in the vegetables, the remaining butter and about half the grated Parmesan. Heat through, then taste and adjust the seasoning and serve with the remaining grated Parmesan handed around separately.

Per portion: Energy 836Kcal/3472kJ; Protein 22.1g; Carbohydrate 79.4g, of which sugars 6g; Fat 42.6g, of which saturates 22.1g; Cholesterol 89mg; Calcium 379mg; Fibre 3.9g; Sodium 462mg.

RISOTTO WITH FOUR CHEESES

THIS IS A VERY RICH DISH. IT IS THE PERFECT CHOICE FOR A DINNER PARTY WITH AN ITALIAN THEME, SERVED WITH A LIGHT, DRY SPARKLING WHITE WINE.

SERVES FOUR

INGREDIENTS
  40g/1½oz/3 tbsp butter
  1 small onion, finely chopped
  1.2 litres/2 pints/5 cups chicken
    stock, preferably home-made
  350g/12oz/1¾ cups risotto rice
  200ml/7fl oz/scant 1 cup dry
    white wine
  50g/2oz/½ cup grated Gruyère cheese
  50g/2oz/½ cup diced taleggio cheese
  50g/2oz/½ cup diced
    Gorgonzola cheese
  50g/2oz/⅔ cup freshly grated
    Parmesan cheese
  salt and ground black pepper
  chopped fresh flat leaf parsley,
    to garnish

1 Melt the butter in a large, heavy pan or deep frying pan and cook the onion over a low heat, stirring frequently, for about 4–5 minutes, until softened and lightly browned. Meanwhile, pour the chicken stock into another pan and heat it to simmering point.

2 Add the rice to the onion mixture, stir until the grains start to swell and burst, then add the wine. Stir until it stops sizzling and most of it has been absorbed by the rice, then pour in a little of the hot stock. Add salt and pepper to taste. Stir over a low heat until the stock has been absorbed.

3 Gradually add the remaining stock, a little at a time, allowing the rice to absorb the liquid before adding more, and stirring constantly. After about 20–25 minutes the rice will be *al dente* and the risotto creamy.

4 Turn off the heat under the pan, then add the Gruyère, taleggio, Gorgonzola and 30ml/2 tbsp of the Parmesan cheese. Stir gently until the cheeses have melted, then taste and adjust the seasoning, if necessary. Spoon the risotto into a warm serving bowl and garnish with parsley. Serve immediately, handing the remaining grated Parmesan separately.

Per portion: Energy 640Kcal/2662kJ; Protein 22.1g; Carbohydrate 67.1g, of which sugars 1.2g; Fat 26g, of which saturates 15.9g; Cholesterol 70mg; Calcium 451mg; Fibre 0.2g; Sodium 473mg.

RISOTTO WITH RICOTTA AND BASIL

THIS IS A WELL-FLAVOURED RISOTTO, WHICH BENEFITS FROM THE DISTINCTIVE PUNGENCY OF BASIL, MELLOWED WITH SMOOTH RICOTTA.

SERVES THREE TO FOUR

INGREDIENTS
45ml/3 tbsp olive oil
1 onion, finely chopped
275g/10oz/1½ cups risotto rice
1 litre/1¾ pints/4 cups hot chicken
 or vegetable stock
175g/6oz/¾ cup ricotta cheese
50g/2oz/2 cups fresh basil leaves,
 finely chopped, plus extra
 to garnish
75g/3oz/1 cup freshly grated
 Parmesan cheese
salt and ground black pepper

1 Heat the oil in a large pan or flameproof casserole and cook the onion over a low heat until soft.

2 Tip in the rice. Cook for a few minutes, stirring constantly, until the rice grains are well coated with oil and are slightly translucent.

3 Pour in about a quarter of the stock. Cook, stirring, until all the stock has been absorbed, then add another ladleful. Continue in this manner, adding more stock when the previous ladleful has been absorbed, until the risotto has been cooking for about 20 minutes and the rice is just tender.

4 Spoon the ricotta into a bowl and break it up a little with a fork. Gently stir it into the risotto along with the chopped basil and grated Parmesan. Taste and adjust the seasoning, if necessary, then cover and leave to stand for 2–3 minutes before serving, garnished with basil leaves.

Per portion: Energy 715Kcal/2975kJ; Protein 22.4g; Carbohydrate 72.6g, of which sugars 2.8g; Fat 36.2g, of which saturates 16.4g; Cholesterol 70mg; Calcium 382mg; Fibre 0.7g; Sodium 442mg.

SEARED SCALLOPS WITH CHIVE SAUCE ON LEEK AND CARROT RICE

SCALLOPS ARE ONE OF THE MOST DELICIOUS SHELLFISH. HERE THEY ARE PARTNERED WITH A DELICATE CHIVE SAUCE AND A PILAFF OF WILD AND WHITE RICE WITH SWEET LEEKS AND CARROTS.

SERVES FOUR

INGREDIENTS
  12–16 shelled scallops
  45ml/3 tbsp olive oil
  50g/2oz/⅓ cup wild rice
  65g/2½ oz/5 tbsp butter
  4 carrots, cut into long thin strips
  2 leeks, cut into thick,
    diagonal slices
  1 small onion, finely chopped
  115g/4oz/⅔ cup long grain rice
  1 fresh bay leaf
  200ml/7fl oz/scant 1 cup white wine
  450ml/¾ pint/scant 2 cups fish stock
  60ml/4 tbsp double (heavy) cream
  a little lemon juice
  25ml/5 tsp chopped fresh chives
  30ml/2 tbsp fresh chervil sprigs
  salt and ground black pepper

1 Lightly season the scallops, brush with 15ml/1 tbsp of the olive oil and set aside.

2 Cook the wild rice in plenty of boiling water for about 30 minutes, until tender, then drain well.

3 Melt half the butter in a small frying pan and cook the carrots over a low heat for 4–5 minutes. Add the leeks and cook for a further 2 minutes. Season with salt and pepper and add 30–45ml/2–3 tbsp water, then cover and cook for a few minutes more. Uncover and cook until the liquid has reduced. Remove from the heat and set aside.

4 Melt half the rest of the butter with 15ml/1 tbsp of the remaining oil in a heavy pan. Add the onion and cook over a low heat for 3–4 minutes, until softened but not browned.

5 Add the long grain rice and bay leaf and cook, stirring constantly, until the rice looks translucent and the grains are coated with oil.

6 Pour in half the wine and half the stock. Season with 2.5ml/½ tsp salt and bring to the boil. Stir, then cover and cook very gently for 15 minutes, or until the liquid is absorbed and the rice is cooked and tender.

7 Reheat the carrots and leeks gently, then stir them into the long grain rice with the wild rice. Add seasoning to taste, if necessary.

8 Meanwhile, pour the remaining wine and stock into a small pan and boil rapidly until reduced by half.

COOK'S TIP
Choose fresh, rather than frozen, scallops as the frozen ones tend to exude water on cooking. Scallops need only the briefest cooking at high heat, just until they turn opaque and brown on each side, so have the pan very hot. Although some people avoid eating the orange-coloured coral, it is delicious and many people consider it to be the best part.

9 Heat a heavy frying pan over a high heat. Add the remaining butter and oil. Sear the scallops for 1–2 minutes on each side. Set aside and keep warm.

10 Pour the reduced stock into the pan and heat until bubbling, then add the cream and boil until thickened. Season with lemon juice, salt and pepper. Stir in the chives and scallops.

11 Stir the chervil into the rice and pile it on to plates. Arrange the scallops on top and spoon the sauce over the rice.

Per portion: Energy 482Kcal/2014kJ; Protein 28.1g; Carbohydrate 42.7g, of which sugars 6g; Fat 18.6g, of which saturates 6.7g; Cholesterol 68mg; Calcium 80mg; Fibre 3g; Sodium 200mg.

SEAFOOD PAELLA

THERE ARE AS MANY VERSIONS OF PAELLA AS THERE ARE REGIONS OF SPAIN. THOSE FROM NEAR THE COAST CONTAIN A LOT OF SEAFOOD, WHILE INLAND VERSIONS ADD CHICKEN OR PORK. HERE THE ONLY MEAT IS THE CHORIZO, ESSENTIAL FOR AN AUTHENTIC FLAVOUR.

SERVES FOUR

INGREDIENTS

  45ml/3 tbsp olive oil
  1 Spanish (Bermuda) onion, chopped
  2 fat garlic cloves, chopped
  150g/5oz chorizo sausage, sliced
  300g/11oz small squid, cleaned
  1 red (bell) pepper, cut into strips
  4 tomatoes, peeled, seeded and
    diced, or 200g/7oz can tomatoes
  500ml/17fl oz/generous 2 cups
    chicken stock
  105ml/7 tbsp dry white wine
  200g/7oz/1 cup short grain Spanish
    rice or risotto rice
  a large pinch of saffron threads
  150g/5oz/1 cup fresh or frozen peas
  12 large cooked prawns (shrimp), in
    the shell, or 8 langoustines
  450g/1lb fresh mussels, scrubbed
  450g/1lb medium clams, scrubbed
  salt and ground black pepper

1 Heat the olive oil in a paella pan or wok, add the onion and garlic and cook until translucent. Add the chorizo and cook until lightly golden.

2 If the squid are very small, leave them whole, otherwise cut the bodies into rings and the tentacles into pieces. Add the squid to the pan and sauté over a high heat for 2 minutes.

3 Stir in the pepper strips and tomatoes and simmer gently for 5 minutes, until the pepper strips are tender. Pour in the stock and white wine, stir well and bring to the boil.

4 Stir in the rice and saffron threads and season well with salt and pepper. Spread the contents of the pan evenly. Bring the liquid back to the boil, then lower the heat and simmer gently for about 10 minutes.

5 Add the peas, prawns or langoustines, mussels and clams, stirring them gently into the rice.

6 Cook the paella over a low heat for a further 15–20 minutes, until the rice is tender and all the mussels and clams have opened. If any remain closed, discard them. If the paella seems dry, add a little more hot chicken stock. Gently stir everything together and serve while piping hot.

Per portion: Energy 618Kcal/2600kJ; Protein 41.4g; Carbohydrate 63.8g, of which sugars 10.3g; Fat 21.9g, of which saturates 5.4g; Cholesterol 290mg; Calcium 179mg; Fibre 4.6g; Sodium 1117mg.

KEDGEREE

THIS CLASSIC DISH ORIGINATED IN INDIA. IT IS BEST MADE WITH BASMATI RICE, WHICH GOES WELL WITH THE MILD CURRY FLAVOUR, BUT LONG GRAIN RICE WILL DO. FOR A COLOURFUL GARNISH, ADD SOME FINELY SLICED RED ONION AND A LITTLE RED ONION MARMALADE.

SERVES FOUR

INGREDIENTS

  450g/1lb undyed smoked
    haddock fillet
  750ml/1¼ pints/3 cups milk
  2 bay leaves
  ½ lemon, sliced
  50g/2oz/¼ cup butter
  1 onion, chopped
  2.5ml/½ tsp ground turmeric
  5ml/1 tsp mild Madras curry powder
  2 green cardamom pods
  350g/12oz/1¾ cups basmati or long
    grain rice, washed and drained
  4 hard-boiled eggs (not *too* hard),
    coarsely chopped
  150ml/¼ pint/⅔ cup single (light)
    cream (optional)
  30ml/2 tbsp chopped fresh parsley
  salt and ground black pepper

1 Put the haddock in a shallow pan and add the milk, bay leaves and lemon slices. Poach gently for 8–10 minutes, until the haddock flakes easily when tested with the tip of a sharp knife. Strain the milk into a jug (pitcher), discarding the bay leaves and lemon slices. Remove the skin from the haddock and flake the flesh into large pieces. Keep hot until required.

2 Melt the butter in the pan, add the onion and cook over a low heat for about 3 minutes, until softened. Stir in the turmeric, the curry powder and cardamom pods and cook for 1 minute.

3 Add the rice, stirring to coat it well with the butter. Pour in the reserved milk, stir and bring to the boil. Lower the heat and simmer the rice for 10–12 minutes, until all the milk has been absorbed and the rice is tender. Season to taste, going easy on the salt.

4 Gently stir in the fish and hard-boiled eggs, with the cream, if using. Sprinkle with the parsley and serve.

VARIATION
Use smoked or poached fresh salmon for a delicious change from haddock.

Per portion: Energy 579Kcal/2421kJ; Protein 34.4g; Carbohydrate 71.1g, of which sugars 0.9g; Fat 17g, of which saturates 8.2g; Cholesterol 257mg; Calcium 76mg; Fibre 0.2g; Sodium 1001mg.

CHICKEN AND PRAWN JAMBALAYA

THE MIXTURE OF CHICKEN, SEAFOOD AND RICE SUGGESTS A CLOSE RELATIONSHIP TO THE SPANISH PAELLA, BUT THE CREOLE NAME IS MORE LIKELY TO HAVE DERIVED FROM JAMBON (THE FRENCH FOR HAM), AND À LA YA (CREOLE FOR RICE). JAMBALAYAS ARE A COLOURFUL MIXTURE OF HIGHLY FLAVOURED INGREDIENTS, AND ARE MADE IN LARGE QUANTITIES FOR FEASTS AND CELEBRATION MEALS.

SERVES TEN

INGREDIENTS

    2 chickens, each about 1.5kg/3–3½lb
    450g/1lb piece raw smoked gammon
      (cured ham)
    50g/2oz/4 tbsp lard or bacon fat
    50g/2oz/½ cup plain (all-
      purpose) flour
    3 onions, finely sliced
    2 green (bell) peppers, seeded
      and sliced
    675g/1½lb tomatoes, peeled
      and chopped
    2–3 garlic cloves, crushed
    10ml/2 tsp chopped fresh thyme
    24 large raw prawns (shrimp), peeled
      and deveined
    500g/1¼lb/3 cups white long grain rice
    2–3 dashes Tabasco sauce
    45ml/3 tbsp chopped fresh flat leaf
      parsley, plus sprigs, to garnish
    salt and ground black pepper

4 Add the diced gammon, onions, green peppers, tomatoes, garlic and thyme. Cook, stirring regularly, for 10 minutes, then add the prawns and mix lightly.

5 Stir the rice into the pan and pour in 1.2 litres/2 pints/5 cups water. Season to taste with salt, pepper and Tabasco sauce. Bring to the boil over a medium heat, then lower the heat, cover and cook gently until the rice is tender and all the liquid has been absorbed. Add a little extra boiling water if the rice looks as if it might be drying out before it is cooked.

6 Add the chopped flat leaf parsley and gently stir it into the finished dish, garnish with tiny sprigs of flat leaf parsley and serve immediately while piping hot.

1 Cut each chicken into 10 pieces and season with salt and pepper. Dice the gammon, discarding the rind and fat.

2 Melt the lard or bacon fat in a large, heavy frying pan. Add the chicken pieces, in batches, brown them all over, then lift them out with a slotted spoon and set them aside.

3 Reduce the heat. Sprinkle the flour into the fat in the pan and stir until the roux turns golden brown. Return the chicken pieces to the pan.

Per portion: Energy 748Kcal/3117kJ; Protein 54.9g; Carbohydrate 50.3g, of which sugars 5.5g; Fat 36.2g, of which saturates 10.8g; Cholesterol 262mg; Calcium 70mg; Fibre 2g; Sodium 588mg.

CARIBBEAN PEANUT CHICKEN

PEANUT BUTTER IS USED A LOT IN MANY CARIBBEAN DISHES. IT ADDS A RICHNESS TO THE DISH, AS WELL AS A DELICIOUS DEPTH OF FLAVOUR ALL OF ITS OWN.

SERVES FOUR

INGREDIENTS
    4 skinless, boneless chicken breast
      portions, cut into thin strips
    225g/8oz/generous 1 cup white long
      grain rice
    30ml/2 tbsp groundnut (peanut) oil
    15g/½oz/1 tbsp butter, plus extra
      for greasing
    1 onion, finely chopped
    2 tomatoes, peeled, seeded
      and chopped
    1 fresh green chilli, seeded
      and sliced
    60ml/4 tbsp smooth peanut butter
    450ml/¾ pint/scant 2 cups
      chicken stock
    lemon juice, to taste
    salt and ground black pepper
    lime wedges and fresh flat leaf
      parsley sprigs, to garnish
For the marinade
    15ml/1 tbsp sunflower oil
    1–2 garlic cloves, crushed
    5ml/1 tsp chopped fresh thyme
    25ml/1½ tbsp medium curry powder
    juice of half a lemon

1 Mix all the marinade ingredients in a large bowl and stir in the chicken. Cover loosely with clear film (plastic wrap) and set aside in a cool place for 2–3 hours.

2 Meanwhile, cook the rice in plenty of lightly salted, boiling water until tender. Drain well and turn into a generously buttered casserole.

3 Preheat the oven to 180°C/350°F/Gas 4. Heat 15ml/1 tbsp of the oil and butter in a flameproof casserole and cook the chicken pieces for 4–5 minutes, until evenly brown. Add more oil if necessary.

4 Transfer the chicken to a plate. Add the onion to the casserole and cook for 5–6 minutes until lightly browned. Stir in the tomatoes and chilli. Cook over a low heat for 3–4 minutes, stirring occasionally. Remove from the heat.

5 Mix the peanut butter with the chicken stock. Stir into the tomato and onion mixture, then add the chicken. Stir in the lemon juice, season to taste, then spoon the mixture over the rice in the casserole.

6 Cover the casserole, transfer it to the oven and cook for 15–20 minutes, or until piping hot. Use a large spoon to toss the rice with the chicken mixture. Serve immediately, garnished with the lime wedges and parsley sprigs.

COOK'S TIP
If the casserole is not large enough to let you toss the rice with the chicken mixture before serving, invert a large, deep plate over the casserole, turn both over and toss the mixture on the plate.

Per portion: Energy 606Kcal/2532kJ; Protein 46.4g; Carbohydrate 52.6g, of which sugars 5.3g; Fat 23.2g, of which saturates 6.6g; Cholesterol 113mg; Calcium 41mg; Fibre 2.3g; Sodium 202mg.

BURRITOS WITH CHICKEN AND RICE

IN MEXICO, BURRITOS ARE A POPULAR STREET FOOD, EATEN ON THE HOOF. THE SECRET OF A SUCCESSFUL BURRITO IS TO HAVE ALL THE FILLING NEATLY PACKAGED INSIDE THE TORTILLA FOR EASY EATING, SO THESE SNACKS ARE SELDOM SERVED WITH A POUR-OVER SAUCE.

SERVES FOUR

INGREDIENTS
    90g/3½oz/½ cup long grain rice
    15ml/1 tbsp vegetable oil
    1 onion, chopped
    2.5ml/½ tsp ground cloves
    5ml/1 tsp dried, or fresh oregano
    200g/7oz can chopped tomatoes
    2 skinless, boneless chicken
      breast portions
    150g/5oz/1¼ cups grated Monterey
      Jack or mild Cheddar cheese
    60ml/4 tbsp sour cream (optional)
    8 x 20–25cm/8–10in fresh wheat
      flour tortillas
    salt
    fresh oregano, to garnish (optional)

1 Bring a pan of lightly salted water to the boil. Add the rice, bring back to the boil and cook for 8 minutes. Drain, rinse and then drain again.

2 Heat the oil in a large pan. Add the onion, with the ground cloves and oregano, and cook, stirring occasionally, for 2–3 minutes. Stir in the rice and tomatoes, with their can juice, and cook over a low heat until all the tomato juice has been absorbed. Remove the pan from the heat and set aside.

VARIATION
For an extra touch of spice, you can add 3–4 canned or bottled jalapeño chillies to the filling, with the chicken, and substitute fresh coriander (cilantro) for the oregano. Rinse, seed and finely chopped the chillies first.

3 Put the chicken portions in a large pan, pour in enough water to cover and bring to the boil. Lower the heat and simmer for about 10 minutes, or until the chicken is cooked through. Lift the chicken out of the pan, put on a plate and leave to cool slightly.

4 Preheat the oven to 160°C/325°F/ Gas 3. Shred the chicken by pulling the flesh apart with two forks, then add the chicken to the rice mixture, with the grated cheese. Gently stir in the sour cream, if using.

COOK'S TIP
If you use very fresh tortillas, you may be able to dispense with the cocktail sticks. Secure the tortilla parcels by damping the final fold with a little water. When you lay the burritos in the dish, place them with the folded surfaces down.

5 Wrap the tortillas in foil and place them on a plate. Stand the plate over boiling water for about 5 minutes. Alternatively, wrap in microwave-safe film and heat in a microwave on full power for 1 minute.

6 Spoon one-eighth of the filling into the centre of a tortilla and fold in both sides. Fold the bottom up and the top down to form a parcel. Secure with a cocktail stick (toothpick).

7 Put the filled burrito in a shallow dish or casserole, cover with foil and keep warm in the oven while you make seven more. Remove the cocktail sticks before serving, sprinkled with fresh oregano.

Per portion: Energy 625Kcal/2628kJ; Protein 37.4g; Carbohydrate 82.2g, of which sugars 4.6g; Fat 17.1g, of which saturates 8.7g; Cholesterol 89mg; Calcium 411mg; Fibre 3.3g; Sodium 617mg.

BEEF BIRYANI

THE MOGULS INTRODUCED THIS DRY, SPICY RICE DISH TO CENTRAL INDIA.

SERVES FOUR

INGREDIENTS
2 large onions
2 garlic cloves, chopped
2.5cm/1in piece of fresh root ginger,
   peeled and coarsely chopped
½–1 fresh green chilli, seeded and
   coarsely chopped
bunch of fresh coriander (cilantro)
60ml/4 tbsp flaked (sliced) almonds
30–45ml/2–3 tbsp water
15ml/1 tbsp ghee or butter, plus
   25g/1oz/2 tbsp butter, for the rice
45ml/3 tbsp sunflower oil
30ml/2 tbsp sultanas (golden raisins)
500g/1¼lb braising or stewing
   steak, cubed
5ml/1 tsp ground coriander
15ml/1 tbsp ground cumin
2.5ml/½ tsp ground turmeric
2.5ml/½ tsp ground fenugreek
good pinch of ground cinnamon
175ml/6fl oz/¾ cup natural
   (plain) yogurt
275g/10oz/1½ cups basmati rice
about 1.2 litres/2 pints/5 cups hot
   chicken stock or water
salt and ground black pepper
2 hard-boiled eggs, quartered,
   to garnish

1 Coarsely chop 1 onion and place it in a food processor or blender. Add the garlic, ginger, chilli, fresh coriander and half the flaked almonds. Pour in the water and process to a smooth paste.

2 Thinly slice the remaining onion into rings or half rings. Heat half the ghee or butter with half the oil in a heavy, flameproof casserole and cook the onion rings over a medium heat for 10–15 minutes, until they are a deep golden brown. Transfer to a plate with a slotted spoon. Cook the remaining flaked almonds briefly until golden and set aside with the onion rings, then quickly cook the sultanas until they swell. Transfer to the plate.

3 Heat the remaining ghee or butter in the casserole with a further 15ml/1 tbsp of the oil. Cook the meat, in batches, until evenly browned. Transfer to a plate and set aside.

4 Wipe the casserole clean with kitchen paper, heat the remaining oil and pour in the onion and ginger paste. Cook over a medium heat, stirring constantly, for 2–3 minutes, until the mixture begins to brown lightly. Stir in the ground coriander, cumin, turmeric, fenugreek and cinnamon, season to taste with salt and pepper and cook for 1 minute more.

5 Lower the heat, then gradually stir in the yogurt, a little at a time. When all of it has been incorporated into the spice mixture, return the meat to the casserole. Stir to coat, cover tightly and simmer over a gentle heat for about 40–45 minutes, until the meat is tender.

6 Meanwhile, place the rice in a large bowl, pour in cold water to cover and leave to soak for 15–20 minutes.

7 Preheat the oven to 160°C/325°F/ Gas 3. Drain the rice, place it in a pan and add the hot chicken stock or water, together with a little salt. Bring back to the boil, cover, lower the heat and cook for 5–6 minutes.

8 Drain the rice and pile it in a mound on top of the meat in the casserole. Using the handle of a spoon, make a hole through the rice and meat mixture, to the base of the pan. Sprinkle the onion rings, almonds and sultanas over the top and dot with butter. Cover the casserole tightly with a double layer of foil and secure with a lid.

9 Cook the biryani in the oven for 30–40 minutes. To serve, spoon the mixture on to a warmed serving plate and garnish with the quartered hard-boiled eggs. Serve with parathas, naan bread or chapatis, if you like.

COOK'S TIP
When you are cooking the onion and ginger paste and the ground spices, reduce the heat to very low and stir constantly to avoid scorching them.

Per portion: Energy 778Kcal/3240kJ; Protein 40g; Carbohydrate 70.4g, of which sugars 13.4g; Fat 37.4g, of which saturates 11.8g; Cholesterol 94mg; Calcium 164mg; Fibre 2.3g; Sodium 183mg.

PASTA, GNOCCHI AND NOODLES

For sheer all-round popularity, pasta dishes top the bill. Pasta cooks quickly and looks as good as it tastes. It is easy to digest and gives slow-release energy. This chapter includes dishes suitable for vegetarians and vegans, as well as such classics as Clams with Neapolitan Tomato Sauce, which features vermicelli. Asian noodles are well represented, too. For a special treat, try Thai Crispy Noodles with Beef, or give your tastebuds a treat with Potato Gnocchi with Simple Tomato and Butter Sauce.

PASTA WITH GARLIC AND CHILLI

THIS IS THE SIMPLEST OF PASTA DISHES AND ONE OF THE BEST. MINT AND OREGANO GIVE VERY DIFFERENT RESULTS, BOTH GOOD. THERE IS NO NEED TO SERVE GRATED PARMESAN WITH THIS DISH — INSTEAD, LET THE CLEAR FLAVOUR OF THE GARLIC AND OLIVE OIL SING OUT.

SERVES THREE TO FOUR

INGREDIENTS
400g/14oz dried spaghetti
105ml/7 tbsp extra virgin olive oil,
  plus extra to taste
1.5ml/¼ tsp dried red chilli flakes or
  2 small whole dried red chillies
6 large garlic cloves, finely chopped
15ml/1 tbsp chopped fresh mint
  or oregano
15g/½ oz chopped fresh flat
  leaf parsley
salt and ground black pepper

1 Cook the spaghetti in lightly salted, boiling water for 9–11 minutes, or according to the packet instructions, until just tender.

2 Meanwhile, heat the oil in a large frying pan or pan over a very gentle heat. Add the chilli flakes or whole chillies and cook very gently for 2–3 minutes.

COOK'S TIP
If you use fresh spaghetti, cook for only 2–3 minutes in salted, boiling water.

3 Add the garlic to the pan. Keep the heat very low, so that the garlic barely bubbles and does not brown, then cook, shaking the pan occasionally, for about 2 minutes. Remove the pan from the heat and cool a little, then add the fresh mint or oregano.

4 Drain the pasta, then immediately add it to the oil and garlic mixture, with the parsley. Toss thoroughly. Season with freshly ground black pepper and transfer to warmed serving bowls. Serve immediately, offering more olive oil for drizzling at the table.

VARIATION
Cook 250g/9oz broccoli florets in salted, boiling water for 4 minutes. Add to the chilli oil and cook for 5–8 minutes.

Per portion: Energy 688Kcal/2897kJ; Protein 16.2g; Carbohydrate 98.9g, of which sugars 4.5g; Fat 28.1g, of which saturates 3.9g; Cholesterol 0mg; Calcium 43mg; Fibre 4.1g; Sodium 6mg.

RIGATONI WITH TOMATOES AND FRESH HERBS

THIS PRETTY AND COLOURFUL PASTA DISH RELIES FOR ITS SUCCESS ON THE BEST ITALIAN CANNED TOMATOES AND TENDER YOUNG HERBS, FRESHLY PICKED. FOR A REAL TREAT, USE FRESH TOMATOES, PEELED AND PURÉED. ADD A LITTLE SUGAR IF THE TOMATOES ARE NOT AT THE PEAK OF RIPENESS.

SERVES SIX TO EIGHT

INGREDIENTS
1 onion
1 carrot
1 celery stick
60ml/4 tbsp olive oil
1 garlic clove, thinly sliced
a few leaves each of fresh basil,
  thyme and oregano or marjoram
2 x 400g/14oz cans chopped Italian
  plum tomatoes
15ml/1 tbsp sun-dried tomato paste
5ml/1 tsp granulated sugar
about 90ml/6 tbsp dry red or white
  wine (optional)
350g/12oz/3 cups dried rigatoni
salt and ground black pepper
coarsely shaved Parmesan cheese,
  to serve

COOK'S TIP
Large pasta tubes are best for this recipe, as they capture the wonderful tomato and herb sauce. If you can't get rigatoni, try penne or penne rigate (ridged penne).

1 Chop the onion, carrot and celery stick finely, either in a food processor or by hand, with a sharp knife.

2 Heat the olive oil in a medium pan, add the garlic slices and stir over a very low heat for 1–2 minutes. Do not let the garlic burn or it will taste bitter.

3 Add the chopped vegetables and the fresh herbs, reserving a few to garnish. Cook over a low heat, stirring frequently, for 5–7 minutes, until the vegetables have softened and are lightly coloured.

4 Add the canned tomatoes, tomato paste and sugar, then stir in the wine, if using. Add salt and pepper to taste. Bring to the boil, stirring, then lower the heat to a gentle simmer. Cook, stirring frequently, for about 45 minutes.

5 Cook the pasta in lightly salted, boiling water for 10–12 minutes, drain and tip into a warmed bowl. Pour the sauce over the pasta and toss well. Garnish with the reserved herbs. Serve immediately, with shavings of Parmesan handed separately.

Per portion: Energy 313Kcal/1323kJ; Protein 8.8g; Carbohydrate 51g, of which sugars 8.8g; Fat 8.6g, of which saturates 1.2g; Cholesterol 0mg; Calcium 43mg; Fibre 3.3g; Sodium 62mg.

CLAMS WITH NEAPOLITAN TOMATO SAUCE

THIS RECIPE TAKES ITS NAME FROM THE CITY OF NAPLES, WHERE BOTH FRESH TOMATO SAUCE AND SHELLFISH ARE TRADITIONALLY SERVED WITH VERMICELLI. HERE THE TWO ARE COMBINED TO MAKE A VERY TASTY DISH THAT IS PERFECT FOR A COLD WINTER'S EVENING.

SERVES FOUR

INGREDIENTS
  1kg/2¼lb fresh clams
  250ml/8fl oz/1 cup dry white wine,
    or vegetable stock
  2 garlic cloves, bruised
  1 large handful fresh flat leaf parsley
  30ml/2 tbsp extra virgin olive oil or
    sunflower oil
  1 small onion, finely chopped
  8 ripe plum tomatoes, peeled, seeded
    and finely chopped
  ½–1 fresh red chilli, seeded and
    finely chopped
  350g/12oz dried vermicelli
  salt and ground black pepper

1 Scrub the clams thoroughly with a brush under cold running water and discard any that are open or do not close their shells when sharply tapped against the work surface.

2 Pour the white wine or vegetable stock into a large, heavy pan and add the bruised garlic cloves. Shred half the parsley finely, add to the wine or stock, then add the clams.

3 Cover the pan tightly with the lid and bring to the boil over a high heat. Cook for about 5 minutes, shaking the pan frequently, until the clams have opened.

4 Tip the clams into a large colander set over a bowl and let the liquid drain through. Leave the clams until cool enough to handle, then remove about two-thirds of them from their shells, tipping the clam liquor into the bowl of cooking liquid. Discard any clams that have failed to open.

5 Set both shelled and unshelled clams aside, keeping the unshelled clams warm in a bowl covered with a lid or thick cloth.

6 Heat the oil in a pan, add the onion and cook gently, stirring frequently, for about 5 minutes, until softened and lightly coloured. Add the tomatoes, then strain in the clam cooking liquid. Add the chilli, and salt and pepper to taste.

7 Bring to the boil, half cover the pan and simmer gently for 15–20 minutes. Meanwhile, cook the pasta according to the packet instructions. Chop the remaining parsley finely.

8 Add the shelled clams to the tomato sauce, stir well and heat through very gently for 2–3 minutes.

9 Drain the cooked pasta well and tip it into a warmed bowl. Taste the sauce for seasoning, then pour the sauce over the pasta and toss everything together well. Garnish with the reserved clams, sprinkle the parsley over the pasta and serve immediately.

Per portion: Energy 500Kcal/2091kJ; Protein 21.6g; Carbohydrate 77.3g, of which sugars 6.9g; Fat 7.1g, of which saturates 1.1g; Cholesterol 50mg; Calcium 134mg; Fibre 2.9g; Sodium 932mg.

PASTA WITH TOMATOES AND SHELLFISH

COLOURFUL AND DELICIOUS, THIS TYPICAL GENOESE DISH IS IDEAL FOR A DINNER PARTY. THE TOMATO SAUCE IS QUITE RUNNY, SO SERVE IT WITH CRUSTY BREAD AND SPOONS AS WELL AS FORKS. FOR A REAL TASTE OF ITALY, CHOOSE A DRY WHITE ITALIAN WINE TO SERVE WITH THE MEAL.

SERVES FOUR

INGREDIENTS
   45ml/3 tbsp olive oil
   1 small onion, chopped
   1 garlic clove, crushed
   ½ fresh red chilli, seeded
     and chopped
   200g/7oz can chopped
     plum tomatoes
   30ml/2 tbsp chopped fresh flat
     leaf parsley
   400g/14oz fresh clams
   400g/14oz fresh mussels
   60ml/4 tbsp dry white wine
   400g/14oz/3½ cups dried trenette
     or spaghetti
   a few fresh basil leaves
   90g/3½oz/⅔ cup cooked, peeled
     prawns (shrimp), thawed and
     thoroughly dried if frozen
   salt and ground black pepper
   lemon wedges and chopped fresh herbs,
     such as parsley or thyme, to garnish

1 Heat 30ml/2tbsp of the oil in a frying pan or medium pan. Add the onion, garlic and chilli and cook over a medium heat for 1–2 minutes, stirring constantly. Stir in the tomatoes, half the parsley and pepper to taste. Bring to the boil, lower the heat, cover and simmer for 15 minutes.

2 Meanwhile, scrub the clams and mussels under cold running water. Discard any that are open and that do not close when sharply tapped against the work surface.

3 In a large pan, heat the remaining oil. Add the clams and mussels, with the rest of the parsley and toss over a high heat for a few seconds. Pour in the wine, then cover tightly. Cook for about 5 minutes, shaking the pan frequently, until the clams and mussels have opened.

4 Transfer the clams and mussels to a bowl, discarding any shellfish that have failed to open. Strain the cooking liquid and set aside. Reserve eight clams and four mussels for the garnish, then remove the rest from their shells.

5 Cook the pasta according to the instructions on the packet. Meanwhile, add 120ml/4fl oz/ ½ cup of the reserved shellfish liquid to the tomato sauce. Add the basil, prawns, shelled clams and mussels to the sauce. Season.

6 Drain the pasta and tip it into a warmed bowl. Add the sauce and toss well to combine. Serve in individual bowls. Sprinkle with herbs and garnish each portion with lemon, two clams and one mussel in their shells.

Per portion: Energy 510Kcal/2160kJ; Protein 27.2g; Carbohydrate 77.1g, of which sugars 5.6g; Fat 11.5g, of which saturates 1.6g; Cholesterol 68mg; Calcium 180mg; Fibre 3.5g; Sodium 193mg.

LOBSTER RAVIOLI

IT IS ESSENTIAL TO USE HOME-MADE PASTA TO OBTAIN THE DELICACY AND THINNESS THAT THIS SUPERB FILLING DESERVES. BEFORE YOU START THE RECIPE, MAKE A WELL-FLAVOURED FISH STOCK, USING THE LOBSTER SHELL AND HEAD.

SERVES FOUR

INGREDIENTS
   1 lobster, about 450g/1lb, cooked
      and taken out of the shell
   2 soft white bread slices, about
      50g/2oz, crusts removed
   200ml/7fl oz/scant 1 cup fish stock
   1 egg
   250ml/8fl oz/1 cup double
      (heavy) cream
   15ml/1 tbsp chopped fresh chives,
      plus extra to garnish
   15ml/1 tbsp finely chopped
      fresh chervil
   salt and ground white pepper
   fresh chives, to garnish
For the pasta dough
   225g/8oz/2 cups strong plain (all-
      purpose) flour
   2 eggs, plus 2 egg yolks
For the mushroom sauce
   a large pinch of saffron threads
   25g/1oz/2 tbsp butter
   2 shallots, finely chopped
   200g/7oz/3 cups button (white)
      mushrooms, finely chopped
   juice of ½ lemon
   200ml/7fl oz/scant 1 cup
      double (heavy) cream

1 Make the pasta dough. Sift the flour with a pinch of salt. Put into a food processor with the eggs and yolks and process until the mixture resembles breadcrumbs. Turn out on to a floured surface; knead to a smooth dough. Wrap in clear film (plastic wrap) and leave to rest in the refrigerator for 1 hour.

2 Meanwhile, make the lobster filling. Cut the lobster meat into large chunks and place in a bowl. Tear the white bread into small pieces and soak them in 45ml/3 tbsp of the fish stock. Place in a food processor with half the egg and 30–45ml/2–3 tbsp of the double cream and process until smooth. Stir the mixture into the lobster meat, then add the chives and chervil and season to taste with salt and white pepper.

3 Roll the ravioli dough to a thickness of 3mm/⅛in, preferably using a pasta machine. The process can be done by hand with a rolling pin but is quite hard work. Divide the dough into four rectangles and dust each rectangle lightly with flour.

4 Spoon six equal heaps of filling on to one sheet of pasta, leaving about 3cm/1¼in between each pile of filling. Lightly beat the remaining egg with a tablespoon of water and brush it over the pasta between the piles of filling. Cover with a second sheet of pasta. Repeat with the other two sheets of pasta and remaining filling.

5 Using your fingertips, press the top layer of dough down well between the piles of filling, making sure each is well sealed. Cut between the heaps with a 7.5cm/3in fluted pastry cutter or a pasta wheel to make twelve ravioli.

6 Place the ravioli in a single layer on a baking sheet, cover with clear film or a damp cloth, and put in the refrigerator while you make the sauces.

7 Make the mushroom sauce. Soak the saffron in 15ml/1 tbsp warm water. Melt the butter in a pan and cook the shallots over a low heat until they are soft but not coloured.

8 Add the chopped mushrooms and lemon juice and continue to cook over a low heat until almost all the liquid has evaporated. Stir in the saffron, with its soaking water, and the cream, then cook gently, stirring occasionally, until the sauce has thickened. Keep warm while you cook the ravioli.

9 In another pan, bring the remaining fish stock to the boil, stir in the rest of the cream and bubble to make a slightly thickened sauce. Season to taste with salt and pepper and keep warm. Bring a large pan of lightly salted water to a rolling boil. Gently drop in the ravioli (left) and cook for 3–4 minutes, until the pasta is just tender.

10 Place three ravioli on to the centre of each of four individual warmed plates, spoon over a little of the mushroom sauce and pour a ribbon of fish sauce around the edge. Serve immediately, garnished with chopped and whole fresh chives.

SEAFOOD LASAGNE

THIS DISH CAN BE AS SIMPLE OR AS ELEGANT AS YOU LIKE. FOR A DINNER PARTY, DRESS IT UP WITH SCALLOPS, MUSSELS OR PRAWNS AND A REALLY GENEROUS PINCH OF SAFFRON IN THE SAUCE; FOR A FAMILY SUPPER, USE SIMPLE FISH, SUCH AS COD AND SMOKED HADDOCK. THE LASAGNE CAN BE PREPARED IN ADVANCE AND BAKED AT THE LAST MOMENT.

SERVES EIGHT

INGREDIENTS
- 350g/12oz monkfish
- 350g/12oz salmon fillet
- 350g/12oz undyed smoked haddock
- 1 litre/1¾ pints/4 cups milk
- 500ml/17fl oz/generous 2 cups fish stock
- 2 bay leaves or a good pinch of saffron threads
- 1 small onion, peeled and halved
- 75g/3oz/6 tbsp butter, plus extra for greasing
- 45ml/3 tbsp plain (all-purpose) flour
- 150g/5oz/2 cups mushrooms, sliced
- 225–300g/8–11oz no-precook or fresh lasagne
- 60ml/4 tbsp freshly grated Parmesan cheese
- salt, ground black pepper, grated nutmeg and paprika
- rocket (arugula) leaves, to garnish

For the tomato sauce
- 30ml/2 tbsp olive oil
- 1 red onion, finely chopped
- 1 garlic clove, finely chopped
- 400g/14oz can chopped tomatoes
- 15ml/1 tbsp tomato purée (paste)
- 15ml/1 tbsp torn fresh basil leaves

1 Make the tomato sauce. Heat the oil in a pan and cook the onion and garlic over a low heat for 5 minutes, until softened and golden. Stir in the tomatoes and tomato purée and simmer for 20–30 minutes, stirring occasionally. Season to taste with salt and pepper and stir in the basil.

COOK'S TIP
It is preferable to use fresh lasagne, if available, as it has a better flavour and texture. Cook the sheets, in batches if necessary, in a large pan of lightly salted, boiling water for 3 minutes. Do not overcrowd the pan or the sheets will stick together.

2 Put all the fish in a shallow flameproof dish or pan with the milk, stock, bay leaves or saffron and onion. Bring to the boil over a medium heat. Poach for 5 minutes, until almost cooked. Leave to cool.

3 When the fish is almost cold, strain it, reserving the liquid. Remove the skin and any bones and flake the flesh.

4 Preheat the oven to 180°C/350°F/ Gas 4. Melt the butter in a pan, stir in the flour; cook for 2 minutes, stirring. Gradually add the poaching liquid and bring to the boil, stirring. Add the mushrooms, cook for 2–3 minutes; season with salt, pepper and nutmeg.

5 Lightly grease a shallow ovenproof dish. Spoon a thin layer of the mushroom sauce over the base of the dish and spread it with a spatula. Stir the fish into the remaining mushroom sauce in the pan.

6 Make a layer of lasagne, then a layer of fish and sauce. Add another layer of lasagne, then spread over all the tomato sauce. Continue to layer the lasagne and fish, finish with a layer of lasagne.

7 Sprinkle over the grated Parmesan cheese. Bake for 30–45 minutes, until bubbling and golden. Before serving, sprinkle with paprika and garnish with rocket leaves.

Per portion: Energy 411Kcal/1724kJ; Protein 32.2g; Carbohydrate 29.8g, of which sugars 3.6g; Fat 18.9g, of which saturates 7.8g; Cholesterol 71mg; Calcium 143mg; Fibre 1.9g; Sodium 525mg.

SPAGHETTI <u>WITH</u> EGGS, BACON <u>AND</u> CREAM

*THIS ITALIAN CLASSIC, FLAVOURED WITH PANCETTA AND A GARLIC AND EGG SAUCE THAT COOKS
AROUND THE HOT SPAGHETTI, IS POPULAR WORLDWIDE. IT MAKES A GREAT LAST-MINUTE SUPPER.*

3 Meanwhile, cook the spaghetti in a large pan of salted, boiling water according to the instructions on the packet until *al dente*.

4 Put the eggs, crème fraîche and grated Parmesan in a bowl. Stir in plenty of black pepper, then beat together well.

5 Drain the pasta thoroughly, tip it into the pan with the pancetta or bacon and toss well to mix.

6 Turn off the heat under the pan, then immediately add the egg mixture and toss thoroughly so that it cooks lightly and coats the pasta.

7 Season to taste, then divide the spaghetti among four warmed bowls and sprinkle with freshly ground black pepper. Serve immediately, with extra grated Parmesan handed separately.

SERVES FOUR

INGREDIENTS
30ml/2 tbsp olive oil
1 small onion, finely chopped
1 large garlic clove, crushed
8 pancetta or rindless smoked
streaky (fatty) bacon rashers
(strips), cut into 1cm/½in strips
350g/12oz fresh or dried spaghetti
4 eggs
90–120ml/6–8 tbsp/½ cup
crème fraîche
60ml/4 tbsp freshly grated
Parmesan cheese, plus extra
to serve
salt and ground black pepper

1 Heat the oil in a large pan, add the onion and garlic and cook gently for about 5 minutes, until softened.

2 Add the pancetta or bacon to the pan and cook for 10 minutes, stirring.

COOK'S TIP
You can replace the crème fraîche with either double (heavy) cream or sour cream, if you like.

Per portion: Energy 686Kcal/2873kJ; Protein 31.1g; Carbohydrate 66.6g, of which sugars 4.2g; Fat 34.5g, of which saturates 14.8g; Cholesterol 213mg; Calcium 243mg; Fibre 2.8g; Sodium 1098mg.

TURKEY LASAGNE

THIS EASY MEAL-IN-ONE BAKED PASTA DISH IS DELICIOUS MADE WITH COOKED TURKEY PIECES AND BROCCOLI IN A RICH, CREAMY PARMESAN SAUCE.

SERVES FOUR

INGREDIENTS

   30ml/2 tbsp light olive oil
   1 onion, chopped
   2 garlic cloves, chopped
   450g/1lb cooked turkey meat,
    finely diced
   225g/8oz/1 cup mascarpone cheese
   30ml/2 tbsp chopped fresh tarragon
   300g/11oz broccoli, broken
    into florets
   salt and ground black pepper
For the sauce
   50g/2oz/¼ cup butter
   30ml/2 tbsp plain (all-purpose) flour
   600ml/1 pint/2½ cups milk
   75g/3oz/1 cup freshly grated
    Parmesan cheese
   115g/4oz no pre-cook lasagne verdi

3 To make the sauce, melt the butter in a pan, stir in the flour and cook for 1 minute, still stirring. Remove from the heat and gradually stir in the milk. Return to the heat and bring the sauce to the boil, stirring constantly. Simmer for 1 minute, then add 50g/2oz/⅔ cup of the Parmesan and plenty of salt and pepper.

4 Spoon a layer of the turkey mixture into a large, shallow ovenproof dish. Add a layer of broccoli and cover with sheets of lasagne. Coat with cheese sauce. Repeat these layers, finishing with a layer of cheese sauce on top. Sprinkle with the remaining Parmesan and bake for 35–40 minutes.

1 Preheat the oven to 180°C/350°F/ Gas 4. Heat the oil in a heavy pan and cook the onion and garlic until softened but not coloured. Remove the pan from the heat and stir in the diced turkey, mascarpone and tarragon and season with salt and pepper to taste.

2 Blanch the broccoli in a large pan of salted, boiling water for 1 minute, then drain and rinse thoroughly under cold water to prevent the broccoli from overcooking. Drain well and set aside.

COOK'S TIP
This is a delicious way of using up any cooked turkey that is left over after Christmas or Thanksgiving celebrations. It is also especially good made with half ham and half turkey.

Per portion: Energy 732Kcal/3072kJ; Protein 61.6g; Carbohydrate 43g, of which sugars 13.1g; Fat 36.2g, of which saturates 19.4g; Cholesterol 138mg; Calcium 539mg; Fibre 3.6g; Sodium 475mg.

POTATO GNOCCHI

GNOCCHI CAN BE MADE EITHER WITH MASHED POTATO AND FLOUR, OR WITH SEMOLINA. TO MAKE SURE THAT THEY ARE LIGHT AND FLUFFY, TAKE CARE NOT TO OVERMIX THE DOUGH.

4 Divide the dough into four pieces. On a lightly floured surface, form each into a roll about 2cm/¾in in diameter. Cut the rolls crossways into pieces about 2cm/¾in long.

5 Hold an ordinary table fork with tines sideways, leaning on the board. Then one by one, press and roll the gnocchi lightly along the tines of the fork towards the points, making ridges on one side, and a depression from your thumb on the other.

SERVES FOUR TO SIX

INGREDIENTS
  1kg/2¼lb waxy potatoes
  250–300g/9–11oz/2¼–2¾ cups
    plain flour (all-purpose), plus more
    if necessary
  1 egg
  pinch of freshly grated nutmeg
  25g/1oz/2 tbsp butter
  salt
  fresh basil leaves, to garnish
  Parmesan cheese cut in shavings,
    to garnish

COOK'S TIP
Gnocchi are also excellent served with a heated sauce, such as Bolognese or a simple cheese sauce.

1 Cook the potatoes in their skins in a large pan of lightly salted, boiling water until tender but not falling apart. Drain and peel while the potatoes are still hot.

2 Spread a layer of flour on a work surface. Pass the hot potatoes through a food mill, dropping them directly on to the flour. Sprinkle with about half of the remaining flour and mix in very lightly. Break the egg into the mixture.

3 Finally, add the nutmeg to the dough and knead lightly, adding more flour if the mixture is too loose. When the dough is light to the touch and no longer moist, it is ready to be rolled.

6 Bring a large pan of salted water to a fast boil, then drop in about half the prepared gnocchi.

7 When the gnocchi rise to the surface, after 3–4 minutes, they are done. Lift them out with a slotted spoon, drain well, and place in a warmed serving bowl. Dot with butter. Cover to keep warm while cooking the remainder. As soon as they are cooked, toss the gnocchi with the butter, garnish with Parmesan shavings and fresh basil leaves, and serve immediately.

Per portion: Energy 454Kcal/1921kJ; Protein 11.7g; Carbohydrate 88.9g, of which sugars 4.2g; Fat 8.1g, of which saturates 4g; Cholesterol 61mg; Calcium 111mg; Fibre 4.5g; Sodium 85mg.

POTATO GNOCCHI WITH SIMPLE TOMATO AND BUTTER SAUCE

GNOCCHI MAKE A SUBSTANTIAL AND TASTY ALTERNATIVE TO PASTA. IN THIS DISH THEY ARE SERVED WITH A VERY SIMPLE, BUT DELICIOUS, FRESH TOMATO SAUCE.

SERVES FOUR

INGREDIENTS
  675g/1½lb floury potatoes
  2 egg yolks
  75g/3oz/¾ cup plain (all-purpose) flour
  60ml/4 tbsp finely chopped fresh
    parsley, to garnish
For the sauce
  25g/1oz/2 tbsp butter, melted
  450g/1lb plum tomatoes, peeled,
    seeded and chopped
  salt

1 Preheat the oven to 200°C/400°F/ Gas 6. Scrub the potatoes, then bake them in their skins in the oven for 1 hour, or until the flesh feels soft when pricked with a fork.

2 While the potatoes are still warm, cut them in half and gently squeeze the flesh into a bowl, or use a spoon to scrape the flesh out of the shells. Mash the potato well, then season with a little salt. Add the egg yolks and mix lightly with a fork or spoon.

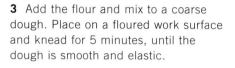

3 Add the flour and mix to a coarse dough. Place on a floured work surface and knead for 5 minutes, until the dough is smooth and elastic.

4 Shape the dough into thumb-sized shapes by making long rolls and cutting them into segments. Press each of these with the back of a fork. Place the gnocchi on a floured work surface.

5 Preheat the oven to 140°C/275°F/ Gas 1. Cook the gnocchi, in small batches, in barely simmering, slightly salted water for about 10 minutes. Remove with a slotted spoon, drain well and tip into a dish. Cover and keep hot in the oven.

6 To make the sauce, heat the butter in a small pan for 1 minute, then add the tomatoes and cook over a low heat until the juice starts to run. Sprinkle the gnocchi with chopped parsley and serve with the sauce.

Per portion: Energy 278Kcal/1174kJ; Protein 6.9g; Carbohydrate 45.3g, of which sugars 6g; Fat 9g, of which saturates 4.4g; Cholesterol 114mg; Calcium 57mg; Fibre 3.4g; Sodium 72mg.

INDIAN MEE GORENG

THIS IS A TRULY INTERNATIONAL DISH COMBINING INDIAN, CHINESE AND WESTERN INGREDIENTS. IT IS A DELICIOUS TREAT FOR LUNCH OR SUPPER AND IN SINGAPORE AND MALAYSIA CAN BE BOUGHT IN MANY STREETS FROM ONE OF THE NUMEROUS HAWKERS' STALLS.

2 If using fried tofu, cut each cube in half, refresh it in a pan of boiling water, then drain well. Heat 30ml/2 tbsp of the oil in a large frying pan. If using plain tofu, cut it into cubes and cook until brown, then lift it out with a slotted spoon and set aside.

3 Beat the eggs with the water and seasoning. Add to the oil in the frying pan and cook without stirring until set. Flip over, cook the other side, then slide it out of the pan, roll up and slice thinly.

4 Heat the remaining oil in a wok and cook the onion and garlic for 2–3 minutes. Add the drained noodles, soy sauce, ketchup and chilli sauce. Toss well over medium heat for 2 minutes, then add the diced potato. Reserve a few spring onions for garnish and stir the rest into the noodles with the chilli, if using, and the tofu.

5 When hot, stir in the omelette. Serve on a hot platter, garnished with the remaining spring onion.

SERVES FOUR TO SIX

INGREDIENTS
    450g/1lb fresh yellow egg noodles
    60–90ml/4–6 tbsp vegetable oil
    115g/4oz fried tofu or 150g/5oz
      firm tofu
    2 eggs
    30ml/2 tbsp water
    1 onion, sliced
    1 garlic clove, crushed
    15ml/1 tbsp light soy sauce
    30–45ml/2–3 tbsp tomato ketchup
    15ml/1 tbsp chilli sauce (or to taste)
    1 large cooked potato, diced
    4 spring onions (scallions), shredded
    1–2 fresh green chillies, seeded
      and thinly sliced (optional)

1 Bring a large pan of water to the boil, add the fresh egg noodles and cook for just 2 minutes. Drain the noodles and immediately rinse them under cold water to halt cooking. Drain again and set aside.

Per portion: Energy 662Kcal/2788kJ; Protein 20.7g; Carbohydrate 95.8g, of which sugars 8.8g; Fat 24.5g, of which saturates 4.9g; Cholesterol 129mg; Calcium 210mg; Fibre 4.5g; Sodium 715mg.

SICHUAN NOODLES WITH SESAME SAUCE

THIS TASTY CHINESE VEGETARIAN DISH RESEMBLES THAMIN LETHOK, A BURMESE DISH, WHICH ALSO CONSISTS OF FLAVOURED NOODLES SERVED WITH SEPARATE VEGETABLES THAT ARE TOSSED AT THE TABLE. THIS ILLUSTRATES NEATLY HOW RECIPES MIGRATE FROM ONE COUNTRY TO ANOTHER.

SERVES THREE TO FOUR

INGREDIENTS

450g/1lb fresh or 225g/8oz dried
   egg noodles
1/2 cucumber, sliced lengthways,
   seeded and diced
4–6 spring onions (scallions)
a bunch of radishes, about 115g/4oz
225g/8oz mooli (daikon), peeled
115g/4oz/2 cups beansprouts, rinsed
   then left in iced water and drained
60ml/4 tbsp groundnut (peanut) oil
   or sunflower oil
2 garlic cloves, crushed
45ml/3 tbsp toasted sesame paste
15ml/1 tbsp sesame oil
15ml/1 tbsp light soy sauce
5–10ml/1–2 tsp chilli sauce, to taste
15ml/1 tbsp rice vinegar
120ml/4fl oz/1/2 cup chicken stock
   or water
5ml/1 tsp sugar, or to taste
salt and ground black pepper
roasted peanuts or cashew nuts,
   to garnish

1 If using fresh noodles, cook them in boiling water for 1 minute, then drain well. Rinse the noodles in fresh water and drain again. Cook dried noodles according to the instructions on the packet, draining and rinsing them as for fresh noodles.

2 Sprinkle the cucumber with salt, leave for 15 minutes, rinse well, then drain and pat dry on kitchen paper. Place in a large salad bowl.

3 Cut the spring onions into fine shreds. Cut the radishes in half and slice finely. Coarsely grate the mooli using a mandolin or a food processor. Add all the vegetables to the cucumber and toss gently.

4 Heat half the oil in a wok or frying pan and stir-fry the noodles for about 1 minute. Using a slotted spoon, transfer the noodles to a large serving bowl and keep warm.

5 Add the remaining oil to the wok. When it is hot, cook the garlic to flavour the oil. Remove from the heat and stir in the sesame paste, with the sesame oil, soy and chilli sauces, vinegar and stock or water. Add a little sugar and season to taste. Warm through over a gentle heat. Do not overheat or the sauce will thicken too much. Pour the sauce over the noodles and toss well. Garnish with peanuts or cashew nuts and serve with the vegetables.

Per portion: Energy 383Kcal/1592kJ; Protein 8.7g; Carbohydrate 24.9g, of which sugars 4.8g; Fat 28.3g, of which saturates 3.9g; Cholesterol 9mg; Calcium 153mg; Fibre 4.2g; Sodium 398mg.

FIVE-FLAVOUR NOODLES

THE JAPANESE NAME FOR THIS DISH IS GOMOKU YAKISOBA, *MEANING FIVE DIFFERENT INGREDIENTS; HOWEVER, YOU CAN ADD AS MANY DIFFERENT INGREDIENTS AS YOU WISH TO MAKE AN EXCITING AND TASTY NOODLE STIR-FRY.*

SERVES FOUR

INGREDIENTS

300g/11oz dried Chinese thin egg
   noodles or 500g/1¼lb fresh yakisoba noodles
200g/7oz lean boneless pork,
   thinly sliced
22.5ml/4½ tsp sunflower oil
10g/¼oz grated fresh root ginger
1 garlic clove, crushed
200g/7oz green cabbage,
   coarsely chopped
115g/4oz/2 cups beansprouts
1 green (bell) pepper, seeded and cut
   into fine strips
1 red (bell) pepper, seeded and cut
   into fine strips
salt and ground black pepper
20ml/4 tsp ao-nori seaweed, to
   garnish (optional)

For the seasoning mix
60ml/4 tbsp Worcestershire sauce
15ml/1 tbsp Japanese soy sauce
15ml/1 tbsp oyster sauce
15ml/1 tbsp sugar
2.5ml/½ tsp salt
ground white pepper

1 Cook the noodles according to the instructions on the packet. Drain well and set aside.

2 Cut the pork into 3–4cm/1¼–1½in strips and season with salt and pepper.

3 Heat 7.5ml/1½ tsp of the oil in a large wok or frying pan. Add the pork and stir-fry until it is just cooked, then remove it from the pan.

4 Wipe the wok with kitchen paper, and heat the remaining oil in it. Add the ginger, garlic and cabbage and stir-fry for 1 minute.

5 Add the beansprouts, stir until softened, then add the green and red peppers and stir-fry for 1 minute more.

6 Return the pork to the pan and add the noodles. Stir in all the ingredients for the seasoning mix and stir-fry for 2–3 minutes. Serve immediately, sprinkled with ao-nori seaweed, if using.

Per portion: Energy 437Kcal/1848kJ; Protein 22.7g; Carbohydrate 65.6g, of which sugars 12.4g; Fat 11.2g, of which saturates 2.8g; Cholesterol 54mg; Calcium 64mg; Fibre 5.1g; Sodium 686mg.

RICE NOODLES WITH PORK

ALTHOUGH RICE NOODLES HAVE LITTLE FLAVOUR THEMSELVES, THEY HAVE A WONDERFUL ABILITY TO TAKE ON THE FLAVOUR OF OTHER INGREDIENTS.

SERVES FOUR TO SIX

INGREDIENTS
   450g/1lb pork fillet (tenderloin)
   225g/8oz dried rice noodles
   115g/4oz/1 cup broccoli florets
   1 red (bell) pepper, quartered
      and seeded
   45ml/3 tbsp groundnut (peanut) oil
   2 garlic cloves, crushed
   10 spring onions (scallions), cut into
      5cm/2in diagonal slices
   1 lemon grass stalk, finely chopped
   1–2 fresh red chillies, seeded and
      finely chopped
   300ml/½ pint/1¼ cups coconut milk
   15ml/1 tbsp tomato purée (paste)
   3 kaffir lime leaves (optional)
For the marinade
   45ml/3 tbsp light soy sauce
   15ml/1 tbsp rice wine
   30ml/2 tbsp groundnut (peanut) oil
   2.5cm/1in piece of fresh root ginger

1 Cut the pork into strips 2.5cm/1in long and 1cm/½in wide. Mix all the marinade ingredients in a bowl, add the pork, stir and marinate for 1 hour.

2 Spread out the rice noodles in a large, shallow dish, pour over enough hot water to cover and leave to soak for 20 minutes, until soft. Drain well and set aside.

3 Meanwhile, blanch the broccoli florets in a small pan of boiling water for 2 minutes, then drain, refresh under cold water and drain well again. Set aside until required.

4 Place the pepper pieces under a hot grill (broiler) for a few minutes until the skin blackens and blisters. Put in a plastic bag for about 10 minutes and then, when cool enough to handle, peel off the skin and slice the flesh thinly.

5 Drain the pork, reserving the marinade. Heat 30ml/2 tbsp of the oil in a large frying pan. Stir-fry the pork, in batches if necessary, for about 3–4 minutes, until the meat is tender. Transfer to a plate and keep warm.

6 Add a little more oil to the pan if necessary and stir-fry the garlic, spring onions, lemon grass and chillies over a low to medium heat for 2–3 minutes. Add the broccoli and pepper slices and stir-fry for a few minutes more.

7 Stir in the reserved marinade, coconut milk and tomato purée, with the kaffir lime leaves, if using. Simmer gently until the broccoli is nearly tender, then add the pork and noodles. Toss over the heat for 3–4 minutes until completely heated through. Transfer to a warm dish and serve immediately.

Per portion: Energy 454Kcal/1901kJ; Protein 30.1g; Carbohydrate 53.2g, of which sugars 7.1g; Fat 12.8g, of which saturates 3.2g; Cholesterol 70mg; Calcium 57mg; Fibre 1.5g; Sodium 428mg.

CANTONESE FRIED NOODLES

CHOW MEIN IS HUGELY POPULAR WITH THE THRIFTY CHINESE WHO BELIEVE IN TURNING LEFTOVERS INTO TASTY DISHES. FOR THIS DELICIOUS DISH, BOILED NOODLES ARE FRIED TO FORM A CRISPY CRUST, WHICH IS TOPPED WITH A SAVOURY SAUCE CONTAINING WHATEVER TASTES GOOD AND NEEDS EATING UP.

SERVES TWO TO THREE

INGREDIENTS
   225g/8oz lean beef steak or pork
      fillet (tenderloin)
   225g/8oz can bamboo shoots, drained
   1 leek, trimmed
   25g/1oz Chinese dried mushrooms,
      soaked for 30 minutes in 120ml/
      4fl oz/½ cup warm water
   150g/5oz Chinese leaves
      (Chinese cabbage)
   450g/1lb cooked egg noodles
      (255g/8oz dried), drained well
   90ml/6 tbsp vegetable oil
   30ml/2 tbsp dark soy sauce
   15ml/1 tbsp cornflour (cornstarch)
   15ml/1 tbsp rice wine or dry sherry
   5ml/1 tsp sesame oil
   5ml/1 tsp caster (superfine) sugar
   salt and ground black pepper

1 Slice the beef or pork, bamboo shoots and leek into thin batons. Drain the mushrooms, reserving 90ml/6 tbsp of the soaking water. Cut off and discard the stems, then slice the caps finely. Cut the Chinese leaves into 2.5cm/1in diamond-shaped pieces and sprinkle with salt. Pat the noodles dry with kitchen paper.

2 Heat a third of the oil in a large wok or frying pan and sauté the noodles. After turning them over once, press the noodles evenly against the base of the pan with a wooden spatula until they form a flat, even cake. Cook over a medium heat for about 4 minutes, or until the noodles on the underside have become crisp.

3 Turn the noodle cake over with a spatula or fish slice or invert on to a large plate and slide back into the wok. Cook for 3 minutes more, then slide on to a heated plate. Keep warm.

4 Heat 30ml/2 tbsp of the remaining oil in the wok. Add the strips of leek, then the meat strips and stir-fry for 10–15 seconds. Sprinkle over half the soy sauce and then add the bamboo shoots and mushrooms, with salt and pepper to taste. Toss over the heat for 1 minute, then transfer this mixture to a plate and set aside.

5 Heat the remaining oil in the wok and sauté the Chinese leaves for 1 minute. Return the meat and vegetable mixture to the wok and sauté with the leaves for 30 seconds, stirring constantly.

6 Mix the cornflour with the reserved mushroom water. Stir into the wok along with the rice wine or sherry, sesame oil, sugar and remaining soy sauce. Cook for 15 seconds to thicken. Divide the noodles among serving dishes and pile the meat and vegetables on top.

Per portion: Energy 695Kcal/2895kJ; Protein 35.3g; Carbohydrate 38.8g, of which sugars 7.7g; Fat 45.3g, of which saturates 8.5g; Cholesterol 79mg; Calcium 79mg; Fibre 4.6g; Sodium 1185mg.

THAI CRISPY NOODLES WITH BEEF

RICE VERMICELLI ARE VERY FINE, DRY, WHITE NOODLES BUNDLED IN LARGE FRAGILE LOOPS AND SOLD IN PACKETS. THEY ARE DEEP-FRIED BEFORE BEING ADDED TO THIS DISH, AND IN THE PROCESS THEY EXPAND TO AT LEAST FOUR TIMES THEIR ORIGINAL SIZE.

SERVES FOUR

INGREDIENTS
about 450g/1lb rump (round) or
  sirloin steak
teriyaki sauce, for sprinkling
175g/6oz rice vermicelli
groundnut (peanut) oil for deep-frying
  and stir-frying
8 spring onions (scallions),
  diagonally sliced
2 garlic cloves, crushed
4–5 carrots, cut into julienne strips
1–2 fresh red chillies, seeded and
  finely sliced
2 small courgettes (zucchini),
  diagonally sliced
5ml/1 tsp grated fresh root ginger
60ml/4 tbsp white or yellow
  rice vinegar
90ml/6 tbsp light soy sauce
about 475ml/16fl oz/2 cups
  spicy stock

1 Using a meat mallet or the side of a rolling pin, beat out the steak, if necessary, to about 2.5cm/1in thick. Place in a shallow dish, brush generously with the teriyaki sauce and set aside for 2–4 hours to marinate.

2 Separate the rice vermicelli into manageable loops and spread several layers of kitchen paper on a very large plate. Pour the oil into a large wok to a depth of about 5cm/2in, and heat until a strand of vermicelli cooks as soon as it is lowered into the oil.

3 Carefully add a loop of rice vermicelli to the oil. It should immediately expand and become opaque. Turn the noodles over so that the strands cook on both sides and then transfer the cooked noodles to the prepared plate to drain. Repeat the process until all the noodles have been cooked. Transfer the cooked rice vermicelli to a separate wok or a deep serving bowl and keep them warm while you are cooking the steak and vegetables.

4 Strain the oil from the wok into a heatproof bowl and set it aside. Heat 15ml/1 tbsp groundnut oil in the clean wok. When it sizzles, cook the steak for about 30 seconds on each side until browned. Transfer to a board and cut into thick slices. The meat should be well browned on the outside but still pink inside. Set aside.

5 Add a little extra oil to the wok and stir-fry the spring onions, garlic and carrots over a medium heat for about 5–6 minutes until the carrots are slightly soft and glazed. Add the chillies, courgettes and ginger and stir-fry for 1–2 minutes more.

6 Stir in the rice vinegar, soy sauce and stock. Cook for about 4 minutes, until the sauce has slightly thickened. Add the steak and cook for a further 1–2 minutes (or longer, if you prefer your meat well done).

7 Pour the steak, vegetables and all the mixture over the noodles and toss lightly and carefully to mix, then serve.

COOK'S TIP
As soon as you add the meat mixture to the noodles, they will soften. If you wish to keep a few crispy noodles, stir some to the surface so they do not come into contact with the hot liquid.

Per portion: Energy 510Kcal/2122kJ; Protein 30.7g; Carbohydrate 41.6g, of which sugars 6.8g; Fat 24.5g, of which saturates 5.7g; Cholesterol 66mg; Calcium 51mg; Fibre 2.1g; Sodium 1262mg.

PAN-FRIED DISHES

Some of the simplest dishes are those that sizzle on top of the stove, leaving the oven free for a baked potato accompaniment, or a hot dessert. With wok or frying pan at the ready, sample such delights as Kofta Kebabs or Salmon with Tequila Cream Sauce. Pan-fried dishes include fritters and fish cakes of various kinds, including completely irresistible Salt Cod Fritters with Aioli. On nights when poultry is on the menu, plump for Stir-fried Chicken with Basil and Chilli for a deliciously spicy stir-fry supper.

CHEESE AND LEEK SAUSAGES WITH TOMATO, GARLIC AND CHILLI SAUCE

THESE ARE BASED ON THE WELSH SPECIALITY OF GLAMORGAN SAUSAGES, WHICH ARE TRADITIONALLY MADE USING WHITE OR WHOLEMEAL BREADCRUMBS ALONE. HOWEVER, ADDING A LITTLE MASHED POTATO LIGHTENS THE SAUSAGES AND MAKES THEM MUCH EASIER TO HANDLE.

SERVES FOUR

INGREDIENTS

25g/1oz/2 tbsp butter
175g/6oz leeks, finely chopped
90ml/6 tbsp cold mashed potato
115g/4oz/2 cups fresh white or
   wholemeal (whole-wheat)
   breadcrumbs
150g/5oz/1¼ cups grated Caerphilly,
   Lancashire or Cantal cheese
30ml/2 tbsp chopped fresh parsley
5ml/1 tsp chopped fresh sage
   or marjoram
2 large (US extra large) eggs, beaten
cayenne pepper
65g/2½oz/1 cup dry
   white breadcrumbs
oil for shallow frying
For the sauce
30ml/2 tbsp olive oil
2 garlic cloves, thinly sliced
1 fresh red chilli, seeded and finely
   chopped, or a good pinch of dried
   red chilli flakes
1 small onion, finely chopped
500g/1¼lb tomatoes, peeled, seeded
   and chopped
few fresh thyme sprigs
10ml/2 tsp balsamic vinegar or red
   wine vinegar
pinch of light muscovado
   (brown) sugar
15–30ml/1–2 tbsp chopped fresh
   marjoram or oregano
salt and ground black pepper

1 Melt the butter and cook the leeks for 4–5 minutes, until softened but not browned. Mix with the mashed potato, fresh breadcrumbs, cheese, parsley and sage or marjoram. Add sufficient beaten egg (about two-thirds of the quantity) to bind the mixture. Season well and add a good pinch of cayenne.

COOK'S TIP
These sausages are also delicious served with garlic mayonnaise.

2 Shape the mixture into 12 sausage shapes. Dip in the remaining egg, then coat with the dry breadcrumbs. Chill the coated sausages.

3 To make the sauce, heat the oil over a low heat in a pan, add the garlic, chilli and onion and cook for 3–4 minutes. Add the tomatoes, thyme and vinegar. Season with salt, pepper and sugar.

4 Cook the sauce for 40–50 minutes, until much reduced. Remove the thyme and purée the sauce in a blender. Reheat with the marjoram or oregano, then adjust the seasoning, adding more sugar, if necessary.

5 Cook the sausages in shallow oil until golden brown on all sides. Drain on kitchen paper and serve with the sauce.

Per portion: Energy 580Kcal/2416kJ; Protein 19.2g; Carbohydrate 35.5g, of which sugars 7g; Fat 40.3g, of which saturates 15.2g; Cholesterol 164mg; Calcium 361mg; Fibre 3.5g; Sodium 604mg.

POTATO AND ONION CAKES WITH BEETROOT RELISH

THESE IRRESISTIBLE PANCAKES ARE BASED ON TRADITIONAL EASTERN EUROPEAN LATKE, GRATED POTATO CAKES. THEY ARE DELICIOUS WITH A SWEET-SHARP BEETROOT RELISH AND SOUR CREAM.

SERVES FOUR

INGREDIENTS
500g/1¼lb potatoes
1 small cooking apple, peeled, cored
  and coarsely grated
1 small onion, finely chopped
50g/2oz/½ cup plain (all-
  purpose) flour
2 large (US extra large) eggs, beaten
30ml/2 tbsp chopped chives
vegetable oil, for shallow frying
salt and ground black pepper
250ml/8fl oz/1 cup sour cream
  or crème fraîche
fresh dill sprigs and fresh chives
  or chive flowers, to garnish
For the beetroot (beet) relish
250g/9oz beetroot (beet), cooked
  and peeled
1 large eating apple, cored and
  finely diced
15ml/1 tbsp finely chopped red onion
15–30ml/1–2 tbsp tarragon vinegar
15ml/1 tbsp chopped fresh dill
15–30ml/1–2 tbsp light olive oil
pinch of caster (superfine) sugar

1 To make the relish, finely dice the beetroot, then mix it with the apple and onion. Add 15ml/1 tbsp of the vinegar, the dill and 15ml/1 tbsp of the oil. Season, adding more vinegar and oil, and a pinch of caster sugar to taste.

2 Coarsely grate the potatoes, then rinse in cold water, drain and dry them on a clean dishtowel.

3 Mix the potatoes, apple and onion in a bowl. Stir in the flour, eggs and chives. Season and mix again.

4 Heat about 5mm/¼in depth of oil in a frying pan and cook spoonfuls of the mixture. Flatten them to make pancakes 7.5–10cm/3–4in across and cook for 3–4 minutes on each side, until browned. Drain on kitchen paper and keep warm until the mixture is used up.

5 Serve a stack of pancakes – there should be about 16–20 in total – with spoonfuls of sour cream or crème fraîche, and beetroot relish. Garnish with dill sprigs and chives or chive flowers and grind black pepper on top just before serving.

VARIATION
To make a leek and potato cake, melt 25g/1oz/2 tbsp butter in a pan, add 400g/14oz thinly sliced leeks and cook until tender. Season well. Coarsely grate 500g/1¼lb peeled potatoes, then season. Melt another 25g/1oz/2 tbsp butter in a medium frying pan and add a layer of half the potatoes. Cover with the leeks, then add the remaining potatoes, pressing down with a spatula to form a cake. Cook for 20–25 minutes over a low heat until the potatoes are browned, then turn over and cook for 15–20 minutes to brown the other side.

Per portion: Energy 471Kcal/1964kJ; Protein 10.3g; Carbohydrate 42.1g, of which sugars 13.4g; Fat 30.2g, of which saturates 10.6g; Cholesterol 152mg; Calcium 118mg; Fibre 3.7g; Sodium 125mg.

CRAB CAKES

UNLIKE FISH CAKES, CRAB CAKES ARE BOUND WITH EGG AND MAYONNAISE OR TARTARE SAUCE INSTEAD OF POTATOES, WHICH MAKES THEM LIGHT IN TEXTURE. IF YOU PREFER, THEY CAN BE GRILLED INSTEAD OF FRIED; BRUSH WITH A LITTLE OIL FIRST.

SERVES FOUR

INGREDIENTS

   450g/1lb mixed brown and white
     crab meat
   30ml/2 tbsp mayonnaise or
     tartare sauce
   2.5–5ml/½–1 tsp mustard powder
   1 egg, lightly beaten
   Tabasco sauce
   45ml/3 tbsp chopped
     fresh parsley
   4 spring onions (scallions), finely
     chopped (optional)
   50–75g/2–3oz/½–¾ cup dried
     breadcrumbs, preferably home-made
   sunflower oil, for frying
   salt, ground black pepper and
     cayenne pepper
   chopped spring onions (scallions),
     to garnish
   red onion marmalade, to serve

1 Put the crab meat in a bowl and stir in the mayonnaise or tartare sauce, with the mustard and egg. Season with Tabasco, salt, pepper and cayenne.

2 Stir in the parsley, spring onions, if using, and 50g/2oz/½ cup of the breadcrumbs. The mixture should be just firm enough to hold together; depending on how much brown crab meat there is, you may need to add some more breadcrumbs.

3 Divide the mixture into eight portions, roll each into a ball and flatten slightly to make a thick flat disc. Spread out the crab cakes on a platter and put in the refrigerator for 30 minutes before frying.

4 Pour the oil into a shallow pan to a depth of about 5mm/¼in. Cook the crab cakes, in two batches, until golden brown all over. Drain on kitchen paper and keep hot. Serve with a spring onion garnish and red onion marmalade.

Per portion: Energy 285Kcal/1187kJ; Protein 23.9g; Carbohydrate 10.3g, of which sugars 0.9g; Fat 16.7g, of which saturates 2.4g; Cholesterol 134mg; Calcium 178mg; Fibre 0.8g; Sodium 768mg.

VEGETABLE-STUFFED SQUID

SHIRLEY CONRAN FAMOUSLY SAID THAT LIFE IS TOO SHORT TO STUFF A MUSHROOM. THE SAME MIGHT BE SAID OF SQUID, EXCEPT THAT THE RESULT IS SO DELICIOUS THAT IT MAKES THE EFFORT SEEM WORTHWHILE. SMALL CUTTLEFISH CAN BE PREPARED IN THE SAME WAY. SERVE WITH SAFFRON RICE.

SERVES FOUR

INGREDIENTS

4 medium squid, or 12 small squid,
    skinned and cleaned
75g/3oz/6 tbsp butter
50g/2oz/1 cup fresh
    white breadcrumbs
2 shallots, chopped
4 garlic cloves, chopped
1 leek, thinly diced
2 carrots, finely diced
150ml/¼ pint/⅔ cup fish stock
30ml/2 tbsp olive oil
30ml/2 tbsp chopped fresh parsley
salt and ground black pepper
fresh rosemary sprigs, to garnish
saffron rice, to serve

3 Heat half the olive oil in the frying pan, add the chopped squid and cook over a high heat for 1 minute. Remove the squid with a slotted spoon and stir into the vegetables. Stir in the parsley.

4 Put the stuffing mixture into a piping (pastry) bag or use a teaspoon to stuff the squid tubes with the mixture. Do not overfill them, as the stuffing will swell lightly during cooking. Secure the openings with cocktail sticks (toothpicks) or sew up with fine thread.

5 Heat the remaining olive oil in the frying pan, place the stuffed squid in the pan and cook until they are sealed on all sides and golden brown. Transfer the frying pan to the oven and roast the squid for 20 minutes.

6 Unless the squid are very small, carefully cut them into three or four slices and arrange on a bed of saffron rice. Spoon the cooking juices over the squid and serve immediately, garnished with sprigs of rosemary.

1 Preheat the oven to 220°C/425°F/ Gas 7. Cut off the tentacles and side flaps from the squid and chop these finely. Set the squid aside. Melt half the butter in a large frying pan that can safely be used in the oven. Add the fresh white breadcrumbs and cook until they are golden brown, stirring to prevent them from burning. Transfer the breadcrumbs to a bowl and set aside until required.

2 Heat the remaining butter in the frying pan and add the chopped and diced vegetables. Cook until softened but not browned, then stir in the fish stock and cook until it has reduced and the vegetables are very soft. Season to taste with salt and ground black pepper and transfer to the bowl with the breadcrumbs. Mix lightly together.

Per portion: Energy 356Kcal/1486kJ; Protein 21.8g; Carbohydrate 15.2g, of which sugars 3.6g; Fat 23.6g, of which saturates 11.1g; Cholesterol 321mg; Calcium 55mg; Fibre 1.9g; Sodium 352mg.

Salt Cod Fritters with Aioli

Aioli is a fiercely garlicky, olive oil mayonnaise from Provence in the south of France and is a traditional accompaniment to salt cod.

SERVES SIX

INGREDIENTS
    450g/1lb salt cod
    500g/1¼lb floury potatoes
    300ml/½ pint/1¼ cups milk
    6 spring onions (scallions),
       finely chopped
    30ml/2 tbsp extra virgin olive oil
    30ml/2 tbsp chopped fresh parsley
    juice of ½ lemon, to taste
    2 eggs, beaten
    60ml/4 tbsp plain (all-purpose) flour
    90g/3½oz/1⅓ cups dry
       white breadcrumbs
    vegetable oil, for shallow frying
    salt and ground black pepper
    lemon wedges and salad, to serve
For the aioli
    2 large garlic cloves
    2 egg yolks
    300ml/½ pint/1¼ cups olive oil
    lemon juice, to taste

1 Soak the salt cod in cold water for 24–36 hours, changing the water 5–6 times. It swells as it rehydrates and a tiny piece should not taste too salty when tried. Drain well.

2 Cook the potatoes, unpeeled, in a pan of boiling salted water for about 20 minutes, until tender. Drain, then peel and mash the potatoes.

3 Poach the cod very gently in the milk with half the spring onions for 10–15 minutes, or until it flakes easily. Remove the cod and flake it with a fork into a bowl, discarding bones and skin.

4 Add 60ml/4 tbsp mashed potato to the flaked cod and beat with a wooden spoon. Work in the olive oil, then gradually add the remaining potato. Beat in the remaining spring onions and the parsley. Season with lemon juice and pepper to taste – the mixture may need a little salt. Beat in one egg, then chill the mixture until firm.

5 Shape the mixture into 12–18 small round cakes. Coat them in flour, then dip them in the remaining egg and coat with the breadcrumbs. Chill.

COOK'S TIPS
• Try to find a thick, creamy white piece of salt cod, preferably cut from the middle of the fish rather than the tail and fin ends. Avoid thin, yellowish salt cod, as it will be too dry and salty.
• Mash potatoes by hand, never in a food processor, as it makes them gluey.
• Aioli traditionally has a sharp bite from the raw garlic. However, if you prefer a milder flavour, blanch the garlic once or twice in boiling water for about 3 minutes each time before using it.

6 Meanwhile, make the aioli. Place the garlic and a good pinch of salt in a mortar and pound to a paste with a pestle. Transfer to a bowl and using a small whisk or a wooden spoon, gradually work in the egg yolks.

7 Add the olive oil, a drop at a time, until half is incorporated. When the sauce is as thick as soft butter, beat in 5–10ml/ 1–2 tsp lemon juice, then continue adding oil until the aioli is very thick. Adjust the seasoning, adding lemon juice to taste.

8 Heat about 2cm/¾in depth of oil in a large, heavy frying pan. Add the salt cod fritters and cook over a medium-high heat for about 4 minutes. Turn them over and cook for a further 4 minutes on the other side, until crisp and golden. Drain on crumpled kitchen paper, then serve with the aioli, lemon wedges and salad leaves.

Per portion: Energy 718Kcal/2980kJ; Protein 21.1g; Carbohydrate 33.1g, of which sugars 1.9g; Fat 56.5g, of which saturates 8.3g; Cholesterol 165mg; Calcium 67mg; Fibre 1.6g; Sodium 196mg.

FRIED FISH WITH TOMATO SAUCE

THIS SIMPLE DISH IS PERENNIALLY POPULAR WITH CHILDREN. IT WORKS EQUALLY WELL WITH LEMON SOLE OR DABS (THESE DO NOT NEED SKINNING), OR FILLETS OF HADDOCK AND WHITING.

SERVES FOUR

INGREDIENTS
60ml/4 tbsp plain (all-purpose) flour
2 eggs, beaten
75g/3oz/¾ cup dried breadcrumbs
4 small plaice or flounder, dark
  skin removed
15g/½oz/1 tbsp butter
15ml/1 tbsp sunflower oil
salt and ground black pepper
1 lemon, quartered, to serve
fresh basil leaves, to garnish
For the tomato sauce
30ml/2 tbsp olive oil
1 red onion, finely chopped
1 garlic clove, finely chopped
400g/14oz can chopped tomatoes
15ml/1 tbsp tomato purée (paste)
15ml/1 tbsp torn fresh basil leaves

1 First make the tomato sauce. Heat the olive oil in a large pan, add the finely chopped onion and garlic and cook gently for about 5 minutes, until softened and pale golden. Stir in the chopped tomatoes and tomato purée and simmer for 20–30 minutes, stirring occasionally. Season with salt and pepper and stir in the basil.

2 Spread out the flour in a shallow dish, pour the beaten eggs into another and spread out the breadcrumbs in a third. Season the fish with salt and pepper.

3 Hold a fish in your left hand and dip it first in flour, then in egg and finally in the breadcrumbs, patting the crumbs on with your dry right hand.

4 Heat the butter and oil in a frying pan until foaming. Cook the fish, one at a time, in the hot fat for about 5 minutes on each side, until golden brown and cooked through, but still juicy in the middle. Drain on kitchen paper and keep hot while you cook the rest. Serve with lemon wedges and the tomato sauce, garnished with basil leaves.

Per portion: Energy 345Kcal/1445kJ; Protein 23g; Carbohydrate 28.3g, of which sugars 5.6g; Fat 16.3g, of which saturates 4.2g; Cholesterol 144mg; Calcium 105mg; Fibre 2g; Sodium 338mg.

TROUT WITH TAMARIND AND CHILLI SAUCE

ALTHOUGH VERY ECONOMICAL, TROUT CAN TASTE RATHER BLAND. THIS SPICY THAI-INSPIRED SAUCE REALLY GIVES IT ZING. IF YOU LIKE YOUR FOOD VERY SPICY, ADD AN EXTRA CHILLI.

SERVES FOUR

INGREDIENTS
  4 trout, 350g/12oz each, cleaned
  6 spring onions (scallions), sliced
  60ml/4 tbsp soy sauce
  15ml/1 tbsp stir-fry oil
  30ml/2 tbsp chopped fresh
    coriander (cilantro)
For the sauce
  50g/2oz tamarind pulp
  105ml/7 tbsp boiling water
  2 shallots, coarsely chopped
  1 fresh red chilli, seeded
    and chopped
  1cm/½in piece fresh root ginger,
    peeled and chopped
  5ml/1 tsp soft brown sugar
  45ml/3 tbsp Thai fish sauce

1 Slash the trout diagonally four or five times on each side with a sharp knife and place in a shallow dish.

2 Fill the cavities with spring onions and douse each fish with soy sauce. Carefully turn the fish over to coat both sides with the sauce. Sprinkle on any remaining spring onions and set aside until required.

3 Make the sauce. Put the tamarind pulp in a small bowl and pour on the boiling water. Mash well with a fork until soft. Tip the mixture into a food processor or blender, add the shallots, fresh chilli, chopped ginger, brown sugar and Thai fish sauce and process to a coarse pulp.

4 Heat the stir-fry oil in a large frying pan or wok and cook the trout, one at a time if necessary, for about 5 minutes on each side, until the skin is crisp and browned and the flesh cooked. Put on warmed plates and spoon over some sauce. Sprinkle with the coriander and serve with the remaining sauce.

Per portion: Energy 352Kcal/1481kJ; Protein 55g; Carbohydrate 3.3g, of which sugars 2.8g; Fat 13.4g, of which saturates 2.8g; Cholesterol 224mg; Calcium 95mg; Fibre 0.4g; Sodium 721mg.

SALMON FISH CAKES

THE SECRET OF A GOOD FISH CAKE IS TO MAKE IT WITH FRESHLY PREPARED FISH AND POTATOES, HOME-MADE BREADCRUMBS AND PLENTY OF INTERESTING SEASONING.

SERVES FOUR

INGREDIENTS

450g/1lb cooked salmon fillet
450g/1lb cooked potatoes, mashed
25g/1oz/2 tbsp butter, melted
10ml/2 tsp wholegrain mustard
15ml/1 tbsp each chopped fresh dill
  and chopped fresh parsley
grated rind and juice of ½ lemon
15g/½oz/1 tbsp plain (all-
  purpose) flour
1 egg, lightly beaten
150g/5oz/1¼ cups dried breadcrumbs
60ml/4 tbsp sunflower oil
salt and ground black pepper
rocket (arugula) leaves, chives and
  lemon wedges to garnish

1 Flake the cooked salmon, discarding any skin and bones. Put it in a bowl with the mashed potato, melted butter and wholegrain mustard and mix well. Stir in the dill and parsley and lemon rind and juice. Season to taste with salt and pepper.

2 Divide the mixture into eight portions and shape each into a ball, then flatten into a thick disc. Dip the fish cakes first in flour, then in egg and, finally, in breadcrumbs to coat evenly.

3 Heat the oil in a frying pan until it is very hot. Cook the fish cakes, in batches, until golden brown and crisp all over. As each batch is ready, drain on kitchen paper and keep hot. Garnish with rocket leaves and chives and serve with lemon wedges.

COOK'S TIP
Almost any fresh white or hot-smoked fish is suitable; smoked cod and haddock are particularly good.

Per portion: Energy 586Kcal/2453kJ; Protein 29.8g; Carbohydrate 49.9g, of which sugars 3.2g; Fat 31g, of which saturates 7.2g; Cholesterol 117mg; Calcium 79mg; Fibre 1.3g; Sodium 266mg.

SALMON WITH TEQUILA CREAM SAUCE

USE REPOSADA TEQUILA, WHICH IS LIGHTLY AGED, FOR THIS SAUCE. IT HAS A SMOOTHER, MORE ROUNDED FLAVOUR, WHICH GOES WELL WITH THE CREAM.

SERVES FOUR

INGREDIENTS

3 fresh jalapeño chillies
45ml/3 tbsp olive oil
1 small onion, finely chopped
150ml/¼ pint/⅔ cup fish stock
grated rind and juice of 1 lime
120ml/4fl oz/½ cup single
  (light) cream
30ml/2 tbsp reposada tequila
1 firm avocado
4 salmon fillets
salt and ground white pepper
strips of green (bell) pepper

1 Roast the chillies in a frying pan until the skins are blistered, being careful not to let the flesh burn. Put them in a strong plastic bag and tie the top to keep the steam in. Set aside for 20 minutes.

2 Heat 15ml/1 tbsp of the oil in a pan. Cook the onion for 3–4 minutes, then add the stock, lime rind and juice. Cook for 10 minutes, until the stock starts to reduce. Remove the chillies from the bag and peel off the skins, slit them and scrape out the seeds.

3 Stir the cream into the onion and stock mixture. Slice the chilli flesh into strips and add to the pan. Cook over a gentle heat, stirring constantly, for 2–3 minutes. Season to taste with salt and white pepper.

4 Stir the tequila into the onion and chilli mixture. Leave the pan over a very low heat. Peel the avocado, remove the stone (pit) and slice the flesh. Brush the salmon fillets on one side with a little of the remaining oil.

5 Heat a frying pan or ridged griddle pan until very hot and add the salmon, oiled side down. Cook for 2–3 minutes, until the underside is golden, then brush the top with oil, turn each fillet over and cook the other side until the fish is cooked and flakes easily when tested with the tip of a sharp knife.

6 Serve the fish on a pool of sauce, with the avocado slices. Garnish with strips of green pepper and fresh flat leaf parsley, if you like.

Per portion: Energy 445Kcal/1846kJ; Protein 27.1g; Carbohydrate 2.5g, of which sugars 1.7g; Fat 34.8g, of which saturates 8.7g; Cholesterol 79mg; Calcium 61mg; Fibre 1.5g; Sodium 68mg.

CHICKEN WITH PEAS

THIS ITALIAN DISH STRONGLY REFLECTS THE TRADITIONS OF BOTH MEDITERRANEAN AND JEWISH COOKING. JEWS FAVOUR THE ENRICHMENT OF MEAT SAUCES WITH EGG BECAUSE OF THE LAWS OF THE KASHRUT, WHICH FORBIDS THE ADDITION OF CREAM TO MEAT DISHES.

SERVES FOUR

INGREDIENTS

    4 skinless, boneless chicken
      breast portions
    plain (all-purpose) flour, for dusting
    30–45ml/2–3 tbsp olive oil
    1–2 onions, chopped
    ¼ fennel bulb, chopped (optional)
    15ml/1 tbsp chopped fresh parsley,
      plus extra to garnish
    7.5ml/1½ tsp fennel seeds
    75ml/5 tbsp dry Marsala
    120ml/4fl oz/½ cup chicken stock
    300g/11oz/2¼ cups petits pois
      (baby peas)
    juice of 1½ lemons
    2 egg yolks
    salt and ground black pepper

1 Season the chicken with salt and pepper, then dust generously with flour. Shake off the excess flour; set aside.

2 Heat 15ml/1 tbsp oil in a pan, add the onions, fennel, if using, parsley and fennel seeds. Cook for 5 minutes.

3 Add the remaining oil and the chicken to the pan and cook for 2–3 minutes on each side, until lightly browned. Remove the chicken and onion mixture from the pan and set aside.

4 Deglaze the pan by pouring in the Marsala and cooking over a high heat until reduced to about 30ml/2 tbsp, then pour in the stock. Add the peas and return the chicken and onion mixture to the pan. Cook over a very low heat while you prepare the egg mixture.

5 In a bowl, beat the lemon juice and egg yolks together, then gradually add about 120ml/4fl oz/½ cup of the hot liquid from the chicken and peas, stirring well to combine.

6 Return the mixture to the pan and cook over a low heat, stirring, until the mixture thickens slightly. (Do not allow the mixture to boil or the eggs will curdle and spoil the sauce.) Serve the chicken immediately, sprinkled with a little extra chopped fresh parsley.

Per portion: Energy 319Kcal/1338kJ; Protein 42g; Carbohydrate 9.1g, of which sugars 5.9g; Fat 10.7g, of which saturates 2.2g; Cholesterol 206mg; Calcium 67mg; Fibre 4.2g; Sodium 150mg.

STIR-FRIED CHICKEN WITH BASIL AND CHILLI

THIS QUICK AND EASY CHICKEN DISH IS AN EXCELLENT INTRODUCTION TO THAI CUISINE. THAI BASIL, WHICH IS SOMETIMES KNOWN AS HOLY BASIL, HAS A UNIQUE, PUNGENT FLAVOUR THAT IS BOTH SPICY AND SHARP. DEEP-FRYING THE LEAVES ADDS ANOTHER DIMENSION TO THIS DISH.

SERVES FOUR TO SIX

INGREDIENTS
- 45ml/3 tbsp vegetable oil
- 4 garlic cloves, thinly sliced
- 2–4 fresh red chillies, seeded and finely chopped
- 450g/1lb skinless boneless chicken breast portions, diced
- 45ml/3 tbsp Thai fish sauce
- 10ml/2 tsp dark soy sauce
- 5ml/1 tsp sugar
- 10–12 Thai basil leaves
- 2 fresh red chillies, seeded and finely chopped and about 20 deep-fried Thai basil leaves, to garnish

1 Heat the oil in a wok or large frying pan. Add the garlic and chillies and stir-fry over a medium heat for 1–2 minutes, until the garlic is golden.

2 Add the pieces of chicken to the wok or pan and stir-fry until the chicken changes colour.

3 Stir in the Thai fish sauce, soy sauce and sugar. Continue to stir-fry the mixture for 3–4 minutes, or until the chicken is fully cooked with the sauce.

4 Stir in the fresh Thai basil leaves. Spoon the entire mixture on to a warm serving platter or individual serving dishes, and garnish with the sliced chillies and deep-fried Thai basil.

COOK'S TIP
To deep-fry Thai basil leaves, first make sure that the leaves are completely dry or they will splutter when added to the oil. Deep-fry the leaves briefly in hot oil until they are crisp and translucent – this will take only about 30–40 seconds. Lift out the leaves using a slotted spoon or wire basket and leave them to drain on kitchen paper.

Per portion: Energy 196Kcal/819kJ; Protein 27.2g; Carbohydrate 0.4g, of which sugars 0.4g; Fat 9.5g, of which saturates 1.3g; Cholesterol 79mg; Calcium 7mg; Fibre 0g; Sodium 424mg.

Turkey or Chicken Schnitzel

In Austria, where this dish originated, Schnitzel was always made from veal, pounded flat, crisply coated and then fried. Nowadays, it may be made from steak, chicken or turkey. This is a popular Israeli version. Serve with a selection of vegetables.

SERVES FOUR

INGREDIENTS

4 boneless turkey or chicken breast
  fillets, each weighing about 175g/6oz
juice of 1 lemon
2 garlic cloves, chopped
plain (all-purpose) flour, for dusting
1–2 eggs
15ml/1 tbsp water
about 50g/2oz/½ cup matzo meal
paprika
a mixture of vegetable and olive oil,
  for shallow frying
salt and ground black pepper
lemon wedges and a selection of
  vegetables, to serve (optional)

1 Lay each piece of meat between two sheets of greaseproof (waxed) paper and pound with a mallet or the end of a rolling pin until it is about half its original thickness and fairly even.

2 In a bowl, combine the lemon juice, garlic, salt and pepper. Coat the meat in it, then leave to marinate.

3 Meanwhile, arrange three wide plates or shallow dishes in a row. Fill one plate or dish with flour, beat the egg and water together in another and mix the matzo meal, salt, pepper and paprika together on the third.

4 Working quickly, dip each fillet into the flour, then the egg, then the matzo meal. Pat everything in well, then arrange the crumbed fillets on a plate and chill for at least 30 minutes and up to 2 hours.

5 In a large, heavy frying pan, heat the oil until it will turn a cube of bread dropped into the oil golden brown in 30–60 seconds. Carefully add the crumbed fillets (in batches if necessary) and cook until golden brown, turning once. Remove and drain on kitchen paper. Serve immediately with lemon wedges and a selection of vegetables.

Per portion: Energy 368Kcal/1546kJ; Protein 45.4g; Carbohydrate 14.7g, of which sugars 0.6g; Fat 14.6g, of which saturates 2.3g; Cholesterol 170mg; Calcium 27mg; Fibre 0.5g; Sodium 125mg.

TURKEY CROQUETTES

IN THESE CRISP PATTIES, SMOKED TURKEY IS MIXED WITH MASHED POTATO AND SPRING ONIONS,
ROLLED IN BREADCRUMBS, AND SERVED WITH A TANGY TOMATO SAUCE.

3 Meanwhile, to make the sauce, heat the oil in a frying pan and fry the onion for 5 minutes until softened. Add the tomatoes and purée, stir and simmer for 10 minutes. Stir in the parsley, season with salt and pepper and keep the sauce warm until needed.

SERVES FOUR

INGREDIENTS
  450g/1lb potatoes, diced
  3 eggs
  30ml/2 tbsp milk
  175g/6oz smoked turkey rashers
  (strips), finely chopped
  2 spring onions (scallions),
  thinly sliced
  115g/4oz/2 cups fresh
  white breadcrumbs
  vegetable oil, for deep-frying
For the sauce
  15ml/1 tbsp olive oil
  1 onion, finely chopped
  400g/14oz can tomatoes, drained
  30ml/2 tbsp tomato purée (paste)
  15ml/1 tbsp chopped
  fresh parsley
  salt and ground black pepper

1 Boil the potatoes for 20 minutes, or until tender. Drain and return the pan to a low heat to make sure all the excess water evaporates.

2 Mash the potatoes with two eggs and the milk. Season well with salt and pepper. Stir in the turkey and spring onions. Chill for 1 hour.

4 Remove the potato mixture from the refrigerator and divide into eight pieces. Shape each piece into a sausage shape and dip in the remaining beaten egg and then the breadcrumbs.

5 Heat the vegetable oil in a pan or deep-fryer to 175°C/330°F and deep-fry the croquettes for 5 minutes, or until golden and crisp. Drain and serve immediately with the sauce.

COOK'S TIP
Test the oil is at the correct temperature by dropping a cube of bread on to the surface. If it sinks, rises and sizzles in 10 seconds, the oil is ready to use.

Per portion: Energy 404Kcal/1698kJ; Protein 19.4g; Carbohydrate 47g, of which sugars 7.7g; Fat 16.7g, of which saturates 2.4g; Cholesterol 73mg; Calcium 93mg; Fibre 3.3g; Sodium 315mg.

KOFTA KEBABS

These spicy patties of minced lamb are spiked with aromatic herbs and seasonings. They are very popular throughout the Middle East right through to the Indian subcontinent. Serve with flat bread and a selection of refreshing and exotic salads, such as oranges sprinkled with cayenne or paprika, onions sprinkled with sumac, and tomato wedges with herbs and chillies.

SERVES FOUR

INGREDIENTS

  450g/1lb minced (ground) lamb
  1–2 large slices of French bread,
    very finely crumbled
  ½ bunch fresh coriander (cilantro),
    finely chopped
  5 garlic cloves, chopped
  1 onion, finely chopped
  juice of ½ lemon
  5ml/1 tsp ground cumin
  5ml/1 tsp paprika
  15ml/1 tbsp curry powder
  pinch each of ground cardamom,
    turmeric and cinnamon
  15ml/1 tbsp tomato purée (paste)
  cayenne pepper or chopped fresh
    chillies (optional)
  1 egg, beaten, if needed
  salt and ground black pepper
  flat bread and salads, to serve

1 Put the lamb, crumbled bread, coriander, garlic, onion, lemon juice, spices, tomato purée, cayenne pepper or chillies and seasoning in a large bowl. Mix well. If the mixture does not bind together, add the beaten egg and a little more bread.

2 With wet hands, shape the mixture into four large or eight small patties.

3 Heat a heavy, non-stick frying pan, add the patties and cook, taking care that they do not fall apart, and turning once or twice, until browned. Serve hot with flat bread and salads.

VARIATION
Mix a handful of raisins or sultanas (golden raisins) into the meat mixture before shaping it into patties.

Per portion: Energy 414Kcal/1740kJ; Protein 29.3g; Carbohydrate 36.9g, of which sugars 4.1g; Fat 17.7g, of which saturates 7.6g; Cholesterol 134mg; Calcium 131mg; Fibre 2.5g; Sodium 470mg.

LAMB BURGERS WITH RED ONION AND TOMATO RELISH

A SHARP-SWEET RED ONION RELISH WORKS WELL WITH BURGERS BASED ON MIDDLE-EASTERN STYLE LAMB. SERVE WITH PITTA BREAD AND TABBOULEH OR WITH FRIES AND A CRISP GREEN SALAD.

SERVES FOUR

INGREDIENTS
    25g/1oz/3 tbsp bulgur wheat
    500g/1¼lb lean minced
      (ground) lamb
    1 small red onion, finely chopped
    2 garlic cloves, finely chopped
    1 green chilli, seeded and
      finely chopped
    5ml/1 tsp ground toasted cumin seeds
    2.5ml/½ tsp ground sumac
    15g/½oz chopped fresh flat
      leaf parsley
    30ml/2 tbsp chopped fresh mint
    olive oil, for frying
    salt and ground black pepper
For the relish
    2 red (bell) peppers, halved
      and seeded
    2 red onions, cut into 5mm/¼in
      thick slices
    75–90ml/5–6 tbsp extra virgin olive oil
    350g/12oz cherry tomatoes, chopped
    ½–1 fresh red or green chilli, seeded
      and finely chopped (optional)
    30ml/2 tbsp chopped fresh mint
    30ml/2 tbsp chopped fresh parsley
    15ml/1 tbsp chopped fresh oregano
    2.5–5ml/½–1 tsp each ground toasted
      cumin seeds
    2.5–5ml/½–1 tsp sumac
    juice of ½ lemon
    caster (superfine) sugar, to taste

1 Pour 150ml/¼ pint/⅔ cup hot water over the bulgur wheat in a bowl and leave to stand for 15 minutes, then drain in a sieve and squeeze out the excess moisture.

2 Place the bulgur wheat in a bowl and add the minced lamb, onion, garlic, chilli, cumin, sumac, parsley and mint. Mix the ingredients thoroughly together by hand, then season with 5ml/1 tsp salt and plenty of black pepper and mix again. Form the mixture into eight small burgers and set aside in the refrigerator while you make the relish.

3 Grill (broil) the peppers, skin side up, until the skin chars and blisters. Place in a bowl, cover and leave to stand for 10 minutes. Peel off the skin, dice the peppers finely and place in a bowl.

4 Brush the onions with 15ml/1 tbsp oil and grill for 5 minutes on each side, until browned. Cool, then chop.

5 Add the onions, tomatoes, chilli to taste, the mint, parsley, oregano and 2.5ml/½ tsp each of the cumin and sumac to the peppers. Stir in 60ml/ 4 tbsp of the remaining oil and 15ml/1 tbsp of the lemon juice. Season with salt, pepper and sugar and leave to stand for 20–30 minutes.

6 Heat a heavy frying pan or a ridged, cast-iron griddle pan over a high heat and grease lightly with olive oil. Cook the burgers for about 5–6 minutes on each side, until cooked at the centre.

7 While the burgers are cooking, taste the relish and adjust the seasoning, adding more salt, pepper, sugar, oil, chilli, cumin, sumac and lemon juice to taste. Serve the burgers as soon as they are cooked, with the relish.

Per portion: Energy 537Kcal/2228kJ; Protein 27.2g; Carbohydrate 19g, of which sugars 13.4g; Fat 39.6g, of which saturates 11.1g; Cholesterol 96mg; Calcium 83mg; Fibre 4.2g; Sodium 105mg.

FILLET OF BEEF STROGANOFF

LEGEND HAS IT THAT THIS FAMOUS RUSSIAN RECIPE WAS DEVISED BY COUNT PAUL STROGANOFF'S COOK TO USE BEEF FROZEN BY THE SIBERIAN CLIMATE. THE ONLY WAY IN WHICH IT COULD BE PREPARED WAS CUT INTO VERY THIN STRIPS. THE STRIPS OF LEAN BEEF WERE SERVED IN A SOUR CREAM SAUCE FLAVOURED WITH BRANDY.

3 Add the mushrooms and stir-fry over a high heat. Transfer the vegetables and their juices to a dish and set aside.

4 Wipe the pan, then add and heat the remaining oil. Coat a batch of meat with flour, then stir-fry over a high heat until browned. Remove from the pan, then coat and stir-fry another batch. When the last batch of steak is cooked, replace all the meat and vegetables. Add the brandy and simmer until it has almost evaporated.

5 Stir in the stock or consommé and seasoning and cook for 10–15 minutes, stirring frequently, or until the meat is tender and the sauce is thick and glossy. Add the sour cream and sprinkle with chopped parsley. Serve with rice and a simple salad.

SERVES EIGHT

INGREDIENTS

   1.2kg/2½lb fillet (tenderloin) of beef
   30ml/2 tbsp plain (all-purpose) flour
   large pinch each of cayenne pepper
     and paprika
   75ml/5 tbsp sunflower oil
   1 large onion, chopped
   3 garlic cloves, finely chopped
   450g/1lb/6½ cups chestnut
     mushrooms, sliced
   75ml/5 tbsp brandy
   300ml/½ pint/1¼ cups beef stock
     or consommé
   300ml/½ pint/1¼ cups sour cream
   45ml/3 tbsp chopped fresh flat
     leaf parsley
   salt and ground black pepper

1 Thinly slice the fillet of beef across the grain, then cut it into fine strips. Season the flour with the cayenne pepper and paprika.

2 Heat half the oil in a large frying pan, add the onion and garlic and cook gently until the onion has softened.

COOK'S TIP

If you do not have a very large pan, it may be easier to cook the meat and vegetables in two separate pans. A large flameproof casserole may be used.

Per portion: Energy 407Kcal/1693kJ; Protein 34.9g; Carbohydrate 8.1g, of which sugars 3.4g; Fat 24g, of which saturates 9.8g; Cholesterol 114mg; Calcium 70mg; Fibre 1.5g; Sodium 87mg.

PAN-FRIED CALF'S LIVER
WITH CRISP ONIONS

SAUTÉED OR CREAMY MASHED POTATOES GO WELL WITH FRIED CALF'S LIVER. SERVE A SALAD OF MIXED LEAVES WITH PLENTY OF DELICATE FRESH HERBS, SUCH AS FENNEL, DILL AND PARSLEY, TO COMPLEMENT THE SIMPLE FLAVOURS OF THIS MAIN COURSE.

SERVES FOUR

INGREDIENTS
  50g/2oz/¼ cup butter
  4 onions, thinly sliced
  5ml/1 tsp caster (superfine) sugar
  4 slices calf's liver, each weighing
    about 115g/4oz
  30ml/2 tbsp plain (all-purpose) flour
  30ml/2 tbsp olive oil
  salt and ground black pepper
  parsley, to garnish

1 Melt the butter in a large, heavy pan with a lid. Add the onions and mix well to coat with butter. Cover the pan with a tight-fitting lid and cook gently for 10 minutes, stirring occasionally.

2 Stir in the sugar and cover the pan. Cook the onions for 10 minutes more, or until they are soft and golden. Increase the heat, remove the lid and stir the onions over a high heat until they are deep gold and crisp. Use a slotted spoon to remove the onions from the pan, draining off the fat.

3 Meanwhile, rinse the calf's liver in cold water and pat it dry on kitchen paper. Season the flour, put it on a plate and turn the slices of liver in it until they are lightly coated in flour.

COOK'S TIP
Take care not to cook the liver for too long as this may cause it to toughen.

4 Heat the oil in a large frying pan, add the liver and cook for about 2 minutes on each side, or until lightly browned and just firm. Arrange the liver on warmed plates, with the crisp onions. Garnish with parsley and serve with sautéed or mashed potatoes.

Per portion: Energy 350Kcal/1458kJ; Protein 23.9g; Carbohydrate 19.7g, of which sugars 8.6g; Fat 20.1g, of which saturates 8.5g; Cholesterol 452mg; Calcium 61mg; Fibre 2.4g; Sodium 162mg.

STEWS, CASSEROLES AND CURRIES

After the fast-food revolution, slow food is enjoying a

renaissance as more and more people take time to make — and

enjoy — delectable stews and casseroles. It's almost mystical,

the way disparate ingredients are transformed by slow cooking

into a dish in which all the different flavours blend to create a

harmonious whole. Beef Carbonade and Lamb and New Potato

Curry are especially fine examples of the genre.

ITALIAN FISH STEW

THIS ROBUST FISH AND TOMATO STEW COMES FROM ITALY WHERE IT IS KNOWN AS BRODETTO. THERE ARE MANY VERSIONS, BUT ALL REQUIRE FLAVOURSOME SUN-RIPENED TOMATOES AND A GOOD FISH STOCK. BUY SOME OF THE FISH WHOLE SO THAT YOU CAN SIMPLY SIMMER THEM, REMOVE THE COOKED FLESH AND STRAIN THE DELICIOUSLY FLAVOURED JUICES TO MAKE THE STOCK.

SERVES FOUR TO FIVE

INGREDIENTS

  900g/2lb mixture of fish fillets or
    steaks, such as monkfish, cod,
    haddock or hake
  900g/2lb mixture of conger eel,
    red or grey mullet, snapper or
    small white fish, prepared
    according to type
  1 onion, halved
  1 celery stick, coarsely chopped
  225g/8oz squid
  225g/8oz fresh mussels
  675g/1½lb ripe tomatoes
  60ml/4 tbsp olive oil
  1 large onion, thinly sliced
  3 garlic cloves, crushed
  5ml/1 tsp saffron threads
  150ml/¼ pint/⅔ cup dry white wine
  90ml/6 tbsp chopped fresh parsley
  salt and ground black pepper
  croûtons, to serve

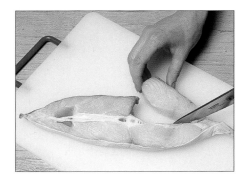

1 Remove any skin and bones from the fish fillets or steaks, cut the fish into large pieces and reserve. Place the bones in a pan with all the remaining fish.

2 Add the halved onion and the celery and just cover with water. Bring almost to the boil, then reduce the heat and simmer gently for about 30 minutes. Lift out the fish and remove the flesh from the bones. Strain the stock.

3 To prepare the squid, twist the head and tentacles away from the body. Cut the head from the tentacles. Discard the body contents and peel away the mottled skin. Wash the tentacles and bodies and dry on kitchen paper.

4 Scrub the mussels, discarding any that are damaged or open ones that do not close when sharply tapped.

5 Plunge the tomatoes into boiling water for 30 seconds, then refresh in cold water. Peel off the skins and chop the flesh coarsely.

6 Heat the oil in a large sauté pan. Add the sliced onion and the garlic, and cook gently for 3 minutes. Add the squid and the uncooked white fish, which you reserved earlier, and cook quickly on all sides. Remove the fish from the pan using a slotted spoon.

7 Add 475ml/16fl oz/2 cups strained reserved fish stock, the saffron and tomatoes to the pan. Pour in the wine. Bring to the boil, then reduce the heat and simmer for about 5 minutes. Add the mussels, cover, and cook for 3–4 minutes, until the mussels have opened. Discard any mussels that remain closed.

8 Season the sauce with salt and pepper and put all the fish in the pan. Cook gently for 5 minutes. Sprinkle with the parsley and serve with the croûtons.

Per portion: Energy 624Kcal/2624kJ; Protein 98.6g; Carbohydrate 12.6g, of which sugars 9.7g; Fat 17.5g, of which saturates 2.9g; Cholesterol 322mg; Calcium 163mg; Fibre 2.8g; Sodium 448mg.

CURRIED PRAWNS IN COCONUT MILK

A WONDERFULLY QUICK AND EASY DISH, THIS FEATURES PRAWNS IN A SPICY YELLOW CURRY GRAVY.

SERVES FOUR TO SIX

INGREDIENTS

600ml/1 pint/2½ cups coconut milk
30ml/2 tbsp yellow curry paste (see
    Cook's Tip)
15ml/1 tbsp Thai fish sauce
2.5ml/½ tsp salt
5ml/1 tsp sugar
450g/1lb raw king prawns (jumbo
    shrimp) peeled, thawed if frozen
225g/8oz cherry tomatoes
yellow and orange (bell) peppers,
    seeded and cut into thin strips,
    chives and juice of ½ lime,
    to garnish

VARIATION

Use cooked prawns (shrimp) for an even
quicker version. Add after the tomatoes
and heat through for 1–2 minutes.

1 Put half the coconut milk in a wok or
pan and bring to the boil. Add the
yellow curry paste, stir until it disperses,
then lower the heat and simmer for
about 10 minutes.

2 Add the Thai fish sauce, salt, sugar
and remaining coconut milk to the
sauce. Simmer for 5 minutes more.

3 Add the prawns and cherry tomatoes.
Simmer very gently for about 5 minutes,
until the prawns are pink and tender.

4 Spoon into a serving dish, sprinkle
with lime juice and garnish with strips
of yellow peppers and chives.

COOK'S TIP

To make yellow curry paste, put into a
food processor or blender 6–8 fresh
yellow chillies, the chopped base of
1 lemon grass stalk, 4 chopped shallots,
4 chopped garlic cloves, 15ml/1 tbsp
chopped peeled fresh root ginger, 5ml/
1 tsp coriander seeds, 5ml/1 tsp mustard
powder, 5ml/1 tsp salt, 2.5ml/½ tsp
ground cinnamon, 15ml/1 tbsp light
brown sugar and 30ml/2 tbsp sunflower
oil. Process to a paste, scrape into a jar,
cover and keep in the refrigerator.

Per portion: Energy 160Kcal/679kJ; Protein 21.5g; Carbohydrate 15.8g, of which sugars 15.5g; Fat 1.7g, of which saturates 0.6g; Cholesterol 219mg; Calcium 144mg; Fibre 2g; Sodium 584mg.

LOUISIANA SEAFOOD GUMBO

GUMBO IS A SOUP, BUT IS SERVED OVER RICE AS A MAIN COURSE. IN LOUISIANA, OYSTERS ARE CHEAP AND PROLIFIC, AND OYSTERS WOULD BE USED THERE INSTEAD OF MUSSELS.

SERVES SIX

INGREDIENTS
450g/1lb fresh mussels
450g/1lb raw prawns (shrimp)
1 cooked crab, about 1kg/2¼lb
small bunch of fresh parsley, leaves
  chopped and stalks reserved
150ml/¼ pint/⅔ cup vegetable oil
115g/4oz/1 cup plain (all-
  purpose) flour
1 green (bell) pepper, chopped
1 large onion, chopped
2 celery sticks, sliced
3 garlic cloves, finely chopped
75g/3oz smoked spiced sausage,
  skinned and sliced
275g/10oz/1½ cups long grain rice
6 spring onions (scallions), shredded
cayenne pepper, to taste
Tabasco sauce, to taste
salt

1 Wash the mussels in several changes of cold water, pulling away the black beards. Discard any mussels that are broken or do not close when you tap them firmly.

2 Bring 250ml/8fl oz/1 cup water to the boil in a deep pan. Add the mussels, cover the pan tightly and cook over a high heat, shaking frequently, for 3 minutes. As the mussels open, lift them out with tongs into a sieve set over a bowl. Discard any that fail to open. Shell the mussels, discarding the shells. Return the liquid from the bowl to the pan and make the quantity up to 2 litres/3½ pints/8 cups with water.

3 Peel the prawns and set them aside, reserving a few for the garnish. Put the shells and heads into the pan.

4 Remove all the meat from the crab, separating the brown and white meat. Add all the pieces of shell to the pan with 5ml/2 tsp salt.

5 Bring the shellfish stock to the boil, skimming it regularly. When there is no more froth on the surface, add the parsley stalks and simmer for 15 minutes. Cool, then strain it into a measuring jug (cup) and make up to 2 litres/3½ pints/8 cups with water.

6 Heat the oil in a heavy pan and stir in the flour. Stir constantly over a medium heat with a wooden spoon or whisk until the roux reaches a golden-brown colour. Immediately add the pepper, onion, celery and garlic. Continue cooking for about 3 minutes, until the onion is softened. Stir in the sausage. Reheat the stock.

7 Stir the brown crab meat into the roux, then ladle in the hot stock, a little at a time, stirring constantly until it has all been smoothly incorporated. Bring to a low boil, partially cover the pan, then simmer the gumbo for 30 minutes.

8 Meanwhile, cook the rice in plenty of lightly salted, boiling water until the grains are tender.

9 Add the prawns, mussels, white crab meat and spring onions to the gumbo. Return to the boil and season with salt if necessary, cayenne and a dash or two of Tabasco sauce. Simmer for a further minute, then add the chopped parsley leaves. Serve immediately, ladling the soup over the hot rice in soup plates.

COOK'S TIP
It is essential to stir constantly to darken the roux without burning. Should black specks occur at any stage of cooking, discard the roux and start again. Have the onion, green (bell) pepper and celery ready to add to the roux the minute it reaches the correct golden-brown stage, as this arrests its darkening.

Per portion: Energy 559Kcal/2336kJ; Protein 31.1g; Carbohydrate 57.6g, of which sugars 3.7g; Fat 23g, of which saturates 3.4g; Cholesterol 183mg; Calcium 145mg; Fibre 1.9g; Sodium 474mg.

GREEN FISH CURRY

ANY FIRM-FLESHED FISH CAN BE USED FOR THIS DELICIOUS CURRY, WHICH GAINS ITS RICH COLOUR FROM A MIXTURE OF FRESH HERBS; TRY EXOTICS, SUCH AS MAHI-MAHI, HOKI OR SWORDFISH, OR HUMBLER FISH, SUCH AS COLEY. SERVE IT WITH BASMATI OR THAI FRAGRANT RICE AND LIME WEDGES.

SERVES FOUR

INGREDIENTS

    4 garlic cloves, coarsely chopped
    5cm/2in piece fresh root ginger,
        peeled and coarsely chopped
    2 fresh green chillies, seeded and
        coarsely chopped
    grated rind and juice of 1 lime
    5–10ml/1–2 tsp shrimp paste
    5ml/1 tsp coriander seeds
    5ml/1 tsp five-spice powder
    75ml/5 tbsp sesame oil
    2 red onions, finely chopped
    900g/2lb hoki fillets, skinned
    400ml/14fl oz/1⅔ cups coconut milk
    45ml/3 tbsp Thai fish sauce
    50g/2oz fresh coriander
        (cilantro) leaves
    50g/2oz fresh mint leaves
    50g/2oz fresh basil leaves
    6 spring onions (scallions), chopped
    150ml/¼ pint/⅔ cup sunflower oil
    sliced fresh green chilli and finely
        chopped fresh coriander (cilantro),
        to garnish
    cooked rice and lime wedges,
        to serve

1 First make the curry paste. Combine the garlic, fresh root ginger, green chillies, the lime juice and shrimp paste in a food processor. Add the coriander seeds and five-spice powder, with half the sesame oil. Process to a fine paste, then set aside until required.

COOK'S TIP
Shrimp paste, also known as blachan or terasi, is available in Asian food stores.

2 Heat a wok or large shallow pan and pour in the remaining sesame oil. When it is hot, stir-fry the red onions over a high heat for 2 minutes. Add the fish and stir-fry for 1–2 minutes to seal the fillets on all sides.

3 Lift out the red onions and fish and put them on a plate. Add the curry paste to the wok or pan and cook for 1 minute, stirring. Return the fish and red onions to the wok or pan, pour in the coconut milk and bring to the boil. Lower the heat, add the Thai fish sauce and simmer for 5–7 minutes, until the fish is cooked through.

4 Meanwhile, process the herbs, spring onions, lime rind and oil in a food processor to a coarse paste. Stir into the fish curry. Garnish with chilli and coriander and serve with rice and lime wedges.

Per portion: Energy 608Kcal/2527kJ; Protein 41g; Carbohydrate 13.3g, of which sugars 9.5g; Fat 43.8g, of which saturates 5.9g; Cholesterol 0mg; Calcium 168mg; Fibre 1.3g; Sodium 313mg.

OCTOPUS STEW

THIS RUSTIC STEW IS A PERFECT DISH FOR ENTERTAINING, AS IT TASTES EVEN BETTER IF MADE A DAY IN ADVANCE. SERVE WITH A COLOURFUL SALAD OF BABY CHARD, ROCKET AND RADICCHIO.

SERVES FOUR TO SIX

INGREDIENTS
1kg/2¼lb octopus, cleaned
45ml/3 tbsp olive oil
1 large red onion, chopped
3 garlic cloves, finely chopped
30ml/2 tbsp brandy
300ml/½ pint/1¼ cups dry
  white wine
800g/1¾lb ripe plum tomatoes,
  peeled and chopped, or 2 × 400g/
  14oz cans chopped tomatoes
1 fresh red chilli, seeded and
  chopped (optional)
450g/1lb small new potatoes
15ml/1 tbsp chopped fresh rosemary
15ml/1 tbsp fresh thyme leaves
1.2 litres/2 pints/5 cups fish stock
30ml/2 tbsp fresh flat leaf
  parsley leaves
salt and ground black pepper
fresh rosemary sprigs, to garnish
For the garlic croûtes
  1 fat garlic clove, peeled
  8 thick slices of baguette or ciabatta
  30ml/2 tbsp olive oil

3 Pour the brandy over the octopus and ignite it. When the flames have died down, add the wine, bring to the boil and bubble gently for about 5 minutes. Stir in the tomatoes, with the chilli, if using, then add the potatoes, rosemary and thyme. Simmer for 5 minutes.

4 Pour in the fish stock and season well. Cover the pan and simmer for 20–30 minutes, stirring occasionally. The octopus and potatoes should be very tender and the sauce should have thickened slightly. At this stage, you can leave the stew to cool, then put it in the refrigerator overnight.

5 Preheat the grill (broiler). To make the garlic croûtes, cut the garlic clove in half and rub both sides of the slices of baguette or ciabatta with the cut side. Crush the garlic, stir it into the oil and brush the mixture over both sides of the bread. Grill (broil) on both sides until the croûtes are golden brown and crisp.

6 To serve the stew, reheat it gently if it has been in the refrigerator overnight, check the seasoning and stir in the parsley leaves. Serve piping hot in individual warmed bowls, garnished with rosemary sprigs and accompanied by the warm garlic croûtes.

1 Cut the octopus into large pieces, put these in a pan and pour in cold water to cover. Season with salt, bring to the boil, then lower the heat and simmer for 30 minutes to tenderize. Drain and cut into bitesize pieces.

2 Heat the oil in a large shallow pan. Cook the onion for 2–3 minutes, until lightly coloured, then add the garlic and cook for 1 minute more. Add the octopus and cook for 2–3 minutes, stirring to colour it lightly on all sides.

Per portion: Energy 588Kcal/2477kJ; Protein 51.6g; Carbohydrate 41.6g, of which sugars 11.5g; Fat 18.1g, of which saturates 2.8g; Cholesterol 120mg; Calcium 163mg; Fibre 3.8g; Sodium 225mg.

RED CHICKEN CURRY WITH BAMBOO SHOOTS

BAMBOO SHOOTS HAVE A LOVELY CRUNCHY TEXTURE. IT IS QUITE ACCEPTABLE TO USE CANNED ONES, AS FRESH BAMBOO IS NOT READILY AVAILABLE IN THE WEST. BUY CANNED WHOLE BAMBOO SHOOTS, WHICH ARE CRISPER AND OF BETTER QUALITY THAN SLICED SHOOTS. RINSE BEFORE USING.

SERVES FOUR TO SIX

INGREDIENTS
   1 litre/1³/₄ pints/4 cups coconut milk
   450g/1lb skinless, boneless chicken
      breast portions, cut into
      bitesize pieces
   30ml/2 tbsp Thai fish sauce
   15ml/1 tbsp sugar
   225g/8oz drained canned bamboo
      shoots, rinsed and sliced
   5 kaffir lime leaves, torn
   salt and ground black pepper
   chopped fresh red chillies and kaffir
      lime leaves, to garnish
For the red curry paste
   5ml/1 tsp coriander seeds
   2.5ml/¹/₂ tsp cumin seeds
   12–15 fresh red chillies, seeded and
      coarsely chopped
   4 shallots, thinly sliced
   2 garlic cloves, chopped
   15ml/1 tbsp chopped galangal
   2 lemon grass stalks, chopped
   3 kaffir lime leaves, chopped
   4 fresh coriander (cilantro) roots
   10 black peppercorns
   good pinch of ground cinnamon
   5ml/1 tsp ground turmeric
   2.5ml/¹/₂ tsp shrimp paste
   5ml/1 tsp salt
   30ml/2 tbsp vegetable oil

1 Make the curry paste. Dry-fry the coriander and cumin seeds for 1–2 minutes, then put in a mortar or food processor with the remaining ingredients, except the oil, and pound or process to a paste.

2 Add the oil, a little at a time, mixing or processing well after each addition. Transfer to a jar and keep in the refrigerator until ready to use.

3 Pour half of the coconut milk into a large, heavy pan. Bring the milk to the boil, stirring constantly until it has separated.

4 Stir in 30ml/2 tbsp of the red curry paste and cook the mixture for 2–3 minutes, stirring constantly. The remaining red curry paste can be kept in the refrigerator for up to 3 months.

5 Add the chicken pieces, Thai fish sauce and sugar to the pan. Stir well, then cook for 5–6 minutes, until the chicken changes colour and is cooked through, stirring constantly to prevent the mixture from sticking to the base of the pan.

6 Pour the remaining coconut milk into the pan, then add the sliced bamboo shoots and torn kaffir lime leaves. Bring the curry back to the boil over a medium heat, stirring constantly to prevent the mixture from sticking, then taste and season with salt and pepper if necessary.

7 To serve, spoon the curry into a warmed serving dish and garnish with chopped chillies and kaffir lime leaves. Boiled Thai jasmine rice would be a good accompaniment.

VARIATION
Instead of, or as well as, bamboo shoots, use straw mushrooms. These are available in cans from Asian stores and supermarkets. Drain well and then stir into the curry at the end of the recipe.

COOK'S TIP
It is essential to use chicken breast portions, rather than any other cut, for this curry, as it is cooked very quickly. Look for diced chicken or strips of chicken (which are often labelled "stir-fry chicken") in the supermarket.

Per portion: Energy 261Kcal/1105kJ; Protein 29.6g; Carbohydrate 19.6g, of which sugars 18.3g; Fat 7.8g, of which saturates 1.5g; Cholesterol 79mg; Calcium 95mg; Fibre 1.1g; Sodium 837mg.

SPANISH PORK AND SAUSAGE CASSEROLE

THIS DISH IS FROM THE CATALAN REGION OF SPAIN, AND COMBINES PORK CHOPS WITH SPICY BUTIFARRA SAUSAGES IN A RICH TOMATO SAUCE. YOU CAN FIND THESE SAUSAGES IN SOME SPANISH DELICATESSENS BUT, IF NOT, SWEET ITALIAN SAUSAGES WILL DO.

SERVES FOUR

INGREDIENTS
    30ml/2 tbsp olive oil
    4 boneless pork chops, about
      175g/6oz each
    4 butifarra or sweet Italian sausages
    1 onion, chopped
    2 garlic cloves, chopped
    120ml/4fl oz/½ cup dry white wine
    6 plum tomatoes, chopped
    1 bay leaf
    30ml/2 tbsp chopped fresh parsley
    salt and ground black pepper
    baked potatoes and green salad,
      to serve

1 Heat the oil in a large, deep frying pan. Cook the pork chops over a high heat until browned on both sides, then transfer to a plate.

2 Add the sausages, onion and garlic to the pan and cook over a medium heat until the sausages are browned and the onion softened, turning the sausages two or three times during cooking. Return the chops to the pan.

3 Stir in the wine, tomatoes, bay leaf and parsley. Season. Cover the pan and cook for 30 minutes.

4 Remove the sausages and cut into thick slices. Return them to the pan and heat through. Serve with baked potatoes and a green salad.

Per portion: Energy 431Kcal/1803kJ; Protein 44.3g; Carbohydrate 12.5g, of which sugars 6.9g; Fat 20.8g, of which saturates 6.5g; Cholesterol 127mg; Calcium 78mg; Fibre 2.4g; Sodium 618mg.

POTATO AND SAUSAGE CASSEROLE

YOU WILL FIND NUMEROUS VARIATIONS OF THIS TRADITIONAL SUPPER DISH THROUGHOUT IRELAND, BUT THE BASIC INGREDIENTS ARE THE SAME WHEREVER YOU GO — POTATOES, SAUSAGES AND BACON.

SERVES FOUR

INGREDIENTS
  15ml/1 tbsp vegetable oil
  4 bacon rashers (strips), cut into
    2.5cm/1in pieces
  2 large onions, chopped
  2 garlic cloves, crushed
  8 large pork sausages
  4 large baking potatoes,
    thinly sliced
  1.5ml/¼ tsp fresh sage
  300ml/½ pint/1¼ cups
    vegetable stock
  salt and ground black pepper
  freshly baked soda bread,
    to serve (optional)

1 Preheat the oven to 180°C/350°F/ Gas 4. Grease a large ovenproof dish and set aside.

2 Heat the oil in a frying pan. Add the bacon and cook for 2 minutes, then add the onions and cook for 5–6 minutes, until golden. Add the garlic and cook for 1 minute, then remove the mixture from the pan and set aside.

3 Add the sausages to the pan and cook for 5–6 minutes, until golden.

4 Arrange the potatoes in the base of the prepared dish. Spoon the bacon and onion mixture on top. Season with the salt and pepper and sprinkle with the fresh sage.

5 Pour on the stock and top with the sausages. Cover and bake for 1 hour. Serve hot with soda bread if you like.

Per portion: Energy 553Kcal/2305kJ; Protein 17.4g; Carbohydrate 48.7g, of which sugars 10g; Fat 33.4g, of which saturates 11.8g; Cholesterol 51mg; Calcium 74mg; Fibre 4g; Sodium 1019mg.

LAMB'S LIVER AND BACON CASSEROLE

BOILED NEW POTATOES TOSSED IN LOTS OF BUTTER GO WELL WITH THIS SIMPLE CASSEROLE. THE TRICK WHEN COOKING LIVER IS TO SEAL IT QUICKLY, THEN SIMMER IT GENTLY AND BRIEFLY. PROLONGED AND/OR FIERCE COOKING MAKES LIVER HARD AND GRAINY.

SERVES FOUR

INGREDIENTS

  30ml/2 tbsp sunflower oil
  225g/8oz rindless unsmoked back
   (lean) bacon rashers (strips), cut
   into pieces
  2 onions, halved and sliced
  175g/6oz/2⅓ cups chestnut
   mushrooms, halved
  450g/1lb lamb's liver, trimmed
   and sliced
  25g/1oz/2 tbsp butter
  15ml/1 tbsp soy sauce
  30ml/2 tbsp plain (all-purpose) flour
  150ml/¼ pint/⅔ cup chicken stock
  salt and ground black pepper

1 Heat the oil in a frying pan and cook the bacon until crisp. Add the onions to the pan and cook for about 10 minutes, stirring frequently, or until softened. Add the mushrooms to the pan and cook for a further 1 minute.

2 Use a slotted spoon to remove the bacon and vegetables from the pan and set aside. Add the liver to the pan and cook over a high heat for 3–4 minutes, turning once to seal the slices on both sides. Remove the liver from the pan and keep warm.

3 Melt the butter in the pan, add the soy sauce and flour and blend together. Stir in the stock and bring to the boil, stirring until thickened. Return the liver and vegetables to the pan and heat through for 1 minute. Season with salt and pepper to taste, and serve with new potatoes and lightly cooked green beans.

Per portion: Energy 434Kcal/1809kJ; Protein 34.7g; Carbohydrate 13g, of which sugars 3.9g; Fat 27.4g, of which saturates 9.4g; Cholesterol 527mg; Calcium 43mg; Fibre 1.6g; Sodium 1258mg.

LAMB AND NEW POTATO CURRY

THIS DISH MAKES THE MOST OF AN ECONOMICAL CUT OF MEAT BY COOKING IT SLOWLY UNTIL THE MEAT IS FALLING FROM THE BONE. CHILLIES AND COCONUT CREAM GIVE IT LOTS OF FLAVOUR.

SERVES FOUR

INGREDIENTS

25g/1oz/2 tbsp butter
4 garlic cloves, crushed
2 onions, sliced into rings
2.5ml/½ tsp each ground cumin,
 ground coriander, turmeric and
 cayenne pepper
2–3 fresh red chillies, seeded and
 finely chopped
300ml/½ pint/1¼ cups hot
 chicken stock
200ml/7fl oz/scant 1 cup
 coconut cream
4 lamb shanks, trimmed of fat
450g/1lb new potatoes, halved
6 ripe tomatoes, quartered
salt and ground black pepper
fresh coriander (cilantro) leaves,
 to garnish
spicy rice, to serve

2 Stir in the hot stock and coconut cream. Place the lamb shanks in the liquid and cover the casserole with foil. Cook in the oven for 2 hours, turning the shanks twice, first after about an hour or so and again about half an hour later.

3 Par-boil the potatoes for 10 minutes, drain and add to the casserole with the tomatoes, then cook uncovered in the oven for a further 35 minutes. Season to taste, garnish with coriander leaves and serve with the spicy rice.

1 Preheat the oven to 160ºC/325ºF/ Gas 3. Melt the butter in a large flameproof casserole, add the garlic and onions and cook over a low heat for 15 minutes, until golden. Stir in the cumin, ground coriander, turmeric, cayenne and chillies, then cook for a further 2 minutes.

COOK'S TIP
Make this dish a day in advance if possible. Cool and chill overnight, then it will be easy to skim off the excess fat that has risen to the surface and solidified. Reheat the curry thoroughly before you serve it.

Per portion: Energy 364Kcal/1528kJ; Protein 23.5g; Carbohydrate 30.5g, of which sugars 12.1g; Fat 17.4g, of which saturates 8.8g; Cholesterol 89mg; Calcium 58mg; Fibre 3.5g; Sodium 205mg.

LAMB STEW <u>WITH</u> SHALLOTS <u>AND</u> NEW POTATOES

THIS FRESH LEMON-SEASONED STEW IS FINISHED WITH AN ITALIAN MIXTURE OF CHOPPED GARLIC, PARSLEY AND LEMON RIND KNOWN AS GREMOLATA, THE TRADITIONAL TOPPING FOR OSSO BUCCO.

SERVES SIX

INGREDIENTS
  1kg/2¼lb boneless shoulder of lamb,
    trimmed of fat and cut into 5cm/
    2in cubes
  1 garlic clove, finely chopped
  finely grated rind of ½ lemon and
    juice of 1 lemon
  90ml/6 tbsp olive oil
  45ml/3 tbsp plain (all-purpose) flour
  1 large onion, sliced
  5 anchovy fillets in olive oil, drained
  2.5ml/½ tsp caster (superfine) sugar
  300ml/½ pint/1¼ cups white wine
  475ml/16fl oz/2 cups lamb stock or
    half stock and half water
  1 fresh bay leaf
  fresh thyme sprig
  fresh parsley sprig
  500g/1¼lb small new potatoes
  250g/9oz shallots, peeled but
    left whole
  45ml/3 tbsp double (heavy)
    cream (optional)
  salt and ground black pepper
For the gremolata
  1 garlic clove, finely chopped
  finely shredded rind of ½ lemon
  45ml/3 tbsp chopped fresh flat
    leaf parsley

1 Mix the lamb with the garlic and the rind and juice of ½ lemon. Season with pepper and mix in 15ml/1 tbsp olive oil, then leave to marinate for 12–24 hours.

2 Drain the lamb, reserving the marinade, and pat the lamb dry with kitchen paper. Preheat the oven to 180°C/350°F/Gas 4.

COOK'S TIP
A mezzaluna (double-handled, half-moon shaped, curved chopping blade) makes a very good job of chopping gremolata ingredients. If using a food processor or electric chopper, take care not to overprocess the mixture as it is easy to reduce the ingredients to a paste.

3 Heat 30ml/2 tbsp olive oil in a large, heavy frying pan. Season the flour with salt and pepper and toss the lamb in it to coat, shaking off any excess. Seal the lamb on all sides in the hot oil. Do this in batches, transferring each batch of lamb to an ovenproof pan or flameproof casserole as you brown it. You may need to add an extra 15ml/1 tbsp olive oil to the pan.

4 Reduce the heat, add another 15ml/ 1 tbsp oil to the pan and cook the onion gently over a very low heat, stirring frequently, for 10 minutes, until softened and golden but not browned. Add the anchovies and caster sugar and cook, mashing the anchovies into the soft onion with a wooden spoon.

5 Add the reserved marinade, increase the heat a little and cook for about 1–2 minutes, then pour in the wine and stock or stock and water and bring to the boil. Simmer gently for about 5 minutes, then pour over the lamb.

6 Tie the bay leaf, thyme and parsley together and add to the lamb. Season with salt and pepper, then cover tightly and cook in the oven for 1 hour. Stir the potatoes into the stew and cook for a further 20 minutes.

7 Meanwhile, to make the gremolata, chop all the ingredients together finely. Place in a dish, cover and set aside.

8 Heat the remaining oil in a frying pan and brown the shallots on all sides, then stir them into the lamb. Cover and cook for a further 30–40 minutes, until the lamb is tender. Transfer the lamb and vegetables to a dish and keep warm. Discard the herbs.

9 Boil the cooking juices to reduce and concentrate them, then add the cream, if using, and simmer for 2–3 minutes. Adjust the seasoning, adding a little lemon juice to taste. Pour this sauce over the lamb, sprinkle the gremolata on top and serve immediately.

Per portion: Energy 553Kcal/2311kJ; Protein 37g; Carbohydrate 26.2g, of which sugars 5.3g; Fat 30.6g, of which saturates 10.4g; Cholesterol 128mg; Calcium 79mg; Fibre 2.7g; Sodium 261mg.

SPICED LAMB WITH TOMATOES AND PEPPERS

SELECT LEAN TENDER LAMB FROM THE LEG FOR THIS LIGHTLY SPICED CURRY WITH SUCCULENT PEPPERS AND ONION WEDGES. SERVE WITH WARM NAAN BREAD TO MOP UP THE TOMATO-RICH JUICES.

SERVES SIX

INGREDIENTS

1.5kg/3¼lb boneless lamb, cubed
250ml/8fl oz/1 cup natural
 (plain) yogurt
30ml/2 tbsp sunflower oil
3 onions
2 red (bell) peppers, seeded and cut
 into chunks
3 garlic cloves, finely chopped
1 red chilli, seeded and chopped
2.5cm/1in piece fresh root ginger,
 peeled and chopped
30ml/2 tbsp mild curry paste
2 x 400g/14oz cans tomatoes
large pinch of saffron threads
800g/1¾lb plum tomatoes, halved,
 seeded and cut into chunks
salt and ground black pepper
chopped fresh coriander (cilantro),
 to garnish

1 Mix the lamb with the yogurt in a bowl. Cover and chill for about 1 hour. (Marinating in yogurt helps to tenderize the meat and reduce the cooking time.)

2 Heat the oil in a karahi, wok or large pan. Drain the lamb and reserve the yogurt, then cook the lamb, in batches, until it is golden on all sides – this takes about 15 minutes in total. Remove from the pan and set aside.

3 Cut two of the onions into wedges (six from each onion) and add to the oil remaining in the pan. Cook the onion wedges over a medium heat for about 10 minutes, or until they are beginning to colour. Add the peppers and cook for a further 5 minutes. Use a slotted spoon to remove the vegetables from the pan and set aside.

4 Meanwhile, chop the remaining onion. Add it to the oil remaining in the pan with the garlic, chilli and ginger, and cook, stirring frequently, until softened.

5 Stir in the curry paste and canned tomatoes with the reserved yogurt marinade. Replace the lamb, add seasoning to taste and stir well. Bring to the boil, reduce the heat and simmer for about 30 minutes.

6 Pound the saffron to a powder in a mortar, then stir in a little boiling water to dissolve it. Add this liquid to the curry. Replace the onion and pepper mixture. Stir in the fresh tomatoes and bring back to simmering point, then cook for 15 minutes. Garnish with chopped coriander to serve.

Per portion: Energy 587Kcal/2456kJ; Protein 54.7g; Carbohydrate 19.5g, of which sugars 17.7g; Fat 33g, of which saturates 13.8g; Cholesterol 191mg; Calcium 143mg; Fibre 4g; Sodium 318mg.

OSSO BUCCO WITH RISOTTO MILANESE

LITERALLY MEANING BONE WITH A HOLE, OSSO BUCCO IS A TRADITIONAL MILANESE STEW OF VEAL, ONIONS AND LEEKS IN WHITE WINE. MANY OF TODAY'S VERSIONS ALSO INCLUDE TOMATOES. RISOTTO MILANESE IS THE ARCHETYPAL ITALIAN RISOTTO AND THE CLASSIC ACCOMPANIMENT FOR OSSO BUCCO.

SERVES FOUR

INGREDIENTS

  50g/2oz/¼ cup butter
  15ml/1 tbsp olive oil
  1 large onion, chopped
  1 leek, finely chopped
  45ml/3 tbsp plain (all-purpose) flour
  4 large portions of veal shin (shank)
  600ml/1 pint/2½ cups dry white wine
  salt and ground black pepper
For the risotto
  25g/1oz/2 tbsp butter
  1 onion, finely chopped
  350g/12oz/1⅔ cups risotto rice
  1 litre/1¾ pints/4 cups boiling
    chicken stock
  2.5ml/½ tsp saffron threads
  60ml/4 tbsp white wine
  50g/2oz/⅔ cup Parmesan cheese,
    coarsely grated
For the gremolata
  grated rind of 1 lemon
  30ml/2 tbsp chopped fresh parsley
  1 garlic clove, finely chopped

1 Heat the butter and oil until sizzling in a large frying pan. Add the onion and leek, and cook gently for about 5 minutes without browning the onions. Season the flour and toss the veal in it, then add it to the pan and cook over a high heat until browned.

COOK'S TIP
When buying veal shin, ask for the pieces to be cut thickly so that they will retain the marrow during cooking (or check that they are prepared this way if purchasing prepacked meat).

2 Gradually stir in the wine and heat until simmering. Cover the pan and simmer for 1½ hours, stirring occasionally, or until the meat is very tender. Use a slotted spoon to transfer the veal to a warm serving dish, then boil the sauce rapidly until reduced and thickened to the required consistency.

3 Make the risotto about 30 minutes before the end of the cooking time for the stew. Melt the butter in a large pan and cook the onion until softened.

4 Stir in the rice to coat all the grains in butter. Add a ladleful of boiling chicken stock and mix well. Continue adding the boiling stock a ladleful at a time, letting each portion be absorbed before adding the next. The whole process takes about 20 minutes.

5 Pound the saffron threads in a mortar, then stir in the wine. Add the saffron-scented wine to the risotto and cook for a final 5 minutes. Remove the pan from the heat and stir in the Parmesan.

6 Mix the lemon rind, parsley and garlic for the gremolata. Spoon some risotto on to each plate, then add the veal. Sprinkle with gremolata and serve immediately.

Per portion: Energy 901Kcal/3764kJ; Protein 49.1g; Carbohydrate 92g, of which sugars 8g; Fat 25.9g, of which saturates 13.7g; Cholesterol 130mg; Calcium 248mg; Fibre 2.9g; Sodium 350mg.

BEEF CARBONADE

THIS RICH, DARK STEW OF BEEF, COOKED SLOWLY WITH LOTS OF ONIONS, GARLIC AND BEER, IS A CLASSIC CASSEROLE FROM THE NORTH OF FRANCE AND NEIGHBOURING BELGIUM.

3 Reduce the heat and return the onions to the pan. Add the garlic, cook briefly, then add the beer or ale, water and sugar. Tie the thyme and bay leaf together and add to the pan with the celery. Bring to the boil, stirring, then season with salt and pepper.

4 Pour the sauce over the beef and mix well. Cover tightly, then place in the oven for 2½ hours. Check the beef once or twice to make sure that it is not too dry, adding a little water, if necessary. Test for tenderness, allowing an extra 30–40 minutes' cooking if necessary.

SERVES SIX

INGREDIENTS
  45ml/3 tbsp vegetable oil or
  beef dripping (drippings)
  3 onions, sliced
  45ml/3 tbsp plain (all-purpose) flour
  2.5ml/½ tsp mustard powder
  1kg/2¼lb boneless beef shin (shank)
  or chuck, cut into large cubes
  2–3 garlic cloves, finely chopped
  300ml/½ pint/1¼ cups dark beer or ale
  150ml/¼ pint/⅔ cup water
  5ml/1 tsp dark brown sugar
  1 fresh thyme sprig
  1 fresh bay leaf
  1 piece celery stick
  salt and ground black pepper
For the topping
  50g/2oz/¼ cup butter
  1 garlic clove, crushed
  15ml/1 tbsp Dijon mustard
  45ml/3 tbsp chopped fresh parsley
  6–12 slices baguette or ficelle loaf

1 Preheat the oven to 160°C/325°F/ Gas 3. Heat 30ml/2 tbsp of the oil or dripping in a frying pan and cook the onions over a low heat until softened. Remove from the pan and set aside.

2 Meanwhile, mix together the flour and mustard and season. Toss the beef in the flour. Add the remaining oil or dripping to the pan and heat over a high heat. Brown the beef all over, then transfer it to a casserole.

5 To make the topping, cream the butter with the garlic, mustard and 30ml/2 tbsp of the parsley. Spread the butter thickly over the bread. Increase the oven temperature to 190°C/375°F/ Gas 5. Taste and season the casserole, then arrange the bread slices, buttered side uppermost, on top. Bake for 20–25 minutes, until the bread is browned and crisp. Sprinkle the remaining parsley over the top and serve immediately.

Per portion: Energy 577Kcal/2410kJ; Protein 42.8g; Carbohydrate 32.8g, of which sugars 9.6g; Fat 28.8g, of which saturates 11.5g; Cholesterol 114mg; Calcium 87mg; Fibre 2.1g; Sodium 414mg.

CHILLI CON CARNE

ORIGINALLY MADE WITH FINELY CHOPPED BEEF, CHILLIES AND KIDNEY BEANS BY HUNGRY LABOURERS WORKING ON THE TEXAN RAILROAD, THIS FAMOUS TEX-MEX STEW HAS BECOME AN INTERNATIONAL FAVOURITE. SERVE WITH RICE OR BAKED POTATOES TO COMPLETE THIS HEARTY MEAL.

SERVES EIGHT

INGREDIENTS
    1.2kg/2½lb lean braising steak
    30ml/2 tbsp sunflower oil
    1 large onion, chopped
    2 garlic cloves, finely chopped
    15ml/1 tbsp plain (all-purpose) flour
    300ml/½ pint/1¼ cups red wine
    300ml/½ pint/1¼ cups beef stock
    30ml/2 tbsp tomato purée (paste)
    fresh coriander (cilantro) leaves
    salt and ground black pepper
For the beans
    30ml/2 tbsp olive oil
    1 onion, chopped
    1 red chilli, seeded and chopped
    2 x 400g/14oz cans red kidney
      beans, drained and rinsed
    400g/14oz can chopped tomatoes
For the topping
    6 tomatoes, peeled and chopped
    1 green chilli, seeded and chopped
    30ml/2 tbsp chopped fresh chives
    30ml/2 tbsp fresh coriander (cilantro)
    150ml/¼ pint/⅔ cup sour cream

2 Use a slotted spoon to remove the onion from the pan, then add the floured beef and cook over a high heat until browned on all sides. Remove from the pan and set aside, then flour and brown another batch of meat.

3 When the last batch of meat is browned, return the first batches with the onion to the pan. Stir in the wine, stock and tomato purée. Bring to the boil, reduce the heat and simmer for 45 minutes, or until the beef is tender.

4 Meanwhile, for the beans, heat the olive oil in a frying pan and cook the onion and chilli until softened. Add the kidney beans and tomatoes and simmer gently for 20–25 minutes, or until thickened and reduced.

5 Mix the tomatoes, chilli, chives and coriander for the topping. Ladle the meat mixture on to warmed plates. Add a layer of bean mixture and tomato topping. Finish with sour cream and garnish with coriander leaves.

1 Cut the meat into thick strips and then cut it crossways into small cubes. Heat the oil in a large, flameproof casserole. Add the chopped onion and garlic, and cook until softened but not coloured. Meanwhile, season the flour and place it on a plate, then toss a batch of meat in it.

VARIATION
This stew is equally good served with tortillas instead of rice. Wrap the tortillas in foil and warm through in the oven.

Per portion: Energy 470Kcal/1969kJ; Protein 42g; Carbohydrate 28.4g, of which sugars 11.2g; Fat 18.9g, of which saturates 6.9g; Cholesterol 106mg; Calcium 124mg; Fibre 8.2g; Sodium 517mg.

STOVE-TOP DISHES

It is remarkable how many main meals can be cooked entirely on top of the stove, from Classic Fish and Chips to steamed specialities like Sea Bass with Orange Chilli Salsa. This is very much hands-on cooking and often achieves better results than when food is cooked in the oven, largely because the cook is more likely to stir and check the dish regularly. The aroma of the cooking food stimulates the appetite, doubling the enjoyment of those lucky enough to tuck into such tasty dishes as Bang Bang Chicken or Pot-roasted Brisket.

MOULES PROVENÇALES

EATING THESE DELECTABLE MUSSELS IS A MESSY AFFAIR, WHICH IS PART OF THEIR CHARM. HAND ROUND PLENTY OF CRUSTY FRENCH BREAD FOR MOPPING UP THE JUICES AND DON'T FORGET FINGERBOWLS OF WARM WATER AND A PLATE FOR DISCARDED SHELLS.

SERVES FOUR

INGREDIENTS

30ml/2 tbsp olive oil
200g/7oz rindless unsmoked streaky (fatty) bacon, cubed
1 onion, finely chopped
3 garlic cloves, finely chopped
1 bay leaf
15ml/1 tbsp chopped fresh mixed Provençal herbs, such as thyme, marjoram, basil, oregano and savory
15–30ml/1–2 tbsp sun-dried tomatoes in oil, chopped
4 large, very ripe tomatoes, peeled, seeded and chopped
50g/2oz/½ cup pitted black olives, chopped
105ml/7 tbsp dry white wine
2.25kg/5–5¼lb fresh mussels, scrubbed and bearded
salt and ground black pepper
60ml/4 tbsp coarsely chopped fresh parsley, to garnish

1 Heat the oil in a large pan. Cook the bacon until golden and crisp. Remove with a slotted spoon; set aside. Add the onion and garlic to the pan and cook gently until softened. Add the herbs, with both types of tomatoes. Cook gently for 5 minutes, stirring frequently. Stir in the olives and season.

2 Put the wine and mussels in another pan. Cover and shake over a high heat for 5 minutes, until the mussels open. Discard any that remain closed.

3 Strain the mussel cooking liquid into the pan containing the tomato sauce through a sieve lined with muslin (cheesecloth) and boil until the mixture is reduced by about one-third. Add the mussels and stir to coat them thoroughly with the sauce. Remove and discard the bay leaf.

4 Divide the mussels and sauce among four heated dishes. Sprinkle over the fried bacon and chopped parsley and serve piping hot.

Per portion: Energy 439Kcal/1836kJ; Protein 34.9g; Carbohydrate 12.8g, of which sugars 6.9g; Fat 25.9g, of which saturates 6.2g; Cholesterol 123mg; Calcium 112mg; Fibre 2.4g; Sodium 1467mg.

FRENCH MUSSELS

THIS IS A TRADITIONAL DISH OF MUSSELS COOKED WITH SHALLOTS, GARLIC AND SAFFRON FROM THE WEST ATLANTIC COAST OF FRANCE. IT TASTES AS SUPERB AS IT LOOKS.

SERVES SIX

INGREDIENTS

2kg/4½lb fresh mussels, scrubbed
  and bearded
250g/9oz shallots, finely chopped
300ml/½ pint/1¼ cups medium white
  wine, such as Vouvray
generous pinch of saffron threads
  (about 12 strands)
75g/3oz/6 tbsp butter
2 celery sticks, finely chopped
5ml/1 tsp fennel seeds,
  lightly crushed
2 large garlic cloves, finely chopped
250ml/8fl oz/1 cup fish or stock
1 bay leaf
pinch of cayenne pepper
2 large (US extra large) egg yolks
150ml/¼ pint/⅔ cup double
  (heavy) cream
juice of ½–1 lemon
30–45ml/2–3 tbsp chopped
  fresh parsley
salt and ground black pepper

1 Discard any mussels that do not shut when tapped sharply.

2 Place 30ml/2 tbsp of the shallots with the wine in a wide pan and bring to the boil. Add half the mussels and cover, then boil rapidly for 1 minute, shaking the pan once. Remove all the mussels, discarding any that remain closed. Repeat with the remaining mussels. Remove the top half-shell from each mussel. Strain the cooking liquid through a fine sieve into a bowl and stir in the saffron, then set aside.

3 Melt 50g/2oz/4 tbsp of the butter in a heavy pan. Add the remaining shallots and celery and cook over a low heat, stirring occasionally, for 5–6 minutes, until softened but not browned. Add the fennel seeds and half of the garlic, then cook for another 2–3 minutes.

4 Pour in the reserved mussel liquid, bring to the boil and then simmer for 5 minutes before adding the stock, bay leaf and cayenne. Season with salt and pepper to taste, then simmer, uncovered, for 5–10 minutes.

5 Beat the egg yolks with the cream, then whisk in a ladleful of the hot liquid followed by the juice of ½ lemon. Whisk this mixture back into the sauce. Cook over a very low heat, without allowing it to boil, for 5–10 minutes until slightly thickened. Taste for seasoning and add more lemon juice if necessary.

6 Stir the remaining garlic, butter and most of the parsley into the sauce with the mussels and reheat for 30–60 seconds. Distribute the mussels among six soup plates and ladle the sauce over. Sprinkle with the remaining parsley and serve.

Per portion: Energy 568Kcal/2360kJ; Protein 26g; Carbohydrate 9.9g, of which sugars 5.4g; Fat 42.1g, of which saturates 23.6g; Cholesterol 272mg; Calcium 149mg; Fibre 1.4g; Sodium 632mg.

STEAMED FISH WITH FIVE WILLOW SAUCE

A FISH KETTLE WILL COME IN USEFUL FOR THIS RECIPE. CARP IS TRADITIONALLY USED, BUT ANY CHUNKY FISH THAT CAN BE COOKED WHOLE, SUCH AS SALMON OR SEA BREAM, CAN BE GIVEN THIS TREATMENT. MAKE SURE YOU HAVE A SUITABLE LARGE PLATTER FOR SERVING THIS SPECTACULAR DISH.

SERVES FOUR

INGREDIENTS
- 1–2 carp or similar whole fish, total weight about 1kg/2¼ lb, cleaned and scaled
- 2.5cm/1in piece fresh root ginger, peeled and thinly sliced
- 4 spring onions (scallions), cut into thin strips
- 2.5ml/½ tsp salt

For the five willow sauce
- 375g/13oz jar chow chow (Chinese sweet mixed pickles)
- 300ml/½ pint/1¼ cups water
- 30ml/2 tbsp rice vinegar
- 25ml/1½ tbsp sugar
- 25ml/1½ tbsp cornflour (cornstarch)
- 15ml/1 tbsp light soy sauce
- 15ml/1 tbsp rice wine or medium-dry sherry
- 1 small green (bell) pepper, seeded and diced
- 1 carrot, peeled and cut into batons
- 1 tomato, peeled, seeded and diced

2 Fold up one or two pieces of foil to make a long wide strip. You will need one for each fish. Place the fish on the foil and then lift the fish on to the trivet. Lower the trivet into the fish kettle and tuck the ends of the foil over the fish.

3 Pour boiling water into the fish kettle to a depth of 2.5cm/1in. Bring to a full rolling boil, then lower the heat and cook the fish until the flesh flakes, topping up the kettle with boiling water as necessary. (See Cook's Tip for cooking times.)

5 In a small bowl, mix the cornflour to a paste with the remaining water. Stir in the soy sauce and rice wine or sherry.

6 Add the mixture to the sauce and bring to the boil, stirring until it thickens and becomes glossy. Add all the vegetables, the chopped pickles and the pickle liquid and cook over a gentle heat for 2 minutes.

7 Using the foil strips as a support, carefully transfer the cooked fish to a platter, then ease the foil away. Spoon the warm sauce over the fish and serve.

COOK'S TIP
If using one large fish that is too long to fit in a fish kettle, cut it in half and cook it on a rack placed over a large roasting pan. Pour in a similar quantity of boiling water as for the fish kettle, cover with foil and cook on top of the stove. Allow about 20–25 minutes for a 1kg/2¼ lb fish; 15–20 minutes for a 675g/1½lb fish. Reassemble the halved fish before coating it with the sauce.

1 Rinse the fish inside and out. Dry with kitchen paper. Create a support for each fish by placing a broad strip of oiled foil on the work surface. Place the fish on the foil. Mix the ginger, spring onions and salt, then tuck the mixture into the body cavity.

4 Meanwhile, prepare the sauce. Tip the chow chow into a sieve placed over a bowl and reserve the liquid. Cut each of the pickles in half. Pour 250ml/8fl oz/1 cup of the water into a pan and bring to the boil. Add the vinegar and sugar and stir until dissolved.

Per portion: Energy 156Kcal/655kJ; Protein 19.1g; Carbohydrate 7.8g, of which sugars 6.3g; Fat 5.1g, of which saturates 1g; Cholesterol 67mg; Calcium 77mg; Fibre 2.4g; Sodium 739mg.

CHINESE-STYLE STEAMED FISH

THIS IS A CLASSIC CHINESE WAY OF COOKING WHOLE FISH, WITH GARLIC, SPRING ONIONS, GINGER AND BLACK BEANS. THE FISH MAKES A SPLENDID CENTREPIECE FOR A CHINESE MEAL OR IT CAN BE SERVED MORE SIMPLY, WITH BOILED RICE AND SOME STIR-FRIED CHINESE GREENS.

SERVES FOUR TO SIX

INGREDIENTS

    2 sea bass, or trout, each weighing
       about 675–800g/1½–1¾lb
    25ml/1½ tbsp salted black beans
    2.5ml/½ tsp sugar
    30ml/2 tbsp finely shredded fresh
       root ginger
    4 garlic cloves, thinly sliced
    30ml/2 tbsp Chinese rice wine or
       dry sherry
    30ml/2 tbsp light soy sauce
    4–6 spring onions (scallions), finely
       shredded or sliced diagonally
    45ml/3 tbsp groundnut (peanut) oil
    10ml/2 tsp sesame oil

1 Wash the fish inside and out under cold running water, then pat them dry on kitchen paper. Using a sharp knife, slash three or four deep cross shapes on each side of each fish.

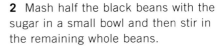

2 Mash half the black beans with the sugar in a small bowl and then stir in the remaining whole beans.

3 Place a little ginger and garlic inside the cavity of each fish and then lay them on a plate or dish that will fit inside a large steamer. Rub the bean mixture into the fish, especially into the slashes, then sprinkle the remaining ginger and garlic over the top. Cover and chill for 30 minutes.

4 Place the steamer over a pan of boiling water. Sprinkle the rice wine or sherry and half the soy sauce over the fish and steam them for 15–20 minutes, or until just cooked.

5 Sprinkle with the remaining soy sauce and sprinkle the spring onions over the fish.

6 In a small pan, heat the groundnut oil until smoking, then trickle it over the spring onions. Sprinkle with the sesame oil and serve immediately.

Per portion: Energy 415Kcal/1741kJ; Protein 54.7g; Carbohydrate 1.6g, of which sugars 1.5g; Fat 20.3g, of which saturates 4.3g; Cholesterol 224mg; Calcium 90mg; Fibre 0.2g; Sodium 739mg.

SEA BASS WITH ORANGE CHILLI SALSA

THE CHILLI CITRUS SALSA HAS A FRESHNESS WHICH PROVIDES THE PERFECT CONTRAST TO THE
WONDERFUL FLAVOUR OF FRESH SEA BASS.

SERVES FOUR

INGREDIENTS
   4 sea bass fillets
   salt and ground black pepper
   fresh coriander (cilantro), to garnish
For the salsa
   2 fresh green chillies
   2 oranges or pink grapefruit
   1 small onion

1 Make the salsa. Roast the chillies in a dry griddle pan until the skins are blistered, being careful not to let the flesh burn. Put them in a strong plastic bag and tie the top to keep the steam in. Set aside for 20 minutes.

COOK'S TIP
If the fish has not been scaled, do this by running the back of a small filleting knife against the grain of the scales. They should come away cleanly. Rinse and pat dry with kitchen paper.

2 Slice the top and bottom off each orange or grapefruit and cut off all the peel and pith. Cut between the membranes and put each segment in a bowl.

3 Remove the chillies from the bag and peel off the skins. Cut off the stalks, then slit the chillies and scrape out the seeds. Chop the flesh finely. Cut the onion in half and slice it thinly. Add the onion and chillies to the orange pieces and mix lightly. Season and chill.

4 Season the sea bass fillets. Line a steamer with greaseproof (waxed) paper, allowing extra to hang over the sides to help lift out the fish after cooking. Place the empty steamer over a pan of water and bring to the boil.

5 Place the fish in a single layer in the steamer. Cover with a lid and steam for about 8 minutes, or until just cooked. Garnish with fresh coriander and serve with the salsa and a vegetable side dish of your choice.

Per portion: Energy 181Kcal/763kJ; Protein 30.2g; Carbohydrate 6.6g, of which sugars 6.3g; Fat 3.9g, of which saturates 0.6g; Cholesterol 120mg; Calcium 232mg; Fibre 1.3g; Sodium 108mg.

FILLETS OF TURBOT WITH OYSTERS

THIS LUXURIOUS DISH IS PERFECT FOR SPECIAL OCCASIONS. IT IS WORTH BUYING A WHOLE TURBOT AND ASKING THE FISHMONGER TO FILLET AND SKIN IT FOR YOU. KEEP THE HEAD, BONES AND TRIMMINGS FOR STOCK. SOLE, BRILL AND HALIBUT CAN ALL BE SUBSTITUTED FOR THE TURBOT.

SERVES FOUR

INGREDIENTS
12 Pacific (rock) oysters
115g/4oz/½ cup butter
2 carrots, cut into julienne strips
200g/7oz celeriac, cut into
   julienne strips
the white parts of 2 leeks, cut into
   julienne strips
375ml/13fl oz/generous 1½ cups
   Champagne or dry white sparkling
   wine (about ½ bottle)
105ml/7 tbsp whipping cream
1 turbot, about 1.75kg/4–4½lb,
   filleted and skinned
salt and ground white pepper

1 Using an oyster knife, open the oysters over a bowl to catch the juices, then carefully remove them from their shells, discarding the shells, and place them in a separate bowl. Set aside until required.

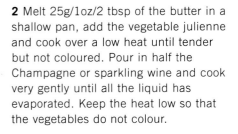

2 Melt 25g/1oz/2 tbsp of the butter in a shallow pan, add the vegetable julienne and cook over a low heat until tender but not coloured. Pour in half the Champagne or sparkling wine and cook very gently until all the liquid has evaporated. Keep the heat low so that the vegetables do not colour.

3 Strain the oyster juices into a small pan and add the cream and the remaining Champagne or sparkling wine. Place over a medium heat until the mixture has reduced to the consistency of thin cream. Dice half the remaining butter and whisk it into the sauce, one piece at a time, until smooth. Season to taste, then pour the sauce into a blender and process until velvety smooth.

4 Return the sauce to the pan, bring it to just below boiling point, then drop in the oysters. Poach for about 1 minute, to warm but barely cook. Keep warm, but do not let the sauce boil.

5 Season the turbot fillets with salt and pepper. Heat the remaining butter in a large frying pan until foaming, then cook the fillets over a medium heat for about 2–3 minutes on each side, until cooked through and golden.

6 Cut each turbot fillet into three pieces and arrange on individual warmed plates. Pile the vegetable julienne on top, place three oysters around the turbot fillets on each plate and pour the sauce around the edge.

Per portion: Energy 752Kcal/3125kJ; Protein 66.7g; Carbohydrate 9.2g, of which sugars 8g; Fat 44.1g, of which saturates 23.9g; Cholesterol 106mg; Calcium 252mg; Fibre 1.4g; Sodium 370mg.

COD CARAMBA

THIS COLOURFUL MEXICAN DISH, WITH ITS CONTRASTING CRUNCHY TOPPING AND TENDER FISH FILLING, CAN BE MADE WITH ANY ECONOMICAL WHITE FISH, SUCH AS COLEY OR HADDOCK.

SERVES FOUR TO SIX

INGREDIENTS
450g/1lb cod fillets
225g/8oz smoked cod fillets
300ml/½ pint/1¼ cups fish stock
50g/2oz/¼ cup butter
1 onion, sliced
2 garlic cloves, crushed
1 green and 1 red (bell) pepper,
  seeded and diced
2 courgettes (zucchini), diced
115g/4oz/⅔ cup drained canned or
  thawed frozen corn kernels
2 tomatoes, peeled and chopped
juice of 1 lime
Tabasco sauce
salt, ground black pepper and
  cayenne pepper
For the topping
75g/3oz tortilla chips
50g/2oz/½ cup grated
  Cheddar cheese
coriander (cilantro) sprigs, to garnish
lime wedges, to serve

1 Lay the fish in a shallow pan and pour over the fish stock. Bring to the boil, lower the heat, cover and poach for about 8 minutes, until the flesh flakes easily when tested with the tip of a sharp knife. Leave to cool slightly, then remove the skin and separate the flesh into large flakes. Keep hot.

2 Melt the butter in a pan, add the onion and garlic and cook over a low heat until soft. Add the peppers, stir and cook for 2 minutes. Stir in the courgettes and cook for 3 minutes more, until all the vegetables are tender.

3 Mix the corn and tomatoes, then add lime juice and Tabasco to taste. Add to the pan, season with salt, black pepper and cayenne. Cook for 2 minutes to heat the corn and tomatoes, then stir in the fish and transfer to a dish that can safely be used under the grill (broiler).

4 Preheat the grill. Make the topping by crushing the tortilla chips, then mixing in the grated cheese. Add cayenne pepper to taste and sprinkle over the fish. Place the dish under the grill until the topping is crisp and brown. Garnish with coriander sprigs and lime wedges.

Per portion: Energy 439Kcal/1834kJ; Protein 39.8g; Carbohydrate 23.7g, of which sugars 11.3g; Fat 20.8g, of which saturates 10.4g; Cholesterol 116mg; Calcium 185mg; Fibre 4.8g; Sodium 1391mg.

CLASSIC FISH AND CHIPS

NOTHING BEATS A PIECE OF COD COOKED TO A CRISP WITH FRESHLY MADE CHIPS ON THE SIDE. THE BATTER SHOULD BE LIGHT AND CRISP, BUT NOT TOO GREASY AND THE FISH SHOULD MELT IN THE MOUTH. SERVE WITH LIME WEDGES IF YOU REALLY WANT TO SHOW OFF. THE SECRET OF COOKING FISH AND CHIPS SUCCESSFULLY IS TO MAKE SURE THE OIL IS FRESH AND CLEAN. HEAT THE OIL TO THE CORRECT TEMPERATURE BEFORE COOKING THE CHIPS AND AGAIN BEFORE YOU ADD THE FISH. SERVE THE DISH IMMEDIATELY, WHILE STILL CRISP AND PIPING HOT.

SERVES FOUR

INGREDIENTS
450g/1lb potatoes
groundnut (peanut) oil for deep-frying
4 x 175g/6oz cod fillets, skinned
lemon wedges, to garnish
For the batter
75g/3oz/⅔ cup plain (all-purpose) flour
1 egg yolk
10ml/2 tsp oil
salt

1 Cut the potatoes into 5mm/¼in thick slices. Cut each slice again to make 5mm/¼in chips (French fries).

2 Heat the oil in a deep-fryer to 180°C/350°F. Add the chips to the fryer and cook for 3 minutes, then remove from the pan and shake off all fat and set to one side.

3 To make the batter, sift the flour into a bowl and add the remaining ingredients with a pinch of salt. Beat well until smooth. Set aside until ready to use.

4 Cook the chips again in the fat for a further 5 minutes or so, until they are really nice and crisp. Drain on kitchen paper and season with salt. Keep hot in a low oven while you cook the pieces of fish.

VARIATION
Although cod is the traditional choice for fish and chips, you can also use haddock. Rock salmon, sometimes sold as huss or dogfish, also has a good flavour. It has a central length of cartilage which cannot be removed before cooking – otherwise the pieces of fish will fall apart – but can be easily prised out once the fish is served.

5 Dip the fish into the batter, making sure they are evenly coated, and shake off any excess.

6 Carefully lower the fish into the fat and cook for 5 minutes. Drain on kitchen paper. Serve with lemon wedges and the chips.

COOK'S TIPS
• Use fresh rather than frozen fish for the very best texture and flavour. If you have to use frozen fish, thaw it thoroughly and make sure it is dry before coating with batter.
• Ideally, you should use fresh oil for deep-frying each time, but it can usually be safely re-used once more. Do not use the same oil repeatedly, as it gradually breaks down and will smoke or even ignite quite easily. Long storage may cause it to turn rancid. After the first use, cool, then strain the oil to remove any debris. Remember, too, that the oil will be flavoured, to some extent, by the food first cooked in it.
• People keeping an eye on their fat intake may not realize that deep-fried foods absorb less fat during cooking than shallow-fried foods. This is because the initial submersion in the oil, providing it has been heated to the correct temperature, quickly seals the outside, preventing any more fat from being absorbed by the food.

Per portion: Energy 740Kcal/3093kJ; Protein 32.8g; Carbohydrate 61g, of which sugars 0.8g; Fat 42.2g, of which saturates 4.2g; Cholesterol 0mg; Calcium 134mg; Fibre 3.6g; Sodium 313mg.

TANDOORI CHICKEN

THE WORD TANDOORI REFERS TO A METHOD OF COOKING IN A CHARCOAL-FIRED CLAY OVEN CALLED A TANDOOR. IN NORTHERN INDIA AND PAKISTAN, A WIDE VARIETY OF FOODS IS COOKED IN THIS TYPE OF OVEN, BUT IN WESTERN COUNTRIES THE METHOD IS MOST POPULAR FOR CHICKEN. WARM NAAN BREAD AND MANGO CHUTNEY MAY BE OFFERED WITH THE CHICKEN AND RICE.

SERVES FOUR

INGREDIENTS

30ml/2 tbsp vegetable oil
2 small onions, cut into wedges
2 garlic cloves, sliced
4 skinless, boneless chicken breast
  portions, cut into cubes
100ml/3½fl oz/⅓ cup water
300g/11oz jar tandoori sauce
salt and ground black pepper
coriander (cilantro) sprigs, to garnish
To serve
5ml/1 tsp ground turmeric
350g/12oz/1⅔ cups basmati rice

1 Heat the oil in a flameproof casserole. Add the onions and garlic, and cook for about 3 minutes, or until the onion is beginning to soften, stirring frequently.

2 Add the cubes of chicken to the casserole and cook for 6 minutes. Stir the water into the tandoori sauce and pour it over the chicken. Bring to the boil, then reduce the heat and simmer for 10 minutes, or until the chicken pieces are cooked through and the sauce is slightly reduced and thickened.

3 Meanwhile, bring a large pan of lightly salted water to the boil, add the turmeric and rice and bring back to the boil. Stir once, reduce the heat to prevent the water from boiling over and simmer the rice for 12 minutes, or according to the time suggested on the packet, until tender.

4 Drain the rice well and serve with the tandoori chicken on warmed individual serving plates, garnished with sprigs of fresh coriander.

COOK'S TIP
You will find jars of ready-made tandoori sauce in large supermarkets.

Per portion: Energy 592Kcal/2479kJ; Protein 44g; Carbohydrate 77.5g, of which sugars 4.5g; Fat 11.4g, of which saturates 1.1g; Cholesterol 105mg; Calcium 54mg; Fibre 0.4g; Sodium 826mg.

CHICKEN AND VEGETABLE TAGINE

MOROCCAN TAGINES ARE USUALLY SERVED WITH COUSCOUS, BUT RICE MAKES AN EQUALLY DELICIOUS ACCOMPANIMENT. HERE, COUSCOUS IS STIRRED INTO THE RICE TO CREATE AN UNUSUAL AND TASTY DISH, ALTHOUGH YOU COULD USE RICE BY ITSELF.

SERVES FOUR

INGREDIENTS
30ml/2 tbsp groundnut (peanut) oil
4 skinless, boneless chicken breast
   portions, cut into large pieces
1 large onion, chopped
2 garlic cloves, crushed
1 parsnip, cut into 2.5cm/1in pieces
1 turnip, cut into 2cm/¾in pieces
3 carrots, cut into 4cm/1½in pieces
4 tomatoes, chopped
1 cinnamon stick
4 cloves
5ml/1 tsp ground ginger
1 bay leaf
1.5–2.5ml/¼–½ tsp cayenne pepper
350ml/12fl oz/1½ cups chicken stock
400g/14oz can chickpeas, drained
   and skinned
1 red (bell) pepper, seeded
   and sliced
150g/5oz green beans, halved
1 piece of preserved lemon peel,
   thinly sliced
20–30 pitted brown or green olives
salt
For the rice and couscous
750ml/1¼ pints/3 cups chicken stock
225g/8oz/generous 1 cup
   long grain rice
115g/4oz/⅔ cup couscous
45ml/3 tbsp chopped fresh
   coriander (cilantro)

1 Heat half of the oil in a large, flameproof casserole and cook the chicken pieces for a few minutes until evenly browned. Transfer to a plate.

2 Heat the remaining oil and cook the onion, garlic, parsnip, turnip and carrots together over a medium heat for 4–5 minutes until the vegetables are lightly flecked with brown, stirring frequently. Lower the heat, cover and sweat the vegetables for 5 minutes more, stirring occasionally.

3 Add the tomatoes, cook for a few minutes, then add the cinnamon stick, cloves, ginger, bay leaf and cayenne. Cook for 1–2 minutes.

4 Pour in the chicken stock, add the chickpeas and browned chicken pieces, and season with salt. Cover and simmer for 25 minutes.

5 Meanwhile, cook the rice and couscous mixture. Bring the chicken stock to the boil. Add the rice and simmer for about 5 minutes until almost tender. Remove the pan from the heat, stir in the couscous, cover tightly and leave for about 5 minutes.

6 When the vegetables in the tagine are almost tender, stir in the pepper slices and green beans and simmer for 10 minutes. Add the preserved lemon and olives, stir well and cook for 5 minutes more, or until the vegetables are perfectly tender.

7 Stir the chopped coriander into the rice and couscous mixture and pile it on to a plate. Serve the chicken tagine in the traditional dish, if you have one, or in a casserole.

Per portion: Energy 707Kcal/2985kJ; Protein 52.6g; Carbohydrate 99.5g, of which sugars 16.9g; Fat 13.7g, of which saturates 2.6g; Cholesterol 105mg; Calcium 164mg; Fibre 10.8g; Sodium 344mg.

BANG BANG CHICKEN

WHAT A DESCRIPTIVE NAME THIS SPECIAL DISH FROM SICHUAN HAS! USE TOASTED SESAME PASTE TO GIVE THE SAUCE AN AUTHENTIC FLAVOUR, ALTHOUGH CRUNCHY PEANUT BUTTER CAN BE USED INSTEAD. BANG BANG CHICKEN IS PERFECT FOR PARTIES AND IDEAL FOR A BUFFET.

SERVES FOUR

INGREDIENTS
   3 skinless, boneless chicken
      breast portions, total weight
      about 450g/1lb
   1 garlic clove, crushed
   2.5ml/½ tsp black peppercorns
   1 small onion, halved
   1 large cucumber, peeled, seeded
      and cut into thin strips
   salt and ground black pepper
For the sauce
   45ml/3 tbsp toasted sesame paste
   15ml/1 tbsp light soy sauce
   15ml/1 tbsp wine vinegar
   2 spring onions (scallions),
      finely chopped
   2 garlic cloves, crushed
   5 × 1cm/2 × ½in piece fresh
      root ginger, peeled and cut
      into thin batons
   15ml/1 tbsp Sichuan peppercorns,
      dry-fried and crushed
   5ml/1 tsp light brown sugar
For the chilli oil
   60ml/4 tbsp groundnut (peanut) oil
   5ml/1 tsp chilli powder

1 Place the chicken in a large, heavy pan. Pour in sufficient water just to cover, add the garlic, peppercorns and onion and bring to the boil over a medium heat. Skim off any foam that rises to the surface, stir in salt and pepper to taste, then cover the pan. Lower the heat and cook for about 25 minutes, or until the chicken is just tender. Drain, reserving the stock.

2 Make the sauce by mixing the toasted sesame paste with 45ml/3 tbsp of the chicken stock, saving the rest for soup. Add the soy sauce, vinegar, spring onions, garlic, ginger and crushed peppercorns to the sesame mixture. Stir in sugar to taste.

3 Make the chilli oil by gently heating the oil and chilli powder together until foaming. Simmer for 2 minutes, cool, then strain off the red-coloured oil and discard the sediment.

4 Spread out the cucumber batons on a platter. Cut the chicken breast portions into pieces of about the same size as the cucumber strips and arrange them on top. Pour over the sauce, drizzle on the chilli oil and serve.

VARIATION
Crunchy peanut butter can be used instead of sesame paste, if you like. Mix it with 30ml/2 tbsp sesame oil and proceed as in Step 2.

Per portion: Energy 297Kcal/1239kJ; Protein 29.7g; Carbohydrate 2.3g, of which sugars 1.8g; Fat 18.9g, of which saturates 2.6g; Cholesterol 79mg; Calcium 94mg; Fibre 1.4g; Sodium 339mg.

POT-COOKED DUCK AND GREEN VEGETABLES

PREPARE THE INGREDIENTS FOR THIS JAPANESE DISH BEFOREHAND, SO THAT THE COOKING CAN BE DONE AT THE TABLE. USE A HEAVY PAN OR FLAMEPROOF CASSEROLE WITH A PORTABLE STOVE.

SERVES FOUR

INGREDIENTS

4 duck breast fillets, about 800g/
   1¾lb total weight
8 large shiitake mushrooms, stalks
   removed, a cross cut into each cap
2 leeks, trimmed and cut diagonally
   into 6cm/2½in lengths
½ hakusai, stalk part removed and
   cut into 5cm/2in squares
500g/1¼lb shungiku or mizuna, root
   part removed, cut in half crossways
For the stock
   raw bones from 1 chicken, washed
   1 egg shell
   200g/7oz/scant 1 cup short grain
      rice, washed and drained
   120ml/4fl oz/½ cup sake
   about 10ml/2 tsp coarse sea salt
For the sauce
   75ml/5 tbsp shoyu
   30ml/2 tbsp sake
   juice of 1 lime
   8 white peppercorns, crushed
For the soup
   130g/4½oz Chinese egg noodles,
      cooked and loosened
   1 egg, beaten
   1 bunch of chives
   ground white pepper

1 To make the stock, put the chicken bones into a pan three-quarters full of water. Bring to the boil and drain when it reaches boiling point. Wash the pan and the bones again, then return to the pan with the same amount of water. Add the egg shell and then bring to the boil. Simmer, uncovered, for 1 hour, skimming frequently. Remove the bones and egg shell. Add the rice, sake and salt, then simmer for 30 minutes. Remove from the heat and set aside.

2 Heat a heavy frying pan until just smoking. Remove from the heat for 1 minute, then add the duck breasts, skin side down. Return to a medium heat and sear for 3–4 minutes, or until crisp. Turn over and sear the other side for 1 minute. Remove from the heat.

3 When cool, wipe the duck fat with kitchen paper and cut the breast and skin into 5mm/¼in thick slices. Arrange on a large serving plate with all the prepared vegetables.

4 Heat through all the ingredients for the sauce in a small pan and transfer to a small jug (pitcher) or bowl.

5 Prepare four dipping bowls, four serving bowls and chopsticks. At the table, bring the pan of soup stock to the boil, then reduce to medium-low. Add half of the shiitake and leeks. Wait for 5 minutes and put in half of the stalk part of the hakusai. Add half of the duck and cook for 1–2 minutes for rare or 5–8 minutes for well-done meat.

6 Each person prepares some duck and vegetables in a serving bowl and drizzles over a little sauce. Add the soft hakusai leaves, shungiku and mizuna to the stock as you eat, adjusting the heat as you go. When the stock is less than a quarter of the pot's volume, top up with 3 parts water to 1 part sake.

7 When the duck has been eaten, bring the reduced stock to the boil. Skim the oil from the surface, and reduce the heat to medium. Add the noodles, cook for 1–2 minutes and check the seasoning. Add more salt if required. Pour in the beaten egg and swirl in the stock. Cover, turn off the heat, then leave to stand for 1 minute. Decorate with the chopped chives and serve with ground pepper.

Per portion: Energy 676Kcal/2846kJ; Protein 53.4g; Carbohydrate 81.6g, of which sugars 9.8g; Fat 19.4g, of which saturates 4.1g; Cholesterol 277mg; Calcium 126mg; Fibre 9.3g; Sodium 1296mg.

LAMB POT-ROASTED <u>WITH</u> TOMATOES, BEANS <u>AND</u> ONIONS

THIS SLOW-BRAISED DISH OF LAMB AND TOMATOES, SPICED WITH CINNAMON AND STEWED WITH GREEN BEANS, SHOWS A GREEK INFLUENCE. IT IS ALSO GOOD MADE WITH COURGETTES INSTEAD OF BEANS.

SERVES EIGHT

INGREDIENTS
    1kg/2¼lb lamb on the bone
    8 garlic cloves, chopped
    2.5–5ml/½–1 tsp ground cumin
    45ml/3 tbsp olive oil
    juice of 1 lemon
    2 onions, thinly sliced
    about 500ml/17fl oz/2¼ cups
      lamb, beef or vegetable stock
    75–90ml/5–6 tbsp tomato
      purée (paste)
    1 cinnamon stick
    2–3 large pinches of ground
      allspice or ground cloves
    15–30ml/1–2 tbsp sugar
    400g/14oz/scant 3 cups
      green beans
    salt and ground black pepper
    15–30ml/1–2 tbsp chopped
      fresh parsley, to garnish

1 Preheat the oven to 160°C/325°F/Gas 3. Coat the lamb with the garlic, cumin, olive oil, lemon juice, salt and pepper.

2 Heat a flameproof casserole. Sear the lamb on all sides. Add the onions and pour the stock over the meat to cover. Stir in the tomato purée, spices and sugar. Cover and cook in the oven for 2–3 hours.

3 Remove the casserole from the oven and pour the stock into a pan. Move the onions to the side of the dish and return to the oven, uncovered, for 20 minutes.

4 Meanwhile, add the beans to the hot stock and cook until the beans are tender and the sauce has thickened. Slice the meat and serve with the pan juices and beans. Garnish with parsley.

Per portion: Energy 333Kcal/1394kJ; Protein 39.1g; Carbohydrate 8.2g, of which sugars 6.9g; Fat 16.2g, of which saturates 5.4g; Cholesterol 125mg; Calcium 41mg; Fibre 2g; Sodium 109mg.

POT-ROASTED BRISKET

THIS JEWISH, POT-ROASTED MEAT DISH INCLUDES THE TRADITIONAL KISHKE, A HEAVY, SAUSAGE-SHAPED DUMPLING, WHICH IS ADDED TO THE POT AND COOKED WITH THE MEAT. SERVE WITH KASHA — MEAT GRAVY WITH KASHA IS ONE OF LIFE'S PERFECT COMBINATIONS.

SERVES SIX TO EIGHT

INGREDIENTS
    5 onions, sliced
    3 bay leaves
    1–1.6kg/2¼–3½lb beef brisket
    1 garlic bulb, broken into cloves
    4 carrots, thickly sliced
    5–10ml/1–2 tsp paprika
    about 500ml/17fl oz/2¼ cups
       beef stock
    3–4 baking potatoes, peeled
       and quartered
    salt and ground black pepper
For the kishke
    about 90cm/36in sausage casing
       (see Cook's Tip)
    250g/9oz/2¼ cups plain
       (all-purpose) flour
    120ml/4fl oz/½ cup semolina
       or couscous
    10–15ml/2–3 tsp paprika
    1 carrot, grated and 2 carrots,
       diced (optional)
    250ml/8fl oz/1 cup rendered
       chicken fat
    30ml/2 tbsp crisp, fried onions
    ½ onion, grated and 3 onions,
       thinly sliced
    3 garlic cloves, chopped
    salt and ground black pepper

1 Preheat the oven to 180°C/350°F/ Gas 4. Put one-third of the onions and a bay leaf in an ovenproof dish, then top with the brisket. Sprinkle over the garlic, carrots and the remaining bay leaves, sprinkle with salt, pepper and paprika, then top with the remaining onions.

2 Pour in enough stock to fill the dish to about 5–7.5cm/2–3in and cover with foil. Cook in the oven for 2 hours.

3 Meanwhile, make the kishke. In a bowl, combine all the ingredients and stuff the mixture into the casing, leaving enough space for the mixture to expand. Tie into sausage-shaped lengths.

4 When the meat has cooked for about 2 hours, add the kishke and potatoes to the pan, re-cover and cook for a further 1 hour, or until the meat and potatoes are tender.

5 Remove the foil from the dish and increase the oven temperature to 190–200°C/375–400°F/Gas 5–6. Move the onions away from the top of the meat to the side of the dish and return to the oven for a further 30 minutes, or until the meat, onions and potatoes are beginning to brown and become crisp. Serve hot or cold.

COOK'S TIP
Traditionally, sausage casings are used for kishke but, if unavailable, use cooking-strength clear film (plastic wrap) or a piece of muslin (cheesecloth).

Per portion: Energy 781Kcal/3271kJ; Protein 44.2g; Carbohydrate 74g, of which sugars 12.7g; Fat 36.4g, of which saturates 14.4g; Cholesterol 113mg; Calcium 124mg; Fibre 5g; Sodium 124mg.

TACOS <u>WITH</u> SHREDDED BEEF

In Mexico, tacos are most often made with soft corn tortillas, which are filled and folded in half. It is unusual to see the crisp shells of corn which are so widely used in Tex-Mex cooking. Tacos are always eaten in the hand.

3 Put the meat on a board, let it cool slightly, then shred it, using two forks. Put the meat in a bowl. Divide the tortilla dough into six equal balls.

4 Open a tortilla press and line both sides with plastic (this can be cut from a new plastic sandwich bag). Put each ball on the press and flatten it into a 15–20cm/6–8in round.

5 Heat a griddle or frying pan until hot. Cook each tortilla for 15–20 seconds on each side, and then for a further 15 minutes on the first side. Keep the tortillas warm and soft by folding them inside a slightly damp dishtowel.

6 Add the oregano and cumin to the shredded meat and mix well. Heat the oil in a frying pan and cook the onion and garlic for 3–4 minutes, until softened. Add the meat mixture and toss over the heat until heated through.

SERVES SIX

INGREDIENTS
    450g/1lb rump (round) steak, diced
    150g/5oz/1 cup masa harina
    2.5ml/½ tsp salt
    120ml/4fl oz/½ cup warm water
    10ml/2 tsp dried oregano
    5ml/1 tsp ground cumin
    30ml/2 tbsp oil
    1 onion, thinly sliced
    2 garlic cloves, crushed
    fresh coriander (cilantro), to garnish
    shredded lettuce, lime wedges and
        tomato salsa, to serve

1 Put the steak in a deep frying pan and pour over water to cover. Bring to the boil, then lower the heat and simmer for 1–1½ hours.

2 Meanwhile, make the tortilla dough. Mix the masa harina and salt in a large mixing bowl. Add the warm water, a little at a time, to make a dough that can be worked into a ball. Knead the dough on a lightly floured surface for 3–4 minutes until smooth, then wrap the dough in clear film (plastic wrap) and leave to rest for 1 hour.

7 Place some shredded lettuce on a tortilla, top with shredded beef and salsa, fold in half and serve with lime wedges. Garnish with fresh coriander.

Per portion: Energy 232Kcal/975kJ; Protein 18.6g; Carbohydrate 21.4g, of which sugars 1.8g; Fat 8.6g, of which saturates 2.6g; Cholesterol 46mg; Calcium 44mg; Fibre 1.1g; Sodium 198mg.

BEEF ENCHILADAS <u>WITH</u> RED SAUCE

ENCHILADAS ARE USUALLY MADE WITH CORN TORTILLAS, ALTHOUGH IN PARTS OF NORTHERN MEXICO WHEAT FLOUR TORTILLAS ARE SOMETIMES USED.

SERVES THREE TO FOUR

INGREDIENTS
    500g/1¼lb rump (round) steak, cut
        into 5cm/2in cubes
    2 ancho chillies, seeded
    2 pasilla chillies, seeded
    2 garlic cloves, crushed
    10ml/2 tsp dried oregano
    2.5ml/½ tsp ground cumin
    30ml/2 tbsp vegetable oil
    7 fresh corn tortillas
    shredded onion and flat leaf parsley
        to garnish
    mango salsa, to serve

1 Put the steak in a deep frying pan and cover with water. Bring to the boil, then lower the heat and simmer for 1–1½ hours, or until very tender.

2 Meanwhile, put the dried chillies in a bowl and pour over the hot water. Leave to soak for 30 minutes, then tip the contents of the bowl into a blender and process to a smooth paste.

3 Drain the steak and let it cool, reserving 250ml/8fl oz/1 cup of the cooking liquid. Meanwhile, cook the garlic, oregano and cumin in the oil for 2 minutes.

4 Stir in the chilli paste and the reserved cooking liquid from the steak. Tear one of the tortillas into small pieces and add it to the mixture. Bring to the boil, then lower the heat. Simmer for 10 minutes, stirring occasionally, until thickened. Shred the steak, using two forks, stir it into the sauce and heat through for a few minutes.

5 Spoon some of the meat mixture on to each tortilla and roll it up to make an enchilada. Keep the enchiladas in a warmed dish until you have rolled them all. Garnish with shreds of onion and fresh flat leaf parsley and then serve immediately with the mango salsa.

VARIATION
For a richer version place the rolled enchiladas side by side in a gratin dish. Pour over 300ml/½ pint/1¼ cups sour cream and 75g/3oz/¾ cup grated Cheddar cheese. Place under a preheated grill (broiler) for 5 minutes, or until the cheese melts and the sauce begins to bubble. Serve with the salsa.

Per portion: Energy 477Kcal/2004kJ; Protein 40.6g; Carbohydrate 39.9g, of which sugars 0.9g; Fat 18.3g, of which saturates 5.5g; Cholesterol 102mg; Calcium 85mg; Fibre 1.6g; Sodium 261mg.

GRILLS AND GRIDDLED DISHES

Whether you grill (broil) inside the oven, on a ridged griddle pan or over an open fire, this is an excellent cooking method. Grilled food looks good, with an all-over tan or the attractive stripes that mark the means of its cooking. There's often a contrast in textures, the outside gaining a crisp crust beneath which the food is beautifully tender. Finally — and perhaps most importantly — grilled food is healthy, as only a minimum amount of oil is used in the process. This chapter includes kebabs, patties and superb grilled vegetable dishes.

GRILLED AUBERGINE PARCELS

THESE ARE DELICIOUS LITTLE ITALIAN BUNDLES OF PLUM TOMATOES, MOZZARELLA CHEESE AND FRESH BASIL LEAVES, WRAPPED IN SLICES OF AUBERGINE.

SERVES FOUR

INGREDIENTS
    2 large, long aubergines (eggplant)
    225g/8oz mozzarella cheese
    2 plum tomatoes
    16 large fresh basil leaves
    30ml/2 tbsp olive oil
    salt and ground black pepper
For the dressing
    60ml/4 tbsp olive oil
    5ml/1 tsp balsamic vinegar
    15ml/1 tbsp sun-dried tomato paste
    15ml/1 tbsp lemon juice
For the garnish
    30ml/2 tbsp roasted pine nuts
    torn basil leaves

1 Remove and discard the stalks from the aubergines and cut them lengthways into thin slices – the aim is to get 16 slices in total (disregarding the first and last slices), each about 5mm/¼in thick.

2 Bring a large pan of salted water to the boil and cook the aubergine slices for about 2 minutes, until just softened. Drain, then dry on kitchen paper.

3 Cut the mozzarella cheese into eight slices. Cut each tomato into eight slices, not counting the first and last slices.

4 Place two aubergine slices on a baking sheet in a cross. Place a tomato slice in the centre, season, then add a basil leaf, followed by a slice of mozzarella, a basil leaf, a tomato slice and more seasoning.

5 Fold the ends of the aubergine slices around the filling to make a neat parcel. Repeat with the rest of the ingredients to make eight parcels. Chill for about 20 minutes. Preheat the grill (broiler).

6 To make the tomato dressing, whisk all the ingredients together and season to taste.

7 Brush the parcels with the oil and cook for about 5 minutes on each side, until golden. Serve, with the dressing, sprinkled with pine nuts and basil.

Per portion: Energy 370Kcal/1532kJ; Protein 12.9g; Carbohydrate 4.4g, of which sugars 4.2g; Fat 33.6g, of which saturates 10.6g; Cholesterol 33mg; Calcium 219mg; Fibre 2.7g; Sodium 237mg.

GRILLED POLENTA <u>WITH</u> CARAMELIZED ONIONS, RADICCHIO <u>AND</u> TALEGGIO CHEESE

SLICES OF GRILLED POLENTA, ONE OF THE STAPLES OF NORTH ITALIAN COOKING, ARE TASTY TOPPED WITH SLOWLY CARAMELIZED ONIONS AND BUBBLING TALEGGIO, ALSO FROM NORTH ITALY.

SERVES FOUR

INGREDIENTS
    900ml/1½ pints/3¾ cups water
    5ml/1 tsp salt
    150g/5oz/generous 1 cup polenta
      or cornmeal
    50g/2oz/⅓ cup freshly grated
      Parmesan cheese
    5ml/1 tsp chopped fresh thyme
    90ml/6 tbsp olive oil
    675g/1½lb onions, halved and sliced
    2 garlic cloves, chopped
    a few fresh thyme sprigs
    5ml/1 tsp brown sugar
    15–30ml/1–2 tbsp balsamic vinegar
    2 heads radicchio, cut into thick
      slices or wedges
    225g/8oz Taleggio cheese, sliced
    salt and ground black pepper

1 In a large pan, bring the water to the boil and add the salt. Adjust the heat so that it simmers. Stirring constantly, add the polenta in a steady stream, then bring to the boil. Cook over a very low heat, stirring frequently, for about 30–40 minutes, until thick and smooth.

2 Beat in the Parmesan and chopped thyme, then turn on to a work surface or tray. Spread evenly, then leave to cool.

3 Heat 30ml/2 tbsp of the oil in a frying pan over a moderate heat. Add the onions and stir to coat in the oil, then cover and cook over a very low heat for 15 minutes, stirring occasionally.

4 Add the garlic and most of the thyme sprigs and cook, uncovered, for another 10 minutes, or until light brown.

5 Add the sugar, 15ml/1 tbsp of the vinegar and salt and pepper. Cook for another 5–10 minutes, until soft and well-browned. Taste and add more vinegar and seasoning as necessary.

6 Preheat the grill (broiler). Cut the polenta into thick slices and brush with a little of the remaining oil, then grill (broil) until crusty and lightly browned.

7 Turn over the polenta and add the radicchio to the grill rack or pan. Season the radicchio and brush with a little oil. Grill for about 5 minutes, until the polenta and radicchio are browned. Drizzle a little vinegar over the radicchio.

8 Heap the onions on to the polenta. Sprinkle the cheese and a few sprigs of thyme over both polenta and radicchio. Grill until the cheese is bubbling. Season with pepper and serve immediately.

Per portion: Energy 608Kcal/2522kJ; Protein 22.3g; Carbohydrate 42.7g, of which sugars 11.4g; Fat 37.5g, of which saturates 15.2g; Cholesterol 65mg; Calcium 352mg; Fibre 3.7g; Sodium 456mg.

YUCATAN-STYLE SHARK STEAK

A FIRM-FLESHED FISH, SHARK IS WIDELY AVAILABLE, EITHER FRESH OR FROZEN. IT NEEDS CAREFUL WATCHING, AS OVERCOOKING WILL MAKE IT DRY AND TOUGH, BUT THE FLAVOUR IS EXCELLENT.

SERVES FOUR

INGREDIENTS

grated rind and juice of 1 orange
juice of 1 small lime
45ml/3 tbsp white wine
30ml/2 tbsp olive oil
2 garlic cloves, crushed
10ml/2 tsp ground achiote seed
  (annatto powder)
2.5ml/½ tsp cayenne pepper
2.5ml/½ tsp dried marjoram
5ml/1 tsp salt
4 shark steaks
fresh oregano leaves, to garnish
4 wheat-flour tortillas and any
  suitable salsa, to serve

COOK'S TIP
Shark freezes successfully, with little or no loss of flavour on thawing, so use frozen steaks if you can't find fresh.

1 Put the orange rind and juice in a shallow non-metallic dish which is large enough to hold all the shark steaks in a single layer. Add the lime juice, white wine, olive oil, garlic, ground achiote (annatto powder), cayenne, marjoram and salt. Mix well.

2 Add the shark steaks to the dish and spoon the marinade over them. Cover and set aside for 1 hour, turning once.

3 Heat a griddle pan until very hot and cook the marinated shark steaks for 2–3 minutes on each side. Alternatively, they are very good cooked on the barbecue, as long as they are cooked after the coals have lost their fierce initial heat. Do not overcook.

4 Garnish the shark steaks with oregano and serve with the tortillas and salsa. A green vegetable would also go well.

Per portion: Energy 239Kcal/1006kJ; Protein 40.6g; Carbohydrate 0.7g, of which sugars 0.1g; Fat 7.5g, of which saturates 1.2g; Cholesterol 77mg; Calcium 33mg; Fibre 0.2g; Sodium 246mg.

SEARED TUNA STEAKS WITH RED ONION SALSA

RED ONIONS ARE IDEAL FOR THIS SALSA, NOT ONLY FOR THEIR MILD AND SWEET FLAVOUR, BUT ALSO BECAUSE THEY LOOK SO APPETIZING. SALAD, RICE OR BREAD AND A BOWL OF THICK YOGURT FLAVOURED WITH CHOPPED FRESH HERBS ARE GOOD ACCOMPANIMENTS.

SERVES FOUR

INGREDIENTS

4 tuna steaks, each weighing about 175–200g/6–7oz
5ml/1 tsp cumin seeds, toasted and crushed
pinch of dried red chilli flakes
grated rind and juice of 1 lime
30–60ml/2–4 tbsp extra virgin olive oil
salt and ground black pepper
lime wedges and fresh coriander (cilantro) sprigs, to garnish

For the salsa
1 small red onion, finely chopped
200g/7oz red or yellow cherry tomatoes, coarsely chopped
1 avocado, peeled, stoned (pitted) and chopped
2 kiwi fruit, peeled and chopped
1 fresh red chilli, seeded and finely chopped
15g/½oz fresh coriander (cilantro), chopped
6 fresh mint sprigs, leaves only, chopped
5–10ml/1–2 tsp Thai fish sauce
about 5ml/1 tsp muscovado (molasses) sugar

1 Wash the tuna steaks and pat dry. Sprinkle with half the cumin, the dried chilli, salt, pepper and half the lime rind. Rub in 30ml/2 tbsp of the oil and set aside in a glass or china dish for about 30 minutes.

2 Meanwhile, make the salsa. Mix the onion, tomatoes, avocado, kiwi fruit, fresh chilli, chopped coriander and mint. Add the remaining cumin, the rest of the lime rind and half the lime juice. Season with Thai fish sauce and sugar to taste. Set aside for 15–20 minutes, then add more Thai fish sauce, lime juice and olive oil if required.

3 Heat a ridged, cast–iron griddle pan. Cook the tuna, allowing about 2 minutes on each side for rare tuna or a little longer for a medium result.

4 Serve the tuna steaks garnished with lime wedges and coriander sprigs. Serve the salsa separately or spoon on to the plates with the tuna.

Per portion: Energy 389Kcal/1628kJ; Protein 43.2g; Carbohydrate 7.9g, of which sugars 6.8g; Fat 20.7g, of which saturates 4.4g; Cholesterol 49mg; Calcium 55mg; Fibre 2.5g; Sodium 180mg.

GRILLED SKEWERED CHICKEN

THESE JAPANESE-STYLE KEBABS, SERVED WITH DELICIOUS YAKITORI SAUCE FOR DIPPING, ARE PERFECT FOR EASY ENTERTAINING AND ABSOLUTELY IDEAL FOR A BARBECUE PARTY. FOR AUTHENTICITY, SERVE WITH JAPANESE CONDIMENTS AND SMALL DRINKING BOWLS OF WARM RICE WINE.

SERVES FOUR

INGREDIENTS
    8 chicken thighs with skin, boned
    8 large, thick spring onions
        (scallions), trimmed
For the yakitori sauce
    60ml/4 tbsp sake
    75ml/5 tbsp shoyu
    15ml/1 tbsp mirin
    15ml/1 tbsp caster (superfine) sugar
To serve
    shichimi togarashi, sansho or
        lemon wedges

1 First, make the yakitori sauce. Mix all the ingredients together in a small pan. Bring to the boil, then reduce the heat and simmer for 10 minutes, or until the sauce has thickened.

2 Cut the chicken into 2.5cm/1in cubes with a sharp knife. Cut the spring onions into 2.5cm/1in long sticks.

3 To grill (broil), preheat the grill (broiler) to high. Oil the wire rack and spread out the chicken cubes on it. Grill both sides of the chicken until the juices run, then dip the pieces in the sauce and put back on the rack. Grill for 30 seconds on each side, repeating the dipping process twice more.

4 Set aside and keep warm. Gently grill the spring onions until soft and slightly brown outside. Do not dip. Thread about four pieces of chicken and three spring onion pieces on to each of eight bamboo skewers.

5 Alternatively, to cook on a barbecue, soak eight bamboo skewers overnight in water. This prevents the skewers from burning. Prepare the barbecue. Thread the chicken and spring onion pieces on to skewers, as above. Place the sauce in a small bowl.

6 Cook the skewered chicken on the barbecue. Keep the skewer handles away from the fire, turning them frequently until the juices start to run. Brush the chicken with sauce. Return to the coals and repeat this process twice more until the chicken is well cooked.

7 Arrange the skewers on a platter or individual plates and serve sprinkled with shichimi togarashi or sansho, or accompanied by lemon wedges.

Per portion: Energy 132Kcal/558kJ; Protein 21.6g; Carbohydrate 5.2g, of which sugars 5.1g; Fat 2.9g, of which saturates 0.8g; Cholesterol 105mg; Calcium 18mg; Fibre 0.3g; Sodium 715mg.

GRILLED CHICKEN BALLS COOKED ON BAMBOO SKEWERS

THESE TASTY CHICKEN BALLS, KNOWN AS TSUKUNE, ARE A YAKITORI BAR REGULAR IN JAPAN, AS WELL AS A FAVOURITE FAMILY DISH, AS THEY ARE EASY FOR CHILDREN TO EAT DIRECTLY FROM THE SKEWER. YOU CAN MAKE THE BALLS IN ADVANCE UP TO THE END OF STEP 2, AND THEY FREEZE VERY WELL.

SERVES FOUR

INGREDIENTS
300g/11oz skinless chicken,
  minced (ground)
2 eggs
2.5ml/½ tsp salt
10ml/2 tsp plain (all-purpose) flour
10ml/2 tsp cornflour (cornstarch)
90ml/6 tbsp dried breadcrumbs
2.5cm/1in piece fresh root
  ginger, grated
For the "tare" yakitori sauce
60ml/4 tbsp sake
75ml/5 tbsp shoyu
15ml/1 tbsp mirin
15ml/1 tbsp caster (superfine) sugar
2.5ml/½ tsp cornflour (cornstarch)
  blended with 5ml/1 tsp water
To serve
shichimi togarashi or
  sansho (optional)

1 Soak eight bamboo skewers overnight in water. Put all the ingredients for the chicken balls, except the ginger, in a food processor and blend well.

2 Wet your hands and scoop about a tablespoonful of the mixture into your palm. Shape it into a small ball about half the size of a golf ball. Make a further 30–32 balls in the same way.

3 Squeeze the juice from the grated ginger into a small mixing bowl. Discard the pulp.

4 Add the ginger juice to a small pan of boiling water. Add the chicken balls, and boil for about 7 minutes, or until the colour of the meat changes and the balls float to the surface. Scoop out using a slotted spoon and drain on a plate covered with kitchen paper.

5 In a small pan, mix all the ingredients for the yakitori sauce, except for the cornflour liquid. Bring to the boil, then reduce the heat and simmer for about 10 minutes, or until the sauce has slightly reduced. Add the cornflour liquid and stir until the sauce is thick. Transfer to a small bowl.

6 Thread three or four balls on to each skewer. Cook under a medium grill (broiler) or on a barbecue, keeping the skewer handles away from the fire. Turn them frequently for a few minutes, or until the balls start to brown. Brush with sauce and return to the heat. Repeat the process twice. Serve, sprinkled with shichimi togarashi or sansho, if you like.

Per portion: Energy 223Kcal/942kJ; Protein 24.2g; Carbohydrate 23.9g, of which sugars 5.1g; Fat 4.1g, of which saturates 1g; Cholesterol 148mg; Calcium 54mg; Fibre 0.6g; Sodium 1031mg.

TURKEY PATTIES

MINCED TURKEY MAKES DELICIOUSLY LIGHT PATTIES, WHICH ARE IDEAL FOR SUMMER MEALS. THE RECIPE IS A FLAVOURFUL VARIATION ON A CLASSIC BURGER. THE PATTIES CAN ALSO BE MADE USING MINCED LAMB, PORK OR BEEF. SERVE THEM IN SPLIT AND TOASTED BUNS OR PIECES OF CRUSTY BREAD, WITH CHUTNEY, SALAD LEAVES AND CHUNKY FRIES.

SERVES SIX

INGREDIENTS
  675g/1½lb minced (ground) turkey
  1 small red onion, finely chopped
  grated rind and juice of 1 lime
  small handful of fresh thyme leaves
  15–30ml/1–2 tbsp olive oil
  salt and ground black pepper

VARIATIONS
• You could try chopped fresh oregano, parsley or basil in place of the thyme, and lemon rind instead of lime.
• Substitute minced (ground) chicken for the turkey.

1 Mix together the turkey, onion, lime rind and juice, thyme and seasoning. Cover and chill for up to 4 hours to allow the flavours to infuse, then divide the mixture into six equal portions and shape into round patties.

2 Preheat a griddle pan. Brush the patties with oil, then place them on the pan and cook for 10–12 minutes. Turn the patties over, brush with more oil and cook for 10–12 minutes on the second side, or until cooked through.

Per portion: Energy 141Kcal/596kJ; Protein 24.8g; Carbohydrate 0.8g, of which sugars 0.6g; Fat 4.4g, of which saturates 1.1g; Cholesterol 69mg; Calcium 15mg; Fibre 0.2g; Sodium 62mg.

TURKEY BREASTS <u>WITH</u> TOMATO-CORN SALSA

ALTHOUGH AN ECONOMICAL AND USEFUL MEAT, TURKEY CAN BE DISAPPOINTINGLY BLAND, SO MARINATING IT BEFORE COOKING AND SERVING WITH A SPICY SALSA IS THE IDEAL APPROACH.

SERVES FOUR

INGREDIENTS
    4 skinless boneless turkey breast
      halves, about 175g/6oz each
    30ml/2 tbsp fresh lemon juice
    30ml/2 tbsp olive oil
    2.5ml/½ tsp ground cumin
    2.5ml/½ tsp dried oregano
    5ml/1 tsp coarse black pepper
    salt
For the salsa
    1 fresh hot green chilli
    450g/1lb tomatoes, seeded
      and chopped
    250g/9oz/1½ cups corn kernels,
      freshly cooked or thawed frozen
    3 spring onions (scallions), chopped
    15ml/1 tbsp chopped fresh parsley
    30ml/2 tbsp chopped fresh
      coriander (cilantro)
    30ml/2 tbsp fresh lemon juice
    45ml/3 tbsp olive oil
    5ml/1 tsp salt

1 With a meat mallet, pound the turkey breasts between two sheets of greaseproof (waxed) paper until thin.

2 In a shallow dish, combine the lemon juice, oil, cumin, oregano and pepper. Add the turkey and turn to coat. Cover and marinate for at least 2 hours, or overnight in the refrigerator.

COOK'S TIP
Use the flat side of a meat mallet to pound the turkey. If you don't have a meat mallet, use the side of a wooden rolling pin.

3 For the salsa, roast the chilli over a gas flame, holding it with tongs, until charred on all sides. Alternatively, char the skin under the hot grill (broiler). Leave to cool for 5 minutes. Wearing rubber gloves, carefully rub off the charred skin. For a less hot flavour, discard the seeds. Chop the chilli finely and place in a bowl.

4 Add the remaining salsa ingredients and toss well to blend. Set aside.

5 Remove the turkey from the marinade. Season lightly on both sides with salt to taste.

6 Heat a ridged griddle pan. When hot, add the turkey breasts and cook for about 3 minutes, until browned on the undersides. Turn and cook the meat on the other side for a further 3–4 minutes, until it is cooked through. Serve the turkey immediately, accompanied by tomato-corn salsa.

VARIATION
Use the cooked turkey, thinly sliced and combined with the salsa, as a filling for warmed flour tortillas.

Per portion: Energy 407Kcal/1711kJ; Protein 45.7g; Carbohydrate 20.6g, of which sugars 9.9g; Fat 16.4g, of which saturates 2.7g; Cholesterol 100mg; Calcium 36mg; Fibre 2.5g; Sodium 761mg.

PORK CHOPS <u>WITH</u> SOUR GREEN CHILLI SALSA

THIN CHOPS OR LOIN STEAKS ARE DELICIOUSLY TENDER AND COOK VERY QUICKLY, SO THIS TASTY DISH IS IDEAL FOR A MIDWEEK FAMILY SUPPER.

SERVES FOUR

INGREDIENTS
  30ml/2 tbsp vegetable oil
  15ml/1 tbsp fresh lemon juice
  10ml/2 tsp ground cumin
  5ml/1 tsp dried oregano
  8 pork loin chops, about
    5mm/¼ in thick
  salt and ground black pepper
For the salsa
  2 fresh hot green chillies
  2 green (bell) peppers, seeded
    and chopped
  1 tomato, peeled and seeded
  ½ onion, coarsely chopped
  4 spring onions (scallions)
  1 pickled jalapeño chilli
  30ml/2 tbsp olive oil
  30ml/2 tbsp fresh lime juice
  45ml/3 tbsp cider vinegar
  5ml/1 tsp salt

1 In a small bowl, combine the vegetable oil, lemon juice, cumin and oregano. Add pepper to taste and stir to mix well.

2 Arrange the pork chops in one layer in a shallow dish. Brush each of them with the oil mixture on both sides. Cover them with clear film (plastic wrap) and set aside to marinate for 2–3 hours or in the refrigerator overnight.

3 For the salsa, roast the chillies over a gas flame, holding them with tongs, until charred on all sides. Alternatively, char the skins under the grill (broiler). Leave to cool for 5 minutes. Wearing rubber gloves, remove the skin. For a less hot flavour, discard the seeds.

4 Place the chillies in a food processor or blender. Add the remaining salsa ingredients. Process until finely chopped but do not purée.

5 Transfer the salsa to a small, heavy pan and simmer 15 minutes, stirring occasionally. Set aside.

6 Season the pork chops to taste with salt and pepper. Heat a ridged griddle pan. Alternatively, preheat the grill (broiler). When hot, add the pork chops and cook for about 5 minutes, until browned on the undersides. Turn and continue cooking for a further 5–7 minutes, until done. Work in batches, if necessary.

7 Serve immediately, with the sour green chilli salsa.

Per portion: Energy 341Kcal/1427kJ; Protein 38.9g; Carbohydrate 5.2g, of which sugars 4.7g; Fat 18.5g, of which saturates 4g; Cholesterol 110mg; Calcium 30mg; Fibre 2.2g; Sodium 623mg.

PORK AND LEEK SAUSAGES WITH MUSTARD MASHED POTATO AND ONION GRAVY

LONG, SLOW COOKING IS THE TRICK TO REMEMBER FOR GOOD ONION GRAVY AS THIS REDUCES AND CARAMELIZES THE ONIONS TO CREATE A WONDERFULLY SWEET FLAVOUR. DO NOT BE ALARMED AT THE NUMBER OF ONIONS — THEY REDUCE DRAMATICALLY IN VOLUME DURING COOKING.

SERVES FOUR

INGREDIENTS
    12 pork and leek sausages
    salt and ground black pepper
For the onion gravy
    30ml/2 tbsp olive oil
    25g/1oz/2 tbsp butter
    8 onions, sliced
    5ml/1 tsp caster sugar
    15ml/1 tbsp plain (all-purpose) flour
    300ml/½ pint/1¼ cups beef stock
For the mash
    1.5kg/3¼lb potatoes
    50g/2oz/¼ cup butter
    150ml/¼ pint/⅔ cup whipping cream
    15ml/1 tbsp wholegrain mustard

1 Heat the oil and butter in a large pan until foaming. Add the onions and mix well to coat them in the fat. Cover and cook gently for about 30 minutes, stirring frequently. Add the sugar and cook for a further 5 minutes, or until the onions are softened, reduced and caramelized.

2 Remove the pan from the heat and stir in the flour, then gradually stir in the stock. Return the pan to the heat. Bring to the boil, stirring, then simmer for 3 minutes, or until thickened. Season.

VARIATION
Pesto and garlic mash is also good with sausages. Instead of the mustard, add 15ml/1 tbsp pesto, 2 crushed garlic cloves and a little olive oil.

3 Meanwhile, cook the potatoes and the pork and leek sausages. First, cook the potatoes in a pan of salted boiling water for 20 minutes, or until tender.

4 Drain the potatoes well and mash them with the butter, whipping cream and wholegrain mustard. Season with salt and pepper to taste.

5 Meanwhile, preheat the grill (broiler) to medium. Arrange the sausages on the grill rack and cook for 15–20 minutes, or until cooked, turning frequently so that they turn an even golden brown all over.

6 Serve the sausages with the creamy mash and plenty of onion gravy.

Per portion: Energy 939Kcal/3913kJ; Protein 19.9g; Carbohydrate 85g, of which sugars 16.7g; Fat 60g, of which saturates 28.6g; Cholesterol 133mg; Calcium 179mg; Fibre 6.6g; Sodium 942mg.

PORK CHOPS WITH CHILLI-NECTARINE RELISH

A FRUITY SALSA MAKES AN INTERESTING AND TASTY CHANGE FROM THE MORE USUAL APPLE SAUCE.

SERVES FOUR

INGREDIENTS
  250ml/8fl oz/1 cup fresh
    orange juice
  45ml/3 tbsp olive oil
  2 garlic cloves, ground
  5ml/1 tsp ground cumin
  15ml/1 tbsp coarsely ground
    black pepper
  8 pork loin chops, about 2cm/¾ in
    thick, well trimmed
  salt
For the relish
  1 small fresh green chilli
  2 nectarines
  30ml/2 tbsp clear honey
  juice of ½ lemon
  250ml/8fl oz/1 cup chicken stock
  1 garlic clove, finely chopped
  ½ onion, finely chopped
  5ml/1 tsp grated fresh root ginger
  1.5ml/¼ tsp salt
  15ml/1 tbsp chopped fresh
    coriander (cilantro)

1 For the relish, roast the chilli over a gas flame, holding it with tongs, until charred on all sides. Alternatively, char the skin under the grill (broiler). Leave to cool for 5 minutes.

2 Wearing rubber gloves, carefully remove the charred skin of the chilli. Discard the seeds if you like a less hot flavour. Finely chop the chilli and place in a heavy pan. Halve the nectarines and remove and discard the stones (pits). Chop the flesh and add to the pan with the chilli.

3 Add the honey, lemon juice, chicken stock, garlic, onion, ginger and salt. Bring to the boil, then simmer, stirring occasionally, for about 30 minutes. Stir in the coriander and set aside.

4 In a small bowl, combine the orange juice, oil, garlic, cumin and pepper. Stir to mix well.

5 Arrange the pork chops, in a single layer, in a shallow, non-metallic dish. Pour over the orange juice mixture and turn to coat. Cover with clear film (plastic wrap) and leave in a cool place to marinate for at least 1 hour or in the refrigerator overnight.

6 Remove the pork chops from the marinade and pat dry with kitchen paper. Season lightly with salt.

7 Heat a ridged griddle pan. When hot, add the pork chops and cook for about 5 minutes, until the undersides are browned. Turn and cook on the other side for a further 10 minutes, until browned. Work in batches if necessary. Serve the chops immediately, with the chilli-nectarine relish.

Per portion: Energy 315Kcal/1321kJ; Protein 43.4g; Carbohydrate 11.4g, of which sugars 11g; Fat 10.9g, of which saturates 3.2g; Cholesterol 126mg; Calcium 28mg; Fibre 0.6g; Sodium 144mg.

ROMANIAN KEBABS

KEBABS ARE POPULAR WORLDWIDE, LARGELY BECAUSE THEY ARE SO EASILY ADAPTED TO SUIT EVERYONE'S TASTE. IN THIS RECIPE, LEAN LAMB IS MARINATED, THEN COOKED WITH CHUNKS OF VEGETABLES TO PRODUCE A DELICIOUS, COLOURFUL AND HEALTHY MEAL.

SERVES SIX

INGREDIENTS
  675g/1½lb lean lamb, cut into
    4cm/1½in cubes
  12 button (pearl) onions
  2 green (bell) peppers, seeded and
    cut into 12 pieces
  12 cherry tomatoes
  12 button (white) mushrooms
  lemon slices and fresh rosemary
    sprigs, to garnish
  freshly cooked rice and crusty bread,
    to serve
For the marinade
  juice of 1 lemon
  120ml/4fl oz/½ cup red wine
  1 onion, finely chopped
  60ml/4 tbsp olive oil
  2.5ml/½ tsp dried sage
  2.5ml/½ tsp chopped fresh rosemary
  salt and ground black pepper

VARIATIONS
• Use rump (round) steak instead of lamb. Cut it into strips, marinate it as suggested, then interleave the strips on the skewers, with the onions, cherry tomatoes and mushrooms. Omit the green (bell) peppers.
• These kebabs are just as delicious cooked on a barbecue.

1 For the marinade, combine the lemon juice, red wine, onion, olive oil, herbs and seasoning in a bowl. Stir the cubes of lamb into the marinade. Cover and chill in the refrigerator for 2–12 hours, stirring occasionally.

2 Remove the lamb pieces from the marinade and thread on six skewers with the onions, peppers, tomatoes and mushrooms. Preheat the grill (broiler).

3 Brush the kebabs with marinade and grill (broil) for 10–15 minutes, turning once. Arrange on cooked rice, with lemon and rosemary. Serve with crusty bread.

Per portion: Energy 259Kcal/1083kJ; Protein 23.6g; Carbohydrate 4g, of which sugars 3.4g; Fat 16.7g, of which saturates 6.5g; Cholesterol 86mg; Calcium 22mg; Fibre 1.9g; Sodium 104mg.

JERUSALEM BARBECUE LAMB KEBABS

IN THE EARLY DAYS OF THE MODERN STATE OF ISRAEL, THE DAYS OF AUSTERITY, "LAMB" KEBABS WOULD HAVE BEEN MADE WITH TURKEY AND A LITTLE LAMB FAT, AND "VEAL" KEBABS WITH CHICKEN AND A SMALL AMOUNT OF VEAL. TURKEY, CHICKEN, BEEF AND VEAL CAN ALL BE COOKED IN THIS WAY.

SERVES FOUR TO SIX

INGREDIENTS
    800g/1¾lb tender lamb, cubed
    1.5ml/¼ tsp ground allspice
    1.5ml/¼ tsp ground cinnamon
    1.5ml/¼ tsp ground black pepper
    1.5ml/¼ tsp ground cardamom
    45–60ml/3–4 tbsp chopped
        fresh parsley
    2 onions, chopped
    5–8 garlic cloves, chopped
    juice of ½ lemon or 45ml/3 tbsp dry
        white wine
    45ml/3 tbsp extra virgin olive oil
    sumac, for sprinkling (optional)
    30ml/2 tbsp pine nuts
    salt
For serving
    flat breads, such as pitta bread,
        tortillas or naan bread
    tahini
    crunchy vegetable salad

3 Thread the cubes of meat on to wooden or metal skewers, then cook on the barbecue for 2–3 minutes on each side, turning occasionally, until cooked evenly and browned.

4 Transfer the kebabs to a serving dish and sprinkle with the reserved onions, parsley, sumac, if using, pine nuts and salt, if you like. Serve the kebabs with warmed flat breads to wrap the kebabs in, a bowl of tahini for drizzling over and a vegetable salad.

COOK'S TIPS
• If sumac is available, its tangy flavour is fresh and invigorating, and its red colour is appealing.
• These kebabs can also be cooked under a hot grill (broiler).

1 Put the lamb, allspice, cinnamon, black pepper, cardamom, half the parsley, half the onions, the garlic, lemon juice or wine and olive oil in a bowl and mix together. Season with salt now, if you like, or sprinkle on after cooking. Set aside and leave to marinate.

2 Meanwhile, light the barbecue and leave for about 40 minutes. When the coals are white and grey, the barbecue is ready for cooking. If using wooden skewers, soak them in water for about 30 minutes to prevent them from burning.

Per portion: Energy 513Kcal/2137kJ; Protein 41.4g; Carbohydrate 6.4g, of which sugars 4.7g; Fat 36g, of which saturates 11.9g; Cholesterol 152mg; Calcium 51mg; Fibre 1.6g; Sodium 177mg.

STEAK BÉARNAISE

BÉARNAISE, AFTER BÉARN IN SOUTH-WEST FRANCE, IS A CREAMY EGG AND BUTTER SAUCE FLAVOURED WITH FRESH TARRAGON. IT IS A CLASSIC COMPLEMENT TO GRIDDLED, GRILLED OR PAN-FRIED STEAK AND ALSO EXCELLENT WITH ROAST BEEF. ROASTED VEGETABLES MAKE A GOOD ACCOMPANIMENT.

SERVES FOUR

INGREDIENTS
    4 sirloin steaks, each weighing about
        225g/8oz, trimmed
    15ml/1 tbsp sunflower oil (optional)
    salt and ground black pepper
For the Béarnaise sauce
    90ml/6 tbsp white wine vinegar
    12 black peppercorns
    2 bay leaves
    2 shallots, finely chopped
    4 fresh tarragon sprigs
    4 egg yolks
    225g/8oz/1 cup unsalted (sweet)
        butter at room temperature, diced
    30ml/2 tbsp chopped fresh tarragon
    ground white pepper

1 Start by making the sauce. Put the vinegar, peppercorns, bay leaves, shallots and tarragon sprigs in a small pan and simmer until reduced to 30ml/2 tbsp. Strain the vinegar through a fine sieve.

2 Beat the egg yolks with salt and freshly ground white pepper in a small, heatproof bowl. Stand the bowl over a pan of very gently simmering water, then gradually beat the strained vinegar into the yolks.

3 Gradually beat in the butter, one piece at a time, allowing each addition to melt before adding the next. Do not allow the water to heat beyond a gentle simmer or the sauce will overheat and curdle.

4 While cooking the sauce, heat a griddle or grill until very hot.

COOK'S TIP
If you are confident about preparing egg and butter sauces, the best method is to reduce the flavoured vinegar before cooking the steak, then finish the sauce while the steak is cooking. This way, the sauce does not have to be kept hot and there is less risk of overheating it or allowing it to become too thick.

5 Beat the chopped fresh tarragon into the sauce and remove the pan from the heat. The sauce should be smooth, thick and glossy.

6 Cover the surface of the sauce with clear film (plastic wrap) or dampened greaseproof (waxed) paper to prevent a skin forming and leave over the pan of hot water, still off the heat, to keep hot while you cook the steak.

7 Season the steaks with salt and plenty freshly ground black pepper.

8 A pan is not usually oiled before cooking steak, but if it is essential to grease the pan, add only the minimum oil. Cook the steaks for 2–4 minutes on each side. The cooking time depends on the thickness of the steaks and the extent to which you want to cook them. As a guide, 2–4 minutes will give a medium-rare result.

9 Serve the steaks on warmed plates. Peel the clear film or dampened greaseproof paper off the sauce and stir it lightly, then spoon it over the steaks.

Per portion: Energy 796Kcal/3297kJ; Protein 51.1g; Carbohydrate 0.5g, of which sugars 0.4g; Fat 65.5g, of which saturates 37.2g; Cholesterol 459mg; Calcium 50mg; Fibre 0.2g; Sodium 450mg.

STUFFED BUTTERFLY OF BEEF WITH CHEESE AND CHILLI SAUCE

THIS RECIPE HAD ITS ORIGINS IN NORTHERN MEXICO OR IN NEW MEXICO, WHICH IS BEEF COUNTRY. IT IS A GOOD WAY TO COOK STEAKS, EITHER UNDER THE GRILL OR ON THE BARBECUE.

SERVES FOUR

INGREDIENTS
    4 fresh serrano chillies
    115g/4oz/½ cup full-fat soft cheese
    30ml/2 tbsp reposada tequila
    30ml/2 tbsp oil
    1 onion
    2 garlic cloves
    5ml/1 tsp dried oregano
    2.5ml/½ tsp salt
    2.5ml/½ tsp ground black pepper
    175g/6oz/1½ cups grated medium
      Cheddar cheese
    4 fillet steaks, at least 2.5cm/
      1in thick

3 Put the full-fat soft cheese in a small heavy pan and stir over a very low heat until it has melted. Add the chilli strips and the tequila and stir to make a smooth sauce. Keep warm over a very low heat.

6 Cut each steak almost but not quite in half across its width, so that it can be opened out, butterfly-fashion. Preheat the grill (broiler) to its highest setting.

1 Dry-roast the chillies in a griddle pan over a moderate heat, turning them frequently until the skins are blistered but not burnt. Put them in a strong plastic bag and tie the top to keep the steam in. Set aside for 20 minutes.

4 Heat the oil in a frying pan and cook the onion, garlic and oregano for about 5 minutes over a moderate heat, stirring frequently until the onion has browned. Season with the salt and pepper.

7 Spoon a quarter of the cheese and onion filling on to one side of each steak and close the other side over it. Place the steaks in a grill pan and grill (broil) for 3–5 minutes on each side, depending on how you like your steak. Serve on heated plates with the vegetables of your choice, and with the cheese and chilli sauce poured over.

2 Remove the chillies from the bag, slit them and scrape out the seeds with a sharp knife. Cut the flesh into long narrow strips, then cut each strip into several shorter strips.

5 Remove the pan from the heat and add the grated Cheddar cheese, in two or three batches. Stir well so that it melts into the onion and garlic mixture without becoming rubbery.

COOK'S TIP
One of the easiest ways of testing whether a steak is cooked is by touch. A steak that is very rare or "blue" will feel soft to the touch; the meat will be relaxed. A rare steak will feel like a sponge, and will spring back when lightly pressed. A medium-rare steak offers more resistance, while a well-cooked steak will feel very firm.

Per portion: Energy 580Kcal/2412kJ; Protein 51.1g; Carbohydrate 3g, of which sugars 2.2g; Fat 39.5g, of which saturates 20.6g; Cholesterol 175mg; Calcium 372mg; Fibre 0.5g; Sodium 735mg.

LONE STAR STEAK WITH POTATO DINNER

*THIS TRADITIONAL AMERICAN MEAL IS USUALLY SERVED WITH CORN ON THE COB, BUT A CRISP,
GREEN SALAD WOULD MAKE A LIGHTER ALTERNATIVE ACCOMPANIMENT.*

SERVES FOUR

INGREDIENTS
    45ml/3 tbsp olive oil
    5 large garlic cloves, crushed
    5ml/1 tsp coarse black pepper
    2.5ml/½ tsp ground allspice
    5ml/1 tsp ground cumin
    2.5ml/½ tsp chilli powder
    10ml/2 tsp dried oregano
    15ml/1 tbsp cider vinegar
    4 boneless sirloin steaks, about
       2cm/¾ in thick
    salt
To serve
    tomato salsa
    freshly cooked corn on the
       cob (optional)
For the potatoes
    50ml/2fl oz/¼ cup vegetable oil
    1 onion, chopped
    5ml/1 tsp salt
    900g/2lb potatoes, boiled and diced
    30–75ml/2–5 tbsp chopped canned
       or bottled green chillies, according
       to taste

1 Heat the olive oil in a heavy frying
pan. When hot, add the garlic and cook,
stirring frequently, for about 3 minutes,
until tender and just brown. Do not let
the garlic burn, as it will become bitter.

2 Transfer the garlic and oil to a shallow
dish large enough to hold the steaks in
a single layer.

3 Add the pepper, allspice, cumin, chilli
powder, oregano and vinegar to the
garlic and stir to blend thoroughly. If
necessary, add just enough water to
obtain a fairly thick paste.

4 Add the steaks to the dish and turn to
coat evenly on both sides with the spice
mixture. Cover and leave to marinate
for 2 hours or place in the refrigerator
overnight. Bring the steaks to room
temperature 30 minutes before cooking.

5 To make the potatoes, heat the oil in
a large non-stick frying pan. Add the
onion and salt. Cook over a medium
heat for 5 minutes, until softened. Add
the potatoes and chillies. Cook, stirring
occasionally, for 15–20 minutes.

6 Season the steaks on both sides with
salt to taste. Heat a ridged griddle pan.
When hot, add the steaks and cook,
turning once, until done to your taste.
Allow about 1–2 minutes on each side
for rare, 2–3 minutes for medium-rare,
and 3–4 minutes for well done.

7 If necessary, briefly reheat the
potatoes. Serve immediately, with the
tomato salsa and corn, if using.

VARIATION
The steaks can also be cooked on a
barbecue. Prepare the fire, and when the
coals are glowing red and covered with
grey ash, spread them in a single layer.
Cook the steaks in the centre of an oiled
grill rack set about 13cm/5in above the
coals for 1 minute per side to sear them.
Move them away from the centre and
cook for 10–12 minutes, or longer for
medium-rare, turning once.

Per portion: Energy 560Kcal/2346kJ; Protein 45.4g; Carbohydrate 39.2g, of which sugars 5g; Fat 25.6g, of which saturates 5.9g; Cholesterol 89mg; Calcium 32mg; Fibre 2.8g; Sodium 640mg.

ROASTS

Although far fewer families sit down to a regular roast dinner every weekend, the fact remains that this is one of the easiest ways of cooking a well-balanced meal — and one of the most delicious. The important thing to remember is that taste really does tell, so it is worth buying the best meat, game, poultry and fish you can afford. Cultivate a good butcher and fish supplier or buy from a recommended source specializing in free-range, additive-free or organic meat or fish. Regard dishes such as Marmalade-glazed Goose or Roast Rib of Beef as special treats and you'll enjoy them all the more.

ROASTED VEGETABLES <u>WITH</u> SALSA VERDE

*THERE ARE ENDLESS VARIATIONS OF THE ITALIAN SALSA VERDE, WHICH MEANS "GREEN SAUCE".
USUALLY A BLEND OF FRESH CHOPPED HERBS, GARLIC, OLIVE OIL, ANCHOVIES AND CAPERS, THIS IS A
SIMPLIFIED VERSION. HERE, IT IS SERVED WITH VEGETABLES AND A RICE DISH FROM CYPRUS.*

SERVES FOUR

INGREDIENTS
  3 courgettes (zucchini),
    sliced lengthways
  1 large fennel bulb, cut
    into wedges
  450g/1lb butternut squash, cut into
    2cm/¾in chunks
  12 shallots
  2 red (bell) peppers, seeded
    and cut lengthways into
    thick slices
  4 plum tomatoes, halved and seeded
  45ml/3 tbsp olive oil
  2 garlic cloves, crushed
  5ml/1 tsp balsamic vinegar
  salt and ground black pepper
For the salsa verde
  45ml/3 tbsp chopped fresh mint
  90ml/6 tbsp chopped fresh flat
    leaf parsley
  15ml/1 tbsp Dijon mustard
  juice of ½ lemon
  30ml/2 tbsp olive oil
For the rice
  15ml/1 tbsp vegetable or olive oil
  75g/3oz/¾ cup vermicelli, broken
    into short lengths
  225g/8oz/generous 1 cup long
    grain rice
  900ml/1½ pints/3¾ cups
    vegetable stock

1 To make the salsa verde, place all
the ingredients, with the exception
of the olive oil, in a food processor or
blender. Blend to a coarse paste, then
add the oil, a little at a time, until the
mixture forms a smooth purée.

2 Transfer the salsa to a bowl, season
to taste with salt and pepper, cover and
set aside.

3 Preheat the oven to 220°C/425°F/
Gas 7. To roast the vegetables, toss the
courgettes, fennel, squash, shallots,
peppers and tomatoes in the olive oil,
garlic and balsamic vinegar. Set aside
for 10 minutes to allow all the flavours
to combine.

4 Place all the vegetables – apart from
the squash and tomatoes – on a large
baking sheet, brush with half the oil
and vinegar mixture and season.

5 Roast the vegetables for 25 minutes,
then remove the baking sheet from
the oven. Using a fork, turn all the
vegetables over and brush with the rest
of the oil and vinegar mixture. Add
the butternut squash and plum
tomatoes, return to the oven and cook
for a further 20–25 minutes, until all
the vegetables are tender and lightly
charred around the edges.

VARIATIONS
• Substitute 45ml/3 tbsp watercress for
half the parsley in the salsa.
• Use sherry vinegar instead of balsamic
vinegar to flavour the vegetables.
• If you like, add a medium aubergine
(eggplant), cut into chunks, to the
mixture of roasted vegetables.

6 Meanwhile, prepare the rice.
Heat the oil in a heavy pan. Add the
vermicelli and cook for about
3 minutes, or until golden and crisp.
Season to taste.

7 Rinse the rice under cold running
water, then drain well and add it to the
vermicelli. Cook for 1 minute, stirring to
coat it in the oil.

8 Add the vegetable stock, then cover
the pan and allow to cook for about
12 minutes, until all the liquid is
absorbed. Stir the rice, then cover and
leave to stand for 10 minutes. Serve
the warm rice with the roasted
vegetables and salsa verde.

COOK'S TIP
The salsa verde will keep for up to
1 week if stored in an airtight container
in the refrigerator.

Per portion: Energy 519Kcal/2160kJ; Protein 12.1g; Carbohydrate 75.3g, of which sugars 14.7g; Fat 18.7g, of which saturates 2.8g; Cholesterol 0mg; Calcium 151mg; Fibre 6.9g; Sodium 27mg.

ROASTED COD WITH FRESH TOMATO SAUCE

REALLY FRESH COD HAS A SWEET, DELICATE FLAVOUR AND A PURE WHITE FLAKY FLESH. SERVED WITH AN AROMATIC TOMATO SAUCE, IT MAKES A DELICIOUS MEAL.

SERVES FOUR

INGREDIENTS

350g/12oz ripe plum tomatoes
75ml/5 tbsp olive oil
2.5ml/½ tsp sugar
2 strips of pared orange rind
1 fresh thyme sprig
6 fresh basil leaves
900g/2lb fresh cod fillet, skin on
salt and ground black pepper
steamed green beans, to serve

COOK'S TIP
Cod is becoming increasingly rare and expensive. You can substitute any firm white fish fillets in this dish. Try haddock, pollock, or that excellent and underrated fish, coley. When raw, coley flesh looks grey, but it turns white on cooking.

1 Preheat the oven to 230°C/450°F/ Gas 8. Coarsely chop the tomatoes.

2 Heat 15ml/1 tbsp of the olive oil in a heavy pan, add the tomatoes, sugar, orange rind, thyme and basil, and simmer for about 5 minutes, until the tomatoes are soft.

3 Press the tomato mixture through a fine sieve, discarding the solids that remain in the sieve. Pour into a small pan and heat gently.

4 Scale the cod fillet and cut on the diagonal into four pieces. Season well.

5 Heat the remaining oil in a heavy frying pan and cook the cod, skin side down, until the skin is crisp. Place the fish on a greased baking sheet, skin side up, and roast in the oven for 8–10 minutes, until the fish is cooked through. Serve the fish on the steamed green beans with the tomato sauce.

Per portion: Energy 319Kcal/1330kJ; Protein 41.8g; Carbohydrate 2.7g, of which sugars 2.7g; Fat 15.6g, of which saturates 2.3g; Cholesterol 104mg; Calcium 27mg; Fibre 0.9g; Sodium 143mg.

ROAST MONKFISH WITH GARLIC

MONKFISH TIED UP AND COOKED IN THIS WAY IS KNOWN IN FRENCH AS A "GIGOT", BECAUSE IT RESEMBLES A LEG OF LAMB. THE COMBINATION OF MONKFISH AND GARLIC IS SUPERB. FOR A CONTRAST IN COLOUR, SERVE IT WITH VIBRANT GREEN BEANS.

SERVES FOUR TO SIX

INGREDIENTS
  1kg/2¼lb monkfish tail, skinned
  14 fat garlic cloves
  5ml/1 tsp fresh thyme leaves
  30ml/2 tbsp olive oil
  juice of 1 lemon
  2 bay leaves
  salt and ground black pepper

1 Preheat the oven to 220°C/425°F/ Gas 7. Remove any membrane from the monkfish tail and cut out the central bone. Peel two garlic cloves and cut them into thin slivers. Sprinkle a quarter of these and half the thyme leaves over the cut side of the fish, then close it up and use fine kitchen string to tie it into a neat shape, like a boned piece of meat. Pat dry with kitchen paper.

2 Make incisions on either side of the fish and push in the remaining garlic slivers. Heat half the olive oil in a frying pan which can safely be used in the oven. When the oil is hot, put in the monkfish and brown it all over for about 5 minutes, until evenly coloured. Season with salt and pepper, sprinkle with lemon juice and then sprinkle over the remaining thyme.

3 Tuck the bay leaves under the monkfish, arrange the remaining (unpeeled) garlic cloves around it and drizzle the remaining olive oil over the fish and the garlic. Transfer the frying pan to the oven and roast the monkfish for 20–25 minutes, until the flesh is cooked through.

4 Place on a warmed serving dish with the garlic and some green beans. To serve, remove the string and cut the monkfish into 2cm/¾in thick slices.

COOK'S TIPS
• The garlic heads can be used whole.
• When serving the monkfish, invite each guest to pop out the soft garlic pulp with a fork and spread it over the monkfish.
• Use two smaller monkfish tails.

Per portion: Energy 253Kcal/1065kJ; Protein 45.2g; Carbohydrate 3.1g, of which sugars 0.3g; Fat 6.6g, of which saturates 1.1g; Cholesterol 40mg; Calcium 26mg; Fibre 0.8g; Sodium 51mg.

ROASTED CHICKEN WITH GRAPES AND FRESH ROOT GINGER

THIS DISH, WITH ITS BLEND OF SPICES AND SWEET FRUIT, IS INSPIRED BY MOROCCAN FLAVOURS. SERVE WITH COUSCOUS, MIXED WITH A HANDFUL OF COOKED CHICKPEAS.

SERVES FOUR

INGREDIENTS
1–1.6kg/2¼–3½lb chicken
115–130g/4–4½oz fresh root
  ginger, grated
6–8 garlic cloves, coarsely chopped
juice of 1 lemon
about 30ml/2 tbsp olive oil
2–3 large pinches of ground cinnamon
500g/1¼lb seeded red and
  green grapes
500g/1¼lb seedless green grapes
5–7 shallots, chopped
about 250ml/8fl oz/1 cup chicken stock
salt and ground black pepper

1 Rub the chicken with half of the ginger, the garlic, half of the lemon juice, the olive oil, cinnamon, salt and lots of pepper. Leave to marinate.

2 Meanwhile, cut the red and green seeded grapes in half, remove the seeds and set aside. Add the whole green seedless grapes to the halved ones.

3 Preheat the oven to 180°C/350°F/ Gas 4. Heat a heavy frying pan or flameproof casserole until hot.

4 Remove the chicken from the marinade, add to the pan and cook until browned on all sides. (There should be enough oil on the chicken to brown it but, if not, add a little extra.)

5 Put some of the shallots into the chicken cavity with the garlic and ginger from the marinade and as many of the red and green grapes that will fit inside. Roast in the oven for 40–60 minutes, or until the chicken is tender.

VARIATIONS
• This dish is good made with duck in place of the chicken. Marinate and roast as above, adding 15–30ml/1–2 tbsp honey to the pan sauce as it cooks.
• Use boneless chicken breast portions, with the skin still attached, instead of a whole chicken. Pan-fry the chicken portions, rather than roasting them.

6 Remove the chicken from the pan and keep warm. Pour off any oil from the pan, reserving any sediment in the base of the pan. Add the remaining shallots to the pan and cook for about 5 minutes until softened.

7 Add half the remaining red and green grapes, the remaining ginger, the stock and any juices from the roast chicken and cook over a medium-high heat until the grapes have cooked down to a thick sauce. Season with salt, ground black pepper and the remaining lemon juice to taste.

8 Serve the chicken on a warmed serving dish, surrounded by the sauce and the reserved grapes.

COOK'S TIP
Seeded Italia or muscat grapes have a delicious, sweet fragrance and are perfect for using in this recipe.

Per portion: Energy 454Kcal/1891kJ; Protein 31.6g; Carbohydrate 19.5g, of which sugars 19.5g; Fat 28.1g, of which saturates 7g; Cholesterol 165mg; Calcium 28mg; Fibre 1g; Sodium 116mg.

GALVESTON CHICKEN

A LIGHTLY SPICED MARINADE TURNS ORDINARY ROAST CHICKEN INTO A SPECIAL MEAL WITH SCARCELY ANY EXTRA EFFORT DEMANDED OF THE COOK. WHAT COULD BE BETTER?

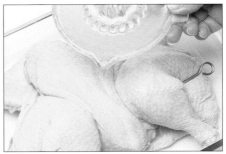

2 Insert a skewer through the chicken, at the thighs, to keep it flat during cooking. Place the chicken in a shallow, non-metallic dish and pour over the lemon juice.

3 In a small bowl, combine the garlic, cayenne, paprika, oregano, pepper, and oil. Mix well. Rub the mixture evenly over the surface of the chicken.

4 Cover and set aside to marinate for 2–3 hours at room temperature or in the refrigerator overnight. Bring the chicken back to room temperature 30 minutes before roasting.

5 Season the chicken well with salt on both sides. Transfer it to a shallow roasting pan.

6 Put the roasting pan in a cold oven and set the temperature to 200°C/400°F/Gas 6. Roast until the chicken is done, about 1–1½ hours, turning occasionally and basting with the roasting juices. To test if it is cooked through, insert a skewer into the thickest part. If the juices that run out are clear, it is ready.

SERVES FOUR

INGREDIENTS
 1.5kg/3½lb chicken
 juice of 1 lemon
 4 garlic cloves, crushed
 15ml/1 tbsp cayenne
 15ml/1 tbsp paprika
 15ml/1 tbsp dried oregano
 2.5ml/½ tsp coarse black pepper
 10ml/2 tsp olive oil
 5ml/1 tsp salt

COOK'S TIP
Roasting chicken in an oven that has not been preheated produces a particularly crispy skin.

1 With a sharp knife or poultry shears, remove the backbone from the chicken. Turn it breast side up. With the heel of your hand, press down to break the breastbone, and open the chicken flat like a book.

Per portion: Energy 407Kcal/1688kJ; Protein 37.2g; Carbohydrate 0g, of which sugars 0g; Fat 28.5g, of which saturates 7.7g; Cholesterol 198mg; Calcium 12mg; Fibre 0g; Sodium 626mg.

ROASTED DUCKLING
ON A BED OF HONEYED POTATOES

THE RICH FLAVOUR OF DUCK COMBINED WITH THESE SWEETENED POTATOES GLAZED WITH HONEY MAKES AN EXCELLENT TREAT FOR A DINNER PARTY OR SPECIAL OCCASION.

SERVES FOUR

INGREDIENTS

  1 duckling, giblets removed
  60ml/4 tbsp light soy sauce
  150ml/¼ pint/⅔ cup fresh
    orange juice
  3 large floury potatoes, cut
    into chunks
  30ml/2 tbsp clear honey
  15ml/1 tbsp sesame seeds
  salt and ground black pepper

1 Preheat the oven to 200°C/400°F/ Gas 6. Place the duckling in a roasting pan. Prick the skin well.

2 Mix the soy sauce and orange juice together and pour over the duck. Cook for 20 minutes.

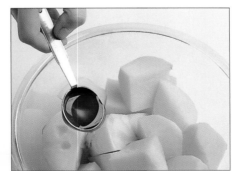

3 Place the potato chunks in a bowl, stir in the honey and toss to mix well. Remove the duckling from the oven and spoon the potatoes all around and under the duckling.

4 Roast for 35 minutes and remove from the oven. Toss the potatoes in the juices so the underside will be cooked and turn the duck over. Put back in the oven and cook for a further 30 minutes.

5 Remove the duckling from the oven and carefully scoop off the excess fat, leaving the juices behind.

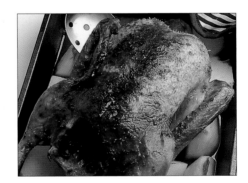

6 Sprinkle the sesame seeds over the potatoes, season and turn the duckling back over, breast side up, and cook for a further 10 minutes. Remove the duckling and potatoes from the oven and keep warm, allowing the duck to stand for a few minutes.

7 Pour off the excess fat and simmer the juices on the hob (stovetop) for a few minutes. Serve the juices with the carved duckling and potatoes.

Per portion: Energy 806Kcal/3341kJ; Protein 20.8g; Carbohydrate 32.3g, of which sugars 6.4g; Fat 66.8g, of which saturates 17.9g; Cholesterol 0mg; Calcium 53mg; Fibre 2.1g; Sodium 403mg.

MARMALADE-GLAZED GOOSE

SUCCULENT ROAST GOOSE IS THE CLASSIC CENTREPIECE FOR A TRADITIONAL CHRISTMAS LUNCH.
RED CABBAGE COOKED WITH LEEKS, AND BRAISED FENNEL ARE TASTY ACCOMPANIMENTS.

SERVES EIGHT

INGREDIENTS
4.5kg/10lb oven-ready goose
1 cooking apple, peeled, cored and
  cut into eighths
1 large onion, cut into eighths
bunch of fresh sage, plus extra sprigs
  to garnish
30ml/2 tbsp ginger
  marmalade, melted
salt and ground black pepper
For the stuffing
  25g/1oz/2 tbsp butter
  1 onion, finely chopped
  15ml/1 tbsp ginger marmalade
  450g/1lb/2 cups ready-to-eat
    prunes, chopped
  45ml/3 tbsp Madeira
  225g/8oz/4 cups fresh
    white breadcrumbs
  30ml/2 tbsp chopped fresh sage
For the gravy
  1 onion, chopped
  15ml/1 tbsp plain (all-purpose) flour
  150ml/¼ pint/⅔ cup Madeira
  600ml/1 pint/2½ cups chicken stock

1 Preheat the oven to 200°C/400°F/
Gas 6. Prick the skin of the goose all
over with a fork and season the bird
generously, both inside and out.

COOK'S TIP
Red cabbage goes well with goose. Cook
1 small leek, sliced, in 75g/3oz/6 tbsp
butter, add 1kg/2¼lb/9 cups shredded
red cabbage, with the grated rind of
1 orange, and cook for 2 minutes. Add
30ml/2 tbsp Madeira and 15ml/1 tbsp
brown sugar and cook for 15 minutes.

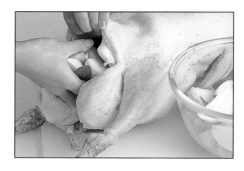

2 Mix the apple, onion and sage leaves
and spoon the mixture into the rump
end of the goose.

3 To make the stuffing, melt the butter
in a large pan and cook the onion for
about 5 minutes, or until softened but
not coloured. Remove the pan from
the heat and stir in the marmalade,
chopped prunes, Madeira, breadcrumbs
and chopped sage.

4 Stuff the neck end of the goose with
some of the stuffing, and set the
remaining stuffing aside in the
refrigerator. Sew up the bird or secure it
with skewers to prevent the stuffing
from escaping during cooking.

5 Place the goose in a large roasting
pan. Butter a piece of foil and use to
cover the goose loosely, then place in
the oven for 2 hours.

6 Baste the goose frequently during
cooking and remove excess fat from the
pan as necessary, using a small ladle or
serving spoon. (Strain, cool and chill the
fat in a covered container: it is excellent
for roasting potatoes.)

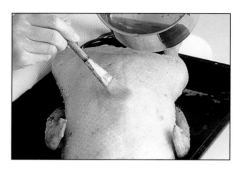

7 Remove the foil from the goose and
brush the melted ginger marmalade
over the goose, then roast for
30–40 minutes more, or until cooked
through. To check if the goose is cooked,
pierce the thick part of the thigh with a
metal skewer; the juices will run clear
when the bird is cooked. Remove from
the oven and cover with foil, then leave
to stand for 15 minutes before carving.

8 While the goose is cooking, shape the
remaining stuffing into walnut-size balls
and place them in an ovenproof dish.
Spoon 30ml/2 tbsp of the goose fat over
the stuffing balls and bake for about
15 minutes before the goose is cooked.

9 To make the gravy, pour off all but
15ml/1 tbsp of fat from the roasting
pan, leaving the meat juices behind.
Add the onion and cook for about
3–5 minutes, or until softened but not
coloured. Sprinkle in the flour and then
gradually stir in the Madeira and stock.
Bring to the boil, stirring constantly,
then simmer for 3 minutes, or until
thickened and glossy. Strain the gravy
and serve it with the carved goose and
stuffing. Garnish with sage leaves.

Per portion: Energy 823Kcal/3443kJ; Protein 57.6g; Carbohydrate 47.1g, of which sugars 23.8g; Fat 43.3g, of which saturates 14g; Cholesterol 177mg; Calcium 106mg; Fibre 4.5g; Sodium 395mg.

SOMERSET CIDER-GLAZED HAM

WILLIAM THE CONQUEROR INTRODUCED CIDER MAKING TO ENGLAND FROM NORMANDY IN 1066.
THIS WONDERFUL OLD WEST-COUNTRY HAM GLAZED WITH CIDER IS TRADITIONALLY SERVED WITH
CRANBERRY SAUCE AND IS IDEAL FOR CHRISTMAS FEASTING.

SERVES EIGHT TO TEN

INGREDIENTS
   2kg/4½lb middle gammon
      (cured ham) in a single piece
   1.3 litres/2¼ pints/5⅔ cups medium-
      dry (hard) cider
   1 large or 2 small onions
   about 30 whole cloves
   3 bay leaves
   10 black peppercorns
   45ml/3 tbsp soft light brown sugar
   bunch of flat leaf parsley, to garnish
For the cranberry sauce
   2 clementines
   350g/12oz/3 cups cranberries
   175g/6oz/¾ cup soft light brown sugar
   30ml/2 tbsp port

1 Weigh the ham and calculate the
cooking time at 20 minutes per 450g/
1lb, then place it in a large casserole or
pan. Stud the onion or onions with
5–10 of the cloves and add to the
casserole or pan with the bay leaves
and peppercorns.

2 Add 1.2 litres/2 pints/5 cups of the
cider and enough water just to cover
the ham. Heat until simmering and then
carefully skim off the scum that rises to
the surface using a large spoon or ladle.
Start timing the cooking from the
moment the stock begins to simmer.

VARIATION
Use honey in place of the soft brown
sugar for the glaze and serve the ham
with redcurrant sauce or jelly.

3 Cover with a lid or foil and simmer
gently for the calculated time. Towards
the end of the cooking time, preheat the
oven to 220°C/425°F/Gas 7.

4 Heat the sugar and remaining cider in
a pan; stir until the sugar has dissolved.

5 Simmer for 5 minutes to make a dark,
sticky glaze. Remove the pan from the
heat and leave to cool for 5 minutes.

6 Lift the ham out of the casserole or
pan using a slotted spoon and a large
fork. Carefully and evenly, cut the rind
from the ham, then score the fat into a
neat diamond pattern. Place the ham in
a roasting pan or ovenproof dish.

7 Press a clove into the centre of each
diamond, then carefully spoon over the
glaze. Roast for 20–25 minutes, or until
the fat is brown, glistening and crisp.

8 Grate the rind and squeeze the juice
from the clementines. Simmer all the
cranberry sauce ingredients in a heavy
pan for 15–20 minutes, stirring
frequently. Transfer the sauce to a jug
(pitcher). Serve the ham hot or cold,
garnished with parsley and with the
cranberry sauce.

COOK'S TIPS
• A large stock pot or preserving pan can
be used in place of the casserole or pan
for cooking the ham.
• Leave the ham until it is just cool
enough to handle before removing the
rind. Snip off the string using a sharp
knife or scissors, then carefully slice off
the rind, leaving a thin, even layer of fat.
Use a narrow-bladed, sharp knife for the
best results – a filleting knife, or a long,
slim ham knife would be ideal.

Per portion: Energy 409Kcal/1712kJ; Protein 44g; Carbohydrate 16.8g, of which sugars 16.8g; Fat 18.8g, of which saturates 6.3g; Cholesterol 58mg; Calcium 27mg; Fibre 0.7g; Sodium 2202mg.

ROAST PORK WITH SAGE AND ONION STUFFING

SAGE AND ONION MAKE A CLASSIC STUFFING FOR ROAST PORK, DUCK AND TURKEY, WITH THE SAGE COUNTERACTING THE FATTINESS OF THE RICH MEATS. SERVE WITH APPLE SAUCE AND ROAST POTATOES.

SERVES SIX TO EIGHT

INGREDIENTS
 1.3–1.6kg/3–3½lb boneless loin of pork
 60ml/4 tbsp fine, dry breadcrumbs
 10ml/2 tsp chopped fresh sage
 25ml/1½ tbsp plain (all-
  purpose) flour
 300ml/½ pint/1¼ cups (hard) cider
 150ml/¼ pint/⅔ cup water
 5–10ml/1–2 tsp crab apple or
  redcurrant jelly
 salt and ground black pepper
 fresh thyme sprigs, to garnish
For the stuffing
 25g/1oz/2 tbsp butter
 50g/2oz bacon, finely chopped
 2 large onions, finely chopped
 75g/3oz/1½ cups fresh
  white breadcrumbs
 30ml/2 tbsp chopped fresh sage
 5ml/1 tsp chopped fresh thyme
 10ml/2 tsp finely grated lemon rind
 1 small (US medium)
  egg, beaten

1 Preheat the oven to 220°C/425°F/ Gas 7. To make the stuffing, melt the butter in a pan and cook the bacon until it begins to brown, then add the onions and cook gently until softened. Mix with the breadcrumbs, sage, thyme, lemon rind and egg, then season well.

2 Cut the rind off the piece of pork in one piece and score it well. Cooking the rind separately makes crisper crackling than leaving it on the pork.

3 Place the pork fat side down, and season. Add a layer of stuffing, then roll up and tie neatly.

4 Lay the rind over the pork and rub in 5ml/1 tsp salt. Roast for 2–2½ hours, basting with the pork fat once or twice. Reduce the temperature to 190°C/375°F/ Gas 5 after 20 minutes. Shape the remaining stuffing into balls and add to the roasting pan for the last 30 minutes.

5 Remove the rind from the pork. Increase the oven temperature to 220°C/425°F/Gas 7 and roast the rind for a further 20–25 minutes, until crisp.

6 Mix the dry breadcrumbs and sage and press them into the fat. Cook the pork for 10 minutes, then cover and set aside in a warm place for 15–20 minutes.

7 Remove all but 30–45ml/2–3 tbsp of the fat from the roasting pan and place it on the hob (stovetop). Stir in the flour, followed by the cider and water. Bring to the boil and then cook gently for 10 minutes. Strain the gravy into a clean pan, add the crab apple or redcurrant jelly, and cook for another 5 minutes. Adjust the seasoning.

8 Serve the pork cut into thick slices and the crisp crackling cut into strips with the cider gravy, garnished with thyme.

Per portion: Energy 426Kcal/1789kJ; Protein 52.4g; Carbohydrate 23.7g, of which sugars 5.3g; Fat 14.1g, of which saturates 5.7g; Cholesterol 180mg; Calcium 67mg; Fibre 1.4g; Sodium 475mg.

ROASTED AND MARINATED PORK

YUAN, A SAUCE MADE FROM SAKE, SHOYU, MIRIN AND CITRUS FRUIT, IS OFTEN USED IN JAPAN TO MARINATE INGREDIENTS EITHER BEFORE OR AFTER COOKING. IN THIS RECIPE, THE SAUCE GIVES A DELICATE FLAVOUR TO PORK. IF POSSIBLE, LEAVE THE MEAT TO MARINATE OVERNIGHT.

SERVES FOUR

INGREDIENTS
    600g/1lb 5oz pork fillet (tenderloin)
    1 garlic clove, crushed
    generous pinch of salt
    4 spring onions (scallions), trimmed,
      white part only
    10g/¼oz dried wakame, soaked in
      water for 20 minutes and drained
    10cm/4in celery stick, trimmed and
      cut in half crossways
    1 carton salad cress
For the yuan sauce
    105ml/7 tbsp shoyu
    45ml/3 tbsp sake
    60ml/4 tbsp mirin
    1 lime, sliced into thin rings

4 Cut the white part of the spring onions in half crossways, then in half lengthways. Remove the round cores, then lay the spring onion quarters flat on a chopping board. Slice them very thinly lengthways to make fine shreds.

5 Soak the shreds in a bowl of ice-cold water. Repeat with the remaining parts of the spring onions. When the shreds curl up, drain and gather them into a loose ball.

6 Cut the drained wakame into 2.5cm/1in squares or narrow strips. Slice the celery very thinly lengthways. Soak in cold water, then drain and gather together as before.

7 Remove the pork from the marinade and wipe with kitchen paper. Slice it very thinly. Strain the marinade and keep it in a gravy boat or jug (pitcher). Arrange the sliced pork on a large serving plate with the vegetables around it. Serve cold with the yuan sauce.

1 Preheat the oven to 200°C/400°F/Gas 6. Rub the pork with crushed garlic and salt, and leave for 15 minutes.

2 Roast the pork for 20 minutes, then turn the meat over and reduce the oven temperature to 180°C/350°F/Gas 4. Cook for a further 20 minutes, or until the pork is cooked. Test by inserting a skewer or the point of a sharp knife into the meat. If the juices run clear, the meat is cooked. If there are any traces of pink in the juices, roast the pork for a little longer.

3 Meanwhile, mix the yuan sauce ingredients in a container that is big enough to hold the pork. When the meat is cooked, immediately put it in the sauce, and leave it to marinate for at least 2 hours, or overnight.

Per portion: Energy 188Kcal/787kJ; Protein 32.5g; Carbohydrate 0.7g, of which sugars 0.6g; Fat 6.1g, of which saturates 2.1g; Cholesterol 95mg; Calcium 18mg; Fibre 0.2g; Sodium 377mg.

ROAST LEG OF LAMB

WHEN YOUNG LAMB WAS SEASONAL TO SPRINGTIME, A ROAST LEG WAS AN EASTER SPECIALITY, SERVED WITH A SAUCE USING THE FIRST SPRIGS OF MINT OF THE YEAR AND EARLY NEW POTATOES. ROAST LAMB IS NOW WELL ESTABLISHED AS A YEAR-ROUND FAMILY FAVOURITE FOR SUNDAY LUNCH, OFTEN SERVED WITH CRISP ROAST POTATOES.

SERVES SIX

INGREDIENTS
 1.5kg/3¼lb leg of lamb
 4 garlic cloves, sliced
 2 fresh rosemary sprigs
 30ml/2 tbsp light olive oil
 300ml/½ pint/1¼ cups red wine
 5ml/1 tsp clear honey
 45ml/3 tbsp redcurrant jelly
 salt and ground black pepper
For the roast potatoes
 45ml/3 tbsp white vegetable fat
  or lard
 1.3kg/3lb potatoes, such as Desirée,
  cut into chunks
For the mint sauce
 about 15g/½oz fresh mint
 10ml/2 tsp caster (superfine) sugar
 15ml/1 tbsp boiling water
 30ml/2 tbsp white wine vinegar

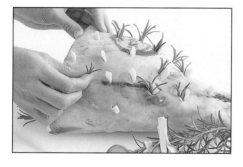

1 Preheat the oven to 220°C/425°F/ Gas 7. Make small slits into the lamb all over the leg. Press a slice of garlic and a few rosemary leaves into each slit, then place the lamb in a roasting pan and season well. Drizzle the oil over the lamb and roast for about 1 hour.

COOK'S TIP
To make a quick and tasty gravy from the pan juices, add about 300ml/½ pint/ 1¼ cups red wine, stock or water and boil, stirring occasionally, until reduced and well-flavoured. Season to taste, then strain into a sauce boat to serve.

2 Meanwhile, mix the wine, honey and redcurrant jelly in a small pan and heat, stirring, until the jelly melts. Bring to the boil, then reduce the heat and simmer until reduced by half. Spoon this glaze over the lamb and return it to the oven for 30–45 minutes.

3 To make the potatoes, put the fat in a roasting pan on the oven shelf above the meat. Boil the potatoes for about 5–10 minutes, then drain them and fluff up the surface of each with a fork.

4 Add the prepared potatoes to the hot fat and baste well, then roast them for 40–50 minutes, or until they are crisp.

5 Meanwhile, make the mint sauce. Place the mint on a chopping board and sprinkle the sugar over the top. Chop the mint finely, then transfer the mint and sugar to a bowl.

6 Add the boiling water and stir until the sugar has dissolved. Add 15ml/ 1 tbsp vinegar and taste the sauce before adding the remaining vinegar. (You may want to add slightly less or more than the suggested quantity.) Leave the mint sauce to stand until you are ready to serve the meal.

7 Cover the lamb with foil and set it aside in a warm place to rest for 10–15 minutes before carving. Serve with the crisp roast potatoes, mint sauce and a selection of seasonal vegetables.

Per portion: Energy 732Kcal/3080kJ; Protein 78g; Carbohydrate 36.4g, of which sugars 4.2g; Fat 31.6g, of which saturates 12.7g; Cholesterol 257mg; Calcium 36mg; Fibre 2.2g; Sodium 182mg.

ROAST VEAL WITH PARSLEY STUFFING

COOKING THIS LOIN OF VEAL, WITH ITS FRAGRANT PARSLEY AND LEEK STUFFING, IN A ROASTING BAG MAKES SURE THAT IT IS SUCCULENT AND FULL FLAVOURED WHEN SERVED.

SERVES SIX

INGREDIENTS
25g/1oz/2 tbsp butter
15ml/1 tbsp sunflower oil
1 leek, finely chopped
1 celery stick, finely chopped
50g/2oz/1 cup fresh
  white breadcrumbs
50g/2oz/½ cup chopped fresh flat
  leaf parsley
900g/2lb boned loin of veal
salt and ground black pepper

VARIATION
Other mild herbs can be used in the stuffing instead of parsley. Try tarragon, chervil and chives, but avoid strong-flavoured herbs, such as marjoram, oregano and thyme, which tend to overpower the delicate flavour of veal.

1 Preheat the oven to 180°C/350°F/ Gas 4. Heat the butter and oil in a frying pan until foaming. Cook the leek and celery until they are just starting to colour, then remove the pan from the heat and stir in the breadcrumbs, parsley and seasoning.

2 Lay the loin of veal out flat. Spread the stuffing over the meat, then roll it up carefully and tie the roll at regular intervals to secure it in a neat shape.

3 Place the veal in a roasting bag and close the bag with an ovenproof tie, then place it in a roasting pan. Roast the veal for 1¼ hours.

4 Pierce the meat with a metal skewer to check whether it is cooked: when cooked the meat juices will run clear. Leave the veal to stand for about 10–15 minutes, then carve it into thick slices and serve with gravy, sautéed potatoes, asparagus and sugar snaps.

ESCALOPES OF VEAL WITH CREAM SAUCE

THIS QUICK, EASY DINNER–PARTY DISH IS DELICIOUS SERVED WITH BUTTERED TAGLIATELLE AND LIGHTLY STEAMED GREEN VEGETABLES.

SERVES FOUR

INGREDIENTS
15ml/1 tbsp plain (all-purpose) flour
4 veal escalopes (US scallops), each
  weighing about 75–115g/3–4oz
30ml/2 tbsp sunflower oil
1 shallot, chopped
150g/5oz/2 cups oyster
  mushrooms, sliced
30ml/2 tbsp Marsala or
  medium-dry sherry
200ml/7fl oz/scant 1 cup
  crème fraîche
30ml/2 tbsp chopped fresh tarragon
salt and ground black pepper

COOK'S TIP
If the sauce seems to be too thick, add 30ml/2 tbsp water.

1 Season the flour and use to dust the veal escalopes, then set aside.

2 Heat the oil in a large frying pan and cook the shallot and mushrooms for 5 minutes. Add the escalopes and cook over a high heat for about 1½ minutes on each side. Pour in the Marsala or sherry and cook until reduced by half.

3 Use a spatula to remove the veal escalopes from the pan. Stir the crème fraîche, tarragon and seasoning into the juices remaining in the pan and simmer gently for 3–5 minutes, or until the sauce is thick and creamy.

4 Return the escalopes to the pan and heat through for 1 minute before serving.

Top per portion: Energy 233Kcal/981kJ; Protein 33.4g; Carbohydrate 7.6g, of which sugars 1.1g; Fat 7.9g, of which saturates 3.6g; Cholesterol 135mg; Calcium 49mg; Fibre 1.3g; Sodium 260mg.
Below per portion: Energy 376Kcal/1564kJ; Protein 25g; Carbohydrate 5.5g, of which sugars 1.5g; Fat 27.5g, of which saturates 14.9g; Cholesterol 108mg; Calcium 44mg; Fibre 0.6g; Sodium 73mg.

ROAST RIB OF BEEF

THIS ROAST LOOKS SPECTACULAR, AND SERVED IN TRADITIONAL STYLE, WITH YORKSHIRE PUDDINGS AND HORSERADISH SAUCE, IT MAKES A PERFECT CELEBRATION MEAL.

SERVES EIGHT TO TEN

INGREDIENTS
45ml/3 tbsp mixed peppercorns
15ml/1 tbsp juniper berries
2.75kg/6lb rolled rib of beef
30ml/2 tbsp Dijon mustard
15ml/1 tbsp olive oil
For the Yorkshire puddings
150ml/¼ pint/⅔ cup water
150ml/¼ pint/⅔ cup milk
115g/4oz/1 cup plain (all-purpose) flour
pinch of salt
2 eggs, beaten
60ml/4 tbsp lard, melted, or sunflower oil (optional)
For the caramelized shallots
20 shallots
5 garlic cloves, peeled
60ml/4 tbsp light olive oil
15ml/1 tbsp caster (superfine) sugar
For the gravy
150ml/¼ pint/⅔ cup red wine
600ml/1 pint/2½ cups beef stock
salt and ground black pepper

1 Preheat the oven to 230°C/450°F/Gas 8. Coarsely crush the peppercorns and juniper berries. Sprinkle half the spices over the meat, then transfer to a roasting pan and roast for 30 minutes.

COOK'S TIP
If you prefer to cook beef on the bone, buy a 3.6kg/8lb forerib. Trim off the excess fat, sprinkle over the spices, then follow the instructions in steps 1 and 2. Roast at the lower temperature for 2 hours for rare beef, 2½ hours for medium rare, and 3 hours for well done.

2 Reduce the oven temperature to 180°C/350°F/Gas 4. Mix the mustard and oil into the remaining crushed spices and spread the resulting paste over the meat. Roast the meat for a further 1¼ hours if you like your meat rare, 1 hour 50 minutes for a medium-rare result or 2 hours 25 minutes for a roast that is medium to well done. Baste the beef frequently during cooking.

3 Make the Yorkshire puddings as soon as the beef is in the oven. Stir the water into the milk. Sift the flour and salt into a bowl. Make a well in the middle and gradually whisk in the eggs followed by the milk and water to make a smooth batter. Cover and leave to stand for about 1 hour. (The batter can be made well in advance and chilled overnight in the refrigerator if convenient.)

4 An hour before the beef is due to be ready, mix the shallots and garlic cloves with the light olive oil and spoon into the roasting pan around the beef. After 30 minutes, sprinkle the caster sugar over the shallots and garlic. Stir the shallots and garlic two or three times during cooking.

5 Transfer the meat to a large serving platter, cover tightly with foil and set aside in a warm place for 20–30 minutes. (This resting time makes carving easier.) Increase the oven temperature to 230°C/450°F/Gas 8. Divide 60ml/4 tbsp dripping from the meat or the lard or oil, if using, among 10 individual Yorkshire pudding tins (muffin pans) and heat in the oven for 5 minutes.

6 Spoon the Yorkshire pudding batter into the hot fat in the tins and bake for 20–30 minutes, or until risen, firm and a golden brown colour. The time depends on the size of the tins: larger Yorkshire puddings will take longer than those in smaller tins.

7 Make the gravy while the Yorkshire puddings are cooking. Simmer the red wine and beef stock together in a pan for about 5 minutes to intensify the flavour of the gravy.

8 Skim the fat from the meat juices in the roasting pan, then pour in the wine mixture and simmer until the gravy is reduced and thickened slightly to a syrupy consistency. Stir frequently with a wooden spoon to remove all of the roasting residue from the roasting pan. Season to taste.

9 Serve the beef with the individual Yorkshire puddings, caramelized shallots and gravy. Offer roast potatoes or game chips as accompaniments, along with a selection of lightly cooked, seasonal vegetables.

Per portion: Energy 828Kcal/3444kJ; Protein 64.8g; Carbohydrate 14.2g, of which sugars 3.3g; Fat 55.7g, of which saturates 22.9g; Cholesterol 229mg; Calcium 74mg; Fibre 0.7g; Sodium 137mg.

BAKED DISHES

Baking is a very versatile cooking method, as this eclectic selection of recipes proves. Crunchy, golden toppings will prove a hit with everyone, and slow baking brings out the full flavour. For a family supper that is sure to please, choose Roasted Ratatouille Moussaka or a hearty Country Meat Loaf. Smoked Haddock and New Potato Pie is another excellent choice, and you can ring the changes by choosing whatever fish is readily available and therefore relatively inexpensive. Do try Fillets of Brill in Red Wine Sauce, which proves once and for all that red wine and fish can go beautifully together.

ROASTED RATATOUILLE MOUSSAKA

BASED ON THE CLASSIC GREEK DISH, THIS MOUSSAKA REALLY HAS A TASTE OF THE MEDITERRANEAN. ROASTING BRINGS OUT THE DEEP RICH FLAVOURS OF THE VEGETABLES, WHICH GIVE A COLOURFUL CONTRAST TO THE LIGHT AND MOUTHWATERING EGG-AND-CHEESE TOPPING. THIS DISH IS PERFECT AS A VEGETARIAN MAIN COURSE, ALTHOUGH IT MAY BE SERVED AS A HEARTY WINTER SIDE DISH, TOO.

SERVES FOUR TO SIX

INGREDIENTS
   2 red (bell) peppers, seeded and cut
     into large chunks
   2 yellow (bell) peppers, seeded and
     cut into large chunks
   2 aubergines (eggplant), cut into
     large chunks
   3 courgettes (zucchini), thickly sliced
   45ml/3 tbsp olive oil
   3 garlic cloves, crushed
   400g/14oz can chopped tomatoes
   30ml/2 tbsp sun-dried tomato paste
   45ml/3 tbsp chopped fresh basil or
     15ml/1 tbsp dried basil
   15ml/1 tbsp balsamic vinegar
   1.5ml/¼ tsp soft light brown sugar
   salt and ground black pepper
   basil leaves, to garnish
For the topping
   25g/1oz/2 tbsp butter
   25g/1oz/¼ cup plain (all-
     purpose) flour
   300ml/½ pint/1¼ cups milk
   1.5ml/¼ tsp freshly grated nutmeg
   250g/9oz ricotta cheese
   3 eggs, beaten
   25g/1oz/⅓ cup freshly grated
     Parmesan cheese

1 Preheat the oven to 230°C/450°F/ Gas 8. Arrange the chunks of red and yellow peppers, aubergines and courgettes in an even layer in a large roasting pan. Season well with salt and ground black pepper.

2 Mix together the oil and crushed garlic cloves and pour them over the vegetables. Shake the roasting pan to thoroughly coat the vegetables in the garlic mixture.

3 Roast in the oven for 15–20 minutes, until slightly charred, lightly tossing the vegetables once during the cooking time. Remove the pan from the oven and set aside. Reduce the oven temperature to 200°C/400°F/Gas 6.

4 Put the chopped tomatoes, sun-dried tomato paste, basil, balsamic vinegar and brown sugar in a large, heavy pan and gently heat to boiling point. Reduce the heat and simmer, uncovered, for about 10–15 minutes, until reduced and thickened, stirring occasionally. Season with salt and freshly ground black pepper to taste.

5 Carefully tip the roasted vegetables out of their pan and into the pan of tomato sauce. Mix well, coating the vegetables thoroughly in the tomato sauce. Spoon into an ovenproof dish.

6 To make the topping, melt the butter in a large, heavy pan over a gentle heat. Stir in the flour and cook for 1 minute. Pour in the milk, stirring constantly, then whisk until blended. Add the nutmeg and continue whisking over a gentle heat until thickened. Cook for a further 2 minutes, then remove from the heat and leave to cool slightly.

7 Mix in the ricotta cheese and beaten eggs thoroughly. Season with salt and plenty of freshly ground black pepper to taste.

8 Level the surface of the roasted vegetable mixture with the back of a spoon. Spoon the moussaka topping over the vegetables and sprinkle with the Parmesan cheese. Bake for 30–35 minutes, until the topping is golden brown. Serve immediately, garnished with basil leaves.

VARIATION
Rather than baking this recipe in one large dish, divide the roasted vegetables and topping among individual gratin dishes. Reduce the baking time to 25 minutes. Individual portions can also be frozen and, when needed, simply removed from the freezer, left to thaw and baked for 30–35 minutes – ideal for those with a solitary vegetarian in the family, or for unexpected guests.

Per portion: Energy 570Kcal/2367kJ; Protein 22.1g; Carbohydrate 27.5g, of which sugars 21.7g; Fat 42.1g, of which saturates 20.3g; Cholesterol 223mg; Calcium 339mg; Fibre 7.1g; Sodium 447mg.

COD, BASIL, TOMATO AND POTATO PIE

FRESH AND SMOKED FISH MAKE A GREAT COMBINATION, ESPECIALLY WITH THE HINT OF TOMATO AND BASIL. SERVED WITH A GREEN SALAD, THIS MAKES AN IDEAL DISH FOR LUNCH OR A FAMILY SUPPER.

2 Melt 75g/3oz/6 tbsp of the butter in a large pan, add the onion and cook for about 5 minutes, until softened and tender but not browned. Sprinkle over the flour and half the chopped basil. Gradually add the reserved fish cooking liquid, adding a little more milk if necessary to make a fairly thin sauce, stirring constantly to make a smooth consistency. Bring to the boil, season with salt and pepper, and add the remaining basil.

3 Remove the pan from the heat, then add the fish and tomatoes and stir gently to combine. Pour into an ovenproof dish.

SERVES EIGHT

INGREDIENTS
  1kg/2¼lb smoked cod fillets
  1kg/2¼lb fresh cod fillets
  900ml/1½ pint/3¾ cups milk
  1.2litres/2 pints/5 cups water
  2 fresh basil sprigs
  1 fresh lemon thyme sprig
  150g/5oz/⅔ cup butter
  1 onion, chopped
  75g/3oz/⅔ cup plain
    (all-purpose) flour
  30ml/2 tbsp chopped fresh basil
  4 firm plum tomatoes, peeled
    and chopped
  12 medium floury potatoes
salt and ground black pepper
crushed black pepper corns,
  to garnish
lettuce leaves, to serve

1 Place both kinds of fish in a roasting pan with 600ml/1 pint/2½ cups of the milk, the water and the herb sprigs. Bring to a simmer and cook gently for about 3–4 minutes. Remove from the heat and leave the fish to cool in the liquid for about 20 minutes. Drain the fish, reserving the cooking liquid for use in the sauce. Flake the fish, removing the skin and any remaining bones.

4 Preheat the oven to 180ºC/350ºF/ Gas 4. Cook the potatoes in boiling water until tender. Drain then add the remaining butter and milk and mash. Season to taste and spoon over the fish mixture, using a fork to create a pattern. You can freeze the pie at this stage. Bake for 30 minutes until the top is golden. Sprinkle with the crushed pepper corns and serve hot with lettuce.

Per portion: Energy 474Kcal/1989kJ; Protein 49.6g; Carbohydrate 30.7g, of which sugars 4.6g; Fat 17.8g, of which saturates 10.2g; Cholesterol 155mg; Calcium 62mg; Fibre 2.5g; Sodium 1672mg.

FISH PIE

THIS DISH CAN BE VARIED TO SUIT YOUR TASTE AND POCKET. THIS IS A SIMPLE PIE, BUT YOU COULD ADD PRAWNS OR HARD-BOILED EGGS, OR MIX THE POTATO TOPPING WITH SPRING ONIONS.

SERVES FOUR

INGREDIENTS

    450g/1lb cod or haddock fillets
    225g/8oz smoked cod fillets
    300ml/½ pint/1¼ cups milk
    ½ lemon, sliced
    1 bay leaf
    1 fresh thyme sprig
    4–5 black peppercorns
    50g/2oz/¼ cup butter
    25g/1oz/¼ cup plain (all-
        purpose) flour
    30ml/2 tbsp chopped fresh parsley
    5ml/1 tsp anchovy essence (extract)
    150g/5oz/2 cups sliced mushrooms
    salt, ground black pepper and
        cayenne pepper
For the topping
    450g/1lb potatoes, cooked and
        mashed with milk
    50g/2oz/¼ cup butter
    2 tomatoes, sliced
    25g/1oz/¼ cup grated Cheddar
        cheese (optional)

1 Put the fish, skin side down, in a shallow pan. Add the milk, lemon slices, bay leaf, thyme and peppercorns. Bring to the boil, then lower the heat and poach gently for about 5 minutes, until just cooked. Strain off and reserve the milk. Remove the fish skin and flake the flesh, discarding any bones.

2 Melt half the butter in a small pan, stir in the flour and cook gently, stirring, for 1 minute. Add the milk and boil, whisking, until smooth and creamy. Stir in the parsley and anchovy essence and season to taste.

3 Heat the remaining butter in a frying pan, add the sliced mushrooms and sauté until tender. Season and add to the flaked fish. Mix the sauce into the fish and stir gently to combine. Transfer the mixture to an ovenproof dish.

4 Preheat the oven to 200ºC/400ºF/ Gas 6. Beat the mashed potato with the butter until very creamy. Season, then spread the topping evenly over the fish. Fork up the surface and arrange the sliced tomatoes around the edge. Sprinkle the exposed topping with the grated cheese, if using.

5 Bake for 20–25 minutes, until the topping is lightly browned. If you prefer, finish browning under a grill (broiler).

VARIATION
Instead of using plain mashed potatoes, try a mixture of mashed potato and mashed swede (rutabaga) or celeriac.

Per portion: Energy 382Kcal/1600kJ; Protein 34.8g; Carbohydrate 24.3g, of which sugars 3.1g; Fat 16.8g, of which saturates 9.9g; Cholesterol 118mg; Calcium 62mg; Fibre 2.7g; Sodium 859mg.

SMOKED HADDOCK AND NEW POTATO PIE

SMOKED HADDOCK HAS A SALTY FLAVOUR AND CAN BE BOUGHT EITHER DYED OR UNDYED. THE DYED FISH HAS A STRONG YELLOW COLOUR, WHILE THE OTHER IS ALMOST CREAMY IN COLOUR.

SERVES FOUR

INGREDIENTS
  450g/1lb smoked haddock fillet
  475ml/16fl oz/2 cups semi-skimmed
    (low-fat) milk
  2 bay leaves
  1 onion, quartered
  4 cloves
  450g/1lb new potatoes
  butter, for greasing
  30ml/2 tbsp cornflour (cornstarch)
  60ml/4 tbsp double (heavy) cream
  30ml/2 tbsp chopped fresh chervil
  salt and ground black pepper
  mixed vegetables, to serve

VARIATIONS
Instead of using all smoked haddock for this pie, use half smoked and half fresh. Cook the two types together, as described in Step 1. A handful of peeled prawns (shrimp) is a good addition to this pie if you want to make it even more filling.

COOK'S TIP
The fish gives out liquid as it cooks, so it is best to start with a slightly thicker sauce than you might think is necessary.

1 Preheat the oven to 200°C/400°F/ Gas 6. Place the haddock in a deep-sided frying pan. Pour the milk over and add the bay leaves.

2 Stud the onion with the cloves and place it in the pan with the fish and milk. Cover the top and simmer for about 10 minutes or until the fish starts to flake.

3 Remove the fish with a slotted spoon and set aside to cool. Strain the liquid from the pan into a separate pan and set aside.

4 To prepare the potatoes, cut them into thin slices, leaving the skins on.

5 Blanch the potatoes in a large pan of lightly salted, boiling water for about 5 minutes. Drain.

6 Grease the base and sides of a 1.2 litre/2 pint/5 cup ovenproof dish. Then using a knife and fork, carefully flake the fish.

7 Reheat the milk in the pan. Mix the cornflour with a little water to form a paste and stir in the cream and the chervil. Add to the milk in the pan and cook until thickened.

8 Arrange one-third of the potatoes over the base of the dish and season with pepper. Lay half of the fish over. Repeat layering, finishing with a layer of potatoes on top.

9 Pour the sauce over the top, making sure that it sinks down through the mixture. Cover with foil and cook for 30 minutes. Remove the foil and cook for a further 10 minutes to brown the surface. Serve immediately with a selection of mixed vegetables.

Per portion: Energy 300Kcal/1266kJ; Protein 23.9g; Carbohydrate 32.4g, of which sugars 1.9g; Fat 9.3g, of which saturates 5.3g; Cholesterol 61mg; Calcium 56mg; Fibre 1.5g; Sodium 881mg.

BAKED SEA BREAM WITH TOMATOES

JOHN DORY, TURBOT OR SEA BASS CAN ALL BE COOKED THIS WAY. IF YOU PREFER TO USE FILLETED FISH, CHOOSE A CHUNKY FILLET, LIKE COD, AND BAKE IT SKIN SIDE UP. ROASTING THE TOMATOES BRINGS OUT THEIR SWEETNESS, WHICH CONTRASTS BEAUTIFULLY WITH THE FLAVOUR OF THE FISH.

SERVES FOUR TO SIX

INGREDIENTS

8 ripe tomatoes
10ml/2 tsp caster (superfine) sugar
200ml/7fl oz/scant 1 cup olive oil
450g/1lb new potatoes
1 lemon, sliced
1 bay leaf
1 fresh thyme sprig
8 fresh basil leaves
1 sea bream, about 900g–1kg/
   2–2¼lb, cleaned and scaled
150ml/¼ pint/⅔ cup dry white wine
30ml/2 tbsp fresh white breadcrumbs
2 garlic cloves, crushed
15ml/1 tbsp finely chopped
   fresh parsley
salt and ground black pepper
fresh flat parsley or basil leaves,
   chopped, to garnish

1 Preheat the oven to 240°C/475°F/ Gas 9. Using a sharp knife, cut the tomatoes in half lengthways and arrange them in a single layer in a large, ovenproof dish, cut side up. Sprinkle with the caster sugar, season to taste with salt and pepper and drizzle over a little of the olive oil. Roast for 30–40 minutes, until the tomatoes are soft and lightly browned on top.

2 Meanwhile, cut the potatoes into 1cm/½in slices. Par-boil for 5 minutes. Drain and set aside.

3 Grease an ovenproof dish with oil. Arrange the potatoes in a single layer with the lemon slices over; sprinkle on the bay leaf, thyme and basil. Season and drizzle with half the remaining olive oil. Lay the fish on top, season; pour over the wine and the rest of the oil. Arrange the tomatoes around the fish.

4 Mix together the breadcrumbs, garlic and parsley and sprinkle over the fish. Bake for 30 minutes, until the flesh comes away easily from the bone. Garnish with chopped parsley or basil.

Per portion: Energy 571Kcal/2383kJ; Protein 25.9g; Carbohydrate 29.4g, of which sugars 7.2g; Fat 37.1g, of which saturates 4.9g; Cholesterol 48mg; Calcium 82mg; Fibre 3g; Sodium 224mg.

FILLETS <u>OF</u> BRILL <u>IN</u> RED WINE SAUCE

FORGET THE OLD MAXIM THAT RED WINE AND FISH DO NOT GO WELL TOGETHER. THE ROBUST SAUCE ADDS COLOUR AND RICHNESS TO THIS EXCELLENT DISH. TURBOT, HALIBUT AND JOHN DORY ARE ALSO GOOD COOKED THIS WAY.

SERVES FOUR

INGREDIENTS
    4 brill fillets, about 175–200g/6–7oz
      each, skinned
    150g/5oz/²⁄₃ cup chilled butter,
      diced, plus extra for greasing
    115g/4oz shallots, thinly sliced
    200ml/7fl oz/scant 1 cup robust
      red wine
    200ml/7fl oz/scant 1 cup fish stock
    salt and ground white pepper
    fresh chervil or flat leaf parsley
      leaves, to garnish

3 Using a fish slice or spatula, carefully lift the fish and shallots on to a serving dish, cover with foil and keep hot.

4 Transfer the dish to the hob (stovetop) and bring the cooking liquid to the boil over a high heat. Cook it until it has reduced by half. Lower the heat and whisk in the chilled butter, one piece at a time, to make a smooth, shiny sauce. Season with salt and ground white pepper, set aside and keep hot.

5 Divide the shallots among four warmed plates and lay the brill fillets on top. Pour the sauce over and around the fish and garnish with the chervil or flat leaf parsley.

1 Preheat the oven to 180°C/350°F/ Gas 4. Season the fish on both sides with salt and pepper. Generously butter a flameproof dish, which is large enough to take all the brill fillets in a single layer without overlapping. Spread the shallots over the base and lay the fish fillets on top. Season.

2 Pour in the red wine and fish stock, cover the dish and bring the liquid to just below boiling point. Transfer the dish to the oven and bake for 6–8 minutes, until just cooked.

Per portion: Energy 511Kcal/2123kJ; Protein 35.7g; Carbohydrate 1.3g, of which sugars 1.3g; Fat 36.7g, of which saturates 19.5g; Cholesterol 156mg; Calcium 97mg; Fibre 0.4g; Sodium 454mg.

SINIYA

The name of this classic Jewish Sephardi dish simply means fish and tahini sauce. In this version, the fish is first wrapped in vine leaves, then spread with tahini and baked. A final sprinkling of pomegranate seeds adds a fresh, invigorating flavour.

SERVES FOUR

INGREDIENTS
4 small fish, such as trout, sea
   bream, red mullet or snapper, each
   weighing about 300g/11oz, cleaned
at least 5 garlic cloves, chopped
juice of 2 lemons
75ml/5 tbsp olive oil
about 20 brined vine (grape) leaves
tahini, for drizzling
1–2 pomegranates
fresh mint and coriander (cilantro)
   sprigs, to garnish

VARIATION
Instead of whole fish, use fish fillets or
steaks such as fresh tuna. Make a bed
of vine (grape) leaves and top with the
fish and marinade. Bake for about
5–10 minutes, until the fish is half
cooked, then top with the tahini as above
and grill (broil) until golden brown and
lightly crusted on top.

1 Preheat the oven to 180°C/350°F/
Gas 4. Put the fish in a shallow, ovenproof
dish, large enough to fit all the fish
without touching each other. In a bowl,
combine the garlic, lemon juice and oil;
spoon over the fish. Turn the fish to coat.

2 Rinse the vine leaves well under cold
water, then wrap the fish in the leaves.
Arrange the fish in the same dish and
spoon any marinade in the dish over
the top of each. Bake for 30 minutes.

3 Drizzle the tahini over the top of each
wrapped fish, making a ribbon so that
the tops and tails of the fish and some
of the vine leaf wrapping still show.
Return to the oven and bake for a
further 5–10 minutes, until the top is
golden and slightly crusted.

4 Meanwhile, cut the pomegranates in
half and scoop out the seeds. Sprinkle
the seeds over the fish, garnish with
mint and coriander, and serve.

Per portion: Energy 402Kcal/1681kJ; Protein 46.8g; Carbohydrate 2.6g, of which sugars 2.6g; Fat 22.8g, of which saturates 4.1g; Cholesterol 192mg; Calcium 86mg; Fibre 0.5g; Sodium 176mg.

BACON-WRAPPED TROUT WITH OATMEAL AND ONION STUFFING

THIS STUFFING IS BASED ON A SCOTTISH SPECIALITY, A MIXTURE OF OATMEAL AND ONION CALLED SKIRLIE. HERRING CAN BE COOKED IN THE SAME WAY. THIS IS VERY GOOD WITH SLICES OF COOKED POTATOES, BRUSHED WITH OLIVE OIL AND GRILLED UNTIL GOLDEN ON EACH SIDE.

SERVES FOUR

INGREDIENTS
  10 dry-cured streaky (fatty) bacon
    rashers (strips)
  40g/1½oz/3 tbsp butter
  1 onion, finely chopped
  115g/4oz/1 cup oatmeal
  30ml/2 tbsp chopped fresh parsley
  30ml/2 tbsp chopped fresh chives
  4 trout, about 350g/12oz each,
    gutted and boned
  juice of ½ lemon
  salt and ground black pepper
  watercress, cherry tomatoes and
    lemon wedges, to serve
For the herb mayonnaise
  6 watercress sprigs
  15ml/1 tbsp chopped fresh chives
  30ml/2 tbsp coarsely
    chopped parsley
  90ml/6 tbsp lemon mayonnaise
  30ml/2 tbsp crème fraîche
  2.5–5ml/½–1 tsp tarragon mustard

1 Preheat oven to 190°C/375°F/Gas 5. Chop two of the bacon rashers. Melt 25g/1oz/2 tbsp of the butter in a large frying pan and cook the bacon briefly. Add the finely chopped onion and cook gently, stirring occasionally, for 5–8 minutes, until softened.

2 Add the oatmeal and cook until the oatmeal darkens and absorbs the fat, but do not allow it to overbrown. Stir in the parsley, chives and seasoning. Cool.

3 Wash and dry the trout, then stuff with the oatmeal mixture. Wrap each fish in two bacon rashers and place in an ovenproof dish. Dot with the remaining butter and sprinkle with the lemon juice. Bake for 20–25 minutes, until the bacon browns and crisps.

4 Meanwhile, make the mayonnaise. Place the watercress, chives and parsley in a sieve and pour boiling water over them. Drain, rinse under cold water, and drain well on kitchen paper.

5 Purée the herbs in a mortar with a pestle. (This is easier than using a food processor for this small quantity.) Stir the puréed herbs into the lemon mayonnaise together with the crème fraîche. Add tarragon mustard to taste and stir to combine.

6 When cooked, transfer the trout to warmed serving plates and serve immediately with watercress, tomatoes and lemon wedges, accompanied by the herb mayonnaise.

Per portion: Energy 870Kcal/3625kJ; Protein 65.9g; Carbohydrate 24.5g, of which sugars 2.6g; Fat 57.1g, of which saturates 17.8g; Cholesterol 300mg; Calcium 115mg; Fibre 2.5g; Sodium 1245mg.

BAKED SALMON WITH WATERCRESS SAUCE

WHOLE BAKED SALMON IS A CLASSIC DISH SERVED AT WEDDING PARTIES AND JUST ABOUT ANY OTHER BIG OCCASION. BAKING THE SALMON IN FOIL PRODUCES A FLESH RATHER LIKE THAT OF A POACHED FISH BUT WITH THE EASE OF BAKING. DECORATING THE FISH WITH THIN SLICES OF CUCUMBER LOOKS PRETTY AND WILL CONCEAL ANY FLESH THAT MAY LOOK RAGGED AFTER SKINNING.

SERVES SIX TO EIGHT

INGREDIENTS
2–3kg/4½–6¾lb salmon, cleaned, with head and tail left on
3–5 spring onions (scallions), thinly sliced
1 lemon, thinly sliced
1 cucumber, thinly sliced
fresh dill sprigs, to garnish
lemon wedges, to serve
For the watercress sauce
3 garlic cloves, chopped
200g/7oz watercress leaves, finely chopped
40g/1½oz fresh tarragon, finely chopped
300g/11oz mayonnaise
15–30ml/1–2 tbsp freshly squeezed lemon juice
200g/7oz/scant 1 cup unsalted (sweet) butter
salt and ground black pepper

1 Preheat the oven to 180°C/350°F/ Gas 4. Rinse the salmon and lay it on a large piece of foil. Stuff the fish cavity with the sliced spring onions and layer the lemon slices inside and around the fish, then sprinkle with plenty of salt and ground black pepper.

2 Loosely fold the foil around the fish and fold the edges over to seal. Bake for about 1 hour.

3 Remove the fish from the oven and leave to stand, still wrapped in the foil, for about 15 minutes, then unwrap the parcel and leave the fish to cool.

4 When the fish is cool, carefully lift it on to a large plate, still covered with lemon slices. Cover the fish tightly with clear film (plastic wrap) and chill for several hours.

5 Before serving, discard the lemon slices around the fish. Using a blunt knife to lift up the edge of the skin, carefully peel the skin away from the flesh, avoiding tearing the flesh, and pull out any fins at the same time.

6 Arrange the cucumber slices in overlapping rows along the length of the fish, to resemble large fish scales.

COOK'S TIP
Do not prepare the sauce more than a few hours ahead of serving as the watercress will discolour it.

7 To make the sauce, put the garlic, watercress, tarragon, mayonnaise and lemon juice in a food processor or blender or a bowl, and process or mix to combine.

8 Melt the butter, then add to the watercress mixture, a little at a time, processing or stirring, until the butter has been incorporated and the sauce is thick and smooth. Cover and chill before serving. Serve the fish, garnished with dill, with the sauce and lemon wedges.

VARIATION
Instead of cooking a whole fish, prepare 6–8 salmon steaks. Place each fish steak on an individual square of foil, then top with a slice of onion and a slice of lemon and season generously with salt and ground black pepper. Loosely wrap the foil up around the fish, fold the edges to seal and place the parcels on a baking sheet. Bake as above for 10–15 minutes, or until the flesh is opaque. Serve cold with watercress sauce, garnished with slices of cucumber.

Per portion: Energy 1044Kcal/4323kJ; Protein 51.6g; Carbohydrate 1.4g, of which sugars 1.2g; Fat 92.4g, of which saturates 28.5g; Cholesterol 231mg; Calcium 135mg; Fibre 0.7g; Sodium 558mg.

BRAISED PORK CHOPS <u>WITH</u> ONION <u>AND</u> MUSTARD SAUCE

THE PIQUANT SAUCE ADDS PUNCH AND EXTRA FLAVOUR TO THIS SIMPLE SUPPER DISH. SERVE IT WITH CELERIAC AND POTATO MASH AND A GREEN VEGETABLE, SUCH AS BROCCOLI OR CABBAGE.

<u>SERVES FOUR</u>

INGREDIENTS
  4 pork loin chops, at least
    2cm/¾in thick
  30ml/2 tbsp plain (all-purpose) flour
  45ml/3 tbsp olive oil
  2 Spanish (Bermuda) onions, sliced
  2 garlic cloves, finely chopped
  250ml/8fl oz/1 cup dry (hard) cider
  150ml/¼ pint/⅔ cup chicken stock
  generous pinch of brown sugar
  2 fresh bay leaves
  6 fresh thyme sprigs
  2 strips lemon rind
  120ml/4fl oz/½ cup double
    (heavy) cream
  30–45ml/2–3 tbsp wholegrain
    mustard
  30ml/2 tbsp chopped fresh parsley
  salt and ground black pepper

1 Preheat the oven to 200°C/400°F/ Gas 6. Trim the chops of excess fat. Season the flour with salt and pepper and use to coat the chops. Heat 30ml/ 2 tbsp of the oil in a frying pan and brown the chops on both sides, then transfer them to an ovenproof dish.

2 Add the remaining oil to the pan and cook the onions over a fairly gentle heat until they soften and begin to brown at the edges. Add the garlic and cook for 2 minutes more.

3 Stir in any leftover flour, then gradually stir in the cider and stock. Season well with salt and pepper and add the brown sugar, bay leaves, thyme sprigs and lemon rind. Bring the sauce to the boil, stirring constantly, then pour over the chops.

4 Cover and cook in the oven for 20 minutes. Reduce the heat to 180°C/ 350°F/Gas 4 and continue cooking for another 30–40 minutes. Remove the foil for the last 10 minutes of the cooking time. Remove the chops from the dish and keep warm, covered with foil.

5 Tip the remaining contents of the dish into a pan or, if the dish is flameproof, place it over a direct heat. Discard the herbs and lemon rind, then bring to the boil.

6 Add the cream and continue to boil, stirring constantly. Taste for seasoning, adding a pinch more sugar if necessary. Finally, stir in the mustard to taste and pour the sauce over the braised chops. Sprinkle with the chopped parsley and serve immediately.

VARIATIONS
• For a less rich sauce, omit the cream and purée the sauce in a blender. Reheat, thinning with a little extra stock if necessary, then adjust the seasoning and add mustard to taste. This will produce a sharper tasting sauce that will need less mustard.
• If you prefer, you can use vegetable or pork stock instead of chicken.
• This recipe also works extremely well with veal chops.

Per portion: Energy 694Kcal/2881kJ; Protein 32g; Carbohydrate 19.8g, of which sugars 9.3g; Fat 53g, of which saturates 21.6g; Cholesterol 131mg; Calcium 80mg; Fibre 2.1g; Sodium 207mg.

PORK ESCALOPES BAKED <u>WITH</u> APPLE <u>AND</u> POTATO RÖSTI

THE JUICES FROM THE PORK COOK INTO THE APPLES AND POTATOES GIVING THEM A WONDERFUL FLAVOUR AS WELL AS MAKING A DELICIOUS SAUCE.

SERVES FOUR

INGREDIENTS

2 large potatoes, finely grated
1 medium cooking apple, grated
2 garlic cloves, crushed
1 egg, beaten
butter, for greasing
15ml/1 tbsp olive oil
4 large prosciutto slices
4 pork escalopes (US scallops), about
  175g/6oz each
4 sage leaves
1 medium cooking apple,
  cut into thin wedges
25g/1oz/2 tbsp butter, diced
salt and ground black pepper
caramelized apple wedges, to serve

COOK'S TIPS
• Do not be tempted to overcook the pork as it will start to dry out.
• If you can't find cooking apples, use an all-purpose eating variety, such as Granny Smith.

1 Preheat the oven to 200°C/400°F/ Gas 6. Squeeze out all the excess liquid from the grated potatoes and apple. Mix the grated ingredients together with the garlic, egg and seasoning.

2 Divide the potatoes into four portions and spoon each quarter on to a baking sheet that has been lined with foil and greased. Form a round with the potatoes and flatten out slightly with the back of a spoon. Drizzle with a little olive oil. Cook for 10 minutes.

3 Meanwhile, lay the prosciutto on a clean surface and place a pork escalope on top. Lay a sage leaf and apple wedges over each escalope and top each piece with the butter. Wrap the prosciutto around each piece of meat, making sure it is covered completely.

4 Remove the potatoes from the oven, place each pork parcel on top and return to the oven for 20 minutes. Carefully lift the pork and potatoes off the foil and serve with caramelized wedges of apple and any cooking juices on the side.

Per portion: Energy 396Kcal/1659kJ; Protein 42.7g; Carbohydrate 19.2g, of which sugars 4.4g; Fat 16.9g, of which saturates 6.7g; Cholesterol 177mg; Calcium 29mg; Fibre 1.5g; Sodium 310mg.

MOUSSAKA

THIS IS A TRADITIONAL EASTERN MEDITERRANEAN DISH, POPULAR IN BOTH GREECE AND TURKEY.
LAYERS OF MINCED LAMB, AUBERGINES, TOMATOES AND ONIONS ARE TOPPED WITH A CREAMY YOGURT
AND CHEESE SAUCE IN THIS DELICIOUS, AUTHENTIC RECIPE.

SERVES FOUR

INGREDIENTS
   450g/1lb aubergines (eggplant)
   150ml/¼ pint/²⁄₃ cup olive oil
   1 large onion, chopped
   2–3 garlic cloves, finely chopped
   675g/1½lb lean minced (ground) lamb
   15ml/1 tbsp plain (all-purpose) flour
   400g/14oz can chopped tomatoes
   30ml/2 tbsp chopped fresh herbs
   450g/1lb fresh tomatoes, sliced
   salt and ground black pepper
For the topping
   300ml/½ pint/1¼ cups yogurt
   2 eggs
   25g/1oz feta cheese, crumbled
   25g/1oz/⅓ cup freshly grated
      Parmesan cheese

1 Cut the aubergines into thin slices and layer them in a colander, sprinkling each layer with salt.

2 Cover the aubergines with a plate and a weight, then leave for about 30 minutes. Pat dry with kitchen paper.

3 Heat 45ml/3 tbsp of the oil in a large, heavy pan. Cook the onion and garlic until softened, but not coloured. Add the lamb and cook over a high heat, stirring frequently, until browned.

4 Stir in the flour until mixed, then stir in the canned tomatoes, herbs and seasoning. Bring to the boil, reduce the heat and simmer gently for 20 minutes.

5 Meanwhile, heat a little of the remaining oil in a large frying pan. Add as many aubergine slices as can be laid in the pan in a single layer, then cook until golden on both sides. Set the cooked aubergines aside. Heat more oil and continue cooking the aubergines, in batches, adding oil as necessary.

COOK'S TIP
Salting and drying the aubergines before cooking reduces the amount of fat that they absorb and helps them to brown more quickly.

6 Preheat the oven to 180°C/350°F/ Gas 4. Arrange half the aubergine slices in a large, shallow ovenproof dish, then add a layer of half the fresh tomatoes.

7 Top the slices with about half of the meat and tomato sauce mixture, then add a layer of the remaining aubergine slices, followed by the remaining tomato slices. Spread the remaining meat mixture over the aubergines and tomatoes.

8 Beat together the yogurt and eggs, then mix in the feta and Parmesan cheeses. Pour the mixture over the meat and spread it evenly.

9 Transfer the moussaka to the oven and bake for 35–40 minutes, or until golden and bubbling.

VARIATION
Use large courgettes (zucchini) instead of aubergines (eggplant), if you like. Cut them diagonally into fairly thick slices.

Per portion: Energy 753Kcal/3132kJ; Protein 46.2g; Carbohydrate 19.4g, of which sugars 17.6g; Fat 55.3g, of which saturates 17.6g; Cholesterol 237mg; Calcium 329mg; Fibre 4.9g; Sodium 425mg.

Country Meat Loaf

Three different kinds of meat are combined with herbs and other flavourings to make this hearty and appetizing traditional meat loaf.

SERVES SIX

INGREDIENTS
  30ml/2 tbsp butter or margarine
  115g/4oz/½ cup chopped onion
  2 garlic cloves, crushed
  50g/2oz/½ cup chopped celery
  450g/1lb lean minced (ground) beef
  225g/½lb minced (ground) veal
  225g/½lb lean minced (ground) pork
  2 eggs
  50g/2oz/1 cup fine fresh
    bread crumbs
  15g/½oz/½ cup chopped
    fresh parsley
  30ml/2 tbsp chopped fresh basil
  2.5ml/½ tsp fresh or dried
    thyme leaves
  2.5ml/½ tsp salt
  2.5ml/½ tsp pepper
  30ml/2 tbsp Worcestershire sauce
  60ml/4 tbsp chilli sauce or
    tomato ketchup
  6 bacon rashers (strips)

1 Preheat the oven to 180°C/350°F/ Gas 4. Melt the butter or margarine in a small frying pan over a low heat. Add the onion, garlic and celery and cook, stirring occasionally, for 8–10 minutes, until softened. Remove from the heat and leave to cool slightly.

COOK'S TIP
To test if the meat loaf is cooked through, insert a skewer. If the juices run clear and skewer comes out fairly clean, then it is ready.

2 In a large mixing bowl combine the onion, garlic and celery with all the other ingredients except the bacon. Mix together lightly, using a fork or your fingers. Do not overwork or the meat loaf will be too compact.

3 Form the meat mixture into an oval loaf. Carefully transfer it to a shallow baking tin (pan).

4 Lay the bacon across the top of the meat loaf. Bake for 1¼ hours, basting occasionally with the juices and bacon fat in the tin.

5 Remove from the oven and drain off the fat. Leave the meat loaf to stand for 10 minutes before serving.

Per portion: Energy 285Kcal/1188kJ; Protein 18.6g; Carbohydrate 11.9g, of which sugars 5.1g; Fat 18.4g, of which saturates 8.3g; Cholesterol 119mg; Calcium 62mg; Fibre 1g; Sodium 572mg.

TAMALE PIE

THIS IS A TEXAN VERSION OF A TRADITIONAL MEXICAN RECIPE, ALTHOUGH SO MANY VARIATIONS EXIST THAT BOTH SIDES OF THE BORDER CAN CLAIM THE ORIGINAL.

SERVES EIGHT

INGREDIENTS
115g/4oz bacon, chopped
1 onion, finely chopped
450g/1lb lean minced (ground) beef
10–15ml/2–3 tsp chilli powder
5ml/1 tsp salt
400g/14oz can tomatoes
40g/1½oz/⅓ cup chopped
  black olives
175g/6oz/1 cup corn kernels, freshly
  cooked or thawed frozen
120ml/4fl oz/½ cup sour cream
115g/4oz/1 cup grated Cheddar or
  Monterey Jack cheese
For the tamale topping
250–300ml/8–10fl oz/1–1¼ cups
  chicken stock
175g/6oz/1½ cups masa harina
  or cornmeal
90ml/6 tbsp margarine or
  vegetable shortening
2.5ml/½ tsp baking powder
50ml/2fl oz/¼ cup milk
salt and ground black pepper

1 Preheat the oven to 190°C/375°F/ Gas 5. Cook the bacon in a large, heavy frying pan for 2–3 minutes, until the fat runs. Pour off any excess fat, leaving 15–30ml/1–2 tbsp. Add the onion and cook, over a medium heat, stirring occasionally, for about 5 minutes, until just softened.

2 Add the beef, chilli powder and salt and cook for 5 minutes, stirring to break up the meat. Stir in the tomatoes and cook for 5 minutes more, breaking them up with a spoon.

3 Add the olives, corn, and sour cream, and mix well. Transfer to a 38cm/15in long rectangular or oval ovenproof dish. Set aside.

4 To make the topping, bring the chicken stock to the boil in a pan over a medium heat and season it with salt and pepper if necessary.

5 In a food processor, combine the masa harina or cornmeal, margarine or shortening, baking powder and milk. Process until combined. With the machine still running, gradually pour in the hot stock until a smooth, thick batter is formed. If the batter is too thick to spread, add additional hot stock or water, a little at a time.

6 Pour the batter over the top of the beef mixture, spreading it evenly with a metal spatula.

7 Bake for about 20 minutes, until the top is just browned. Sprinkle the surface evenly with the grated cheese and continue baking for a further 10–15 minutes, until the cheese has melted. Serve immediately.

Per portion: Energy 492Kcal/2044kJ; Protein 23.3g; Carbohydrate 26.6g, of which sugars 6.1g; Fat 32.1g, of which saturates 17.4g; Cholesterol 96mg; Calcium 206mg; Fibre 1.6g; Sodium 827mg.

PIZZAS, TARTS AND PIES

Although pizzas are now commonplace, filling supermarket freezers and fast becoming the world's favourite takeaway food, the home-made variety is almost always superior. Making your own dough enables you to tailor the toppings to the tastes of your guests. We've supplied recipes for basics like Fiorentina Pizza and Hot Pepperoni Pizza, but you can add extra ingredients or invite diners to invent their own combinations. This chapter also includes delectable pastries like Cheese and Onion Flan, Filo-wrapped Fish and Rich Game Pie.

SUN-DRIED TOMATO CALZONE

CALZONE IS A TRADITIONAL FOLDED PIZZA. IN THIS TASTY VEGETARIAN VERSION, YOU CAN ADD MORE OR FEWER RED CHILLI FLAKES, DEPENDING ON PERSONAL TASTE.

SERVES TWO

INGREDIENTS
    4 baby aubergines (eggplant)
    3 shallots, chopped
    45ml/3 tbsp olive oil
    1 garlic clove, chopped
    50g/2oz/⅓ cup sun-dried tomatoes
      in oil, drained
    1.5ml/¼ tsp dried red chilli flakes,
      if using
    10ml/2 tsp chopped fresh thyme
    75g/3oz mozzarella cheese, cubed
    salt and ground black pepper
    15–30ml/1–2 tbsp freshly grated
      Parmesan cheese, plus extra to serve
For the dough
    225g/8oz/2 cups strong white
      bread flour
    5ml/1 tsp salt
    2.5ml/½ tsp easy-blend (rapid-rise)
      dried yeast
    15ml/1 tbsp olive oil
    150ml/¼ pint/⅔ cup warm water

1 Make the dough. Place the dry ingredients in a bowl and mix to form a soft dough with the oil and water. Knead for 10 minutes. Put in an oiled bowl, cover and leave in a warm place until doubled in size.

2 Preheat the oven to 220°C/425°F/ Gas 7. Dice the aubergines. Cook the shallots in a little oil until soft. Add the aubergines, garlic, sun-dried tomatoes, chilli, if using, thyme and seasoning. Cook for 5 minutes. Divide the dough in half and roll out each piece on a lightly floured work surface to an 18cm/7in round.

3 Spread the aubergine mixture over half of each round, leaving a 2.5cm/1in border, then sprinkle on the mozzarella. Dampen the edges with water, then fold over the dough to enclose the filling. Press the edges firmly together to seal. Place on greased baking sheets.

4 Brush with half the remaining oil and make a small hole in the top of each calzone to allow steam to escape. Bake for 15–20 minutes, until golden. Remove from the oven and brush with the remaining oil. Sprinkle over the Parmesan and serve immediately.

Per portion: Energy 777Kcal/3259kJ; Protein 25.3g; Carbohydrate 92.2g, of which sugars 6.2g; Fat 36.7g, of which saturates 11.8g; Cholesterol 37mg; Calcium 494mg; Fibre 7g; Sodium 323mg.

CLASSIC MARINARA PIZZA

THE COMBINATION OF SIMPLE INGREDIENTS, FRESH GARLIC, GOOD QUALITY OLIVE OIL AND A TASTY TOMATO SAUCE GIVES THIS PIZZA AN UNMISTAKABLY ITALIAN FLAVOUR. ALTHOUGH PLAIN IN LOOKS, THE TASTE OF THE MARINARA IS UTTERLY DELICIOUS.

SERVES TWO

INGREDIENTS
  60ml/4 tbsp extra virgin olive oil or
    sunflower oil
  675g/1½lb plum tomatoes, peeled,
    seeded and chopped
  4 garlic cloves, cut into slivers
  15ml/1 tbsp chopped
    fresh oregano
  salt and ground black pepper
For the pizza base
  225g/8oz/2 cups plain (all-purpose)
    white flour
  pinch of salt
  10ml/2 tsp baking powder
  50g/2oz/4 tbsp margarine
  about 150ml/¼ pint/⅔ cup milk

1 Preheat the oven to 220°C/425°F/ Gas 7. Use non-stick baking parchment to line a baking sheet. Sift the flour, salt and baking powder in a bowl and rub the margarine lightly into the flour until it resembles breadcrumbs.

2 Pour in enough milk to form a soft dough and knead. Roll the dough out to a round about 25cm/10in in diameter.

3 Place the dough on the prepared baking sheet and make the edges slightly thicker than the centre.

4 Heat 30ml/2 tbsp of the oil in a pan. Add the seeded and chopped plum tomatoes and cook, stirring frequently for about 5 minutes, until soft.

5 Place the tomatoes in a sieve over a bowl and leave to drain for about 5 minutes.

6 Empty the juice from the bowl and force the tomatoes through the sieve into the bowl with the back of a spoon. You may also use a food processor or blender and process until smooth.

7 Brush the pizza base with half the remaining oil. Spoon over the tomatoes and sprinkle with garlic and oregano. Drizzle over the remaining oil and season with salt and pepper.

8 Bake for 15–20 minutes, until the pizza is crisp and golden. Serve immediately, while piping hot.

Per portion: Energy 858Kcal/3597kJ; Protein 15.6g; Carbohydrate 101.7g, of which sugars 16g; Fat 46.2g, of which saturates 4.5g; Cholesterol 4mg; Calcium 272mg; Fibre 6.9g; Sodium 266mg.

FIORENTINA PIZZA

AN EGG ADDS THE FINISHING TOUCH TO THIS SPINACH PIZZA; TRY NOT TO OVERCOOK IT THOUGH, AS IT'S BEST WHEN THE YOLK IS STILL SLIGHTLY SOFT IN THE MIDDLE.

SERVES TWO TO THREE

INGREDIENTS
45ml/3 tbsp olive oil
1 small red onion, thinly sliced
175g/6oz fresh spinach,
  stalks removed
1 pizza base, about
  25–30cm/10–12in diameter
1 small jar pizza sauce
freshly grated nutmeg
150g/5oz mozzarella cheese
1 egg
25g/1oz/¼ cup grated Gruyère cheese

1 Heat 15ml/1 tbsp of the oil and cook the onion until soft. Add the spinach and cook until wilted. Drain any liquid.

2 Preheat the oven to 220°C/425°F/Gas 7. Brush the pizza base with half the remaining olive oil. Spread the pizza sauce evenly over the base, using the back of a spoon, then top with the spinach mixture. Sprinkle over a little freshly grated nutmeg.

3 Thinly slice the mozzarella and arrange over the spinach. Drizzle over the remaining oil. Bake for 10 minutes, then remove from the oven.

4 Make a small well in the centre of the pizza topping and carefully break the egg into the hole.

5 Sprinkle over the grated Gruyère cheese and return to the oven for a further 5–10 minutes, until crisp and golden. Serve immediately.

VARIATION
Italians make a folded pizza called calzone. It is made in the same way as a pizza but is folded in half to conceal the filling. Add the egg with the rest of the pizza topping, fold over the dough, seal the edges and bake for 20 minutes.

Per portion: Energy 808Kcal/3377kJ; Protein 33.1g; Carbohydrate 72g, of which sugars 10.3g; Fat 44.8g, of which saturates 16.3g; Cholesterol 151mg; Calcium 640mg; Fibre 5.3g; Sodium 911mg.

PEPPERY TOMATO PIZZA

PUNGENT ROCKET AND AROMATIC FRESH BASIL ADD COLOUR AND FLAVOUR TO THIS CRISP PIZZA,
A PERFECT ADDITION TO ANY PICNIC, BUFFET OR OUTDOOR MEAL.

SERVES TWO

INGREDIENTS
    10ml/2 tsp olive oil
    1 garlic clove, crushed
    150g/5oz can chopped tomatoes
    2.5ml/½ tsp caster (superfine) sugar
    30ml/2 tbsp torn fresh basil leaves
    2 tomatoes, seeded and chopped
    150g/5oz mozzarella cheese, sliced
    20g/¾oz rocket (arugula) leaves
For the pizza base
    225g/8oz/2 cups strong white
        bread flour
    5ml/1 tsp salt
    2.5ml/½ tsp easy-blend (rapid-rise)
        dried yeast
    30ml/2 tbsp olive oil

1 To make the pizza base, place the dry ingredients in a bowl. Add the oil and 150ml/¼ pint/⅔ cup warm water. Mix to form a soft dough.

2 Turn out the dough and knead until it is smooth and elastic. Place in an oiled bowl and cover. Leave in a warm place for 45 minutes, or until doubled in bulk.

3 Preheat the oven to 220°C/425°F/ Gas 7. Make the topping. Heat the oil in a frying pan and cook the garlic for 1 minute. Add the canned tomatoes and sugar and cook for 10 minutes.

4 Knead the risen dough lightly, then roll out to form a rough 30cm/12in round. Place on a lightly oiled baking sheet and push up the edges of the dough to form a shallow, even rim.

5 Season the tomato mixture and stir in the basil. Spoon it over the pizza base, then top with the chopped fresh tomatoes. Arrange the mozzarella slices on top of the tomato mixture. Season with sea salt and pepper and drizzle with a little olive oil.

6 Bake for 10–12 minutes, until crisp and golden. Scatter the rocket leaves over the pizza just before serving.

Per portion: Energy 735Kcal/3087kJ; Protein 26.1g; Carbohydrate 93g, of which sugars 7.3g; Fat 31.3g, of which saturates 12.7g; Cholesterol 44mg; Calcium 459mg; Fibre 5.5g; Sodium 330mg.

PISSALADIÈRE

THIS FAMOUS ONION AND ANCHOVY DISH IS A TRADITIONAL MARKET FOOD OF NICE IN SOUTHERN
FRANCE. IT CAN BE MADE USING EITHER SHORTCRUST PASTRY OR, AS HERE, YEASTED DOUGH, SIMILAR
TO A PIZZA BASE. EITHER WAY, IT IS MOST DELICIOUS EATEN LUKEWARM RATHER THAN PIPING HOT.

SERVES SIX

INGREDIENTS
  250g/9oz/2¼ cups strong white bread
    flour, plus extra for dusting
  50g/2oz/⅓ cup fine polenta
    or semolina
  5ml/1 tsp salt
  175ml/6fl oz/¾ cup lukewarm water
  5ml/1 tsp dried yeast
  5ml/1 tsp caster (superfine) sugar
  30ml/2 tbsp extra virgin olive oil
For the topping
  60–75ml/4–5 tbsp extra virgin
    olive oil
  6 large sweet Spanish (Bermuda)
    onions, thinly sliced
  2 large garlic cloves, thinly sliced
  5ml/1 tsp chopped fresh thyme, plus
    several sprigs
  1 fresh rosemary sprig
  1–2 × 50g/2oz cans anchovies in
    olive oil
  50–75g/2–3oz small black olives,
    preferably small Niçoise olives
  salt and ground black pepper

1 Mix the flour, polenta or semolina and salt in a large mixing bowl. Pour half the water into a bowl. Add the yeast and sugar, then leave in a warm place for 10 minutes, until frothy. Pour the yeast mixture into the flour mixture with the remaining water and the olive oil.

2 Using your hands, mix all the ingredients together to form a dough, then turn out and knead for 5 minutes, until smooth, springy and elastic.

3 Return the dough to the clean, floured bowl and place it in a plastic bag or cover with oiled clear film (plastic wrap), then set the dough aside at room temperature for 30–60 minutes to rise and double in bulk.

4 Meanwhile, start to prepare the topping. Heat 45ml/3 tbsp of the olive oil in a large, heavy pan and add the sliced onions. Stir well to coat the onions in the oil, then cover the pan and cook over a very low heat, stirring occasionally, for 20-30 minutes. (Use a heat-diffuser mat to keep the heat low, if possible.)

5 Add a little salt to taste and the garlic, chopped thyme and rosemary sprig. Stir well and continue cooking for another 15–25 minutes, or until the onions are soft and deep golden yellow but not browned at all. Uncover the pan for the last 5–10 minutes' cooking if the onions seem very wet. Remove and discard the rosemary. Set the onions aside to cool.

6 Preheat the oven to 220°C/425°F/ Gas 7. Roll out the dough thinly and use to line a large baking sheet, about 30 × 23–25cm/12 × 9–10in. Taste the onions for seasoning before spreading them over the dough.

7 Drain the anchovies, cut them in half lengthways and arrange them in a lattice pattern over the onions. Sprinkle the olives and thyme sprigs over the top of the pissaladière and drizzle with the remaining olive oil. Bake for about 20–25 minutes, or until the dough is browned and cooked. Season with pepper and serve warm, cut into slices.

VARIATIONS
• Shortcrust pastry can be used instead of yeast dough as a base: bake it blind for 10–15 minutes before adding the filling.
• If you enjoy anchovies, try spreading about 60ml/4 tbsp anchovy purée (paste) – *anchoïade* – over the base before adding the onions. Alternatively, spread black olive paste over the base.

Per portion: Energy 431Kcal/1797kJ; Protein 9.9g; Carbohydrate 51.6g, of which sugars 10g; Fat 21.7g, of which saturates 3.1g; Cholesterol 8mg; Calcium 138mg; Fibre 3.8g; Sodium 825mg.

BRESAOLA AND ROCKET PIZZA

ALTHOUGH THE ARMENIANS ORIGINATED THE IDEA OF TOPPING FLATTENED DOUGH WITH SAVOURY INGREDIENTS BEFORE BAKING IT, IT WAS THE ITALIANS — THE NEAPOLITANS IN PARTICULAR — WHO DEVELOPED THE PIZZA IN THE 1830s.

SERVES FOUR

INGREDIENTS
  150g/5oz packet pizza base mix
  120ml/4fl oz/½ cup lukewarm water
  225g/8oz/3¼ cups mixed
    wild mushrooms
  25g/1oz/2 tbsp butter
  2 garlic cloves, coarsely chopped
  60ml/4 tbsp pesto
  8 slices bresaola
  4 tomatoes, sliced
  75g/3oz/⅓ cup cream cheese
  25g/1oz rocket (arugula)

1 Preheat the oven to 200°C/400°F/ Gas 6. Tip the packet of pizza base mix into a large mixing bowl and pour in enough of the water to mix to a soft, not sticky, dough, following the instructions on the packet.

2 Turn out the dough on to a lightly floured surface and knead for about 5 minutes, or until smooth and elastic. Divide the dough into two equal pieces, knead lightly to form two balls, then pat out the balls of dough into flat rounds with your hands.

3 Roll out each piece of dough on a lightly floured surface to a 23cm/9in round and transfer to baking sheets.

4 Slice the wild mushrooms. Melt the butter in a frying pan and cook the garlic for 2 minutes. Add the mushrooms and cook over a high heat for about 5 minutes, or until the mushrooms have softened but are not overcooked.

5 Spread pesto on the pizza bases, to within 2cm/¾in of the edge of each one. Arrange the bresaola and tomato slices around the rims of the pizzas, then spoon the cooked mushrooms into the middle.

6 Dot the cream cheese on top of the pizzas and bake for 15–18 minutes, or until the bases are crisp and the cheese just melted. Top each pizza with a handful of rocket leaves just before serving. Serve immediately.

COOK'S TIP
If you are in a hurry, buy two ready-made pizza bases instead of the pizza mix and bake for 10 minutes.

Per portion: Energy 448Kcal/1873kJ; Protein 16.6g; Carbohydrate 34.7g, of which sugars 6g; Fat 28g, of which saturates 12.8g; Cholesterol 56mg; Calcium 179mg; Fibre 3.5g; Sodium 213mg.

HOT PEPPERONI PIZZA

THERE IS NOTHING MORE MOUTHWATERING THAN A FRESHLY BAKED PIZZA, ESPECIALLY WHEN THE TOPPING INCLUDES TOMATOES, MOZZARELLA CHEESE, PEPPERONI AND RED CHILLIES.

SERVES FOUR

INGREDIENTS
225g/8oz/2 cups strong white
  bread flour
10ml/2 tsp easy-blend (rapid-rise)
  dried yeast
5ml/1 tsp granulated sugar
2.5ml/½ tsp salt
15ml/1 tbsp olive oil
175ml/6fl oz/¾ cup mixed lukewarm
  milk and water
For the topping
400g/14oz can chopped
  tomatoes, strained
2 garlic cloves, crushed
5ml/1 tsp dried oregano
225g/8oz mozzarella cheese, grated
2 dried red chillies, crumbled
225g/8oz pepperoni, sliced
30ml/2 tbsp drained capers
fresh oregano, to garnish

1 Sift the flour, stir in the yeast, sugar and salt and make a well in the centre. Stir the oil into the milk and water, then stir into the flour. Mix to a soft dough.

2 Knead the dough on a lightly floured surface for 10 minutes until it is smooth and elastic. Cover and leave in a warm place for about 30 minutes, or until the dough has doubled in bulk.

3 Preheat the oven to 220°C/425°F/ Gas 7. Turn the dough out on to a lightly floured surface and knead lightly for 1 minute. Divide it in half and roll each piece out to a 25cm/10in round. Place on lightly oiled pizza trays or baking sheets. To make the topping, mix the strained tomatoes, garlic and dried oregano in a bowl.

4 Spread half the tomato mixture over each base, leaving a border around the edge. Set half the mozzarella aside. Divide the rest between the pizzas, sprinkling it over evenly. Bake for 7–10 minutes, until the dough rim on each pizza is pale golden.

5 Sprinkle the crumbled chillies over the pizzas, then arrange the pepperoni slices and capers on top. Sprinkle with the remaining mozzarella. Return the pizzas to the oven and bake for 7–10 minutes more. Sprinkle over the fresh oregano and serve immediately.

Per portion: Energy 631Kcal/2638kJ; Protein 28.8g; Carbohydrate 47.6g, of which sugars 4.7g; Fat 37.5g, of which saturates 16.8g; Cholesterol 80mg; Calcium 317mg; Fibre 2.7g; Sodium 1498mg.

CHEESE AND ONION FLAN

THE USE OF YEAST DOUGHS FOR TARTS AND FLANS IS POPULAR IN VARIOUS REGIONS OF FRANCE.
CHOOSE A STRONG CHEESE SUCH AS LIVAROT, MUNSTER OR PORT SALUT IN THIS RECIPE.

SERVES FOUR

INGREDIENTS
    15g/½oz/1 tbsp butter
    1 onion, halved and sliced
    2 eggs
    250ml/8fl oz/1 cup single
      (light) cream
    225g/8oz strong semi-soft
      cheese, sliced
    salt and ground black pepper
    salad leaves, to serve
For the yeast dough
    10ml/2 tsp dried yeast
    120ml/4fl oz/½ cup milk
    5ml/1 tsp sugar
    1 egg yolk
    225g/8oz/2 cups plain (all-purpose)
      flour, plus extra for kneading
    2.5ml/½ tsp salt
    50g/2oz/4 tbsp butter, softened

1 To make the dough, place the yeast in a bowl. Warm the milk in a small pan until it is at body temperature and stir into the yeast with the sugar. Continue stirring until the yeast has dissolved completely. Leave the yeast mixture to stand for about 3 minutes, then beat in the egg yolk.

COOK'S TIP
If you prefer to use easy-blend (rapid-rise) yeast, omit step 1. Beat the egg yolk and milk together in a jug (pitcher). Add the dry yeast to the flour and salt in the food processor and pulse to combine. Pour in the egg and milk mixture and proceed with the recipe as normal.

2 Put the flour and salt in a food processor fitted with a metal blade and pulse to combine. With the machine running, slowly pour in the yeast mixture. Scrape down the sides and continue processing for 2–3 minutes. Add the softened butter and process for another 30 seconds.

3 Transfer the dough to a lightly greased bowl. Cover the bowl with a dishtowel and leave to rise in a warm place for about 1 hour, until the dough has doubled in bulk.

4 Remove the dough from the bowl and place on a lightly floured surface. Knock back (punch down) the dough by hitting it with your fist. Sprinkle a little more flour on the work surface and roll out the dough to a 30cm/12in round.

5 Line a 23cm/9in flan tin (quiche pan) with the dough. Gently press it into the tin and trim off any overhanging pieces, leaving a 3mm/⅛in rim around the flan case (pie shell). Cover with a dishtowel, set aside in a warm place and leave the dough to rise again for about 30 minutes, or until puffy.

6 Meanwhile, melt the butter in a heavy pan and add the onion. Cover the pan and cook over a medium-low heat, stirring occasionally, for about 15 minutes, until softened and lightly coloured. Remove the lid and continue cooking, stirring frequently, until the onion is very soft and caramelized.

7 Preheat the oven to 180°C/350°F/Gas 4. Beat together the eggs and cream. Season and stir in the cooked onion.

8 Arrange the cheese on the base of the flan case. Pour over the egg mixture and bake for 30–35 minutes, until the base is golden and the centre is just set. Cool slightly on a wire rack and serve warm with salad leaves.

Per portion: Energy 747Kcal/3113kJ; Protein 27.1g; Carbohydrate 49.6g, of which sugars 5.9g; Fat 49.2g, of which saturates 29.9g; Cholesterol 271mg; Calcium 619mg; Fibre 2.3g; Sodium 576mg.

TUNA AND EGG GALETTE

THIS FLAKY PASTRY TART COMBINES SOFT-CENTRED EGGS AND A SLIGHTLY PIQUANT FISH FILLING.
IT MAKES A WONDERFUL DISH FOR A SUMMER SUPPER AND IS ALSO A GREAT BUFFET-TABLE STANDBY.

SERVES FOUR

INGREDIENTS

    2 sheets of ready-rolled puff pastry
    plain (all-purpose) flour, for dusting
    beaten egg, to glaze
    60ml/4 tbsp olive oil
    175g/6oz tuna steak
    2 onions, sliced
    1 red (bell) pepper, seeded
      and chopped
    2 garlic cloves, crushed
    45ml/3 tbsp capers, drained
    5ml/1 tsp grated lemon rind
    30ml/2 tbsp lemon juice
    5 eggs
    salt and ground black pepper
    chopped flat leaf parsley, to garnish

1 Preheat the oven to 190°C/375°F/
Gas 5. Lay a sheet of pastry on a lightly
floured baking sheet and cut to a
28 × 18cm/11 × 7in rectangle. Brush
the whole sheet with beaten egg.

2 Cut the second sheet of pastry to the
same size. Cut out a rectangle from
the centre and discard, leaving a
2.5cm/1in border. Lift the border on to
the first sheet. Brush the border with
beaten egg and prick the base.

3 Bake the pastry case (pie shell) for
about 15 minutes until golden.

COOK'S TIP
If you are using fresh, unfrozen pastry,
the remaining rectangle of pastry can
be wrapped in clear film (plastic wrap)
and frozen. Allow to thaw at room
temperature for 1 hour before using.

4 Heat 30ml/2 tbsp of the oil in a frying
pan and cook the tuna steak for
2–3 minutes on each side, until golden
but still pale pink in the middle. Transfer
to a plate and flake into small pieces.

5 Add the remaining oil to the pan and
cook the onions, red pepper and garlic
for 6–8 minutes, until softened, stirring
occasionally. Remove the pan from the
heat and stir in the tuna, capers and
lemon rind and juice. Season well.

6 Spoon the filling into the pastry case
and level the surface with the back of a
spoon. Break the eggs into the filling
and return the galette to the oven for
about 10 minutes, or until the eggs
have just cooked through. Garnish with
chopped parsley and serve immediately.

COOK'S TIP
To make sure the eggs do not become
hard on top during baking, cover the tart
with lightly oiled foil.

Per portion: Energy 544Kcal/2263kJ; Protein 21.7g; Carbohydrate 27.7g, of which sugars 4.7g; Fat 39.5g, of which saturates 10.1g; Cholesterol 260mg; Calcium 102mg; Fibre 1.9g; Sodium 320mg.

FILO-WRAPPED FISH

THIS DELICIOUS DISH COMES FROM JERUSALEM, WHERE WHOLE FISH ARE WRAPPED IN FILO PASTRY AND SERVED WITH A ZESTY TOMATO SAUCE. THE CHOICE OF FISH CAN BE VARIED ACCORDING TO WHAT IS IN SEASON AND WHAT IS FRESHEST ON THE DAY OF PURCHASE.

SERVES THREE TO FOUR

INGREDIENTS
- 450g/1lb salmon or cod steaks or fillets
- 1 lemon
- 30ml/2 tbsp olive oil, plus extra for brushing
- 1 onion, chopped
- 2 celery sticks, chopped
- 1 green (bell) pepper, diced
- 5 garlic cloves, chopped
- 400g/14oz fresh or canned tomatoes, chopped
- 120ml/4fl oz/½ cup passata (bottled strained tomatoes)
- 30ml/2 tbsp chopped fresh flat leaf parsley
- 2–3 pinches of ground allspice or ground cloves
- cayenne pepper, to taste
- pinch of sugar
- about 130g/4½oz filo pastry (6–8 large sheets)
- salt and ground black pepper

1 Sprinkle the salmon or cod steaks or fillets with salt and black pepper and a squeeze of lemon juice. Set aside while you prepare the sauce.

2 Heat the olive oil in a pan, add the chopped onion, celery and pepper and cook for about 5 minutes, until the vegetables are softened. Add the garlic and cook for a further 1 minute, then add the tomatoes and passata and cook until the tomatoes have softened and the mixture is of a sauce consistency.

3 Stir the parsley into the sauce, then season with allspice or cloves, cayenne pepper, sugar and salt and pepper.

4 Preheat the oven to 200°C/400°F/Gas 6. Take a sheet of filo pastry, brush with a little olive oil and cover with a second sheet. Place a piece of fish on top of the pastry, towards the bottom edge, then top with 1–2 spoonfuls of the sauce, spreading it evenly.

5 Roll the fish in the pastry, taking care to enclose the filling completely. Arrange on a baking sheet and repeat with the remaining fish and pastry. You should have about half the sauce remaining, to serve with the fish.

6 Bake for 10–15 minutes, or until golden. Meanwhile, reheat the remaining sauce if necessary. Serve immediately with the remaining sauce.

Per portion: Energy 509Kcal/2135kJ; Protein 36.2g; Carbohydrate 37.2g, of which sugars 10.4g; Fat 25.1g, of which saturates 4.2g; Cholesterol 75mg; Calcium 137mg; Fibre 5g; Sodium 192mg.

SALMON IN PUFF PASTRY

THIS IS AN ELEGANT PARTY DISH, MADE WITH RICE, EGGS AND SALMON ENCLOSED IN PUFF PASTRY.

SERVES SIX

INGREDIENTS
    450g/1lb puff pastry, thawed
        if frozen
    1 egg, beaten
    3 hard-boiled eggs
    90ml/6 tbsp single (light) cream
    200g/7oz/1¾ cups cooked long
        grain rice
    30ml/2 tbsp finely chopped
        fresh parsley
    10ml/2 tsp chopped fresh tarragon
    675g/1½lb salmon fillets
    40g/1½oz/3 tbsp butter
    juice of ½ lemon
    salt and ground black pepper

2 In a bowl, mash the hard-boiled eggs with the cream, then stir in the cooked rice. Add the parsley and tarragon and season well. Spoon this mixture on to the prepared pastry.

5 Roll out the remaining pastry and cut out a semi-circular piece to cover the head portion and a tail shape to cover the tail. Brush both pieces of pastry with a little beaten egg and place on top of the fish, pressing down firmly to secure. Score a criss-cross pattern on the tail.

1 Preheat the oven to 190°C/375°F/ Gas 5. Roll out two-thirds of the pastry into a large oval, measuring about 35cm/14in in length. Cut into a curved fish shape and place on a lightly greased baking sheet. Use the trimmings to make narrow strips. Brush one side of each strip with a little beaten egg and secure in place around the rim of the pastry to make a raised edge. Prick the base all over with a fork, then bake for 8–10 minutes until the sides are well risen and the pastry is lightly golden. Leave to cool.

3 Cut the salmon into 2cm/¾in chunks. Melt the butter until it starts to sizzle, then add the salmon. Turn the pieces over in the butter so that they begin to colour but do not cook through.

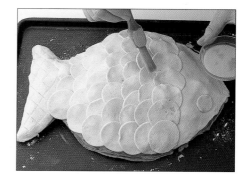

6 Cut the remaining pastry into small rounds and, starting from the tail end, arrange the rounds in overlapping lines to represent scales. Add an extra one for an eye. Brush the whole fish shape with the remaining beaten egg.

7 Bake for 10 minutes, then reduce the temperature to 160°C/325°F/Gas 3 and cook for a further 15–20 minutes, until the pastry is evenly golden. Slide the fish on to a serving plate and serve.

COOK'S TIP
If the pastry seems to be browning too quickly, cover it with foil during cooking and remove from the oven for the last 5 minutes. It is important that the "fish" cooks for the recommended time, so that the salmon is sufficiently cooked through.

4 Remove from the heat and arrange the salmon pieces on top of the rice, piled in the centre. Stir the lemon juice into the butter in the pan, then spoon the mixture over the salmon pieces.

VARIATION
If time is short you may prefer to use this simplified method. Roll out the pastry into a rectangle, then make pastry edges to contain the filling. Part bake the pastry, add the filling, top with plain, rolled out pastry and return it to the oven.

Per portion: Energy 668Kcal/2782kJ; Protein 31g; Carbohydrate 36.6g, of which sugars 0.7g; Fat 45.3g, of which saturates 14g; Cholesterol 209mg; Calcium 98mg; Fibre 1.1g; Sodium 389mg.

CHICKEN-MUSHROOM PIE

THIS IS A GREAT FAMILY FAVOURITE, ESPECIALLY POPULAR ON A COLD WINTER'S EVENING. IT'S ALSO A GOOD WAY TO USE UP LEFTOVER ROAST CHICKEN.

SERVES SIX

INGREDIENTS

- 15g/½oz dried porcini mushrooms
- 50g/2oz/¼ cup butter
- 30ml/2 tbsp flour
- 250ml/8fl oz/1 cup simmering chicken stock
- 50ml/2fl oz/¼ cup whipping cream or milk
- 1 onion, coarsely chopped
- 2 carrots, sliced
- 2 celery sticks, coarsely chopped
- 50g/2oz fresh mushrooms, quartered
- 450g/1lb cooked chicken meat, cubed
- 50g/2oz/½ cup shelled fresh or frozen peas
- beaten egg, for glazing
- salt and ground black pepper

For the pastry

- 225g/8oz/2 cups plain (all-purpose) flour
- 1.5ml/¼ tsp salt
- 115g/4oz/½ cup cold butter, cut into pieces
- 75g/3oz/⅓ cup shortening
- 60–120ml/4–8 tbsp iced water

1 For the pastry, sift the flour and salt into a bowl. With a pastry blender or two knives, cut in the butter and shortening until the mixture resembles coarse breadcrumbs. Sprinkle with 90ml/6 tbsp iced water and mix until the dough holds together. If the dough is too crumbly, add a little more water, 15ml/1 tbsp at a time. Gather the dough into a ball and flatten into a round. Wrap in greaseproof (waxed) paper and chill for at least 30 minutes.

2 Place the dried porcini mushrooms in a small bowl. Add hot water to cover and leave to soak for about 30 minutes until softened. Lift out of the water with a slotted spoon, leaving any grit behind, and drain. Discard the soaking water.

3 Preheat the oven to 190°C/375°F/ Gas 5. Melt 30ml/2 tbsp of the butter in a heavy pan. Stir in the flour and cook, whisking constantly, for about 1 minute, until bubbling. Gradually, add the warm stock and cook over a medium heat, whisking constantly, until the mixture comes to the boil. Cook, still whisking, for 2–3 minutes more. Whisk in the cream or milk and season to taste with salt and pepper. Remove the pan from the heat and set aside.

4 Heat the remaining butter in a large, non-stick frying pan until foaming. Add the onion and carrots and cook over a medium heat, stirring occasionally, for about 5 minutes, until softened. Add the celery and fresh mushrooms and cook, stirring occasionally, for a further 5 minutes. Stir in the cubed chicken meat, fresh or frozen peas, and drained porcini mushrooms.

5 Add the chicken mixture to the cream sauce and stir to mix. Taste for seasoning. Transfer to a 2 litre/4 pint/ 10 cup rectangular ovenproof dish.

6 Roll out the dough on a lightly floured surface to about 3mm/⅛in thickness. Cut out a rectangle about 2.5cm/1in larger all around than the dish. Lay the rectangle of dough over the filling. Make a decorative edge, crimping the dough by pushing the index finger of one hand between the thumb and index finger of the other hand.

7 Cut several vents in the top of the pie to allow steam to escape. Brush the dough with the egg glaze.

8 Press together the dough trimmings, then roll out again. Cut into strips and lay them over the top of the pie. Glaze again. If you like, roll small balls of dough and set them in the "windows" in the lattice.

9 Bake for about 30 minutes, until the top of the pie is browned and the filling is piping hot. Serve the pie hot, straight from the dish.

Per portion: Energy 600Kcal/2501kJ; Protein 23.7g; Carbohydrate 38.8g, of which sugars 3.7g; Fat 40g, of which saturates 21.8g; Cholesterol 132mg; Calcium 92mg; Fibre 2.7g; Sodium 226mg.

RICH GAME PIE

TERRIFIC FOR STYLISH PICNICS OR JUST AS SMART FOR A FORMAL WEDDING BUFFET, THIS PIE LOOKS SPECTACULAR WHEN BAKED IN A FLUTED RAISED PIE MOULD. SOME SPECIALIST KITCHEN STORES HIRE THE MOULDS SO THAT YOU CAN AVOID THE EXPENSE OF PURCHASING THEM; ALTERNATIVELY A 20CM/8IN ROUND SPRINGFORM TIN CAN BE USED.

SERVES TEN

INGREDIENTS
25g/1oz/2 tbsp butter
1 onion, finely chopped
2 garlic cloves, finely chopped
900g/2lb mixed boneless game
   meat, such as skinless pheasant
   and/or pigeon (US squab) breast,
   venison and rabbit, diced
30ml/2 tbsp chopped mixed fresh
   herbs such as parsley, thyme
   and marjoram
salt and ground black pepper
For the pâté
50g/2oz/¼ cup butter
2 garlic cloves, finely chopped
450g/1lb chicken livers, rinsed,
   trimmed and chopped
60ml/4 tbsp brandy
5ml/1 tsp ground mace
For the hot water crust pastry
675g/1½lb/6 cups strong white
   bread flour
5ml/1 tsp salt
115ml/3½fl oz/scant ½ cup milk
115ml/3½fl oz/scant ½ cup water
115g/4oz/½ cup lard, diced
115g/4oz/½ cup butter, diced
beaten egg, to glaze
For the jelly
300ml/½ pint/1¼ cups game or
   beef consommé
2.5ml/½ tsp powdered gelatine

1 Melt the butter in a small pan, then add the onion and garlic and cook until softened but not coloured. Remove from the heat and mix with the diced game meat and the chopped mixed herbs. Season well, cover and chill.

2 To make the pâté, melt the butter in a pan until foaming. Add the garlic and chicken livers and cook until the livers are just browned. Remove the pan from the heat and stir in the brandy and mace. Process the mixture in a blender or food processor to a smooth purée, then set aside and leave to cool.

3 To make the pastry, sift the flour and salt into a bowl and make a well in the centre. Place the milk and water in a pan. Add the lard and butter and heat gently until melted, then bring to the boil and remove from the heat as soon as the mixture begins to bubble. Pour the hot liquid into the well in the flour and beat until smooth. Cover and leave until cool enough to handle.

4 Preheat the oven to 200°C/400°F/ Gas 6. Roll out two-thirds of the pastry and use to line a 23cm/9in raised pie mould. Spoon in half the game mixture and press it down evenly. Add the pâté and then top with the remaining game.

5 Roll out the remaining pastry to form a lid. Brush the edge of the pastry lining the mould with a little water and cover the pie with the pastry lid. Trim off excess pastry from around the edge. Pinch the edges together to seal in the filling. Make two holes in the centre of the lid and glaze with egg. Use pastry trimmings to roll out leaves to garnish the pie. Brush with egg.

6 Bake the pie for 20 minutes, then cover it with foil and cook for a further 10 minutes. Reduce the oven temperature to 150°C/300°F/Gas 2. Glaze the pie again with beaten egg and cook for a further 1½ hours, keeping the top covered loosely with foil.

7 Remove the pie from the oven and leave it to stand for 15 minutes. Increase the oven temperature to 200°C/400°F/Gas 6. Stand the mould on a baking sheet and remove the sides. Quickly glaze the sides of the pie with beaten egg and cover the top with foil, then cook for a final 15 minutes to brown the sides. Leave to cool completely, then chill the pie overnight.

8 To make the jelly, heat the game or beef consommé in a small pan until just beginning to bubble, whisk in the gelatine until dissolved and leave to cool until just setting. Using a small funnel, carefully pour the jellied consommé into the holes in the pie. Chill until set. This pie will keep in the refrigerator for up to 3 days.

Per portion: Energy 731Kcal/3058kJ; Protein 44g; Carbohydrate 54.3g, of which sugars 2.5g; Fat 32g, of which saturates 17.9g; Cholesterol 223mg; Calcium 163mg; Fibre 2.3g; Sodium 444mg.

STEAK, MUSHROOM AND ALE PIE

THIS ANGLO-IRISH DISH IS A FIRM FAVOURITE ON MENUS AT RESTAURANTS SPECIALIZING IN TRADITIONAL FARE. PIPING HOT, CREAMY MASHED POTATOES OR PARSLEY-DRESSED BOILED POTATOES AND SLIGHTLY CRUNCHY CARROTS AND GREEN BEANS OR CABBAGE ARE PERFECT ACCOMPANIMENTS; FOR A BAR-STYLE MEAL, CHIPS OR BAKED POTATOES AND A SIDE SALAD CAN BE SERVED WITH THE PIE.

SERVES FOUR

INGREDIENTS

25g/1oz/2 tbsp butter
1 large onion, finely chopped
115g/4oz/1½ cups chestnut or button
 (white) mushrooms, halved
900g/2lb lean beef in one piece,
 such as braising steak
30ml/2 tbsp plain (all-purpose) flour
45ml/3 tbsp sunflower oil
300ml/½ pint/1¼ cups stout or
 brown ale
300ml/½ pint/1¼ cups beef stock
 or consommé
500g/1¼lb puff pastry, thawed if frozen
beaten egg, to glaze
salt and ground black pepper

1 Melt the butter in a large, flameproof casserole, add the onion and cook gently, stirring occasionally, for about 5 minutes, or until it is softened but not coloured. Add the halved mushrooms and continue cooking for a further 5 minutes, stirring occasionally.

2 Meanwhile, trim the meat and cut it into 2.5cm/1in cubes. Season the flour and toss the meat in it.

COOK'S TIP

To make individual pies, divide the filling among four individual pie dishes. Cut the pastry into quarters and cover as above. If the dishes do not have rims, press a narrow strip of pastry around the edge of each dish to seal the lid in place. Cook as above, reducing the cooking time slightly.

3 Use a slotted spoon to remove the onion mixture from the casserole and set aside. Add and heat the oil, then brown the steak, in batches, over a high heat to seal in the juices.

4 Replace the vegetables, then stir in the stout or ale and stock or consommé. Bring to the boil, reduce the heat and simmer for about 1 hour, stirring occasionally, or until the meat is tender. Season to taste and transfer to a 1.5 litre/2½ pint/6¼ cup pie dish. Cover and leave to cool. If possible, chill the meat filling overnight as this allows the flavour to develop. Preheat the oven to 230°C/450°F/Gas 8.

5 Roll out the pastry in the shape of the dish and about 4cm/1½in larger all around. Cut a 2.5cm/1in strip from the edge of the pastry. Brush the rim of the dish with water and press the pastry strip on it. Brush the pastry rim with beaten egg and cover the pie with the pastry lid. Press the lid firmly in place and then trim the excess from around the edge.

6 Use the blunt edge of a knife to tap the outside edge of the pastry, pressing it down with your finger as you seal in the filling. (This technique is known as knocking up.)

7 Pinch the pastry between your fingers to flute the edge. Roll out any remaining pastry trimmings and cut out shapes to garnish the pie, brushing the shapes with a little beaten egg before pressing them lightly in place.

8 Make a hole in the middle of the pie to allow steam to escape, brush the top carefully with beaten egg and chill for 10 minutes to rest the pastry.

9 Bake the pie for 15 minutes, then reduce the oven temperature to 200°C/400°F/Gas 6 and bake for a further 15–20 minutes, or until the pastry is risen and golden.

Per portion: Energy 1061Kcal/4423kJ; Protein 58.8g; Carbohydrate 59.3g, of which sugars 7.6g; Fat 65.3g, of which saturates 24g; Cholesterol 164mg; Calcium 129mg; Fibre 3.2g; Sodium 622mg.

INDEX